Sexual Exploitation of Teenagers

Sexual Exploitation of Teenagers

Adolescent Development, Discrimination, and Consent Law

JENNIFER ANN DROBAC

THE UNIVERSITY OF CHICAGO PRESS   CHICAGO AND LONDON

JENNIFER ANN DROBAC is professor at the Indiana University Robert H. McKinney School of Law.

The University of Chicago Press, Chicago 60637
The University of Chicago Press, Ltd., London

Printed in the United States of America
25 24 23 22 21 20 19 18 17 16 1 2 3 4 5

ISBN-13: 978-0-226-30101-3 (cloth)
ISBN-13: 978-0-226-30115-0 (e-book)

DOI: 10.7208/chicago/9780226301150.001.0001

Library of Congress Cataloging-in-Publication Data

Drobac, Jennifer Ann, author.
Sexual exploitation of teenagers : adolescent development, discrimination, and consent law / Jennifer Ann Drobac.
pages cm
Includes bibliographical references and index.
ISBN 978-0-226-30101-3 (cloth : alk. paper) — ISBN 978-0-226-30115-0 (ebook)
1. Sexual harassment of women—Law and legislation—United States. 2. Teenagers—Legal status, laws, etc.—United States. 3. Sexual consent—United States. 4. Sexual harassment—United States—Prevention. 5. Teenagers—Sexual behavior—United States. I. Title.
KF3467.D758 2016
345.73′0253—dc23

2015020842

♾ This paper meets the requirements of ANSI/NISO Z39.48–1992 (Permanence of Paper).

FOR THE DOES AND JOES,
THE TEENAGERS WHO SPEAK OUT FOR A WISER WORLD

AND, ESPECIALLY, FOR "SARA"

Contents

CHAPTER ONE

Introductions

Sara's Case, Sexual Exploitation, and Legal Terms

When "Sara" (an alias) was fifteen, Michael Cosio, the forty-year-old manager of the movie theater where she worked, befriended her and gained her confidence. Cosio also befriended other teenage employees. He provided them with alcohol, gave them free theater tickets, and even offered to teach sixteen-year-old Sara to drive. Cosio encouraged Sara "to speak with him about her problems, how her parents did not understand her, and about things that mattered to her, a teenage girl." He gave Sara expensive gifts, took her to nice dinners, and gave her cash. Sara had no idea that Cosio was a registered sex offender, convicted of molesting his twelve-year-old niece.[1]

Cosio's attention became increasingly intimate and physical with Sara. At first, Sara rebuffed his physical advances. However, after repeatedly soliciting sexual favors from her, Cosio lied to Sara. He told Sara that he was suffering from a potentially inoperable brain tumor and was not sure how long he had to live. He told her that he loved her. Convinced that she loved her "desperately ill" manager, Sara eventually acquiesced to his sexual advances. After Cosio kissed her, Sara "remember[ed] feeling 'numb' at first. Everything was moving so quickly. Everything was a blur to her." When she was sixteen, Sara had sexual intercourse with him. Cosio promoted Sara to projectionist so that they could engage in sex more easily and frequently in the secluded projection room. When Sara's brother, also a theater employee, observed Cosio kissing his sister in a storage room, Cosio again lied, stating that Sara had forced herself on him. Sara felt ashamed and was concerned about how her brother thought of her.[2]

Cosio's behavior turned increasingly hostile. He began calling Sara a "whore" and a "slut." When Sara and Cosio argued, he threatened to tell her parents about their relationship. Sara was ashamed and fearful of how her parents would respond to her conduct with Cosio. So, she kept their "relationship" a secret. After Sara became pregnant, Cosio had his adult girlfriend take Sara to have an abortion. By this time, Cosio was already in jail, serving time on a larceny conviction. Believing that Cosio was wrongly convicted, Sara continued to write to Cosio in jail.[3]

Sara's parents knew nothing about the "affair." When they finally discovered the cause of her plummeting grades and disturbing behavior, they notified the police. A police officer explained to Sara that Cosio had no tumor and was a registered sex offender. Sara cooperated with the district attorney, who successfully prosecuted Cosio for statutory rape.[4]

I met Sara months later when her mother brought Sara to speak with me about a civil suit against Cosio and the theater that hired him, allegedly in violation of the conditions of his parole. An initial concern was how the law would treat Sara if she and her parents sued the theater owner for sexual harassment. What legal meaning, if any, would Sara's "consent" carry? Should she even consider a lawsuit?

Sara's options at the time were limited. She could have just dropped the matter and moved on to reconstruct her life. Michael Cosio was already in jail, ultimately convicted of unlawful sex with a minor (Sara) under California Penal Code section 261.5. While he was not a source for financial relief, Sara needed the vindication of her own dignity and of the righteousness of her offense regarding his treatment of her. A lawsuit offered that potential because, under California antidiscrimination law, a sexual harassment target may sue the individual perpetrator. The employer, the movie theater, was not initially responsive to overtures by Sara's counsel concerning financial reimbursement for Sara's medical and counseling expenses, physical injuries, and emotional distress. As long as the company ignored her private appeals, only official intervention could have spurred resolution and closure for Sara. California case and statutory laws at that time regarded a minor's consent to sex as irrelevant in the criminal context. Therefore, it was logical to think that Sara's consent would have no bearing on a civil complaint for sexual harassment, sex discrimination in employment, and personal injury. Sara was still a minor, however, so she could not sue in her own name. She had to proceed initially with her mother as the named plaintiff. After she turned eighteen, however, she refiled under her own name against Cosio and the movie theater. Sara endured a lengthy deposition and fruitless arbitration proceedings. After over a year of litigation and discovery, the case settled confidentially out of court shortly before trial. No one will ever know how a judge and jury might have responded ultimately to Sara's claims and the respondents' defenses.

How would you have advised Sara? How *should* the law have treated her? How should the law have responded to Cosio and the movie theater owners?

Aspirations for This Book

Sexual Exploitation of Teenagers explores the very common problem of the sexual harassment and exploitation of maturing teenagers by adults. It examines in particular detail Sara's case and those of five other "consenting" teenagers: Kati (*Starbucks* Doe), *Oberweis* Doe, *Donaldson* Doe, "Joe" (*Mama Taori's* Doe), and *Willits* Doe.[5] These adolescents and millions of their peers are out in the world, experiencing its riches and joys, but also its dangers and challenges. These youth may not have the wisdom—the emotional, intellectual, and experiential tools—to handle the challenges they may face, such as sexual exploitation and harassment. They may not make wise choices in response to sexual advances by their supervisors, teachers, coaches, or mentors.

I originally titled this book *Worldly but Not Yet Wise* because that name describes the condition of many adolescents who are the subjects of this investigation. However, this more poetic title fails to inform readers that this book analyzes primarily adult sexual predation of teenagers and the exploitation of teen naiveté and new worldliness. I have retained many of the chapter headings, though, to remind readers of the precarious transitional state of these youth, who navigate the world but often without sufficient protection.

Inspired by the stories of many Does and Joes, *Sexual Exploitation of Teenagers* considers three fundamental questions. First, do teenagers face more sexual harassment than adults? Second, are they developmentally different than adults, and if so, might these differences influence how they deal with sexual abuse by adults? Third, is civil law, as opposed to criminal law, congruent with adolescent "developing capacity"?

In other words, does current sexual harassment law adequately protect teenagers? With an interdisciplinary approach, this book answers these overarching questions and tackles logical follow-up questions. For the six profiled teenagers and numerous more, this book considers how the law treated these juveniles and the adults involved. It highlights the conflicts between responsive laws—where the law arguably failed to protect these teenagers—and how civil law reforms might better serve adolescents.

Sexual Exploitation of Teenagers begins by identifying the scope and nature of the sexual harassment of teenagers at work and school. Chapter 2 reveals some disturbing statistics about the sexual abuse of adolescents. It also discusses how adolescents face sexual harassment and exploitation in other surroundings, such as the mall, social and sports clubs, prisons, and the military. Chapter 2's statistics often incorporate harassment by peers (between teenagers) as well as abuse by adults. I acknowledge that peer sexual harassment is a serious problem; however, this book focuses on the abuse of power by adults who target teenagers. It does so for two major reasons. First, I think that training teenagers how to behave respectfully and lawfully with each other is very important but difficult when adults fail to model the appropriate behavior that society expects from juveniles. Second, I believe that adults can usually best handle inappropriate teenage behavior in the locales where the behaviors occur, and not in court. The correction of adult behavior often necessitates operation of law when informal measures do not work. Adults who sexually exploit children should be subject to the operation of corrective legal response.

In addition to targeted harassment, *Sexual Exploitation of Teenagers* and particularly chapter 2 examine sexually charged messaging and discriminatory situations, often called "hostile" work or school environments in legal parlance. Many incidents of sexual harassment of teens are not severe enough to meet thresholds required for legal remedies. However, every incident contributes to a teenager's ambient influences. These influences may reinforce harmful sex-role stereotypes and discriminatory attitudes about women, girls, and disempowered minorities. They may also subtly facilitate more serious sexual harassment. Appendix 1 provides a list of common sexually harassing behaviors to provide an understanding of the conduct under scrutiny in this book.

Following this discussion of the prevalence of sexual harassment, this book reviews the new cutting-edge science of adolescent development. Chapter 3 explains how teenagers, as a group, are different from mature adults. It explores adolescent neurobiological, psychosocial, and sexual maturation. Adolescents are not simply mini-adults. Chapter 3 provides the background for an evaluation of whether laws designed for adult targets can adequately protect juveniles and their "developing capacities." Thus, chapter 3's review of adolescent development informs a discussion of the law that affects and purportedly protects teenagers.

In chapters 4 and 5, *Sexual Exploitation of Teenagers* explains in lay terms how law addresses sexual harassment and abuse generally, but also how it may do so inadequately for teenagers. The book highlights conflicting criminal and civil laws, detailing the legal mixed message sent to adults and teenagers. These chapters analyze the public regulation of sexuality and how teenagers first tried to access protection under civil laws. Similar to early sexual harassment adult complainants, these teenagers faced numerous legal difficulties and occasionally apparent hostility from courts.

Chapters 6, 7, and 8 look more particularly at the development of antidiscrimination laws and how they fared in protecting minors. Chapter 6 starts by reviewing the theoretical underpinnings of sexual harassment law. It surveys historical attitudes concerning sexuality and various theoretical perspectives regarding equality. Most foundational support for sexual harassment law assumes that the targets possess legal capacity. Chapter 6 compares theoretical justifications for law with the unique aspects of adolescent sexual abuse and the minors' responses. This chapter highlights the disconnect between sexual harassment legal theory and the actual problems involving minors.

Chapter 7 explains that Title VII of the 1964 Civil Rights Act never contemplated juvenile workers. State fair employment practices statutes, which often mirror Title VII, also fail to address working minors. These lapses create odd results in civil courts when courts conflate adolescent developmental capacity with *legal* capacity and actual consent with *legal* consent. Chapter 7 carefully examines the legal decision in Joe's case to trace how and why the law fails to protect American adolescents adequately.

Chapter 8 analyzes California criminal and civil law related to the sexual abuse of minors to show how the laws often conflict in their treatment of adolescent consent. This chapter also follows the precedential influence of California case law, including the case of *Donaldson* Doe. From California to New York, laws fail to protect minors while treating their consent inconsistently.

Chapter 9 extends the review of sexual harassment laws with the application of Title IX of the Education Amendments of 1972. These amendments, distinct from the CRA, modified several statutes, including the Higher Education Act of 1965. The Education Amendments specifically prohibit sex discrimination at school, and courts have interpreted them to prohibit the sexual harassment by adults of teenagers at school.[6] Chapter 9 ends with a discussion of judicial bias and how judicial attitudes have, in some cases, thwarted efforts to protect abused teenagers.

Sexual Exploitation of Teenagers concludes in chapter 10 with a discussion of possible reforms, some more attractive than others. This chapter posits that, while the sexual harassment of teenagers remains a significant problem, corrective remedies that are more congruent with adolescent developing capacity exist. In particular, chapter 10 offers the idea of "legal assent," the mechanism of a new approach to adolescent consent. Adolescents will engage in sex, sometimes with adults. The challenge is to protect teenagers while they explore the adult world. The adolescent assent proposal affords teenagers the chance to revoke their consent when an adult behaves abusively, takes unfair advantage, or breaches a duty owed to that minor. The assent approach contemplates that adults will treat minors with care, as would a fiduciary, or will "just say no," especially if the law permits maturing teenagers to revoke their "yes" to sex. (A *fiduciary* is a person in a position of trust and confidence who acts for the benefit of another, often called a beneficiary.) This revocation mimics the operation of traditional contract law defenses, such as unconscionability, undue influence, and duress, that work to invalidate contracts. Once the adolescent abrogates the assent and the court confirms the abrogation, a court must prohibit or exclude any further discussion of the original consent. Chapter 10 provides greater detail regarding this proposed legal reform.

Throughout, *Sexual Exploitation of Teenagers* tracks the stories of the Doe teenagers who were involved in federal or state civil cases. While Joe and *Oberweis* Doe were from Tennessee and Illinois respectively, all the other cases involved California teenagers. Of course, it makes a difference that California is a populous state with laws that provide reasonable protection for workers and students. So, many of the high profile cases begin there. In contrast, for example, Indiana has almost no state sexual harassment case law because Indiana's code mandates that a plaintiff obtain written permission to sue from the employer before the aggrieved worker can initiate an action in court under the Indiana Civil Rights Act.[7] Not surprising, employers either don't grant the permission or plaintiffs don't bother to ask. While it is beyond the scope of this book to cover the laws of every state, the discussion of the profiled case histories is relevant for a broad understanding of the issues. Teenagers across the nation face similar exploitation and all (should) have access to federal law. These cases highlight the similarities and variations and they commence a discussion of the problems, inconsistencies, and gaps in protection.

From these case stories, including Sara's, one can evaluate the predicament of teenagers who function in a heavily sexualized culture with mature adults. One can weigh whether adolescent development, immaturity, and naiveté played a role in the controversies and whether these teens may have sent initiating sexual cues, not fully realizing (or, to the contrary, fully aware) how adults might receive their flirtation or acquiescence. I found these cases shocking because I saw sexual imposition, exploitation, and the abuse of power by adults in positions of trust. However, contemporaneous and judicial responses to complaints by these minors ranged from claims that they were misguided juveniles to speculation by Judge Richard Posner that *Oberweis* Doe was possibly a "siren"! Lay readers may wonder whether these were promiscuous teenagers looking to win the jackpot with a civil suit. (Although, as minors they could not even bring suit in their own names.) Readers might conclude that these were shamefully abused and exploited adolescents for whom others sought redress. Another interpretation is that they were maturing human beings, suddenly aware of the injustice of what occurred to them and looking within the legal system for a fair resolution. Perhaps threads of all three explanations run through a case. Readers might conclude that one or more possibly was a siren, luring a consort to his legal demise. Or one might decide that the perpetrators deliberately cultivated the trust of these teenagers and then exploited them sexually. By analyzing the cases, one can evaluate whether the adult perpetrators took advantage of ineffectual laws to manipulate and abuse their juvenile targets. I argue that they did, if the perpetrators thought about the law at all. This book concludes that current civil sexual harassment law inadequately protects maturing teenagers.

With an interdisciplinary approach, *Sexual Exploitation of Teenagers* supports this overarching conclusion by offering scientific evidence and legal analysis. It demonstrates that teens face more sexual harassment than adults and that adolescents may respond differently to sexual harassment than adults. It discusses how teenagers are developmentally different from adults and how these differences change throughout the adolescent years. These differences may manifest in the context of their social interactions and influence their response to sexual overtures. Additionally, this book evinces why sexual harassment law that protects teenage targets should be different from that which protects adult targets. Focusing also on perpetrators, in addition to targets, this book finds that teenage and adult harassers should answer to different laws. Arguably, current law is not congruent with teenage developmental maturity. This book offers concrete responses to many of the concerns that arise during the discussion. It contemplates legal and administrative reforms as well as extralegal responses that might alleviate the problem. What the book cannot answer definitively, due to inconclusive science or a dearth of research, it showcases for further discussion and exploration. At the end, you, the reader, can decide whether legal assent might serve to ameliorate the problems exposed in the coming chapters.

Worldly Terms

Any exploration of law and behavior benefits from an early review of key terms and phrases that guide and cabin the discussion. For example, although the term *teenager* technically includes eighteen-and nineteen-year-olds, I concentrate on minors in this book. I focus particularly on girls, for whom legal redress is more often expected and sought. Girls also report more and may endure more sexual harassment and exploitation than boys. I also use the term *adolescents* when referring to minors, even though new research indicates that adolescence continues into the early twenties. This is discussed in more depth in chapter 3.

Most states set the *age of majority*, the age at which society considers a person a fully mature adult, at eighteen. At that threshold, people assume full legal control over their lives and choices. In Alabama, Delaware, and Nebraska, people reach their majority at nineteen. In Mississippi, the age is twenty-one. A few states, including Arkansas, Nevada, Ohio, Tennessee, Utah, and Wisconsin, vary the age of majority depending on graduation from high school.[8] At the age of majority, the law affords a person most (but not all) the rights associated with adulthood. The right to purchase and consume alcoholic beverages is one of the few rights consistently bestowed at twenty-one, which is after the attainment of the age of majority in most states.

Another milestone is the *age of consent*. This age introduces even more complexity for a variety of reasons. First, most people think of the age of consent as the age at which the law allows a person to engage in sexual relations with another person. However, as evidenced for *Donaldson* Doe, some courts treat the age of consent as the age at which a person can legally marry without parental permission. This book explores the interconnection between marriage and sexual activity in chapters 4 and 5. For the purposes of our discussion throughout this book, though, I associate the age of consent with the more colloquial meaning, in other words, the legal right to engage in sexual intercourse with another adult. A second complicating factor concerning the age of consent arises in that not all states rely on the same bright-line (or clearly defined) rule. Chapter 4 also discusses how the fifty states have more than fifty differing laws regarding *the* age of consent. Even within states, different ages legitimate various types of sexual activity. Appendix 2 provides a summary of state juvenile sex crime statutes across the nation. Third, even if one can pinpoint the age of consent under criminal law, some states give the same consent by a minor different legal effect in the civil law context. Thus, consent might constitute no defense to criminal law charges but a complete defense in a civil law case. I found that thirteen states had such conflicts in their treatment of juvenile consent.

Finally, while the pinpointing of an age associated with a particular activity may have value, what does *consent* really mean? I use quotations at the first instances of the words *consent*, *consensual*, and *consenting* in reference to consent by a minor because even explicit verbal consent by a minor may not constitute *legal* consent and may equate more realistically with acquiescence.

Consent, Acquiescence, and Assent

Consent means to give "permission for something to happen . . . agree to do something."[9] Slightly different from *consent*, *assent* means, "to express approval or agreement."[10] By this definition, *assent* denotes cooperation or secondary status. Both terms arguably include two prerequisites: knowledge regarding the choice and volition. In the first aspect, consent and assent must be informed and correspond to the activity they legitimate. Ignorant cooperation does not indicate consent or assent. Additionally, any misrepresentation taints responsive consent or assent. The individual must also possess the cognitive ability to reason about a choice. In the second aspect, consent and assent must indicate freedom of choice and volition. The individuals must be able to guide their own responsive choices. In contrast, to *acquiesce* means "to accept something reluctantly but without protest"[11] and indicates neither full consent nor assent.

In distinguishing acquiescence further, I would add another requirement for consent and assent: a measure of autonomy and power. For example, if someone has no opportunity or authority to dissent, can society value that person's consent? No, consent and assent must be free of duress and coercion. The notion of genuine consent assumes a level of mutuality and equality between the people coming to an agreement. Consent presumes emotional, intellectual, and developmental capacity.[12] These characteristics undergird *legal* capacity.

RESTATEMENTS (SECOND) OF TORTS AND CONTRACTS. This elucidation of consent is consistent with its interpretation in section 892A of the *Second Restatement of Torts*. While not binding on courts, the restatements of law offer legal guidance to assist courts in making fair and just decisions by summarizing common law precedent and juridical consensus. The *Restatement of Torts* provides guidance regarding personal injury law. Section 892A, subsection (2)(a) elaborates on the "effect of consent" to behavior that might otherwise constitute a tort, a wrongful act. Section 892A specifies that, in order to extinguish tort liability, consent must be "by one who has the capacity to consent."[13] A comment to this subsection provides,

> If, however, the one who consents is not capable of appreciating the nature, extent or probable consequences of the conduct, the consent is not effective to bar liability unless the parent, guardian, or other person empowered to consent for the incompetent has given consent, in which case the consent of the authorized person will be effective even though the incompetent does not consent. . . .[14]

This passage clarifies that those who consent must understand what they are doing and be able to anticipate the results of their actions. Such appreciation requires what psychologists refer to as "counterfactual thinking" about different outcomes for events, or "what if–then" reasoning. This explanation focuses on the cognitive aspects of consent.

Contract law has also examined the notions of legal consent and capacity. For hundreds of years, contract law has held that minors lack the capacity to give legal (as opposed to actual) consent.[15] Therefore, the law often permits minors to void their actual consent without penalty. This conclusion about a minor's legal capacity results, in part, from the fear that adults may take legal advantage of minors who make contractual agreements.[16]

Contract law also distinguishes between cognitive and volitional incapacity, especially in the context of mental disabilities. Section 15(1) of the *Second Restatement of Contracts* states,

> A person incurs only voidable contractual duties by entering into a transaction if by reason of mental illness or defect
>
> (a) he is unable to understand in a reasonable manner the nature and consequences of the transaction, or
> (b) he is unable to act in a reasonable manner in relation to the transaction and the other party has reason to know of his condition.[17]

Subsection (a) mirrors the torts guidance above. However, (b) relates to *volitional incapacity*, or the inability to regulate one's responses in a social context. Some incapacitated individuals may understand the nature of a transaction or conduct but not be able to control their responsive behavior reasonably. For example, a gambler might understand cognitively that she has no money with which to bet but might not be able to stop herself from gambling. An elderly person suffering from dementia might understand in one moment that he has a perfectly fine roof on his house but might hours later sign a contract with an unscrupulous salesperson for a new roof.

Comment b to section 15 explains,

> Even though understanding is complete, [an incapacitated man] may lack the ability to control his acts in the way that [a] normal individual can and does control them; in such cases the inability makes the contract voidable only if the other party has reason to know of his condition. Where a person has some understanding of a particular transaction which is affected by mental illness or defect, the controlling consideration is whether the transaction in its result is one which a reasonably competent person might have made.[18]

This passage naturally prompts the question whether some teenagers may suffer from a similar volitional incapacity or "defect." One might argue that a teenager "may lack the ability to control his acts in the way that [a] normal individual [adult] can and does control them."[19] For example, she may understand the facts regarding sexual activity but not be able to control her conduct the way an adult would.

Several disciplines use a variety of terms to express the notion of adolescent behavior as markedly dissimilar to adult behavior. Psychologists refer to this phenomenon as *psychosocial immaturity*.[20] Legal scholars sometimes refer to this difference as *diminished capacity*.[21] I find the term *diminished capacity* inappropriate because the word *diminished* carries a negative connotation. Additionally, it suggests that full capacity should exist or may once have existed. Most teenagers suffer not from impairment but from immaturity—a blameless condition and a natural phase of growth. I prefer the term *developing capacity* because of teenagers' transitional status from childhood to adulthood and their developing maturity.

Capacity clearly has different meanings depending on the context. Full *legal* capacity, required for legal responsibility and the exercise of many legal rights, means just that—"complete capacity and maturity." Neither diminished capacity nor developing capacity satisfies the legal requirements regarding mature understanding, autonomy, and capacity. Full legal capacity is an all-or-nothing proposition. There is no sliding scale for legal capacity. Moreover, as demonstrated in chapters 3, 4, and 5, adolescents have not reached that legal threshold. Even in the criminal system, prosecutors try adolescents in juvenile court as children or in adult court as adults. Jurists do not try them in adult court as mature children. Semantics aside, one might consider whether contract law's guidance on incapacity accurately describes many adolescents, at one point or another in their development. I suggest that it does.

MEDICAL ASSENT. While this discussion of key terms has highlighted the similarities between consent and assent, government regulation of human-subject medical research brings nuanced meaning to assent as it applies to children in that context. The Code of Federal Regulations mandates that Institutional Review Boards (IRBs) may approve research on children if "adequate provisions are made for soliciting the assent of the children and the permission of their parents or guardians."[22] The IRB decides whether the child is even "capable of providing assent" by considering the child's age, maturity, and psychological state.[23] IRBs may waive parental permission only under special circumstances.[24] No additional guidance suggests how IRBs should weigh these factors.

Thus, *medical* assent does not equate with legal consent because parental permission—consent—typically bolsters a child's assent. Moreover, Drs. Elizabeth Cauffman and Laurence Steinberg cautioned, "Adolescents who demonstrate that they meet the criteria for informed [medical] consent may nevertheless lack the psychosocial maturity required to make consistently mature judgments."[25] Additionally, one might argue that capacity for medical assent does not equate with legal capacity because the contemplated medical decisions are so narrowly defined and well informed. The responsibility for any decision to conduct medical research on a minor is typically shared by the researchers, IRB, the parents, and lastly, the juvenile.

Consent in Different Contexts

People considering juvenile legal autonomy might agree that teenagers are capable of assent and acquiescence. Similarly, even a six-year-old may "know" or recognize Hillary Clinton and Jeb Bush and may "voluntarily" pick one or the other for president. The law does not allow that child to cast a political vote, however.[26] Additionally, people might agree that many juveniles understand the concept of sexual intercourse.[27] Their knowledge of the mechanics of sexual activity does not necessarily qualify them, however, as competent decision makers or as ready to engage maturely in the behavior. Many adults, judges, and courts disagree. For them, relative cognitive maturity, or even apparent physical maturity, equates with adult legal capacity. They ignore or are ignorant of the level of psychosocial maturity required for competent decision making in uncontrolled or stressful situations. These adults may not be mindful of or familiar with the emphasis on legal capacity evident in the traditional restatements of law.

As *Sexual Exploitation of Teenagers* considers whether or not adolescents have the threshold level of competence, sufficient power, and status to give legally significant consent to sex with an adult, the book also takes into account the context. Sexual harassment by definition is not consensual. People rarely choose to be sexually harassed or exploited. Some adolescents, however, may consent to sexual activity without fully appreciating to what they are consenting or why. For example, social conditioning may prompt consent. Professor R. George Wright once noted that noncoercive factors can influence a person's consent when it "has social antecedents." He explained, "We do not have pure personalities apart from the social formation of our preferences, including our preferences to consent or refuse to consent." Wright cautioned that "not all processes of the social formation of preferences are equal in the degree to which they respect freedom and dignity. There is a real difference . . . between a broad education and brainwashing."[28] Chapter 2 explores some of the social antecedents that may influence teenagers.

Second, teens may not have the power to refuse a sex solicitation in a particular situation. Professor Katherine Federle has argued against the pervasive emphasis on capacity for the justification of children's rights. She suggested, "We must reconstruct rights talk about children in terms of power, and only when we make explicit the role of capacity is a new theory of rights for children possible." Federle explained that social oppression and political inequality foster hierarchy and status. Give children rights and they can "access existing political and legal structures in order to make claims. Permitting these types of rights claims also has the salutary effect of redistributing power and altering hierarchies."[29]

Sexual Exploitation of Teenagers explores the hierarchical world of teenagers. It highlights abuses of power in the form of sexual harassment, exploitation, and discrimination. It shows how jurists confuse developing capacity with legal capacity and actual consent with legal consent. *Sexual Exploitation of Teenagers* demonstrates how compounded confusion and inadequate legal protections leave some minors without remedies or recourse. Finally, it offers legal assent and, more particularly, the revocation of assent as a method for empowering the teenagers whom adults have exploited.

CHAPTER TWO

Adolescent Worldliness

Sexual Harassment Targeting Teenagers

This chapter details how and in what contexts adults sexually exploit teenagers. It helps readers understand the world that teens navigate and the constant sexual messaging and behaviors that they experience. Chapter 2 also provides definitions of *sexual harassment* to clarify legal proscriptions. This chapter provides concrete examples of offending conduct and some statistical data. The description of teen sexual abuse is shorter than you might think it would be. This is not because people don't harass teenagers. They do. In middle school, in high school, in club sports, at church, at work—anywhere that one can imagine adolescents gathering or meeting with adults individually, one still finds teen sexual abuse and harassment. Researchers cannot tell exactly how prevalent sexual harassment is, however, because no single institution or agency collects such information or complaints for much of the abuse of adolescents that occurs.[1]

Researchers do know that authorities, including state child protective service agencies, documented about forty-one thousand cases of sexually abused adolescents ages nine to seventeen in 2011.[2] That same year the Department of Justice (DOJ) and Centers for Disease Control and Prevention (CDC) conducted a survey of over 4,500 children ages one to seventeen and found that among girls ages fourteen to seventeen almost a quarter (22.8%) had been sexually victimized and almost 11 percent (10.8%) had been sexually assaulted (the equivalent of contact sexual abuse) in the last year. "Among this group, 8.1% had reported an attempted or completed rape, 13.6% experienced sexual harassment, and 12.9% were exposed to an unwanted Internet sexual solicitation in the last year."[3] Many, if not most, cases of sexual harassment are not reported.[4]

Defining Sexual Harassment

Before one reviews the statistics from the Equal Employment Opportunity Commission (EEOC) and the American Association of University Women (AAUW), one should understand what constitutes sexual harassment. One might look to a variety of guiding sources for clarification, but because *Sexual Exploitation of Teenagers* focuses on legal avenues for redress, I concentrate on legal definitions of sexual harassment and exploitation. Nothing in the US Constitution or the US Code specifically prohibits sexual harassment in nonmilitary contexts. Title VII of the Civil Rights Act of 1964 (CRA) does not mention it but prohibits discrimination in employment based on sex.[5] In its 1980 Guidelines on Sexual Harassment, the EEOC explained that sexual harassment is a form of sex discrimination. The EEOC advised, "Unwelcome sexual advances, requests for sexual favors, and other verbal or physical conduct of a sexual nature constitute sexual harassment when . . . interfering with an individual's work performance or creating an intimidating, hostile or offensive work environment."[6] A request for a date does not by itself constitute sexual harassment. Under Title VII and most state fair employment practices statutes, the conduct must be either severe or pervasive to qualify as actionable sexual harassment for which the target could file a lawsuit.[7] Typically, a jury decides what conduct qualifies as severe or pervasive. Severity is inversely related to frequency so one incident of rape constitutes actionable sexual harassment. Additionally, a judge or jury must consider "all the circumstances" when evaluating abuse because "no single factor is required."[8]

Title IX of the Education Amendments of 1972 similarly prohibits sex discrimination in federally funded schools.[9] The US Department of Education (ED), Office for Civil Rights (OCR), states, "Sexual harassment is unwelcome conduct of a sexual nature[,] . . . unwelcome sexual advances, requests for sexual favors, and other verbal, nonverbal, or physical conduct." The definition continues, "Sexual harassment . . . can deny or limit . . . the student's ability to participate in or to receive benefits, services, or opportunities in the school's program."[10] Note the similarity between this definition and that from the EEOC. Both the EEOC and OCR definitions require that the conduct be unwelcome and sexual. These definitions are narrow and do not highlight nonsexual forms of abuse. For example, they do not explain that gender animosity may motivate some forms of hostile, sex-based harassment.

What if a teacher, Dr. Summers, suggests that girls don't succeed in math and science because of "issues of intrinsic aptitude"?[11] Is that harassment, even though it is not a sexual advance or severe? Sex-based harassment is actionable if it is severe *or* pervasive under Title VII (or both severe *and* pervasive under Title IX). Summers's comment is sex-based harassment, even if the remark is not actionable. It contributes to gender stereotypes and perpetuates a hostile environment for female students. It sensitizes girls to the notion that they lack talent in those fields. However, it falls within neither of the definitions just reviewed.

So what if a physics teacher, Mr. Smith, flatters a teenage student with sexual attention? Is it still harassment, even though she "welcomed" the kisses and caresses?[12] In its own educational pamphlet, the OCR posed the question, "Must the sexual conduct be unwelcome?" The answer reads, "Yes. Conduct is considered unwelcome if the student did not request or invite it and considered the conduct to be undesirable or offensive." The OCR added, "The age of the student, the nature of the conduct and other relevant factors affect whether a student *was capable* of welcoming the sexual conduct. A student's submission to the conduct or failure to complain does not *always* mean that the conduct was welcome."[13]

From a legal perspective and by this OCR definition, a compliant fifteen-year-old usually "welcomes" the sexual advances of a teacher perhaps twenty years her senior? Really? How will the OCR, or even an expert psychologist or psychiatrist, know whether the minor was "capable of welcoming the conduct" when it happened? Adults will be evaluating the teen's capacity months or years after-the-fact when the issue lands in the superintendent's office or in court. How will judges and jurors, who conceivably have no training in adolescent development, know if the teen was mature and capable when the alleged incidents occurred? And, doesn't this question miss the point? Arguably, society outlaws sex with minors because they *don't* have the *legal capacity* to consent. The OCR sends a troublesome message to our children, teenagers, younger grammar school students, and adult sexual predators when it presumes juvenile legal capacity to welcome sex with an adult.

Some clubs and youth-oriented associations use a broader definition than the one developed by the EEOC for sexual harassment by adults at work.[14] For example, Rotarians do not emphasize that conduct must be "unwelcome." They also acknowledge sexual harassment as grooming behavior, behavior engaged in by a sexual predator intent on serious sexual exploitation.[15] Adult seduction and molestation of adolescents at work, school, or play are fundamentally different from adult abuse of other adults because, as chapter 3 explains, these teen targets are not adults and do not function like adults. Therefore, I suggest another definition: "To sexually harass is to dominate another person physically or psychologically by annoying, frightening, demeaning, or taking unfair advantage of that person through the exploitation of human sexuality or gender stereotypes." This definition takes care of both Mr. Smith and Dr. Summers. However, this definition is not the foundation of law.

Does one comment make a sexual harassment legal case? No and that clarification is important. This discussion addresses the refinement of a legal definition. This refinement should factor in the "environment" that molds and affects our children and that, arguably, influences their responsive behavior. The requirements of a prima facie ("on its face" or "at first view") legal case for sexual harassment receive clarification in chapters 6 and 7. Dr. Summers's comment may be harassing by my definition but it would not merit legal action under current sexual harassment law. A legal case requires at least severe or pervasive harassment and sometimes both. For the moment, readers must accept the standard definitions of sexually harassing conduct, aware that seduced children will fall through the technical, legal cracks.

Sexual Harassment at School

In 2001 the AAUW announced that 83 percent of girls and 79 percent of boys reported experiencing sexual harassment at some point during their school career.[16] These are staggering numbers. Ten years later the AAUW published results from another survey but limited the time frame to one academic year, 2010–11. It still found that almost half of the students (48%) in grades 7–12 reported being sexually harassed during that year.[17] Educating a projected sixteen million students in US high schools alone,[18] schools are dealing with a huge problem. Appendix 1 contains a list of behaviors about which the AAUW polled in 2011.[19]

Other studies confirm similar rates.[20] "Some researchers claim that sexual harassment is so common for girls that many fail to recognize it as sexual harassment when it happens."[21] For example, many girls might not consider a smack on the butt by a coach to be harassment. However, this conduct is almost never acceptable at the workplace and is not appropriate at school.[22] Certainly, one smack on the butt is neither severe nor indicative of pervasive harassment. However, such behavior multiplied could add to the creation of a hostile educational environment. Take another example. According to the top definition (of more than eighty) on *Urban Dictionary*, the word *biatch* "has found it's [sic] way into the mouths of every white teen in america [sic]."[23] This word is a "gangster" substitute for *bitch*.[24] Oddly, teen girls might recognize *bitch* as insulting but not *biatch* because of the common and popular usage of the new version in "teen speak." Just as youths may not recognize discrimination and gender-based slurs, they may not immediately identify sexual harassment. Thus, the prevalence of sexual harassment in schools may be even higher than that reported by the AAUW. *Sexual Exploitation of Teenagers* will further review the failure to recognize sexual harassment in the section on enculturation below.

The AAUW also reports that sexual harassment in schools almost always occurs between students. The 2011 AAUW study noted, "Nearly all the behavior documented in the survey was peer-to-peer sexual harassment."[25] For students sexually harassed by peers, schools and parents should be the first line of protection and guidance. Most cases do not require federal or state police involvement, a lawyer, or a court filing. The high incidence of reported harassing behaviors, however, suggests that schools, parents, and other adults could do more to train and protect all students and appropriately discipline transgressing students.

Additionally, legal liability for Romeo and Juliet (or Romeo and Romeo) may make no sense, given chapter 3's revelations regarding adolescent psychosocial and sexual development. Not all adolescent consent requires formal legal analysis. When a six-year-old steals a kiss from a classmate, the child needs adult supervision and age-appropriate parental guidance, not legal intervention.[26] Arguably, Romeo and Juliet need similar and age-appropriate adult supervision and guidance. (I note here that in *Romeo and Juliet*, Juliet was thirteen and sword-wielding Romeo was perhaps sixteen to nineteen years old, although William Shakespeare never specifies his exact age.)[27] Responsible parenting and other informal strategies, such as peer counseling and mentoring by qualified youth leaders, teachers, counselors, and coaches, allow concerned adults to sidestep formal legal intervention to avoid the misplaced application of law regarding offensive adolescent sex-based behavior.

In contrast to peer sexual harassment, there is much less information about educator sexual misconduct. A 2004 ED study by Professor Charol Shakeshaft found "few empirical studies of educator sexual misconduct. . . . The report recommends a series of studies to deepen the understanding of educator sexual misconduct and strategies to prevent the abuse of students."[28] Rigorous scientific analysis and legal reform must remedy haphazard and misguided treatment of adolescent exploitation. When power imbalances, adult-teen sexual predation, and more serious forms of unaddressed youth sexual abuse put children at risk of significant injury and trauma, legal responses should be swift and targeted.

While the AAUW surveys focused on peer sexual harassment, Professor Shakeshaft analyzed the data from AAUW reports predating the 2011 study that also contained information on educator sexual misconduct. In her 2003 article, she determined that almost *10 percent* (9.6%) of students in the eighth through twelfth grades had experienced *unwanted* educator sexual misconduct.[29] The 2004 Shakeshaft ED report explained, "Teachers whose job description includes time with individual students, such as music teachers or coaches, are more likely to sexually abuse than other teachers. . . . The majority of allegations of educator sexual misconduct are not reported to the police by the school districts."[30] It also found, "There are no systematic studies of false accusations of educators, but studies of child sexual abuse in general indicate that false allegations are not common."[31] Shakeshaft concluded, "Based on the assumption that the AAUW surveys accurately represent the experiences of all K–12 students, more than 4.5 *million* students are subject to sexual misconduct by an employee of a school sometime between kindergarten and 12th grade."[32]

The question arises why the OCR and the schools, to which parents must send their children, do not track and publish this information. Thankfully, the AAUW has been on the alert. At the very least, this issue deserves immediate attention.[33]

Sexual Harassment at Work

While the schoolhouse appears to be the most likely place that a teenager will experience sexual harassment, more and more teenagers are now working part-time. Therefore, they fall at risk to predators at the workplace too. Researchers estimate that over 4.4 million adolescents between the ages of sixteen and nineteen worked in 2012.[34] The EEOC reported, however, that of over 7,500 sexual harassment charges filed in 2012,[35] only thirty-nine working minors filed a formal complaint of sexual harassment.[36] That news suggests teenagers are safe at work. However, one must question why so many youth experience sexual harassment at school and so few do at work, according to the EEOC. Something may be wrong with the EEOC charge numbers. Consider some other perspectives on this question.

In 2009 *NOW on PBS* (Public Broadcasting Service) collaborated with Brandeis University's Schuster Institute for Investigative Journalism to create *Is Your Daughter Safe At Work?*, a television documentary concerning the sexual harassment of working teenagers. During the show, host Maria Hinojosa learned from journalist E. J. Graff that, according to Schuster's research, about 200,000 teenagers are sexually harassed on the job each year.[37] Graff and the Schuster Institute created a website that further documents the problem with a list of cases, anecdotal stories, and helpful resources.[38] In stark contrast to the Schuster/PBS claim, the EEOC reported that of almost 12,700 sexual harassment charges, only sixty-eight minors filed charges in 2009.[39]

The same year as the Schuster/PBS documentary, professors Susan Fineran and James E. Gruber published the results of their study concerning a small sample of working high school females. Seventy-two percent of these girls were under eighteen and most worked primarily in two types of jobs: restaurant service (44%) and retail sales (36%). Fineran and Gruber found that more than 52 percent had experienced some form of sexual harassment during the past year at their part-time jobs and that a "large majority of the perpetrators were older than the girls, with nearly half (46%) described as older than 30."[40] Fineran and Gruber compared their data with similar studies of adult female workers and determined that "teenage girls not only experienced more harassment [than the adults] but also that it occurred in a shorter time period." Fineran and Gruber concluded, "These findings may seem somewhat predictable given that teenagers are young, single, and have low job status. All three factors are cited in the literature as strong and consistent predictors of sexual harassment victimization."[41] Again, the question arises why the Fineran and Gruber study reveals so much more sexual harassment than the EEOC charge statistics substantiated. If minors face more sexual harassment than adult women, then why didn't the EEOC and state fair employment practices agencies see at least 13,000 charges by minors (or 268 more than the 12,632 actually filed by adults)?

In 2010 Mary O'Neill, a regional attorney for the EEOC, confirmed that the sexual harassment of teenagers "continues to be an epidemic in many workplaces, restaurants, retails, etc., where young people work."[42] However, that year the EEOC posted only forty-five charges by minors for sexual harassment, compared to the over 11,700 total charges filed.[43]

Several reasons related to non-reporting explain the very low EEOC charge statistics for teenagers. First, teenagers fail to report harassment because of their immaturity and embarrassment. Second, they may be ignorant about their rights. Third, adolescents may fear that adult supervisors will not believe them or will retaliate. Fourth, teens have a desire to do well in their first jobs "and not rock the boat."[44] Presumably, these teenagers hope to get good job references, recommendations they may not get if they complain about sexual harassment. A working teenager may fear being labeled "a trouble maker," thereby ruining her chances of employment in the future. Teenagers rightfully feel concerned about their future employment prospects whether or not they have good job references. Teenagers ages sixteen to nineteen faced an unemployment rate of 24 percent in 2012, as compared to the 8-percent rate for adults.[45] Given the high unemployment rate for teenagers, one can imagine the pressure they must feel to keep a job.

Additionally, the EEOC charge forms do not require a date of birth.[46] The EEOC intake charge form provides a space for date of birth, but information was not available regarding whether complainants fill in that information. Many teens may be filing charges of sexual harassment that the EEOC fails to categorize accurately because the charge documents do not properly reflect that the charging party is a minor. Finally, even if a charge contains the complainant's age, that information may not be transferred from the paper intake forms to computer records. Sadly, the EEOC charge statistics are almost irrelevant for documenting the sexual harassment of teenagers at work.

The initial response to the sexual harassment of teenagers is not acceptable. Schools don't adequately track sexual harassment (let alone prevent it) and neither does the EEOC, the commission specifically created to enforce Title VII. Instead, EEOC press releases, court filings, newspaper reports, and the occasional academic study tell us some of what's really going on for working teenagers and students. One wonders if, because of this inattention, harassers target teenage workers more than they do adults.

Youth Sexual Harassment in the Restaurant Industry

The Fineran and Gruber study indicated that more than three quarters (80%) of the teenagers in their study worked in restaurants or entertainment and retail sales. So did Sara and most of our profiled Doe plaintiffs. EEOC lawsuits document the sexual harassment of youth in the restaurant industry. According to EEOC District Director Lynn Y. Bruner, no other industry receives as many complaints or sees as many cases filed in the civil court system as the restaurant industry.[47] In 2002 the EEOC filed eighteen sexual harassment lawsuits against restaurants,[48] including Taco Bell, Church's Chicken, Applebee's, Denny's, Colonial Café & Ice Cream, Pepe's Mexican Restaurants, and others.[49]

One cannot always tell from EEOC press releases whether the alleged targets were minors at the time the incidents occurred; nevertheless, two EEOC press releases from 2003 documented the sexual harassment of female teenagers at Burger King, Church's Chicken,[50] Jack in the Box, and Taco Bell.[51] For example, on January 31, 2003, the *St. Louis Post Dispatch* reported the case of a Burger King manager who sexually harassed six women, five of whom were high school students.[52] The manager, in his late twenties, allegedly fondled the workers, made vulgar comments, and demanded sex. Initially, the women did not know how to make a complaint to someone more senior than their manager.[53]

A 2012 EEOC press release announced a $1 million settlement that included injunctive relief involving the franchisee of twenty-five McDonald's restaurants: "According to the EEOC's complaint, since at least 2006, several male employees subjected female co-workers to sexual harassment, including sexual comments, kissing, touching of their private areas, and forcing their hands onto the men's private parts." The announcement noted that "some" of the harassed workers were teenagers, but it did not indicate how many or whether these teens had filed charges individually. As EEOC General Counsel P. David López commented, "harassment no longer can be accepted as simply 'part of the culture' of the restaurant industry. . . . As seen in this case," he added, "many younger workers' first experience with the workplace is in this industry and it is important that harassment of these workers not be tolerated."[54]

In the EEOC press release concerning the Burger King case, Lynn

Bruner expressed her concern for vulnerable adolescents in the restaurant industry. She commented, "We as a society fail when teenagers—as part of their first employment experience—are subjected to graphic language, inappropriate touching, and requests for sexual favors by the very adults who are supposed to make sure they're safe." She further explained that sexual harassment might be a particular problem in the restaurant industry because restaurants often hire young, inexperienced workers.[55] High employee turnover contributes to the problem, presumably because of monitoring difficulties and the need to train new employees continually.[56] Bruner also suggested that "restaurants often try to create an 'entertainment atmosphere' that can cloud the rules for appropriate conduct in the workplace."[57] Identification of this work sector, plagued by the sexual harassment of its teen workers, enables concerned adults to target it for remediation.

Youth Sexual Harassment in Retail Sales and at Work Generally

As discussed in chapter 3, facts regarding adolescent development suggest that responsible adults should not shelter teens from experimentation and gradual learning. Teens need to develop a strong work ethic, workplace relationships, and concrete skills useful for their future employment. Responsible adults should facilitate their learning and maturation under circumstances that safeguard their developmental vulnerabilities.

San Francisco Legal Aid Society—Employment Law Center Staff Attorney David Pogrel agrees that teenagers face unique risks at the workplace. He explained, "Teenagers on the job are often seen as fungible. A lot of employers don't treat them with the same respect [as adult workers]." Pogrel suggested that employers violate "a whole myriad of rights . . . of young workers," do not pay them properly, and fail to prevent their sexual harassment.[58] Adolescents face this treatment at a time in their development when they are learning new interpersonal skills and how to function in a workplace environment. They may not yet understand the boundaries between what may be tolerated outside the workplace but illegal within it.

Sexual harassers target not only young restaurant workers, but also teens working in other industries. In 1999 the EEOC filed suit against Footaction USA. A manager in his late thirties allegedly sexually harassed a teenage employee. The manager, coworkers, and customers subjected the teenager to sexual jokes, propositions, and threats, culminating in a physical assault. San Francisco EEOC District Director Susan L. McDuffie commented, "Sexual harassment—at what is very often the teenaged employee's first job—can have a devastating psychological effect, causing the victim to feel shame, to change the way she dresses, to drop out of school, and to be afraid to tell anyone what is happening." About litigation that the EEOC had filed McDuffie said, "We hope this suit will send two messages. Employers must have zero tolerance for sexual harassment. In addition, teens should know they have a right to report unwelcome, offensive sexual conduct . . . and that if they come to the EEOC, we will take action."[59]

In these quotes, McDuffie raised several important points. First, she acknowledged the phenomenon of teen harassment. Second, she briefly explored sexual harassment's devastating effects on adolescents and mentioned their fear of reporting harassment. Third, she called for zero tolerance by employers in order to protect these teens. Fourth, she emphasized the need for teens to know their rights and that the EEOC responds to complaints. This fourth point supports the notion that some teens do not know their rights and are unaware that an agency exists to help them.

Schools and state fair-employment agencies must improve their reporting and response systems. At the very least, the EEOC must start accurately reporting incidents of sexual harassment by updating its reporting processes to ensure accessibility by minors. Concerned adults need to know the prevalence and scope of the sexual harassment of working adolescents. Is sexual harassment of teenagers as pervasive as sexual harassment of adults? Is it even more pervasive? Fineran and Gruber's small study suggests that it is more pervasive.

Responsible adults must also determine whether the presence of adolescent workers in an industry correlates with a high incidence of sexual harassment. An investigation into adolescent harassment will lead to other, more sophisticated questions. For example, if sexual harassment of teenagers is pervasive, do they tolerate harassment and, if so, why? Are they ignorant of their rights? Are they immobilized by shame? Is it shame or do they fear economic retaliation, or even physical violence? The American Academy of Child & Adolescent Psychiatry (AACAP) suggested in a policy statement, "It is common for children and adolescents to conceal these offenses [sexual harassment] because they feel afraid, ashamed, vulnerable, and humiliated. They may actually believe their own behavior may have precipitated the sexual harassment. These incidents are often not revealed for many years, if ever."[60] This AACAP statement raises other questions. To what extent do teenagers fail to report harassment? If teenagers are not complaining, do they have unique coping techniques? Do they consent to sexual activity and then complain? Is Sara's case unique? Answers to these questions will enable jurists, educators, health-care professionals, and employers to address problems through training, counseling, and legal reform.

Sexual Harassment in Other Contexts

The survey and anecdotal evidence about workplaces and schools highlight the need for more rigorous empirical research and comprehensive action to prevent the sexual harassment of adolescents. These two venues, however, are not the only arenas in which teenagers face sexual harassment and abuse. Adolescents encounter harassment on sports teams and in church youth groups, the military, and juvenile detention centers, among other places.

Sexual Harassment of Adolescent Athletes

In its policy statement, the Women's Sports Foundation declares, "Sexual harassment is a recognized social problem in sport. Sexual harassment in sport deters girls and women from participating and developing as athletes."[61] Nowhere that I could find does the Women's Sports Foundation, or anyone else, describe the prevalence of this problem in youth athletics. Safe4Athletes explains on its website, "While there is no consistently collected data on the prevalence of these transgressions, there is reason to believe that news reports and limited data from national sport governing bodies represent the proverbial 'tip of the iceberg.'" This organization then details that 159 coaches in Washington State were fired or reprimanded for sexual misconduct, fifty-nine swim coaches have resigned or been banned from USA Swimming because of conduct violations, and eighty-two coaches associated with USA Gymnastics are now ineligible for membership.[62]

Sexual harassment is a serious problem for male athletes as well as females. Pennsylvania State University is settling approximately twenty-five civil law claims by boys abused by former assistant coach Gerald

Sandusky. A jury convicted Sandusky of forty-five counts of criminal sex charges involving ten boys over a period of more than a decade. Allegations of a university cover-up complicate the cases.[63] Weighing witness testimony, the report of the special investigative counsel determined "that, in order to avoid the consequences of bad publicity, the most powerful leaders at the University—Spanier, Schultz, Paterno and Curley—repeatedly concealed critical facts relating to Sandusky's child abuse from the authorities, the University's Board of Trustees, the Penn State community, and the public at large."[64] Thus, not only did school officials fail to report abuse, they actively concealed it to avoid negative publicity.

Sports clubs and leagues, as well as universities, have an interest in attracting and keeping healthy adolescent athletes, both male and female. Unless these organizations start tracking sexual harassment charges and remediating problems, they will not know if their prevention and education efforts are effective.[65]

Sexual Harassment at Church

Volumes have been written about the sexual abuse of children by priests, pastors, church youth leaders, and other adults affiliated with religious institutions.[66] *Sexual Exploitation of Teenagers* does not review that material in depth. Suffice it to say that the US Conference of Catholic Bishops commissioned a voluntary survey conducted of the US dioceses, commonly known as the *John Jay Report*. The study indicated that about 4 percent (4,392) of US Catholic priests were accused of sexual abuse between 1950 and 2002 in 10,992 individual reports of abuse.[67] The majority of the victims (81%) were boys, and most (78%) were between the ages of eleven and sixteen.[68] Perhaps the days of sexual abuse scandals involving religious institutions and youth are behind us. Concerned adults won't know, however, unless those institutions become aggressive about continuously tracking the problem.

Sexual Harassment in the Military

The military enlists teenagers as young as seventeen if they have a parent's signature. It engages in heavy marketing and recruiting in high schools and shopping malls, at sporting events and convenience stores, wherever older teenagers gather. Young soldiers are vulnerable to abuse, despite strict military discipline. In 2011 the military acknowledged

3,000 cases of *reported* sexual assault. Female soldiers are 180 times more likely to be sexually assaulted by another US soldier than killed by enemy fire. "Victims tend to be young, of low rank, and too intimidated to speak out."[69] A new Pentagon study on sexual assault "estimated that 26,000 service members experienced unwanted sexual contact in 2012, up from 19,000 in 2010. Of those cases, the Pentagon says, 53 percent involved attacks on men, mostly by other men."[70] This study highlights that young men, as well as women, face sexual harassment and abuse in the military.

Despite the recent military scandals regarding rape and sexual assault, the military does prohibit sexual harassment.[71] "Pentagon leaders and their 13,800 recruiters have made tackling the issue of sexual assault a priority in their efforts to enlist 280,000 young men and women annually for active and reserve forces, said Defense Department spokesman Lt. Cmdr. Nate Christensen."[72]

In 2013 the Department of Defense (DoD) published an analysis concerning reports of unwanted sexual contact for fiscal year 2012. It confirmed that 18 percent (~470) of the 2,610 completed investigations of unrestricted reports involved teenage victims ages sixteen to nineteen.[73] Only 5 percent of the investigated subject perpetrators from completed reports were teenagers.[74] Neither the DoD survey nor recent media reports make clear how many of the reported and suspected sexual abuse and rape cases involved minors. However, young soldiers are being blamed for the sexual abuse. Having studied teen sexuality for years, Dr. Mike Males suggests that "scapegoating [has] shifted to children and youth, who have proven perpetually easy to malign and sensationalize for the purpose of quick funding and popularity scorings."[75]

Dr. Males's assertion may apply in the context of the military sex scandals. For example, Senator Saxby Chambliss of the Senate Armed Services Committee suggested to the Joint Chiefs of Staff at a 2013 military sex scandal hearing, "The young folks coming in to each of your services are anywhere from 17 to 22 or 23. Gee whiz, the hormone level created by nature sets in place the possibility for these types of things to occur."[76] I found no science to support the assertion that hormones cause rape or sexual assault. This comment suggests that Chambliss believes stereotypes concerning youthful sexual behavior and that he confuses natural sexual development with violent sexual assault.

"Air Force Chief of Staff Gen. Mark Welsh suggested in recent Senate testimony that the spike in reports of sexual assaults in the military could be blamed on the 'hook up mentality' of the country's young people."[77] This assertion raises several concerns. First, "hooking up" refers to casual consensual sex, and that is not the same as assault and rape. The conflation of consensual sexual activity and sexual abuse highlights why the military might be having problems eradicating sexual violence. Second, the implication of Welsh's remark is that Army, Navy, Air Force, and Marine leaders cannot control sexual harassment or assault in the military, in part because they are not even able to identify it.

This discussion begs the question whether the perpetrators are actually young people. Certainly, not all of them are. Lt. Col. Jeffrey Krusinski, who led the Air Force's sexual assault prevention program and was arrested for sexual assault, was in his forties.[78] Brigadier General Bryan T. Roberts, who faced allegations of adultery and misconduct involving a physical altercation, became a commissioned officer through Reserve Officers' Training Corp (ROTC) in 1983 and so was in his fifties.[79] Master Sgt. Brad Grimes, who was charged with several sex-related crimes, is an eighteen-year veteran of the Army.[80] Sgt. First Class Michael McClendon, who was accused of videotaping West Point female cadets undressing and in the showers, joined the Army in 1990, twenty-four years ago.[81] In 2011 Tech. Sgt. Jaime Rodriguez was thirty-two and a recruiter when he sent a seventeen-year-old recruit "lewd text messages and naked photos of himself." Seventeen other women claim he tried to initiate sexual relationships with them.[82] In sum, these are not young, inexperienced soldiers, but seasoned officers and soldiers who allegedly took advantage of their rank and positions.[83]

As it deals with the thousands of pending rape, sexual assault, and harassment cases, the military should reform its complaint and response procedures and start noting the actual numbers of minor victims and perpetrators. DoD should address whether even greater numbers of minor service members, who allegedly consent to sexual activity, even have the capacity to do so. Additionally, the *Feres* doctrine that prevents the application of Title VII in the context of military employment begs for reconsideration of legal remedies.[84]

Sexual Harassment in Juvenile Detention Centers and Prisons

One might think that juveniles in detention might avoid sexual abuse because of the secure nature of their living circumstances. Not so. A 2003 survey of youth victimization in detention facilities found that 4 percent of youth in a sample population of over seven thousand had experienced not simply sexual harassment but actual sexual assault. "For the victims, these sexual assaults are not isolated occurrences. Youth who report any sexual assault experienced an average of six or more similar events during their time in residence."[85]

During 2005 and 2006, juvenile correction authorities received over four thousand allegations of sexual violence. The DOJ reported that more than a third of these (36%) concerned "youth-on-youth nonconsensual sexual acts, such as rape and forcible sodomy." Another 21 percent involved peers engaged in "unwanted touching or grabbing with the intention to exploit sexually." Another third (32%) pertained to "staff sexual misconduct, defined as any act of a sexual nature directed toward a youth, either consensual or nonconsensual." Finally, 11 percent "involved staff sexual harassment, including repeated comments or demeaning references of a sexual nature to a youth."[86] Of the substantiated allegations about staff, juvenile correction officers characterized almost two-thirds "as 'a romantic relationship' or as 'appeared to be willing.'" Fifty-four percent of the adult perpetrators were male, and 63 percent were under thirty years old. In only 40 percent of these cases did the adults face arrest and prosecution.[87]

According to a 1988 DOJ study, juveniles housed in adult prisons were five times more likely to be sexually assaulted than if housed in juvenile detention facilities. "Clearly, safely housing juveniles in adult facilities and protecting younger inmates from predatory, older inmates are important issues for correctional administrators."[88]

Sexual Harassment in Public

In her 2010 book *Stop Street Harassment: Making Public Places Safe and Welcoming for Women*, Holly Kearl documents and discusses street harassment, including whistles, catcalls, obscene comments, and other more threatening behaviors, such as stalking. Kearl explains that friends, family, and others had told her the calls and whistles were "a compliment." She writes, "I did not see my experiences in the larger context of women's inequality in society or piece together how many of us can't go about our daily lives without men objectifying, insulting, or threatening us."[89]

Senator Kirsten Gillibrand documents similar comments but from other members of Congress. One member told her, "You know, Kirsten, you're even pretty when you're fat." She explains in her memoir, "I believed his intentions were sweet, even if he was being an idiot."[90] Also similar to Kearl, Gillibrand accepted this comment as a compliment. Yet, she understood that this man was "an idiot" and that his comment was insulting or somehow just wrong.

I remember as a young child that automobile repair garages and many male-dominated workplace locations used to display "adult" (male) calendars and pin-up pictures of busty nude women. If you are familiar with the popular television show *Mad Men*,[91] you will know how sexist even a white-collar office was back in the 1960s. Some patrons and workers found these displays vulgar, but no one really questioned the legality of the images of naked, sexually available women. No one blinked when men "rated" passing secretaries or women on the street on a scale of one to ten. Such behavior and displays were "art," "free speech," and "adult entertainment." They were examples of men just being men as they appreciated the (sometimes spread-eagle) female form.

Today, one might be surprised to see such centerfold displays in a ticket office, dispatch trailer, garage, or repair shop. Men do not hang around the Keurig machine and discuss their latest sexual conquests or "rate" the latest female executive recruits. Workers have been alerted to the harassing nature of such displays and conversations that demean women and cast them as sexual objects. Most workers understand how such images contribute to the enculturation of a workforce that thinks nothing of the domination and sexual stereotyping of women. While this behavior does not target one woman, it arguably subjects a class (all female workers) to annoying behavior that results in hostile or intimidating work environments. It keeps women, as a class, from moving beyond such stereotypes. It changes the expectations of both men and women about the dignity of women and possible contributions that women might make in the world.

Is this behavior actionable? Not if the controversy fails to meet legal thresholds. For example, Title VII applies only to workplaces that employ fifteen or more workers. However, the failure to meet a legal threshold does not negate the fact that the underlying conduct or message is harassing. It demeans or takes advantage of someone through the exploitation of human sexuality or gender stereotypes. It leads to the domination of women by those (usually men but not always) who control the harassing behavior and messaging. It changes the perception of women and girls. It conditions women and girls to sexual objectification and the futility of resistance.

So, why is such harassment still prevalent outside the workplace—in public? Because despite the pervasiveness of public sexual harassment, women lack the resources and means to implement effective reform. Whom do you sue for public harassment? What laws can you use? How expensive is it? How do you prove damages? The damage caused by pervasive public harassment is a bit like the damage to the pyramids caused by the polluted winds. This damage is subtle, accumulating over time. State laws may not adequately address street harassment, and many people do not even realize that some forms of street harassment are unlawful in many jurisdictions.[92] Rather than further outlaw street harassment, I would like to see targeted public service announcements and other media campaigns raise consciousness about street harassment. A good way to curb rude behavior is to point it out and denounce it.

A review of media content prevalent in public places and malls reveals, however, much sexist and demeaning content that shoppers and others fail to notice. Messaging on the street, at the mall, or in a song arguably contributes to the enculturation of the next generation—one that is spending lots of time at the mall or accessing media and, therefore, being exposed to sexual messaging. Consider for a moment that harassment, once camouflaged as art, free speech, or "adult entertainment" is now fashion, free cultural self-expression, and is still "adult entertainment."

One might argue that commercial sexual messaging is not sexual harassment. Others contend that such sexual messaging constitutes subtle and sometimes blatant discriminatory harassment. The Stop Street Harassment website currently has a page that lists seven prominent companies whose advertisements and products arguably condone street harassment. One New Jersey mall sign read, "We apologize for the whistling construction workers, but man you look good! So will we soon, please pardon our dust, dirt, and assorted inconveniences." A Lucy Activewear advertisement in a mall displayed women bent over in yoga pants. The caption read, "Let the compliments begin. Try the new Perfect Booty Pant." These ads minimize street harassment, perpetuate stereotypes about construction workers and other street/mall observers, and objectify women by reducing them to visual entertainment or body parts.[93]

As one considers how far American culture has come in the appreciation of human dignity and cooperative respect since the 1960s, one might further consider how far society could progress in the next fifty years. Are today's public and retail messages holding us back or propelling us forward?

Sexual Harassment at the Mall

Ten years ago, when my daughter was a teenager, I called the "fashion statement" that was then pervasive in the teen departments at most chain department stores the "Après Molestation" look. My daughter and I could not avoid the torn jeans, thongs visible over pants cut just above the pubic bone, T-shirts that fell off shoulders, and shoes that had teens tottering as if they were still reeling from an attack. I also heard the style called the "Come Fuck Me" look. I found this appellation doubly offensive but apt because, in addition to its crudity, it suggests, as some adults believe, that young girls invite their own sexual violation. You may recall the Billings, Montana, judge who asserted that the fourteen-year-old student, seduced by her fifty-four-year-old teacher, was "older than her chronological age" and that she was "as much in control of the situation as was the defendant."[94] The implication of these comments is that this girl may have invited the statutory rape. Such attitudes are not rare, as chapter 3 demonstrates.

My daughter saw no problem with the apparel offered her. When I bluntly delivered my opinion, she was appalled and asserted that she was not attempting to foster that look. I told her that, at thirteen, she did not have the experience to know how the rest of the world would view and interpret her fashion statement. Was this interaction an example of timeless parent-child conflict or feminist pushback against a culture intent on grooming our girls? Perhaps both. However, if beauty is in the eye of the beholder, then so is the vision of a teenage "tramp." Arguably, this fashion funneling (the herding of fashion consumers to a narrow set of fashion options) is the result of aspirational advertising directed at girls and their parents.

Many people are not familiar with the concept of *aspirational advertising*, but it is a common marketing tool. Aspirational advertising specifically appeals to people through images that portray them as they wish to be. Many middle-aged women (my peers) want to feel and appear younger than their actual age. They purchase products, such as cosmetics, hair color, and clothing, which advertisers market for their goal. You may have noticed that teenagers want to want to "fit in" and appear older than they are.[95] No one who has seen the Abercrombie & Fitch mega-posters of scantily clad teenagers in their mall stores doubts what CEO Mike Jeffries recently acknowledged, "A&F is an aspirational brand that, like most specialty apparel brands, targets its marketing at a particular segment of customers."[96]

Marketers even developed an aspirational name for targeted juvenile consumers between ages eight and twelve: "tweens."[97] One reporter commented that "a quick visit to the mall makes it clear that marketers believe what girls . . . want to be is an 18-year-old starlet on the make. Snakeskin pants, belly shirts, faux leopard jackets and bikini underwear are this season's offerings for little girls."[98] I suspect that reporter shopped at the same stores my daughter and I frequented. One vice president at a marketing firm commented, "There is significantly less rebellion in young people today . . . and a more aspirational relationship between parent and child."[99] Does this new marketing foster parent-teen bonding? Maybe not. Certainly not for feminist parents and their commercially seduced young daughters.

Researchers who focus on safety for adolescents comment, "Especially in a society where images of adolescent sexuality abound in the media, it may not be clear to many adolescents and adults that [sexual] relationships between adults and underage adolescents are criminal."[100] Academics caution that our culture is saturated with sexual messaging. Parents may not realize how their children are processing these sexual images. "It's harder and harder to think about what it means for someone who's fresh, who doesn't understand, who can't *think* the way we do."[101] Chapter 3 explores adolescent *thinking* in more depth. Forever 21 and other mall stores, however, are not the only commercial enterprises selling stereotypical sex to teens (and adults).

Sexual Harassment in Air Waves and Cyberspace

American teens fully embrace their digital gadgets. During any weekend, one can find adolescents at the mall, often talking on their cell phones or listening to music. iPhones and similar devices keep them in touch (so to speak) and stream digital messages, including music.[102] "Nearly four in five teens (79%) have an iPod or other mp3 player."[103] Youth, ages eleven to eighteen, are exposed to approximately *eight* hours of media content *per day* on average. Television, audio, and video/movie are, respectively, the top three consumed forms of media in a typical adolescent's day.[104]

THE INTERNET. As plugged-in as teens are, one would not be surprised to hear that 93 percent of adolescents ages twelve to seventeen use the Internet.[105] The Internet is a marvelous educational tool and, occasionally, a gateway for sexual predators who harass youth. Reports of the prevalence of abuse confuse concerned Internet users because of the differing measures such as harassment versus solicitation and the different venues.

A Girl Scout Research Institute study found that 30 percent of teenage girls who had visited an online chat room had been sexually harassed. Adolescent girls received "photos of naked men," requests "for bra sizes," and solicitations for "'cyber,' which is slang for having cyber sex."[106] Most teens, however, do not encounter sexual solicitations. Researchers distinguish between direct sexual solicitations and more general sexual harassment. According to one study, "[f]ifteen percent of all of the youth reported an unwanted sexual solicitation online in the last year; 4% reported an incident on a social networking site specifically. Thirty-three percent reported an online harassment in the last year; 9% reported an incident on a social networking site specifically."[107] Thus, Facebook and Myspace, for example, harbor fewer threats to youth than other forums.

Internet chat rooms and instant messaging offer seemingly private access to youth whose parents may not be monitoring their traffic. Researchers explained, "Among targeted youth, solicitations [i.e., requests for meetings or sexual favors] were more commonly reported via instant messaging (43%) and in chat rooms (32%), and harassment [e.g., sexist remarks, sexual comments or images] was more commonly reported in instant messaging (55%) than through social networking sites (27% and 28%, respectively)."[108] Again, the distinctions between sexual solicitations and more general harassment, and between venues, make a significant difference in the statistics.

Teens who meet in person with an online predator usually know the adult's age and expect to engage in sexual activity. "In the [National Juvenile Online Victimization] Study, only 5% of offenders pretended to be teens when they met potential victims online."[109] Previously abused youth experience more sexual victimization via the Internet than other teens. Researchers suggest that "prior abuse may trigger risky sexual behavior that directly invites online sexual advances. But delinquency, depression, and social interaction problems unrelated to abuse also may increase vulnerability."[110]

By early adolescence, teens understand the need to exercise caution while surfing on the Internet. So, why do teens meet with online solicitors and engage in risky Internet behavior? Some experts suggest that "as youths [12–17] get older and gain experience online, they engage in more complex and interactive Internet use. . . . [I]t was those 15 to 17 years of age who were most prone to take risks involving privacy and contact with unknown people."[111] Scholars attribute risks taken by older adolescents to "growing sexual curiosity, knowledge, and experience as youths make the transition from childhood to adulthood." Researchers also explain that relationships that develop online "typically take place in isolation and secrecy, outside of oversight by peers, family members, and others in the youths' face-to-face social networks. This isolation may lead to relationships that form more quickly, involve greater self-disclosure, and develop with greater intensity than face-to-face relationships among peers."[112] Chapter 3 discusses impulsivity and risk-taking behavior more in-depth.

Referencing maturity of judgment, a concept also discussed in chapter 3, experts suggest, "Few youths of those ages have the mature judgment and emotional self-regulation required to engage in healthy relationships that include sexual intimacy." Adolescent emotional control (or lack thereof) may explain why Internet seducers might gain access to teenagers. "In summary, what creates risk for teens online is not innocence about sex. The factors that make youths vulnerable to seduction by online molesters are complex and related to immaturity, inexperience, and the impulsiveness with which some youths respond to and explore normal sexual urges."[113] Again, chapter 3 covers all of this territory more completely.

CELLULAR TELEPHONES. If teen communication were confined to in-home desktop computer use, parents might have an easier time monitoring their traffic. However, according to a Pew Research Center Survey, 78 percent of adolescents ages twelve to seventeen had a cell phone in 2012.[114] The number of twelve-year-olds who owned a cell phone jumped from 18 percent in 2004 to 58 percent in 2009.[115] Moreover, cell phone technology has rapidly improved within the past few years. "Even the simplest, voice-only phones have more complex and powerful chips than the 1969 on-board computer that landed a spaceship on the moon."[116] Many cell phones allow the user to access the Internet, take digital pictures, send text messages with attachments, and conduct myriad other functions. Nearly half of all teen cell phone users (47%) have these multifunction smartphones.[117] What are teens doing with these technologically advanced gadgets?

Sexting, the distribution of sexually explicit messages or pictures, concerns many Americans. Several sexting scandals at schools in Pennsylvania, Washington, and Florida highlighted the phenomenon.[118] A 2009 Pew Research Center survey found that 4 percent of 800 surveyed teens ages twelve to seventeen had texted a sexually suggestive, nude, or seminude picture of themselves to another person. Fifteen percent of teens had received a sexually suggestive, nude, or seminude picture of another person through a text message. Researchers suspect that surveyed teens underreported their sexting activities because "sexting is a topic with a relatively high level of social disapproval." While not a representative sample, teen focus groups provided information that supported suspected underreporting.[119]

Another small 2012 study determined that almost 10 percent of 149 survey participants ages ten to seventeen reported sending nude or nearly nude images of themselves or receiving nude or nearly nude images of others. In response to the query whether the nude or nearly nude images showed "breasts, genitals, or someone's bottom," 54 percent of senders and 84 percent of receivers answered affirmatively. The other 46 percent of senders and 16 percent of receivers considered "nude or nearly nude" to include people wearing bathing suits, underwear, or pictures focused on clothed genitals.[120] "The percentage of youth who have, in the past year, appeared in or created sexually explicit sexual images that potentially violate child pornography laws is low (1%)."[121] While the sexting prevalence data differs depending on the study, a considerable number of adolescents send or receive sexual images and texts.

Underage teens can face serious criminal penalties for distributing or receiving nude pictures of themselves or other teens. The Federal Sex Offender Registration and Notification Act mandates registration for any convicted sex offender age fifteen or older.[122] "Today, every state has a statute criminalizing the creation, possession and distribution of child pornography and federal law mandates state enforced sexual offender registration. As a result, teens engaged in sexting may be charged under child pornography laws and become subject to federally mandated sex offender registration rules."[123] "[M]ost youth who simply produce or transmit images are not being treated as offenders." However, in 18 percent of cases involving no other criminal or malicious conduct, officers arrested teenagers. "This suggests that some youth may be facing exposure to criminal treatment in cases that might be better handled informally by families and clinicians."[124] One might ask, What are they thinking? This time, the *they* in that question refers to both the teens who sext *and* the prosecutors who pursue otherwise innocent adolescents with the threat of lifetime sex offender registration. The teenagers are developing capacity to evaluate whether or not an action might be inconsistent with the law and to conform their behavior to any such laws. The prosecutors already have that capacity.

TELEVISION. In addition to their access to modern media gadgets, teenagers still watch television. According to a study by the Henry J. Kaiser Family Foundation, 99 percent of minors ages eight to eighteen have a television in their home. Sixty-eight percent have a television in their bedroom.[125] On average, teens spend approximately three hours per day watching television programs.[126] Research discussed below indicates that much of this programming contains sexual content.

Television treatment of sexual harassment has attracted little academic attention in recent years. A 1997 study found that 84 percent of prime-time television programs depicted at least one incident of sexual harassment, with 3.4 incidents per show on average.[127] While most targets responded negatively, almost none took any legal action. In addition, a number of victims and witnesses responded "with humor, laughter, even sexual interest. The laugh track that is heard after nearly every exchange in situation-comedies reinforces the idea that sexual harassment is acceptable, and even light-hearted behavior between men and women."[128] This study found that women made many of the most sexist comments to other women. Researchers explained, "Such behaviors are not necessarily uncommon among any minority group that is psychologically oppressed and participates in its own oppression but such comments are more disarming and much harder to refute (after all, they come from the 'expert')."[129] This portrayal lends credibility to the notion that women who complain about sexual harassment are overreacting troublemakers.

More recent research demonstrates a connection between sexualized prime-time programming and teen behavior and perceptions. "Eighty-three percent of parents say exposure to sex on TV contributes to children becoming involved in sexual situations before they're ready. . . . Most teens agree: nearly three out of four 15–17 year-olds say sex on TV influences the sexual behaviors of kids their age."[130] Experts found a positive correlation between exposure to "sexy" prime-time television programs and teen acceptance of sex as recreation and support of stereotypical gender roles. In addition, teens who watched television for companionship more readily reflected attitudes that men are sexually driven and women are sexual objects.[131] Finally, researchers reported that "frequent viewing of music videos and talk shows, and strong identification with same-sex characters were each associated with greater levels of dating/sexual experience." These researchers stressed that findings indicated correlations, not causation, but the associations were clear.[132] This correlation becomes relevant as one evaluates whether the Does and Joes of profiled sexual harassment cases were sexually promiscuous or like many other teens raised in a culture saturated with sexual messaging.

MUSIC. Most teenagers might laugh if one suggested to them that music was sexually harassing. Moreover, I suspect that sophisticated music scholars might challenge my portrayal in a variety of ways. I could not find a relevant survey to support my perspective; however, several feminist scholars have analyzed rap and other popular music. Professor Margaret Hunter suggests, "Rap music sells a 'lifestyle.'" This lifestyle valorizes "cars, women ['hos'], drugs, and strip clubs." Hunter lists products that symbolize the lifestyle, including "PimpJuice energy drink (Nelly), Roc-a-Wear sunglasses (Jay-Z), Sean John jeans (Diddy), or Conjure Cognac (Ludacris)."

Hunter further explains,

> This lifestyle product is reinforced through lyrics, music video, online fan gossip, and constant marketing. The consumer-driven lifestyle product is epitomized in 50 Cent's newest product in his G-Unit line: the interactive pornography video. The pornography trade magazine, Adult Video News, reports that the interactive DVD, Groupie Love, will "take viewers inside his X-rated lifestyle." "You're banging their girls backstage at the concerts and hanging with them on the tour bus. . . . The viewer will be able to choose which girls to have sex with and where the sex will take place."[133]

Apparently *Groupie Love* facilitates "consensual" virtual sex with young "groupies"—*love* being a euphemism for group sex. Professor bell hooks argues, "To take 'gangsta rap' to task for its sexism and misogyny while critically accepting and perpetuating those expressions of that ideology which reflect bourgeois standards (no rawness, no vulgarity) is not to call for a transformation of the culture of patriarchy."[134] First, concerned adults and teens need to recognize the racist, sexist patriarchal culture. Then, they can attempt to reform it.

One might think that an attack on hip-hop is the same corruption-of-youth argument that stodgy adults laid against the music industry decades ago. "The King's" gyrating hips, however, didn't destroy Western civilization in the 1950s. Unlike Elvis's rock 'n' roll, however, hip-hop glamorizes misogynistic lifestyles and sexually degrading acts against women. Four aspects characterize hip-hop: (1) a sexually insatiable actor (usually male), (2) objectifies a target (usually female), (3) for sexual pleasure, (4) that focuses almost exclusively on physical characteristics.[135] Among musical genres, rap and R&B music contain the majority of references to degrading sex. These messages aren't silent trees falling in an unpopulated forest. Rap and R&B are the most popular forms of music among young people.[136] However, misogynistic lyrics exist in many music genres. One Tumblr website, "Misogynistic Lyrics that aren't Rap," contains links to thirty-nine pages of offensive lyrics from other music genres.[137]

Beyond shocking lyrics, musicians take pride in notoriously racy music videos. One study asked Dutch adolescents to provide a label for "sexually suggestive music videos." The participants chose rap/hip-hop as synonymous with sexually suggestive.[138] Researchers then provided 384 teenagers with a questionnaire that assessed how often the teens watched rap/hip-hop videos and how realistically the videos reflected life and adult relationships. Additionally, the researchers asked whether girls often said "no" when they meant "yes" and whether "it [was] alright for a boy to lean hard on a girl to have sex with him." The researchers hoped to assess teen receptiveness to the notion that women are sex objects and that men are supposed to be sexually dominant.

The study revealed that, among both males and females, as the frequency of exposure to rap/hip-hop videos and the perceived realistic nature of the videos increased, perceptions of women as sex objects and acceptance of male sexual dominance increased as well. Researchers also determined that perceptions of women as sex objects decrease over time as teens age. Stereotypes of female objectification and male sexual dominance may lay the psychological groundwork, however, for the commission of sexual harassment by adolescent males and its tolerance, if not acceptance, by their female peers. According to another expert, "Sexual harassment is also related to objectification. Objectification refers to the tendency of American culture to treat women's bodies as objects to be looked at and enjoyed by other people." In contrast, "[m]en's bodies . . . are primarily agentic and functional. They are supposed to do things, while women are just decorative and available for men's sexual gratification. This perception gives men permission to sexually harass and, again, encourages women to be passive, compliant—and silent."[139] Arguably, rap music expresses misogynistic degradation and, at its worst, contributes to a culture that valorizes and encourages sexual harassment.

Increased governmental censorship is not the answer to this problem. Censorship typically makes a message more interesting and alluring, not less so. I also appreciate the artistry in hip-hop music and acknowledge that it speaks for (some) disenfranchised people in our culture. It may express male sexual fear as it describes a fantasy. However, as with satire, the question is whether the audience will understand the underlying message.

Rather than increased governmental censorship, the solution involves *more* speech and education. Creative efforts are already underway to combat sexist cyber harassment. WAM! (Women, Action & the Media) is "an independent North American nonprofit dedicated to building a robust, effective, inclusive movement for gender justice in media."[140] It has just teamed up with Twitter to study harassment and abuse on the Twitter platform to improve Twitter's response to this phenomenon. WAM! explains, "Twitter recognizes that the best way to ensure equally free speech for all users on their platform is to ensure that all users are equally free to speak without being targeted by harassment, abuse and threats."[141] This WAM! initiative is just one example of efforts that might be made to eradicate harassment in public.

Education budget cuts that slash music and art classes from school curriculums limit our ability to review artistic trends with our children. If students analyze both the beauty and harm of artistic expression with qualified experts, those adults may empower teens to think critically about the messages they absorb in their daily lives. When teenagers recognize the potential damage caused by the toxic winds of public harassment, if they see with adult assistance the satire and pain in artistic works, they are more likely to respond appropriately. Once-banned books such as Toni Morrison's *Beloved* and Vladimir Nabokov's *Lolita* showcase how our appreciation of art evolves. The proper response to teen fashion offerings may also be more awareness and conversation. Singer-songwriter Dar Williams speaks to fashion, "And now I'm in this clothing store, and the signs say less is more / More that's tight means more to see, more for them, not more for me / That can't help me climb a tree in ten seconds flat."[142]

Conclusions Regarding Adolescent Worldliness

Depressed and disgusted? Teenagers are not safe from sexual abuse and harassing behavior. No matter where they go, they are potentially at risk. Educators, employers, jurists, legislators, and parents need to notice and understand the influences brought to bear on American teens as these adult guardians consider how the law should assist sexually harassed adolescents. Conceivably, the conditioning and aspirational brainwashing that bathes our teens—through magazines, on television, in music, on DVDs, in movies, and at the mall—influence how they respond to sexual advances from adult teachers, coworkers, prison officials, and their peers. Assuming this brainwashing occurs (and one knows it when one sees it) while teen brains are developing, responsible adults need to evaluate whether the commercial seduction of teens and their repeated bombardment with sexual chatter and behavior influences their vulnerability to seduction in the more traditional sense. And should the law account for this phenomenon? I suggest that laws should. Before considering the law, however, one should understand the science of adolescent neurological and psychosocial development.

CHAPTER THREE

Adolescent Development

Wisdom Regarding Teen Capacity

To evaluate the civil sexual harassment cases filed by Sara and her peers, one benefits from first considering whether adolescent consent to sex with their adult consorts equates with adult legal consent. If it does, these young people may not have justiciable claims of harm under civil law. Therefore, an understanding of adolescent development informs any evaluation of whether teenagers are capable of making wise, adultlike choices concerning sexual activity. Simply put, do teenagers have the *legal* capacity to opt for and handle sex with a work supervisor such as Michael Cosio, a teacher, or another adult authority figure? The science of adolescent development informs this legal analysis.

This chapter not only surveys adolescent physical and psychosocial maturation, it also addresses how society and adult behaviors influence adolescent development and capacity. The chapter considers whether cultural stereotypes and attitudes regarding teen capacity and sexual behavior may influence that development. In a similar way, this chapter examines how adolescent traits and development influence adult sexual predators. Adults intent on the sexual exploitation of children know how to groom their targets. They intuitively understand how adolescent vulnerabilities enable predatory conduct. Finally, this chapter briefly reviews how sexual abuse may dramatically influence adolescent physical and psychosocial maturation.

This chapter begins with a question. Do teenagers really think and function like adults? I imagine that most teens would respond, "Duh, no!" However, certain laws, drafted by arguably competent adults, presume that some adolescents do think and function like adults. So, why do other adults automatically assume that teens do not? In part, these people rely on what they remember. We were all teenagers once. Most adults recall their youth and have thought on occasion, What was I thinking? In part, these adults also rely on what they have observed in their own children, young friends, and neighbors. Such observations may have prompted the question, What were they thinking?

Persistent cultural messages seduce many adults into believing that something is *wrong* with American teenagers and the way they naturally behave. Playing with this belief in 2002, Dr. Michael Bradley titled his book *Yes, Your Teen Is Crazy! Loving Your Kid Without Losing Your Mind.* Two years later, he published *Yes, Your Parents Are Crazy! A Teen Survival Guide.* It's possible that the second title more accurately describes reality—that adults are a little crazy in the way they treat teenagers and that teenagers navigate to survive the guardians charged with their care. This notion takes on literal meaning when one considers that as late as 2005 judges and juries could subject serious teen criminal offenders to the death penalty![1] Less drastic treatment of teenagers persists in a variety of contexts, despite the science that proves teenagers are not simply mini-adults.

To frame the new scientific information reviewed below, this chapter poses several questions. First, have most teenagers formed a coherent independent identity, and if not, should jurists treat teen consent to sex with an adult supervisor, teacher, or coworker as legally significant? Second, do adolescent impulsivity and moodiness combine with stress (including pressure for sex) to influence a teen's decision-making process? Third, who influences an adolescent's decision to have sex with a supervisor or teacher (assuming that a minor does actually consent)? The teen's parents? Peers? Social media? Only the supervisor? Finally, should the law regard teen consent that was arguably given impulsively and under stress, and perhaps as a result of pressure by an authority figure, as significant and legally binding? In sum, does the law even go in the right direction given what scientists know from the group data about adolescent development and decision making?

Assume for a moment that adolescent consent should not be legally binding because adolescents do not have the power, (equal) status, and competence to consent to sex with an adult. Will jurists account for adolescent developing capacity, neurological and psychosocial immaturity, status, and power in their allocation of rights and liabilities? While many people claim to base the attribution of rights on competency, they often judge competency and assign rights based on physical appearance.[2] Thus, society sometimes treats those children who look physically mature as adults, whether or not they are emotionally, neurologically, and psychosocially mature. Scientists have demonstrated that an adolescent may look like an adult but may not have the same cognitive capacity as one.[3] This information is vitally important to judges and jurors who must evaluate consent and capacity. Chapter 1 reviewed the conflation of capacity, acquiescence, and consent. This chapter presents information about adolescent development that many jurists don't know. One can now see how the science of adolescent development might guide legal reasoning. One can also see the harm in assuming capacity based on physical maturity.

For an example of the importance of this assumption of maturity based on physiognomy, consider the statutory rape defenses, which chapter 4 covers in more depth. Under the US criminal law scheme, minors (under the age of consent) lack capacity even if they consent to sex with an adult. Thus, their consent is no defense. Their physical maturity, however, may constitute a defense. In California, for example, the perpetrator's mistake of age, particularly of older teenagers—arguably based on physical maturity—comprises a defense.[4] Even if scientists cannot yet make firm conclusions regarding adolescent developing capacity and judgmental maturity, adults should at least avoid confusing physical maturity with neurological and psychosocial maturity when assigning legal rights and duties. Neither the blooming of the adult body nor its withering with disease or old age necessarily equates with mental maturity or acuity.

The Short Answer on Adolescent Development

So how are teenagers different from mature adults? While no biological markers precisely define the beginning and end of adolescence, most researchers agree that it starts during the second decade of life and ends in the third decade. Increasingly, scientists argue that adolescence (or "emerging adulthood") extends to about age twenty-five. Adolescents experience physical, cognitive, sexual, and psychosocial development during this long maturation phase.[5] The survey of transitional changes highlighted below indicates that adolescent functioning differs significantly from both childhood and adult behavior. Translation: "This is *how* they are thinking!"

Before one delves into the details of adolescent neurobiological and psychosocial development, however, one should cover the basics. One might imagine teenagers as people whose eyeballs are directed inward. Relative to adults, they have trouble "seeing" the outside world in the sense that they are limited in their ability to see something from another's perspective. Experts have written extensively on the development of "theory of mind," this ability to perceive the world from someone else's perspective. Adolescents are also very self-absorbed, in part because their brains and bodies undergo many changes during adolescence. Teens are noticing and adapting to these changes. They are rediscovering and learning to manage themselves. Most readers are familiar with the facts of adolescent secondary sex characteristic development. However, not everyone knows that adolescents' brains are also changing. For example, gray matter, composed of neurons, in a teen's brain almost doubles in some regions. The frontal lobes develop last and are partially responsible for the type of mature outward-focused thinking that one recognizes as adult thinking. Not until the frontal lobes mature do adolescents begin to focus effectively on how their behavior affects others and may result in long-term consequences.

The changes in the teen brain and the development of more finely tuned electrochemical pathways also influence social functioning. Peer influence peaks at age fourteen, but a coherent sense of self and identity does not emerge until about eighteen. Impulsivity becomes particularly prominent in the late teen years when adults grant adolescents more autonomy at about age sixteen. Impulsivity restabilizes again in the twenties. Improvements in abstract thinking continue until about age seventeen or eighteen. However, teens have trouble postponing short-term rewards for those more distant, even if they are greater. This ability to delay gratification continues developing until about twenty-one or twenty-two, when teenagers resemble adults. Thus, teens behave in ways that are consistent with their rapidly changing physical and neuropsychological characteristics.

Think of a daisy ("day's eye") that closes at night or during bad weather. The daisy transitions from closed bud to full bloom. One doesn't see its yellow disk "eye" until it sees the light of day. Similarly, one doesn't see the fully mature beauty of an adult until the teenager, the budding adult, turns its eyes outward.[6]

Neurological Development

In 1999 the intramural program at the National Institute of Mental Health (NIMH) announced that the adolescent brain undergoes dramatic changes, changes not previously documented. NIMH neuroscientist Dr. Jay Giedd examined adolescent brains using advanced imaging technology. Giedd discovered that over one year gray matter nearly doubled in some regions, including the prefrontal cortex. The gray matter consists of brain cells, neurons, and neuronal connections, synapses. Depending upon the brain region, nonlinear increases in gray matter peak between ages eleven and sixteen for girls and about a year later, respectively, for boys. Along this growth curve unnecessary, underused connections are purged, thus reorganizing the functioning of the brain. Prior to Giedd's discovery, scientists knew that such growth and reorganization phases occurred during gestation and the first eighteen months after birth; however, they did not know about this second wave of overproduction and winnowing that occurs throughout puberty.[7]

These dramatic changes that occur during puberty influence adolescent reasoning and the ability to formulate consent because of the functions of the particular areas of the brain that are involved. "Neuropsychological studies show that the frontal lobes are essential for such functions as response inhibition, emotional regulation, planning and organization. Many of these aptitudes continue to develop between adolescence and young adulthood."[8] The more mature the frontal cortex, sometimes called "the area of sober second thought," the better teenagers can reason, control their impulses, and make considered judgments. "Thus, there is fairly widespread agreement that adolescents take more risks at least partly because they have an immature frontal cortex, because this is the area of the brain that takes a second look at something and reasons about a particular behavior."[9] This conclusion has serious implications regarding adolescent consent and legal capacity.

Researchers caution that adults should not oversimplify adolescent brain development. The "imbalance model of brain development" emphasizes teen reliance on the reward-related subcortical regions that develop earlier than the prefrontal cortex. Recent studies suggest that the adolescent ventral-striatum, an area responsible for the detection and understanding of new and rewarding environmental cues, may trump or override the immature prefrontal cortical response. "With age and experience, the connectivity between these two regions is strengthened and provides a mechanism for top-down modulation of the subcortically driven emotional behavior that increases the capacity for self-control."[10] In emotionally neutral contexts that scientists studied, adolescent impulse control equated with or was even better than that of adults.[11] As teenagers mature, their responses in emotionally heated situations begin to mirror their more adultlike responses in less emotional situations.

Other areas of the brain also influence teen judgment and behavior. Like the frontal cortex, the cerebellum continues to mature well into adolescence. Dr. Giedd wrote that the cerebellum enhances functioning in all forms of higher thought, from mathematics to decision making and social skills. The corpus callosum connects the two hemispheres of the brain and appears to influence creativity and problem solving.[12] The amygdala, a key component of the limbic system, likely governs emotional and gut responses. Dr. Leslie Hulvershorn commented that both adults and teenagers rely on the amygdala and the frontal cortex.[13] However, she explained that the frontal cortex is not as able to regulate the amygdala of teenagers. Some scientists hypothesize that less regulation of the amygdala by the prefrontal cortex also helps explain why children and teenagers experience trouble regulating their emotional responses.[14]

As noted, a big-picture view of adolescent development contributes to the understanding of how teen neurobiological maturation affects behavior. Behavior may also influence physical development. The pruning and organization of the new neural connections in the brain continue throughout the teen years. Giedd asserted, "Maturation does not stop at age 10, but continues into the teen years and even the 20s."[15] The mechanism of synaptic pruning is not yet well understood. One might think that more gray matter means higher functioning. Not so, said Giedd: "Bigger isn't necessarily better, or else the peak in brain function would occur at age 11 or 12. . . . The advances come from actually taking away and pruning down of certain connections themselves."[16] Drawing conclusions from the research, some scientists suggest that the pruning occurs on a "use-it-or-lose-it" principle.[17] Used connections survive and unused connections "wither and die." Added Giedd, "If a teen is doing music or sports or academics, those are the cells and connections that will be hardwired. If they're lying on the couch or playing videogames or MTV, those are the cells and connections that are going to survive."[18]

During the gray matter pruning phase, white matter increases. The white matter supports neuronal connections in the brain.[19] White matter is made up of a "layer of insulation called myelin [which] progressively envelops these nerve fibers, making them more efficient, just like insulation on electric wires improves their conductivity."[20] More recently, scientists discovered that myelin also "modulates the timing and synchrony of the neuronal firing patterns that create functional networks in the brain."[21] Evidence indicates that environmental experiences influence myelination.[22] Myelination levels in adolescents increase into their early twenties. "During child development, myelination correlates with maturing patterns of behavior."[23] For example, infants cannot move an index finger independently because their neurons are not sufficiently myelinated. Myelination increases again in the forties, growing 50 percent by the mid-fifties.[24] Additional myelination may occur again in the early seventies.[25] In lay terms, the brain reinforces itself periodically to foster those synaptic connections most needed and used.

This new research confirms that adolescent brain development extends into the twenties, beyond the age of consent set in every state. Critical abilities, including impulse control, emotional regulation, planning, decision making, and organization, may not fully mature until the third decade of life. Additionally, behaviors and experiences may influence myelination and determine the extent of winnowing and reorganization of gray matter during adolescence. It's possible that teenagers hard wire experiences, such as algebra homework or sex in a movie-theater projection booth, into their brains. What they are *doing* may be mapped into the brain and become what they are *thinking*. Moreover, Hulvershorn noted that gene expression changes as a result of environmental factors and this may also influence myelination and pruning. While the genetic aspects of adolescent development are beyond the scope of this book, they should influence the research concerning adolescent legal rights and theories about consent in the future.[26]

Cognitive and Emotional Development

Adolescents mature cognitively as well as physically. Cognitive changes include the development of the ability to think more abstractly than a child. Adolescents engage in counter-factual reasoning (if-then reasoning about events and their possible consequences), consider hypothetical situations, and can adopt a variety of perspectives on a subject. They think introspectively, examining their own thoughts and emotions. The evolution of these cognitive and emotional skills happens in unpredictable ways. Some teenagers employ advanced reasoning skills earlier and more often than many of their peers. Additionally, situational factors influence individual reasoning performance. For example, when the environment and situations are familiar, everyone (including a teenager) tends to employ more advanced cognitive reasoning. Some transient developmental declines appear for certain tasks, particularly for those involving stressful or anxiety-provoking circumstances.[27] In other words, teenagers may temporarily *regress* cognitively and behaviorally when under stress, as they are slowly maturing.

This information, combined with the theory on hard wiring, highlights the possible benefits of not sheltering teens from experimentation with respect to sexuality, workplace relationships, and other concrete skills. Instead, the facilitation of their learning and maturation under circumstances that safeguard their developmental vulnerabilities might better prepare teens for adulthood. Thus, attributing full capacity to minors may not safeguard them, just as insulating them from all experimentation could stunt their maturation and cognitive development. "Just say no!" may not be the right advice for a teenager. Government officials do not give teenagers a driver's license before requiring that they practice driving with a licensed adult driver in the vehicle. Similarly, adults should not deem teenagers mature until they have practiced being adult-like under relatively regulated conditions.

While every child's needs are different and some parents (and jurists) may disagree, I advocate a child-raising model that affords juveniles a considerable measure of experimentation autonomy within controlled circumstances. For example, I permitted my teenagers to close their bedroom door when hosting a boyfriend or girlfriend, as long as the three of us (parent, child, and teen guest) had had "the talk." "The talk" was an individualized review of direct communication, sexuality, sexual risks, and sexual safety. Most teens have to be fairly mature and desperate for that closed door to endure the talk from Mom or Dad. I emphasized for my teenagers that I wanted them at home (as opposed to the backseat of a car) so that they could come to me at any time with questions and concerns. At my house, teenagers had to agree to behave responsibly, consider the safety and dignity of themselves and their partner, and acknowledge the trust I extended them. My teenagers are now healthy, young adults. While I understand that this system will not work for all families, I wonder what might happen if more parents had the talk with their teens and then afforded them a fair measure of autonomy.

This discussion highlights that context matters regarding teen cognitive development and capacity. Adults should not take one developmental or functional milestone and extrapolate it to pronounce that any given adolescent has matured in all ways. For example, research from the 1980s suggested that adolescent cognitive development enabled youth to make hypothetical decisions comparable to adults. Lawyers employed these studies in legal briefs to advocate in favor of abortion rights for teenage women. Following the dissemination of these data concerning the cognitive abilities of teenagers and a number of high-profile violent crimes involving youth, prosecutors began trying more children as adults.[28] This increase in the number of adolescents tried in criminal court as adults at the end of the twentieth century prompted researchers to revisit the issue of adolescent cognitive competence.

The MacArthur Juvenile Adjudicative Competence Study investigated whether adolescents are intellectually and emotionally competent to stand trial in adult criminal court. The study indicated many juveniles under fifteen were probably not capable of functioning like adults at trial: "[Y]ounger individuals were less likely to recognize the risks inherent in different choices and less likely to think about the long-term consequences of their choices."[29] This finding is consistent with the neuroscientific evidence regarding maturity in those brain regions responsible for inhibitory control and decision making. The performance of sixteen- and seventeen-year-olds did not differ from the adults. MacArthur researchers were quick to point out, however, that the functioning of older juveniles was not necessarily equivalent to that of adults. Researchers emphasized that further inquiry into age differences regarding other capacities and abilities was ongoing for these older teenagers.[30]

Further scientific research concerning adolescent brain function confirmed findings that teenage brains continue to mature beyond mid-adolescence. Adolescent cognitive development does not cease at sixteen. Reflective judgment, logical reasoning, and working memory—all complex skills—improve during adolescence. Additionally, these skills vary dynamically across contexts. Factors such as stress, novelty, and self-organization drive variations. Harking back to the original uses of the early studies of adolescent cognition, Dr. Kurt Fischer explained, "Reasoning about abortion, where a doctor or health-care worker can support the teen's thinking over a length of time, is very different from acting violently in the heat of the moment." Fischer distinguished between the supported reasoning used in a medical decision and the reasoning that a teen might use when encountering gang pressure to commit a violent act. Fischer emphasized the importance of context and teen emotional states. He asserted, "Teenagers are not simply cognitively mature and psychosocially immature. Context is radically implicated in the nature of capabilities. . . . Depending on context and support, the same individual can function in drastically different ways, and there is not one condition that represents the true capacity."[31]

These quotes highlight, as psychologists have determined, that emotional states and other factors influence cognitive capability in young people. Dr. Linda Spear summarized that "brain development through adolescence may be characterized not so much by increases in task associated activation of the PFC [prefrontal cortex] and other frontal regions, per se, but by an increased reliance on distributed brain regions that function in 'collaborative' networks of activity with frontal regions such as the PFC."[32] Moreover, cognitive ability is not the only trait instrumental in effective functioning and decision making. Other traits also come into play. In essence, teenagers are elaborate symphonies!

Psychosocial Development

Evidence of psychosocial maturation supports the notion that adolescents experience significant changes not only during their teenage years, but also into their early twenties and beyond. Dr. Laurence Steinberg's research identified four psychosocial traits that distinguish adolescents from adults: capacity for self-regulation, reward sensitivity, future orientation, and peer influence.[33] These traits are reviewed below.

Self-regulation and Reward Sensitivity

Particular characteristics signal the transition from adolescence to adulthood. Studies have shown, for example, that adolescents take more and greater risks than do adults. Such behaviors include unprotected sex, drunk driving, use of illegal drugs, and minor criminal activity. Scientists once believed that teenagers differed from adults in their ability to perceive or calculate risks. However, researchers now believe that neither a lack of information about a particularly risky behavior (such as unprotected sex) nor cognitive capacity fully explains their risk-taking tendency. Studies have demonstrated that increasing knowledge does not necessarily lead people to make better decisions.[34]

New evidence demonstrates that age differences in reward sensitivity may also explain adolescent risk taking. Dr. Silvia Bunge has compared the prefrontal cortex of healthy children with the prefrontal cortex of adults suffering from brain injuries, who take more risks than healthy adults. She has determined that healthy children make riskier choices than adults, in part because they enjoy doing so; it is rewarding for them. She tied these choices to activity in the prefrontal cortex. Bunge suggested that teens are less able to resist the temptation of a new reward. She explained, "If your friend says, 'Hey let's try this drug; it will be fun,' you might not be able to use the information you know about the possible negative consequences to resist."[35] In sum, teens value rewards over risks more highly than do adults.

Dr. Laurence Steinberg explained adolescent risk-taking behavior by examining two interacting neurobiological systems. The first, a socioemotional system, governs the processing of social and emotional information. The second system, a cognitive control system, directs deliberative thinking, impulse control, foresight, and the evaluation of risks and rewards. Dramatic changes within the socioemotional system take place over the course of puberty. These changes involve a significant increase in dopaminergic activity within the socioemotional system, which Steinberg suggested leads to reward-seeking behavior.

What is so important about dopamine? Any kind of reward or pleasurable event, including sex and good food, increases dopamine levels. People naturally want more of a good thing. Cocaine and methamphetamine act, in part, by amplifying the effects of dopamine. Therefore, people take these drugs, at least initially, to increase the pleasurable effect. The increase in dopaminergic activity during puberty may possibly explain why teens might want more of it and will engage in risky behaviors to get it. This hypothesis is somewhat controversial, but further research in the area will test it. These changes in the socioemotional system precede the structural maturation of the cognitive control system. Steinberg argued that because the cognitive control system matures later in adolescence, the temporal gap in the development of these two systems "creates a period of heightened vulnerability to risk taking during middle adolescence."[36]

Dr. Abigail Baird contributed to our understanding of the two systems. Baird explained that the bottom-up system helps us understand "what is 'right' or 'safe' and what is 'wrong' or 'dangerous.'" In describing the top-down system she first asked, "Have you ever jumped from the second-story window of a house?" She guessed that most adults have not and would refuse. Baird asserted, "This is a prime example of how abstract reasoning is able to generate a visceral response and in turn inform cognition about potential emotional consequence. The prefrontal cortex is able to draw on previous experiences, and by integrating them with current situational demands, generate 'possible scenarios.'"[37] Adults have the ability and experience to engage in an effective philippic calculus about the window jumping "opportunity." In a top-down way, they know not to go there.

In contrast, an adolescent might consider how to tie pillows to himself in order to jump from the window and soften the fall. Or a teen might open up an umbrella to act as a parachute! You are cringing, I imagine. That is because your prefrontal cortex is already helping you to imagine what might happen to these young jumpers. Baird concluded, "Together these two systems provide the means by which individuals are able to follow both obvious and abstract moral or legal ideals. In order to follow the law, one needs to either *feel* that the deed she is about to commit is wrong or *think* that it is wrong."[38] The question is, What are young jumpers thinking? Not the same thing as you and me. They are getting ready to jump! *Sexual Exploitation of Teenagers* will return to the second-floor window when discussing Sara's case later.

Future Orientation

Other studies suggest that adolescents hold different priorities than do adults. In particular, teens value long-term consequences less than short-term consequences. For example, teenagers engage in more delay discounting than do adults, preferring smaller immediate awards to larger but delayed rewards.[39] In other words, teens might opt for a couple of evenings of Xbox gaming before the Scholastic Aptitude Test (SAT) college admission examination. For those teens, immediate Xbox gaming fun beats a great SAT score, an admission letter to Stanford, and years of future rewards. Fortunately, self-regulation develops during high school and into early adulthood. Research suggests that development of future-time orientation continues until about age twenty-two.[40] New evidence links future orientation with prefrontal cortex structural and functional maturation.[41] Over time, teenagers develop the ability to anticipate, plan for, and wait for future rewards. Thus, as a young adult anticipates graduating from Stanford (because his parents restricted Xbox usage during the days before the SAT), he might *think* and *choose* to get a good night's sleep before the Medical College Admission Test. At least potentially, he has developed the requisite maturity, skills, and life experience to make that choice for himself, without parental intervention.

On average, teenagers also engage in more impulsive behavior than average adults. *Impulsivity* might be defined as the tendency to react without really thinking about the consequences.[42] Preliminary studies of juvenile impulsivity suggest that it remains relatively stable until age sixteen when it increases and then again stabilizes at age nineteen. Impulsivity declines during adulthood.[43] Adolescents may make decisions more impulsively than adults because they "may have less time than adults to assess and appropriately integrate rewards with goal-oriented behavior."[44] In other words, adolescent brains take longer to pull together all the related information for a decision due to the immaturity of their prefrontal cortices. Teens then have less time remaining to decide and execute. This finding might explain why "cool" decisions, those made when calm and collected and not in response to potential rewards, seem more adultlike and those under stress or in response to goal-oriented behavior appear more impulsive.

Parents and teen mentors need more investigation regarding the relationships between impulsivity, sensation-seeking, and judgmental maturity. Scientists believe, however, that stress and mood also influence temperate decision making. Studies indicate that older teenagers exhibit greater mood volatility than do adults.[45]

Peer Influence

Most people understand that teenagers respond to peer pressure. You may recall your parent asking whether you would jump off a cliff (out of a second-floor window?) simply because your friends were. Neuroscientists and juvenile psychologists have studied this phenomenon too. As juveniles form a sense of their own identity during adolescence and young adulthood they "develop a greater capacity for autonomous decision making and begin to resist peer influence."[46] Until a sense of adult identity and autonomy matures, teenagers make choices influenced both directly and indirectly by their peers. For example, a 2009 report for the United States Department of Health and Human Services (HHS) details that the "odds of an adolescent engaging in sex are 2–4 times higher if the same-sex closest friend of that adolescent is sexually active."[47] Direct coercion affects some decisions, but many other decisions result from an adolescent's concern for peer approval and fear of rejection.[48] Evidence confirms that teens are preoccupied with their social status. Drs. Elizabeth Cauffman and Laurence Steinberg reported that adolescents are most susceptible to peer influence at about age fourteen, after which that influence declines. Some studies, however, indicate that a coherent sense of identity does not emerge until about age eighteen. Ego development, or individuation, according to some studies, increases throughout adolescent years.[49]

As teens individuate, other people's influences affect various aspects of adolescent life. For example, parents influence adolescents in matters of religion and career choice; whereas, peers sway choices regarding daily concerns such as clothing and music preferences. Cauffman and Steinberg suggested that "adolescents' display of independence—and hence, maturity of judgment—may be highly situation-specific, with youngsters being influenced more on some topics than others, and by different sources of influence to differing degrees, depending on the decision in question."[50]

Recent studies confirm that peer influence, even the *perceived* presence of peers, reinforces adolescent risk taking. The subjective value of immediately available rewards increases for adolescents who engage in tasks in the presence of their peers. The presence of peers also increases preferences for short-term benefits of risky choices over safer alternatives with long-term value. The data highlight the interconnected nature of adolescent psychosocial traits, in this case peer influence, reward sensitivity, and future orientation (or the lack thereof). "[A]dolescents may not only be particularly sensitive to the reward-sensitizing effects of social stimuli, . . . this sensitization may further undermine their capacity to 'put the breaks' on impulsive responding."[51]

Discussion about Developmental Science

As with the developing neuroscience, the research regarding psychosocial traits, various specific ages, and maturity of judgment is quite new. Understandably, psychologists hesitate to draw specific conclusions for the practical application of what they now know.[52] The neuroscientific research, in particular, provides group data and insights concerning developmental trajectories for the adolescent brain and behavior. These group-related discoveries do not lend themselves to conclusions about individual subjects, however. Too much variability within age groups and across developmental phases means that the scientific measures do not yet accurately assess behavioral maturity.[53] Given the nature of the scientific information, a focus on structural legal and educational support for the teenage population seems more appropriate than recommendations for individual teenagers.

Teen priorities involved in decision making, including social status and immediate rewards discussed above, help explain how sex with an adult, for example a teacher, might seem like a good idea from an adolescent's perspective. De-emphasizing the long-term academic career, reputation, and health risks, some immature teenagers might choose an exciting sexual relationship and the concomitant status increase with an older, more "sophisticated" man or woman offering such rewards. A focus on teen priorities, including immediate rewards and social status, has value but only if one also considers what teens are thinking about—sex.

Adolescent Sexuality

As adolescents change, they mature sexually as well as neurobiologically and psychosocially. In addition to the physiological changes, most teenagers experience new sexual behaviors. Some researchers highlight that American adults conceptualize adolescent sexuality in a risk-based frame. The CDC's Youth Risk Behavior Survey (YRBS) added credence to this claim by its name alone. Programs that focus on abstinence-only education and sexually transmitted infections (STIs) capture only the negative aspects of adolescent sexuality. Positive aspects of adolescent sexual maturation include the development of a sense of intimacy and the exploration of love and sexual pleasure. Some researchers suggest that Americans need to take a more holistic and balanced perspective when considering teen sex.[54] I endorse this more nuanced and comprehensive approach.

According to the CDC, almost half of all high school students (47.4%) engage in sexual intercourse.[55] Table 3.1, drawn from the CDC 2011 YRBS, shows that nearly two-thirds (64%) of twelfth-grade females

TABLE 3.1. **Percentage of high school students who ever had sexual intercourse . . . by sex, race/ethnicity, and grade—United States, Youth Risk Behavior Survey, 2011**

	Female		Male		Total	
Category	%	CI*	%	CI	%	CI
Race/Ethnicity						
White†	44.5	41.8–48.3	44.0	40.9–47.2	**44.3**	**41.1–47.4**
Black†	53.6	48.7–58.5	66.9	63.6–70.0	**60.0**	**56.6–63.4**
Hispanic	43.9	40.8–47.1	53.0	50.6–55.4	**48.6**	**46.1–51.0**
Grade						
9	27.8	24.0–31.9	37.8	34.8–41.0	**32.9**	**29.9–36.0**
10	43.0	38.8–47.2	44.5	39.9–49.2	**43.8**	**40.0–47.6**
11	51.9	48.8–55.0	54.5	51.1–57.9	**53.2**	**50.4–56.1**
12	63.6	59.3–67.7	62.6	58.7–66.4	**63.1**	**59.6–66.5**
Total	**45.6**	**43.0–48.3**	**49.2**	**46.6–51.8**	**47.4**	**45.0–49.9**

Source: Danice K. Eaton et al., CDC, *Youth Risk Behavior Surveillance–United States, 2011*, 61. Morbidity and Mortality Weekly Report No. 4, June 8, 2012, Table 63 at 110.
* 95% confidence interval.
† Non-Hispanic.

have had sex. The occurrence of first intercourse is slightly higher for high school boys than girls before twelfth grade. However, when one considers that sixteen is the age of consent in many states and that most students reach that age in or before eleventh grade, one realizes that more than 40 percent of US teenagers have sex for the first time while still under the age of consent. Even if these teens are exploring intimacy, love, and sexual pleasure, they often do so in violation of state law.

In his 2010 book, *Teenage Sex and Pregnancy*, Dr. Mike Males challenged the notion that teen sex comprises something fundamentally different from adult sexuality. He suggested, "[I]t is safe to say that teenage and adult sexual behaviors under similar economic and social conditions *are one and the same*. We are not looking at two separate sexualities, the adult version of which can be accepted and encouraged while the teenage version is deplored and prevented. We are looking at *the same behaviors*."[56]

One reason for Males's criticism of labels such as "teenage sex and pregnancy" is that "6 in 10 men who impregnate teenagers are adults. The younger the pregnant teen, the bigger the partner age gap and the more likely she was to have suffered family chaos, including sexual abuse and other violence."[57]

Dr. Males also explored the correlations between race, poverty, and early sexual activity. He explained, "In 2005, among females under age 20, 60 percent of all live births, 64 percent of abortions, 62 percent of fetal losses, and 61 percent of all pregnancies involved black, Hispanic, and other nonwhite minorities. More than four in five involve impoverished and low-income teens."[58] Dr. Males made a compelling case that so-called teenage pregnancy indicates not a problem with irresponsible youth, but an economic and, therefore, also a race-based phenomenon involving adults.[59] The CDC 2011 YRBS (table 3.1) also documented higher percentages of early sexual activity for black adolescents (almost 70% for males) than for white and Hispanic teenagers. These facts support Males's correlation of early sexual activity and race.

Additional YRBS facts support conclusions by Dr. Males. For example, the 2011 YRBS also revealed a significant minority of juveniles (6.2%) have their first intercourse before turning thirteen years old. More than a fifth (21%) of black males and many more black females than white ones (7% and 2.6%, respectively) have experienced sexual intercourse before age thirteen.[60] These data suggest that many adolescents have sex several *years* before they reach the age of consent in their home state.

The YRBS data combined with Males's reflections about teen pregnancy compel further inquiry and even reconsideration about whether adults have appropriately labeled teen pregnancy and sexuality. Dr. Males may be correct that the problem is not so much teen pregnancy and sex between peers but rather that "the presentation of teen pregnancy reflects both traditional sexism of blaming females for unwanted fertility and America's disturbing legacy of singling out society's *least* powerful groups—in this case, younger girls—to blame for social and moral problems."[61] This quote finds support in the statements made by one senator and an air force officer who blamed teenagers for the recent sexual assaults in the military. *Sexual Exploitation of Teenagers* will return to the claim that society scapegoats teenagers, and especially so-called hooking-up, queen bee, bad girl sirens. These data about adolescent sexual activity with adults should prompt serious consideration of adolescent volition and sexual abuse more generally. This book's discussion about teen capacity and consent in the context of adult-teen consensual sex and sexual exploitation constitutes only one aspect of the larger issue of teen sexual development and capacity.

Volition and Sexual Activity

Given the information on the occurrence of first sexual intercourse, questions arise whether teenagers welcome and are prepared for their first sexual activity. The 2011 CDC YRBS detailed that 8 percent of high school students (11.8% of females and 4.5% of males) reported being physically forced to have sexual intercourse.[62]

Another CDC study confirmed that nearly 11 percent of females ages eighteen to twenty-four when interviewed, who first had intercourse before age twenty noted, "I really didn't want it to happen at the time." The percentage jumps to over 18 percent for females who were fourteen or younger and to 17 percent for females whose male partner was three or more years older. If one totals the percentages of females who had negative or mixed feelings about their first sexual intercourse under twenty years (58.8%), one finds that only about 40 percent (41.2%), less than half, "really wanted it to happen at the time."[63]

A 2003 Kaiser Family Foundation study explained, "Nearly two-thirds of adolescents (15–17, 63%) and young adults (18–24, 61%) think that delaying sex may be a 'nice idea, but nobody really does.' And over half agree that once you do have sex it is harder to say 'no' the next time." The same study revealed that 31 percent of adolescent females ages fifteen to seventeen, compared to 18 percent of males, reported that they "have done something sexually they didn't really want to [do]." Thirty-three percent of females in the same age group, compared to 18 percent of males, reported engaging in oral sex "to avoid having sexual intercourse." Kaiser reported, "Twenty nine percent of adolescents and just over a third of young adults report having personally experienced pressure to have sex."[64]

Age differences between partners also contribute to questions of volition. For adolescents ages fifteen to seventeen, the earlier a young girl engages in sex, the older her partner likely is and the greater their respective age gap. As a result, the younger an adolescent is, the more likely the sex is unwanted or nonvoluntary.[65] Additionally, pregnancy rates for adolescents with partners more than six years older were 3.7 times the rate of those adolescents dating someone no more than two years older. These data suggest that when minors become sexually involved with substantially older adults, the relationships may be unbalanced because of individual differences in maturity, experience, socioeconomic status, and even physical size. Such imbalances may foster and shield abuse by older partners.[66] Based on the statistics, the National Campaign for the Prevention of Teen Pregnancy cautioned that "there is evidence from small area studies that some young teens, like older teens, can get into situations where they feel sexual pressure or coercion. By virtue of their young age, however, they may be less able to handle these situations effectively than older teens."[67]

Survey responses and data, regarding volition and desire, underscore issues of emotional readiness with respect to adolescent sexual activities. However, no one can really measure psychosexual maturity. Dr. Males is right to equate teen and adult sexual *behavior*, but questions remain about adolescent emotional and psychological maturity and readiness for sexual activity, especially with a more experienced adult. Adults help to prepare teenagers for team sports with daily practices, for musical recitals with lessons (and more daily practice), for war with boot camp (and even more daily practice). But how do adults prepare teenagers for a lifetime of sexual fulfillment? That's the point; adults do not.

Information about adolescent sexuality facilitates a discussion about legal capacity. Teenagers are sexually active; they have some experience. However, some sexual experience may not create legal capacity, informed consent, or sexual maturity. Acquiescence does not necessarily indicate consent under the law. Moreover, information concerning adolescent cognition, psychosocial maturity, and brain function should at least inform conclusions about teen volition and capacity. Traits pertaining to self-regulation, reward sensitivity, future orientation, and peer influence may be guiding adolescent sexual behavior in ways that are quite different from adult thinking and resulting conduct. One can see differences even in the ways adults and teens communicate about sex.

Adolescent Communication Concerning Sexuality

Because survey questions differ so radically, it is difficult to track changes in parent-adolescent communication. For example, a 1995 survey reported that most parents—almost 75 percent—did not know that their children fourteen or younger were having sex. The statistics were only moderately better for parents of sexually active teens fifteen and older: only about half of them (54%) knew.[68] The 2009 HHS study detailed that 93 percent of parents who were "most knowledgeable" (MKPs) about their adolescent had "talked about sex or sexual issues."[69] This recent statistic is encouraging but does not elucidate how many MKPs knew their teenagers were having sex. A 2012 Planned Parenthood/*Family Circle* survey indicated that 81 percent of parents of sexually active teens knew that their children were having intercourse. However, only 45 percent of parents knew that their children were having oral sex.[70]

Common sense suggests that most parents don't know everything about their children's sexual behavior. On most days ignorance may not be problematic. However, communication about teen-adult pregnancy, sexually transmitted disease, sexting and violations of privacy, adult-teen sexual predation, sexual abuse more generally, sexual harassment, and the emotional downsides of a sexual relationship gone awry may be important to assist adolescents in avoiding or coping with these problems. Recall how Sara's parents had no idea that a registered sex offender had seduced their daughter, who had gone with his adult girlfriend to obtain an abortion.

Statistics tell us that parents and their teenagers disagree concerning their communications about sex. In one California study, 69 percent of parents said that they had spoken with their children about sex or birth control.[71] Only 41 percent of their children confirmed those conversations had occurred.[72] According to the 2012 Planned Parenthood/*Family Circle* survey, 42 percent of parents asserted that they had spoken to their teens "'many times' about how to say no to sex." Only 27 percent of their teenagers confirmed these conversations. Ninety percent of parents but only 84 percent of teenagers say they have had open conversations with each other about sexuality. Fifty percent of these surveyed teens felt "uncomfortable talking to their parents about sex."[73] In the 2009 HHS study, researchers concluded, "MKPs consistently reported greater levels of communication than their adolescents did." The researchers could not determine whether the discrepancy was due to MKP overreporting, adolescent inattention to MKPs, adolescent inability to process the information, or some other undetermined explanation.[74]

Anecdotal stories confirm the research. For example, one parent explained, "I want to relay the message that his sexual health is *his* responsibility, not just a girl's. That alcohol and drugs interfere with the ability to make smart choices. Also that girls are not objects to be cast aside, but cherished." The teenage son reported his parent said, "Use Protection."[75] From her research, Dr. Deborah Yurgelun-Todd concluded that "the teenager is not going to take the information that is in the outside world, and organize it and understand it the same way we do. . . . [I]f you're assuming they understood everything you said—they may not have. Or they may have understood it differently."[76] Yurgelun-Todd confirmed what many parents have long suspected: they are often talking to a wall.

Researchers interpreted the 2009 HHS survey results concerning parent-adolescent communication about sex and suggested "that a lack of parent-adolescent communication may cause adolescents to turn to peers, who may in turn influence adolescent behavior."[77] Teenagers who have grounded, informed, and wise peers are probably getting good advice. For the rest, adults should be concerned. A 2010 Data Brief by the National Center for Health Statistics concluded, "Parental communication about sex education topics with their teenagers is associated with delayed sexual initiation and increased birth control method and condom use among sexually experienced teenagers."[78]

Additionally, a 2002 Kaiser Family Foundation and *Seventeen* magazine survey revealed that only 16 percent of fifteen- to seventeen-year-olds (13% boys, 20% girls) had talked to a health-care provider about their decision to have sex. Only 28 percent (18% boys, 39% girls) had ever discussed birth control and protection with a health-care provider.[79] According to a 2003 Kaiser Family Foundation survey of women's sexual health, one-third of adolescents and young adult women ages fifteen to twenty-four say that they strongly or somewhat agree with the statement that "buying condoms is embarrassing." Just over one-quarter said that "it is hard to 'bring up' the subject of condoms."[80] Not surprisingly, the percentage of teens reporting embarrassment increases for younger teens.[81]

In 2011 the Kaiser Family Foundation explained, "Confidentiality of care is a primary concern for many adolescents. Research has found that teenagers will go without care, withhold information about themselves, delay, or not seek help in order to keep their parents from finding out about a health issue." The Kaiser Family Foundation added that state parental consent and notification laws influence confidentiality. Kaiser suggested, "Insurance companies may contribute to a lack of confidentiality by sending an 'Explanation of Benefits' (EOB) to the primary insurance holder, usually a parent, when a teenager seeks a healthcare service. This reporting may deter teens from seeking important care for sensitive health concerns."[82]

Sexuality and Psychosocial Development

The psychosocial changes that occur during adolescence appear to bear a direct correlation with developing sexual maturity. Experts in adolescence suggested, "How teens are educated about and exposed to sexuality will largely determine whether they develop a healthy sexual identity."[83] These experts asserted that teens (and others) equate intimacy with sex and explained,

> In fact, intimacy and sex are not the same. Intimacy is usually first learned within the context of same-sex friendships, then utilized in romantic relationships. Intimacy refers to close relationships in which people are open, honest, caring and trusting. Friendships provide the first setting in which young people can practice their social skills with those who are their equals. . . . Rather than exploring a deep emotional attachment first [in sexual relationships], teens tend to assume that if they engage in the physical act, the emotional attachment will follow.[84]

In this passage, one sees the importance of equality in how teens practice social skills that build intimacy. Ideally, teens will practice social skills through friendships with peers—their equals. Additionally, this analysis highlights that teens engage in sex hoping to find intimacy.

A study published in 2006 confirmed that teens look for intimacy in their sexual relationships: "Participants made significant discriminations in the relative importance of the three relationship goals. They rated intimacy as the most important goal in a relationship, followed by social status and, finally, sexual pleasure. Males and females ranked the three goal items in the same order."[85] Of the 637 ninth graders surveyed, females considered intimacy more important than the males did.[86] Researchers also found gender differences concerning the goal of social status. That difference "provides empiric support for the gender double standard, by which sex improves social status for young men, but jeopardizes it for young women. . . . This association between sexual experience and lower social status goals suggests that sex is a social liability for females."[87] If this conclusion is true, it explains some of the gendered language, such as the label "Jezebel," associated with teenage victims, discussed in chapter 9.

Another Kaiser Family Foundation poll revealed other motivations that prompted teen sexual behavior. Forty-five percent, almost half, answered that a "major reason" they had sex was because the "other person wanted to."[88] This response suggests that many teens succumb to pressure by their romantic partners and indicates a clear lack of mutuality, at least with respect to first-time sexual experiences. The Kaiser survey noted several other major reasons teens decided to have sex. Thirty-two percent expressed that they were "just curious." Sixteen percent listed that "many friends already had" had sex, which prompted them to have sex. Alcohol influenced 5 percent of teens. Finally, 51 percent noted they had "met the right person."[89] While this last and most common reason reflects a sense of readiness, most of the other reasons alert adults to external pressures applied by friends and partners. Teens in the Kaiser study supported this conclusion when 86 percent agreed that "young people today face pressure when it comes to sex and relationships."[90] The Kaiser Family Foundation survey supports the MacArthur Network hypothesis that psychosocial factors, such as peer pressure, influence adolescent decision making.

Society and Adolescent Sexuality

As this chapter reviews the science of teen psychosocial development and sexuality, it also considers the society in which our teens live. Some feminists would argue that American society is a predominantly patriarchal culture (e.g., Sheryl Sandberg's advice to "lean in" assumes a male-dominated business environment[91]). If that description is accurate, adults must acknowledge patriarchy's impact on adolescent females. Professor Michelle Oberman summarized the psychological literature on this subject. She said that "among girls, adolescence is a time of acute crisis, in which self-esteem, body image, academic confidence, and the willingness to speak out decline precipitously."[92]

The theory is that our patriarchal culture creates a stereotype of women that portrays them in sexual terms and as less valuable than men. This stereotype may be changing, but recent studies substantiated the sexual double standard for adolescents.[93] "A distressing six in ten teens (61% of boys and 57% of girls) and fully three-quarters of adults (74%) believe that teen girls often receive the message that attracting boys and looking sexy is one of the most important things girls can do."[94] These statistics support (or are created by) the sexual messaging marketed at the mall and discussed in chapter 2. As girls change physically and psychosocially, they may be adopting the cultural stereotypes. Oberman asserted that "the most significant external manifestation . . . [of their gendered psychosocial development] is their increasing unwillingness to speak their opinions or voice their desires. . . . Girls equate compliance and cooperation with 'niceness,' and they perceive that being nice is central to being 'feminine.'"[95]

Girls are not manufacturing this notion all by themselves. Success in business often entails female compliance with stereotypes. Girls pick up this message. For example, niceness and femininity were central issues in the sex discrimination case brought by Ann Hopkins, an accountant at Price Waterhouse. In *Price Waterhouse v. Hopkins*, the Supreme Court explained, "[I]n order to improve her chances for partnership, Thomas Beyer [speaking for Price Waterhouse's Policy Board] advised, Hopkins should 'walk more femininely, talk more femininely, dress more femininely, wear make-up, have her hair styled, and wear jewelry.'"[96] The Court responded in one comment, "We sit not to determine whether Ms. Hopkins is nice, but to decide whether the partners reacted negatively to her personality because she is a woman."[97]

Sexual objectification, low self-esteem, and the desire to be "nice" or "feminine" may impair girls' ability to fend off or recover from unwanted sexual attention.[98] For example, while both girls and boys experience sexual harassment in school (56% and 40%, respectively), more often girls report feeling its negative effects.[99] The AAUW study discussed in chapter 2 found that "girls' [harassment] experiences tend to be more physical and intrusive than boys' experiences. . . . Girls were more likely than boys to say that they had been negatively affected by sexual harassment—a finding that confirms previous research by AAUW (2001) and others." The AAUW stressed that girls felt the negative consequences for longer than boys: "Too often, these negative emotional effects take a toll on students' and especially girls' education, resulting in decreased productivity and increased absenteeism from school."[100]

The AAUW study also documented peer policing of student conduct and the enforcement of gender stereotypes. "For example, a boy who wears colorful clothing might be called gay, and a girl who plays sports might be called a lesbian."[101] The prevalence of sexual harassment and gender norm enforcement in schools (and in American culture more generally), combined with the psychosocial changes of adolescent development, pose a formidable set of challenges for maturing teenagers.

Add cultural attitudes about teenagers who engage in sexual behavior to this picture. "In 1996, 69 percent of US adults indicated that it was 'always wrong' for adolescents between the ages of 14–16 to have sex."[102] US adults may not be worried so much about the type of sex or its meaning but just the fact that teenagers engage in it at all. The Alan Guttmacher Institute elaborated, "Because teens are often regarded and portrayed as being incapable of using contraception effectively, having sex is often equated with becoming pregnant and a teen parent; the slogan of one state's current teen pregnancy campaign is 'You play, you pay.'"[103] Guttmacher emphasized that the US was the only country with formal policies that directed funds solely at the promotion of sexual abstinence.

If one takes the perspective of an evolutionary biologist, then sex, reproduction, and the survival of our species are natural and biologically mandated activities. Promoting sexual abstinence is a bit like funding the cessation of sleeping, breathing, or using the toilet. You can "hold it" for a while, but it's just not natural and certainly isn't good for you in the long-term. On the other hand, every biological activity and function has efficiencies and socially acceptable times and places. Hyperventilation is not healthy either. Breathing heavily into the telephone without speaking can be viewed as rude, and just plain weird. Cultural norms play a role in dictating those "normal" times and places. However, when cultural norms (and laws) extend beyond biological reason and mandates, one needs to question those norms.

In 2000 Dr. Suzanne M. Sgroi put her research focused on child sexual abuse in context: "There was also widespread belief (then [during the 1970s] as now) that engaging in sexual interaction was a transforming experience that marked an individual's rite of passage into adulthood." Sgroi added, "A sexually experienced child was viewed as an anomaly by most of the general public, who believed that youthful victims of sexual abuse had 'lost their innocence' and become contaminated in a way that made them seductive and dangerous."[104] In coming chapters, this attitude surfaces in judicial opinions and social reactions to teen-adult sexual liaisons.

In addition, research shows that attitudes have not changed much. According to a 2009 HHS report, most parents (~70%) disapprove of premarital sex generally and for their own adolescent children in particular.[105] Ninety percent disagreed that it was "[o]kay for adolescents to have sex while in high school."[106] These views help to explain court decisions that credit adolescent consent to sexual activity as adultlike behavior and, therefore, legally significant.[107] The reasoning works like this: sex is an "adult" activity and therefore those who engage in it must be adults. These cultural attitudes explain why society might make adolescents "pay" for "playing." These norms account for court opinions that treat a sexually active teen as a seductress, "a voluntary participant, with strong financial incentive to shape evidence that determines the outcome."[108] These negative judgments do not emphasize the power, age, and maturity disparities between adolescents and their workplace supervisors or adult teachers. They do not acknowledge psychosocial immaturity that might prompt a different response to developing capacity.

Sexual exploration and experimentation is a natural part of the human maturation process.[109] However, if an adolescent does not or cannot consent to specific sexual conduct with an adult, that conduct (by the adult pursuing the sex) should be labeled sexual abuse. To map a strategy for dealing with adolescent consent to sex under the law, one must understand, at least superficially, the consequences of child and adolescent sexual abuse.

Sexual Abuse of Adolescents

The American Psychological Association (APA) defined *child sexual abuse*: "Child[1] sexual abuse is any interaction between a child and an adult (or another child) in which the child is used for the sexual stimulation of the perpetrator or an observer." In its first footnote and for purposes of clarity, the APA defined *child* to include "adolescents below the age of consent." The APA continued, "A central characteristic of any abuse is domination of the child by the perpetrator through deception, force, or coercion into sexual activity. Children, due to their age, **cannot** give meaningful consent to sexual activity."[110] While a full discussion of sexual abuse is beyond the scope of this book, a brief review serves to provide context for the sexual harassment of teenagers.[111]

The AACAP estimated that up to 80,000 cases of child sexual abuse are reported each year but that many more cases exist because children often do not report their abuse.[112] This calculation is consistent with the AAUW finding that only about 9 percent of sexually harassed students report the abuse to an adult at school. Only about 27 percent talk about it with a parent or other family member.[113] In 2011 HHS's Children's Bureau documented 61,472 cases of child sexual abuse. Of those cases, about two-thirds (40,936) involved adolescents ages nine to seventeen.[114]

Researchers from the American Bar Association (ABA) Center on Children and the Law describe some behaviors common to child abuse victims as "child sexual abuse accommodation syndrome." This syndrome explains five behaviors of children who (first) often feel that they cannot escape or who (second) adapt to survive. Secrecy, delayed disclosure, and retraction are three more purported syndrome characteristics. Even in cases involving children with confirmed sexually transmitted diseases, over 40 percent of the children denied any sexual contact.[115] "The main reasons for nondisclosure to parents included the child's feeling that the parents could not be relied on, fear of being blamed or not believed, feelings of shame, and not wanting to burden parents."[116]

Abusers typically share common traits as well. Most abusers know their targets. Abusers "are usually beloved and trusted members of their schools, churches, or communities, and they 'groom' their victims patiently until they can trap the child into sex and silence." One scholar noted, "Affection, admiration, and trust are typically a vital part of the complex relationship."[117]

How perpetrators operate may relate to or explain teen concealment of workplace sexual abuse. Therefore, one should become familiar with common abuse profiles. Perpetrators often groom their targets and gradually sexualize their relationship with the targets. The ABA Center on Children and the Law noted that abusers may use force or threaten injury or death to keep their targets from reporting the abuse:

> In other cases, offenders achieve compliance through the abuse of adult authority. They may disguise the meaning of the abuse (e.g., sex education, hygiene), normalize the behavior, (e.g., all fathers show love this way), conceal the intent (e.g., accidental contact during play), or offer tangible or intangible rewards (e.g., money, gifts, attention). . . . [O]ffenders may also convince children that they will not be believed or they will be responsible for negative consequences to themselves, their families, or offenders.[118]

This brief summary of common characteristics of sexual abuse targets and perpetrators permits us to compare these features to sexual harassment cases.

Worldly Application

Compare the profiles of sexual abuse to Sara's case. Recall that Sara did not report her seduction by the movie theater manager even after he impregnated her and had his adult girlfriend take her to have an abortion. Not until police told Sara that the manager did not have a brain tumor and was a registered sex offender did she agree to cooperate with the district attorney. Whether or not Sara was "in love" with her manager or suffered from sexual abuse is debatable. The fact remains that she did not discuss her problems with her parents or any adult besides her manager.[119] All of our Does and Joe initially kept their liaisons secret. Secrecy allowed their consorts to continue unchecked.

Sara's harasser fits the perpetrator profile described by the ABA. Sara's manager clearly wielded adult authority: He was approximately twenty-five years her senior. He was also her workplace supervisor and carried additional authority conferred by the theater owner. He could terminate her employment and did on one occasion. Arguably, her manager disguised the meaning of his sexual overtures when he told her that he loved her and had a brain tumor and did not know how long he had to live. He implied that he wanted to share a level of intimacy and bonding with her before he died, not just have sex. He also normalized this workplace behavior by suggesting that a mature, romantic involvement existed, that they were in love. He concealed his relationship with his adult girlfriend, his prior conviction as a sex offender, and additional facts to conceal his true sexual, predatory intentions. He offered tangible and intangible rewards: a workplace promotion, driving lessons, gifts, cash, and adult guidance and attention.[120] This man used every trick in the ABA book.

For her part, Sara exhibited classic teen characteristics. She took unnecessary risks, such as having unprotected sex and undergoing an abortion without the support of her parents.[121] She suggested in letters to her manager, who was in jail at the time, that she wanted to emancipate herself from her parents. Upon his release, she would run away with him to Canada where she would have his baby.[122] No one can know for sure what Sara was actually thinking. It does not seem a stretch to suggest, however, that she felt that her parents would not "understand." Why else would she prefer that her lover's adult girlfriend drive her to the abortion clinic?

Possibly, Sara felt shame, embarrassment, and humiliation that she did not protect herself from an unwanted pregnancy (not to mention potentially fatal STIs). Those feelings might have prevented her from approaching her parents or other counselors. Those feelings might also have combined with a heightened level of self-consciousness to cloud her judgment about her "boyfriend." After all, she actually believed his story about the brain tumor. At the very least, Sara's conduct with her manager was uninhibited. This former A student demonstrated poor judgment and made a tragic choice to trust (and have sex with) her managerial seducer.[123] Because Sara "played," some states would have her "pay" (even more than she already did). Metaphorically, she jumped out the second-floor window! She needed an ambulance, not a paddy wagon. Sara was *thinking* like a teenager, exactly as Dr. Baird might have predicted.

Experts confirm that sexually abused children and adolescents can suffer long-term negative effects. In 2000 McLean Hospital researchers hypothesized at least four types of brain abnormalities linked to child abuse or neglect. (*Child abuse* refers to harmful conduct done to a child. *Child neglect* refers to when an adult fails to provide necessary support for a child. Therefore, the failure to feed a child constitutes child neglect. The vicious beating of a child constitutes child abuse.) First, researchers associated limbic irritability with more self-destructive and aggressive behavior. Second, they speculated that arrested development of the left hemisphere relates to the development of depression and increased risk of memory impairments. Third, deficient integration of the left and right hemispheres can lead to dramatic mood or personality shifts. Fourth, increased vermal activity may impair the maintenance of emotional balance. Dr. Martin Teicher explained, "A child's interaction with the outside environment causes connections to form between brain cells. . . . Then these connections are pruned during puberty and adulthood. So whatever a child experiences, for good or bad, helps determine how his brain is wired."[124] Researchers stress that some of these changes are permanent. Other studies detail behavioral and psychiatric disorders, including depression, and post-traumatic stress disorder (PTSD).[125] While not all adolescent targets of sexual abuse will suffer such trauma, it is important to understand that some will.

Sexual Abuse and Brain Damage

As noted the abnormalities linked to child abuse or neglect documented by McLean scientists included limbic irritability, arrested development of the left hemisphere, deficient integration of the right and left hemispheres, and increased vermal activity. The limbic system, also known as the "emotional brain," controls emotions associated with survival responses. Evidence suggests that child abuse may cause electrical disturbances in limbic connectivity. Such disturbance can result in seizures or abnormalities on electroencephalograms, or EEGs, which measure brain waves. Follow-up studies at McLean documented that abused children were twice as likely as non-abused patients to have an abnormal EEG. Researchers associated these abnormalities "with more self-destructive behavior and more aggression."[126]

The second condition, arrested development of the left hemisphere, suggests that the right hemisphere of abused children may be more active than that in non-abused children. The left hemisphere controls language. The right hemisphere controls perception and "expression of negative affect," among other functions. Researchers hypothesized that the imbalance "may contribute to the development of depression and increase the risk of memory impairments."[127]

In making the third finding pertaining to brain integration, McLean researchers noticed an abnormally small corpus callosum in abused children. The corpus callosum acts as the brain's information highway between the hemispheres. McLean scientists associated neglect "with a 24 percent to 42 percent reduction in the size of various regions of the corpus callosum in boys, but sexual abuse had no effect. In girls, sexual abuse was associated with an 18 to 30 percent smaller size in the corpus callosum, but neglect had no effect." McLean researchers "theorize that a smaller corpus callosum leads to less integration of the hemispheres. This in turn can result in dramatic shifts in mood or personality."[128] Other studies have confirmed this effect on the corpus callosum.[129]

Finally, McLean researchers noted an increased level of vermal activity in abused children. The cerebellar vermis helps regulate the limbic system and control emotions and attention. By studying blood flow to this area, researchers concluded that higher vermal activity levels served to "quell electrical irritability within the limbic system." They speculated that abuse interfered with the ability to maintain emotional balance. McLean researchers also used animal studies to explain the possible impact of child abuse. They suggested that abuse or neglect may "trigger the release of [some] hormones and neurotransmitters while inhibiting others, in effect remolding the brain so that the individual is 'wired' to respond to a hostile environment."[130] How ironic that jurists call a workplace replete with sexual harassment a hostile environment.

Another study compared magnetic resonance imaging, or MRI, scans of eighteen healthy women's brains to twenty brain scans of women who had reported prolonged histories of abuse before the age fifteen. Brain scans of abused victims showed "markedly smaller hippocampal volume."[131] This damage could result in poor academic performance and difficulty adjusting to new social situations, among other negative consequences.[132]

Am I suggesting that an adolescent like Sara will suffer brain damage because of workplace sex? No, one cannot assume or predict individual outcomes based on population or anecdotal studies. However, I raise several questions based on new evidence and collected statistical information. Scientific studies demonstrate that child sexual abuse can negatively impact brain development. Studies also show that adolescent brains are works in progress. Survey evidence indicates that young teens are having sex, some at the workplace or at school. Many teen sexual encounters involve peer pressure. Some teen-adult liaisons, if not many, involve deception and subtle coercion and may not be completely voluntary for the teens.

Is it possible that a less than voluntary sexual encounter can produce permanent brain changes? If not after just one encounter, then what about after six or twelve or fifty? Is it possible that even voluntary sexual encounters by a young adolescent (immature by definition) with an adult can produce negative neurological consequences? Even if such encounters will not produce permanent neurological changes, can they produce temporary or chronic disabilities that lead to other problems? For example, might sex at the workplace create emotional or psychological conditions that could in turn affect performance on standardized academic tests or college entrance examinations? Can and should the law deal with these issues?

States have statutory rape laws because adults believe that it is harmful for minors below a certain age to engage in sex, particularly with adults. Adults have concluded that teens do not have the capacity to consent. Should jurists discourage, both legally and financially, workplace or school teen-adult sex for the same reason and because of what might be true, given the new evidence? Or do adult guardians risk hardwiring immaturity if they do not allow for teenage sexual experimentation—including mistakes? More information is needed for one to answer these questions with confidence.

Other Negative Effects

In addition to critical changes in brain development, child sexual abuse results in other negative consequences. First, sexually abused children suffer a variety of psychiatric disorders.[133] While a full discussion of the effects of child sexual abuse is beyond the scope of this book, research suggests that sexually abused children experience more PTSD, depression, and anxiety than non-abused children.[134] Children tend to internalize their negative emotions rather than act aggressively or violently.

Anxiety, depression, and withdrawal are common symptoms of sexual abuse.[135] Children who experience PTSD because of sexual abuse also present with a smaller corpus callosum and total brain volume than those children who do not suffer from PTSD. Boys seem to experience this particular physical side effect more often than girls, which suggests "that males may be more vulnerable to the effects of severe stress on brain structures than females." Adverse effects of PTSD associated with sexual abuse were observed in both sexes, no matter the difference in corpus callosum and intracranial size.[136] "However, only about one-third of individuals with childhood sexual abuse have a lifetime diagnosis of PTSD."[137]

Abuse survivors mentioned above with smaller hippocampal volume also reported having more PTSD-like symptoms such as dissociation, recurring nightmares, amplified reactions when startled, and emotional numbing.[138] Reports indicate that 42 to 90 percent of sexual abuse victims suffer from some sort of PTSD, with many symptoms appearing closely after the maltreatment. Inhibited intellectual ability, reflected by low IQ scores and poor school performance, is one of the more apparent manifestations of sexual abuse and altered brain development.[139] Thus, research suggests that sexual abuse can cause not only physical brain damage, but also severe and intense social repercussions for the victims. Dr. Leslie Hulvershorn commented that the most common outcome of childhood sexual abuse is borderline personality disorder.[140]

Second, young adults ages fifteen to twenty-four account for almost 50 percent of the more than nineteen million new STIs each year, even though they make up only 25 percent of the sexually active population.[141] In 2013 the Kaiser Family Foundation reported "that 37% of young men and 70% of young women had an STI test in the past year."[142] According to Advocates For Youth (AFY), "Cultural traditions that value women's passivity and subordination also diminish the ability of many women to adequately protect themselves, to refuse unwanted sex, and to negotiate condom use." AFY added that "half of girls who reported HIV or STIs had been physically or sexually abused."[143]

In a survey of high school students, only 67 percent of males and 54 percent of females reported using a condom when they last had sexual intercourse.[144] Statistics reveal that following one incident of unprotected sex a girl faces "a 1% risk of acquiring HIV, a 30% risk of getting genital herpes, and a 50% chance of contracting gonorrhea."[145] Sexually active females under twenty are two to four times more likely than their male peers to contract an STI.[146] Anatomical differences between males and females make women more susceptible to STIs.[147] In 1992 Dr. Males emphasized that 90 percent of the HIV infections, caused when minors have heterosexual sex, occur in females. From his research, he concluded, "HIV and AIDS transmission to teens may be less due to teenage sexual practices, on which it is often blamed, than on the pattern of liaison between teenage girls and adult men."[148] Chapter 6 revisits this conclusion as it reviews Professor William Eskridge's opinions on adult-teen liaisons and the spread of HIV.

During Sara's "affair" with her forty-year-old manager, Sara withdrew from family and friends.[149] She locked herself in her room. She quit the swim team and lost interest in continuing her education. After she found out about how her lover deceived her, she had nightmares and anxiety attacks. She exhibited many of the symptoms of sexual abuse. Was she a "normal," withdrawn, and self-conscious teen or an abused adolescent? One cannot know for sure. Certainly, Sara was lucky that she did not get an incurable or fatal STI.[150]

This brief review of adolescent development permits one to return to the law's treatment of adolescents with a fresh perspective. At the very least, one can begin to evaluate whether the law, as it now stands, takes American society in the right direction. I argue in the following chapters that the law does not.

CHAPTER FOUR

Legal Treatment of Worldly Adolescents and Criminal Law Treatment of Unwise Adults

To make sense of the current legal treatment of adolescent sexual exploitation and harassment by adults covered in chapters 7, 8 and 9, one benefits from an understanding of the historical context. A review of the law's treatment of teenagers and their "consent," and traditional criminal law responses to the sexual abuse of women and adolescents, facilitates such an understanding. The US criminal and civil legal systems have historically but inconsistently distinguished adolescents and adults. For example, juvenile advocates have argued, sometimes successfully, that laws should not subject teenagers to adult prison sentences.[1] Similarly, juveniles should not have to accept full financial and civil responsibility for the consequences of consensual sex, which in many jurisdictions is labeled statutory rape. Chapter 5 focuses primarily on the civil law response to sexual exploitation while this chapter covers the criminal law response to teenagers and their sexual abuse. This chapter also begins the discussion of how criminal law treatment of consent influences civil law. The discussion in both chapters reveals that the law treats adolescent capacity inconsistently. There is no national standard.

Adolescent Legal Rights and Capacity

Children, including teenagers, have legal rights and status. The US Supreme Court confirmed in *Planned Parenthood of Central Missouri v.*

Danforth (1976) that "[c]onstitutional rights do not mature and come into being magically only when one attains the state-defined age of majority. Minors, as well as adults, are protected by the Constitution and possess constitutional rights."[2] The Supreme Court gave this conclusion fuller analysis in *Thompson v. Oklahoma* (1988).

Thompson v. Oklahoma

In *Thompson v. Oklahoma*, the US Supreme Court considered and rejected the death penalty for juveniles fifteen and younger. The *Thompson* Court acknowledged,

> there are differences [between children and adults] which must be accommodated in determining the rights and duties of children as compared with those of adults. Examples of this distinction abound in our law: in contracts, in torts, in criminal law and procedure, in criminal sanctions and rehabilitation, and in the right to vote and hold office.[3]

The *Thompson* Court noted many of the legal limitations on the rights of minors, including eligibility to vote, serve on a jury, marry, and drive without parental consent; purchase alcohol, pornographic materials, and cigarettes; and gamble. [4]

The *Thompson* Court's explanation for the different legal treatment of minors relied in part on legal precedent but also on then-current studies regarding adolescent psychosocial development. The Court concluded, "Inexperience, less education, and less intelligence make the teenager less able to evaluate the consequences of his or her conduct while at the same time he or she is much more apt to be motivated by mere emotion or peer pressure than is an adult."[5] While scientific inquiry has far to go for a complete understanding of adolescent neurological and psychosocial development, jurists do have significantly more neuroscientific information now than they did in 1988 when the Court decided *Thompson*.

Beyond Thompson

The law limits adolescent legal liability in many other respects not covered in the *Thompson* decision. For example, common law declared that contracts with a minor were not void but were voidable by the minor.[6]

Thus, if Doe purchased a used car and discovered that the salesperson had taken advantage of her and charged double its worth, she could void the contract and get her money back. However, she could also repudiate without reason. This practice remains the majority rule although many state laws now require that Doe return the car.[7] In *Stanford v. Kentucky* (1989), the dissent noted that thirty-seven states restrict a minor's access to general medical treatment without parental consent.[8] Many states prohibit minors from filing lawsuits unless represented by a parent or guardian.[9] Additionally, the law limits the right of adolescents to work. The federal Fair Labor Standards Act specifies a minimum work age of fourteen for nonagricultural work and child labor standards.[10]

On the other hand, not all laws treat adolescents as "infants" or as children with a legal disability. Some laws grant adolescents adult privileges. For example, all fifty states now allow minors to consent, without parental approval or notification, to testing and treatment for HIV and other STIs. Twenty-eight states permit a minor mother to place her child for adoption without legal counsel and without consulting her own parents.[11] States also attribute adult responsibilities to adolescents.[12] For example, California gives prosecutors discretion to charge a minor of fourteen or older as an adult for the crimes of murder, rape, and certain other sex offenses.[13]

What becomes clear from this preliminary review of youth rights is that Americans do not have a consistent approach to juvenile legal capacity. At the same time, the law regarding teenagers is not static. Since the publication of recent neuroscientific and psychosocial discoveries concerning adolescent development, the Supreme Court has begun to implement legal changes based on the new science. The Supreme Court's recent *Graham v. Florida* (2010) opinion relied on amici briefing (supplemental briefs from friends of the Court) regarding the science of adolescent development and provides valuable guidance relevant to adolescent maturity, consent, and legal capacity.[14]

Graham v. Florida

The *Graham* Court held that, similar to a death penalty, a life sentence without the possibility of parole for particular juvenile offenders violates the Eighth Amendment protection against cruel and unusual punishment.[15] This decision also reaffirms evidence regarding adolescent neurological and psychosocial development, discussed in *Roper v. Sim-*

mons (2005).[16] In *Roper* the Court invalidated the death penalty for sixteen- and seventeen-year-olds. The *Graham* Court noted that "developments in psychology and brain science continue to show fundamental differences between juvenile and adult minds. For example, parts of the brain involved in behavior control continue to mature through late adolescence."[17]

The *Graham* Court found that society might still hold a teenager responsible for his behavior but that "his transgression 'is not as morally reprehensible as that of an adult.'"[18] This distinction between responsibility and moral culpability is important. If a toddler knocks over a vase while stumbling to a table, adults might find her responsible but not morally culpable because she did not intend to break the vase and lacked the motor coordination to control her steps and body. Extend this example to a teenager who may be technically responsible for saying yes to sex but who cannot fully anticipate the consequences of her conduct and may lack the psychosocial skills to control her behavior in context. Remember that this same teenager consents not in a vacuum but with an adult who solicits, encourages, or at least abets her behavior. But for the adult's conduct, this adolescent would not have had the opportunity to consent.

The *Graham* Court highlighted several developmental factors that might influence a decision to spare adolescents from *legal* responsibility for their behavior, even as adults recognize their *personal* responsibility. The Court affirmed, "As compared to adults, juveniles have a 'lack of maturity and an underdeveloped sense of responsibility;' they 'are more vulnerable or susceptible to negative influences and outside pressures, including peer pressure;' and their characters are 'not as well formed.'"[19] The Court also noted that "juveniles' 'lack of maturity and underdeveloped sense of responsibility . . . often result in impetuous and ill-considered actions and decisions. . . .'"[20]

The *Graham* Court recognized that even a psychological evaluation of a given adolescent might not yield enough information for jurists to make critical legal determinations about a youth. The Court stated that "even expert psychologists" might find it difficult to differentiate between adolescent conduct that results from "transient immaturity" and that which reflects "irreparable corruption."[21] In other words, the Court confirmed that experts might not be able to tell whether a juvenile offender will "outgrow" a tendency to engage in destructive, unlawful behavior. This finding suggests that a case-by-case determination of adolescent maturity in a criminal or civil case might produce unsatisfactory or flawed results concerning the capacity of a teenager to control his behavior or consent to sex. Conceivably, the same individual could continue to engage in similar irresponsible conduct as an adult. However, an overwhelming amount of statistically significant evidence establishes that immature, risky behavior is much more prevalent in teenagers. Therefore, jurists should give teenagers the benefit of any remaining doubts about legal capacity.

Recent Supreme Court focus on adolescent neurological and psychosocial development and the differences between adolescent and adult conduct emphasizes the need to consider these differences, as well as adolescent capacity, in contexts other than the criminal trials of juvenile offenders accused of heinous crimes. Note that none of these Supreme Court cases find that juveniles possess adult *legal* capacity. Nor do they create a separate *legal* status for adolescents, although certain specific laws limit adolescent rights and others assign to adolescents *adult* responsibilities. The Court acknowledges differences between adults and adolescents in their ability to regulate behavior and to evaluate the consequences of their conduct. The differences do not translate, however, to a clear legal conclusion about adolescent capacity. Where one finds more consistent treatment of adolescent legal capacity is in statutory rape laws. These laws still dominate the criminal field and are worth exploring for an understanding of the cultural backdrop for civil sexual exploitation law.

Statutory Rape Laws

As noted, statutory rape laws historically defined the *age of consent* as a girl's age when her consent to sexual intercourse earned legal significance and insulated the male participant from criminal prosecution. During the nineteenth century, states raised the age of consent from ten to as high as twenty-one.[22] As late as 1994, only thirty-five states had gender-neutral laws protecting both male and female minors.[23] Now all fifty states protect both sexes.[24]

The Evolution of Modern Statutory Rape Laws

In 1997 Professor Charles Phipps surveyed state sex crime laws and found that most states distinguish among sex crimes against children by the severity of the offense and the age of the child. He concluded that most states classify crimes against children under thirteen or fourteen as the most serious. The least serious were non-forcible sex crimes with older teenagers. Most penal codes specify an age difference of at least two to five years between the perpetrator and the victim as a required element of the case.[25]

Phipps also discussed the Model Penal Code's treatment of sex crimes and highlighted its gendered approach. The Model Penal Code is a statutory text that was first drafted by the American Law Institute (ALI) in 1962 to assist states in standardizing and modernizing their own penal codes. At press time, the ALI was updating the sexual assault and related sections. The Model Penal Code classifies sexual intercourse between an adult female and juvenile male not as a third-degree felony as it does for adult males, but only as a misdemeanor. Thus, under the code, adult males face harsher penalties than do adult females for sexual intercourse with a minor. Moreover, the code sets the age of consent at ten—an age no longer accepted by any state. Phipps explained, "The drafters were worried about the seductive powers of adolescents as well as the application of a rule of strict liability and they wanted to draw a clear line for the most serious offense."[26] As discussed in chapter 2, Senator Chambliss and Gen. Mark Welsh share views similar to those of the drafters of the Model Penal Code concerning the sexual power of teenagers. This fear, of the seductive powers of female teenagers especially, is a theme in the sexual exploitation cases and surfaces in the individual cases of profiled Does.

More than fifteen years after Phipps's survey, a definitive age of consent is elusive. Some states set a baseline age of consent but then increase the age when a case involves special facts, such as an adult in a position of trust or authority, a relative, or a school employee. For example, at least seventeen states set the age of consent at fourteen *or younger* but increase it to sixteen or older under special circumstances, such as when the adult is much older or in a position of trust or authority.[27] More than twenty-five states increase the age of consent from their respective bases to eighteen (or older) under special circumstances.[28] Many states recognize an enhancement of the severity of the offense when a member of the family or an adult in a position of authority commits the offense.[29]

Teachers and other school employees, guardians, babysitters, employers and shift supervisors, psychotherapists, and medical professionals are all examples of people who wield authority over adolescents.[30] In

Doe v. Estes, the court explained, "Schoolchildren are particularly vulnerable to mistreatment at the hands of adults, especially where those adults are cloaked with the authority of the state."[31] The Model Penal Code creates an offense of statutory rape by one in a position of authority but narrowly defines that position and excludes the teacher-student relationship.[32] The 1980 commentary to the Model Penal Code explains, "Coverage of every instance of sexual relations with an employee, student, or other person under one's supervision would reach too far."[33]

If one takes the highest age for intercourse with an adult in each state, thirty-two states set the age of consent at eighteen or older,[34] four at seventeen,[35] and fifteen at sixteen.[36] These laws demonstrate that 38 percent of the states (19) set the age of consent below the age of majority. Less than 10 percent of the states (4) set it at the age of majority, eighteen, absent special circumstances.[37]

While statutory rape is a strict liability offense, a few states retain now uncommon elements of the offense or unusual defenses. For example, in California, mistake of age, particularly of older victims, may still constitute a defense.[38] Presumably, society wants to avoid punishing adults who honestly believe their partners are old enough to consent. However, no such rationale explains the defense in Massachusetts where chastity remains an element of the crimes against older children.[39] Thus, if the child was not virginal at the time of the offense, the perpetrator may use that as a complete defense to the crime of statutory rape. In 1998 Mississippi repealed laws requiring that the target be "chaste."[40] The chastity defense suggests a possible public policy motivation for statutory rape laws, moral norms enforcement. Chapter 9 discusses moral bias later. For now, however, consider that even though most states do not have a chastity defense, chastity can become an issue for juvenile victims. It did for a California Doe—Kati—in her case against Starbucks. Therefore, the case of *Starbucks* Doe and the broader application of this legal defense warrant further examination. One can find a worst-case application of the chastity offense in a relatively recent Texas case, *Hernandez v. State.*

A CASE EXAMPLE OF THE CHASTITY DEFENSE: *HERNANDEZ V. STATE.* Even though only Massachusetts still retains a codified criminal defense concerning chastity, a number of sexual abuse cases echo reasoning common in the now dated chastity defense cases. Until 1993 in Texas a perpetrator could argue capacity to consent to sex based on a promiscuity defense.[41] In *Hernandez v. State*[42] the court emphasized,

> We do observe that the State's brief acknowledges "that children aged fourteen to seventeen who have voluntarily become sexually active are, unlike their sexually inactive peers, imputed by the law with the capacity to consent to sexual conduct like an adult." It then adds, "Stated conversely, the law which imputes to children an incapacity to consent to sexual activity makes a logical exception for those in their mid-teens who have chosen to become sexually active."[43]

The court did not explain exactly how the choice to have sex elevated a minor's legal capacity to that of adult with full maturity, understanding, and appreciation. So, if a fourteen-year-old such as Kati "chose" to have sex with an adult, Texas law declared that she was then transformed from a normal eighth grader (junior high school student) into a woman with full legal capacity?

The *Hernandez* decision prompts several more serious questions. First, did the law really impute capacity because these minors made a choice? Did the law assume that every teenager who "chose" to have sex weighed the decision carefully, considering all the potential ramifications? The *Hernandez* court's reasoning flies in the face of the common (and new scientific) understanding of teenage reward sensitivity, sexuality, and willingness to engage in risky behavior. Second, did the *Hernandez* facts justify the attribution of capacity? In *Hernandez*, the minor's mother allegedly "sold" her daughter to the accused rapist and other men.[44] Although the minor's "choice" not to resist the accused may have reflected a well-reasoned decision, I would hardly grant her adult status based on those facts.

To follow this analysis further, let us ask why both the *Hernandez* prosecution and the court suggested that the law made a logical exception for sexually active teens. If teen virgins are incapable of offering *legal* consent, shouldn't the law protect them from their own naïve and misguided choices? How is it logical for the law to credit their choice to have sex in the first place? If the law places such responsibility and resulting consequences on fourteen- to seventeen-year-olds, if it affords their perpetrators the ability to invoke a promiscuity defense, then it is not logical to keep statutory rape laws on the books for youth over thirteen.

What do the experts say? Former Federal Bureau of Investigation (FBI) Special Agent Kenneth V. Lanning spent more than thirty years fighting crime against children. Concerning promiscuous or "bad" children, Lanning explained,

> Society seems to have a problem addressing any sexual-victimization case in which the adult offender is not completely "bad" or the child victim is not completely "good." . . . It [child prostitution] is the form of sexual victimization of children most unlike the stereotype of the innocent child victim. Child prostitutes, by definition, participate in and sometimes initiate their victimization but often do so rather than face subsequent consequences such as abuse at home, homelessness, and violence at the hands of those manipulating them to participate in this illegal activity. . . . Whether or not it seems fair, when adults and children have nonforced sex, the child is *always* the victim.[45]

In this passage, Lanning discounts the myth of the innocent child participant. These children, even if they act willingly, are still *victims.* They are still victims, even if they ultimately recover sufficiently to bring claims against their abusers (or their parents do so on their behalf).

Another interpretation of the *Hernandez* court's reasoning is that the law imputed capacity because sex elevates minors to a new level of understanding. One could argue, using this reasoning, that if parents simply introduced their teenage children to sex, those juveniles would all develop adult wisdom and legal capacity. Unlikely.

Arguably, the law in *Hernandez* reflected adult moral norms and moralistic prejudice. Apparently, lawmakers in Texas believed that those teenagers who had sex chose an immoral path and were, therefore, promiscuous and "bad." These adults refused to "reward" or even protect "bad" teenagers in Texas. The promiscuity defense, which presumably reflected this morality-based perspective, died only about twenty years ago in Texas. Did moral bias (the double standard) die with it? That assessment is harder to make, but readers can evaluate whether it was a factor in Kati's case.

DOE V. STARBUCKS, INC. Kati, a California Doe, alleged that her twenty-four-year-old supervisor, Tim Horton, convinced her to have sex with him when she was a sixteen-year-old barista at Starbucks in 2005. Kati reported that Horton repeatedly asked her out and that she initially spurned his advances.[46] In pleadings, Kati claimed that while at work and in front of coworkers, Horton made "perhaps hundreds" of profane, sexually explicit remarks concerning his sexual interest in her.[47] Eventually, Kati acquiesced to Horton's advances in the hopes that he would stop.[48] In November or December 2005, they allegedly engaged in sexual activity.[49] Kati stated, "[Horton] demanded that I perform oral sex on him, which I did. I felt like I had to—that I had no choice." She explained, "I felt that, because he had given me marijuana and I had smoked it with him, I had to do what he said, because he was my Supervisor and I didn't want to lose my job."[50] Kati and Horton engaged in sexual activities regularly through June 2006.[51] In addition to "vaginal intercourse and oral copulation" at work and offsite, "[t]hey exchanged explicit sexual comments and text messages at work."[52] Horton insisted that Kati not disclose their relationship to anyone.[53] In 2006 Kati left her job to enroll in a mental health treatment facility.[54] State authorities charged Horton with criminal unlawful sexual intercourse with a minor for his conduct with Kati, to which he pled guilty. In a parallel 2009 civil action, Kati alleged sexual harassment and torts claims against Starbucks and Horton.[55] *Sexual Exploitation of Teenagers* discusses Kati's civil case briefly in chapter 5 and more thoroughly in chapter 8, but readers can now evaluate the chastity issue in the context of Federal Rule of Evidence 412.

FEDERAL RULE OF EVIDENCE 412. The criminal law chastity and promiscuity defenses clearly contradict the provisions of Federal Rule of Evidence 412 and parallel state statutes that specifically prohibit introduction of the victim's prior sexual history into evidence as grossly prejudicial.[56] The first section of rule 412 reads, "The following evidence is **not** admissible in any civil or criminal proceeding involving alleged sexual misconduct except as provided in subdivisions (b) and (c): (1) Evidence offered to prove that any alleged victim engaged in other sexual behavior. (2) Evidence offered to prove any alleged victim's sexual predisposition."[57] Limited exceptions to these evidentiary rules exist and require that parties who wish to offer such evidence satisfy certain procedural requirements. When courts fail to invoke rule 412 (or similar state equivalents)[58] or misapply the procedural safeguards, to protect the sexual history of minor victims, then any evaluation of a minor's maturity could conceivably include a discussion of the minor's sexual maturity and sexual history. This circumstance leaves minors vulnerable to the grossest legal abuses that legislators intended rule 412 (and state equivalents) to combat.[59] Even if a court errs in admitting such evidence, an appeal does not retract sensitive information that has already been released in the record or in open court.

For example, after Kati agreed to appear on ABC's *20/20* television news show, Federal Judge Andrew J. Guilford, the presiding judge in her civil case, released records of her prior sexual history. He acknowledged that while Kati had a right to privacy, Starbucks and its employees had a right to "defend themselves [sic] in the court of public opinion." The *Orange County Register* recounted that when Kati was between fourteen and sixteen years old, she engaged in sexual activity with seven male partners. She did so with another five during the time she knew Horton. Kati responded, "They are trying to defend themselves by calling me a slut." The *Register* reported, "One of Starbucks' arguments is that Moore has not sought criminal or civil action against any of the other men, all but one of whom were older than 18."[60] Where to start? How is it relevant that this young teen had sex with other men? Because she said yes to a dozen men, she must say yes to the thirteenth at Starbucks? Does rule 412 mean nothing? Apparently so in "the court of public opinion."

Kati was fourteen when she began to engage in this sexual, risky behavior. This timing coincides with the common advent of adolescent impulsivity, experimentation, and attraction to "rewarding" risks. Sadly, when Kati jumped out of the metaphorical, developmental second floor window, her umbrella parachute did not open. Judge Guilford ruled to release her sexual history to the court of public opinion. Whether or not the judge actually believed Kati was a "slut," California retains an unofficial promiscuity defense "in the [unofficial] court of public opinion." Moreover, California is not the only state where this release could have resulted. If the judge had applied the reasoning of *Hernandez* in Texas or still-current Massachusetts law, Kati's "choice" made her capable of adult decision making under the law.

Because Sara, *Donaldson* Doe, and *Willets* Doe also lived in California, a state that sets the age of consent for penetration at eighteen,[61] the district attorneys successfully prosecuted criminal charges against their respective adult seducers.[62] As with Starbucks's Horton, Sara's manager, Michael Cosio, could not raise mistake of age as a defense. He knew (or should have known) Sara's age from her work permit, which California required her to obtain from her school. Donaldson must have known how old his underage target—his sister-in-law—was. Clint Smith, a teacher, should have known that his *Willits* paramour, a sophomore in high school, was only fifteen.

Had Sara, *Donaldson* Doe, and Kati lived in fourteen other states, however, their consent would have insulated their seducers from prosecution under criminal statutory rape law because all three were sixteen, the age of consent in those other states, by the time their adult consorts seduced them.[63] Thus, the state in which a Doe consents, and where the district attorney prosecutes the claim, can make a difference at least initially in her case. How does such variation make logical sense? It's difficult to believe that teenagers in Indiana, where the age of consent is sixteen, are so much more mature than those in California. These laws also mean that a fast-food restaurant doing business in all the states within the Seventh Circuit contends with three different ages of consent: sixteen in Indiana, seventeen in Illinois, and eighteen in Wisconsin. Furthermore, the inconsistencies create additional complexity for the corporation and concomitant difficulties training staff for compliance with the myriad requirements. Such complexity increases the chances that problems will arise.

Public Policy, Consent, and Criminal Statutory Rape Laws

The gendered nature and unstable age demarcations of the statutory rape laws prompt further inquiry regarding the public policy goals that support state statutory rape laws. Presumably, criminal law prevents harm to society as well as individuals within society. The law's designation of the "State" or the "People" to prosecute perpetrators serves as a constant reminder of that broad utilitarian goal.[64] Another goal of the criminal justice system centers on punishment of the perpetrator who commits the bad act, or *actus reus*. Punishment serves several subsidiary aims: deterrence (both general and specific), rehabilitation, retribution, and incapacitation.[65] With a strict liability offense such as statutory rape, society demonstrates its concern not with the actor's guilty mind, or *mens rea*, but with the harm to teenage and younger children.

What harm results from consensual teen-adult sexual contact? How is this illegal conduct between the adolescent and the adult so different from the same, legal behavior between consenting adults? The question, properly framed for teenagers, analyzes not so much the sexual conduct but the quality of the consent. The physical acts between teenagers and adults may be the same as those between two mature adults. Chapter 3 noted that idea from Dr. Mike Males. What differs between adolescents and adults are the expectations, motivations, and experiential wisdom (or lack thereof) that produce the problematic consent. In sum, jurists cannot tell if teens have *legal* capacity. Additionally, because adolescent expectations and motivations differ, and because the nature of the consent differs, the consequences of the exact same behavior also differ for adolescents.

Historically, other harms justified the statutory rape laws. In addition to protecting children, statutory rape laws protected "the weaker sex," vindicated the interests of fathers and husbands, and facilitated the prevention of unwanted pregnancy.[66] In *Michael M. v. Superior Court*, a case involving the statutory rape prosecution of a seventeen-year-old male who had sexual intercourse with a sixteen-year-old female, the US Supreme Court reviewed other possible justifications for the law, as it validated pregnancy prevention. The *Michael M.* Court suggested, "Some legislators may have been concerned about preventing teenage pregnancies, others about protecting young females from physical injury or from the loss of 'chastity,' and still others about promoting various religious and moral attitudes towards premarital sex."[67] Those reasons may still motivate some people to favor strict statutory rape laws.

After studying statutory rape cases, Professor Michelle Oberman suggested that "there is at least one important difference between girls and women when it comes to consensual sex: the sexual bargains struck by girls often are so painfully one-sided that it is difficult for adults to understand what prompted the girl to consent." Oberman categorized a national Westlaw database of statutory rape cases into four groups: consensual relationships, acquaintance rape, stranger rape, and overreaching and/or age range of more than ten years. Eighty-one percent of the national group and 91 percent of the Illinois cases fell into the overreaching category. Oberman concluded that prosecutors targeted the cases with a greater age gap between the parties because of the greater "risk of significant power disparity between the parties."[68] Her findings suggest that the public is concerned with preventing coercion and power disparities in sexual relationships involving minors.

The notion that juvenile capacity, and therefore "consent," differs qualitatively from adult consent engenders passionate debate.[69] This idea, however, dates back hundreds of years.[70] Because adults have historically deemed children incapable of giving informed consent, the law pertaining to children differs from that concerning adults in everything from contract formation to fundamental civil rights.

If adults accept that children cannot give informed consent because they lack capacity, the sexual taking of a child's body constitutes a theft of the most intimate kind—a rape. This violation, or *actus reus*, justifies the punishment. In *Virginia v. Black*, Justice Clarence Thomas explained that statutory rape carries no scienter requirement. The government need not prove that the minor did not consent. Justice Thomas wrote, "The legislature has determined in such cases that children under the age of sixteen (16) cannot, as a matter of law, consent to have sexual acts performed upon them, or consent to engage in a sexual act with someone over the age of sixteen (16)."[71] Justice Thomas emphasized, "The legislature finds the behavior so reprehensible that the intent is satisfied by the mere act committed by a perpetrator."[72]

As the child approaches the age of consent and maturity, however, society becomes less certain of the disability of immaturity. This uncertainty becomes apparent in statutes that set lower ages of consent for sexual contact than for sexual penetration.

Children's rights advocates, who take a self-determinist approach, maintain that children should enjoy the right to make decisions for themselves whenever practicable.[73] Some argue that statutory rape laws disregard adolescent capabilities and sexual autonomy. In her book *Harmful to Minors: The Perils of Protecting Children from Sex*, Judith Levine argued that adult fears concerning juvenile sexuality combined with the "politics of child protectionism" dominate adult governance of children's sexuality.[74] She advocated for "not only protection and schooling in safety but also the entitlement to pleasure."[75] She explained, "There is no distinct moment at which a person is ready to take on adult responsibilities, nor is it self-evident that only those who have reached the age of majority are mature enough to be granted adult privileges." Levine added, "Criminal law, which must draw unambiguous lines, is not the proper place to adjudicate family conflicts over youngsters' sexuality."[76] Whether *Michael M.* was more a family matter than a criminal one is difficult to discern. It reminds us, however, that district attorneys do prosecute teenagers for statutory rape. Levine raised a valid criticism. Her critique of American treatment of child sexuality deserves attention.

Every child is different, and so is every family. Without complete sex education, careful supervision, and a dramatic change in the way American culture deals with sexuality more generally, teenagers will not be prepared for sexual experimentation and will not enjoy their "entitlement to [sexual] pleasure." Additionally, if law operates to negate teen consent, such negation creates other undesirable effects.

CONSENT BEYOND STATUTORY RAPE LAW—PARTICULARLY CONSENT TO MEDICAL SERVICES. The consideration of whether or not adolescents have the threshold level of competence, sufficient power, and status to give legally significant consent to sex reintroduces a concern about context. Sexual harassment by definition is not consensual. No one freely chooses to be sexually harassed. Some adolescents, however, may consent to sexual activity without fully appreciating to what they are consenting or why. The context and nature of the decision may veil the nature of the proposed activity. Additionally, teens may not have the power to refuse a sex solicitation. If one accepts, however, that adolescents may be incapable of consenting to sex with an adult coworker, one necessarily creates other problems. For example, one risks the invalidation of consent in contexts in which most adults might wish to permit teen consent, such as for medical care, including STI treatment and abortion services. I do not want to craft a theoretical basis for sexual harassment law or propose law reform that undermines a teen's access to abortion or other medical services.

A responsible abortion choice typically requires information and will lead to change: the termination—or not—of an undesired pregnancy. When confronted with an undesired pregnancy, most women who contemplate abortion have access to information and professional guidance from the people providing the medical service. They may also have the benefit of advice from a partner, parents, and other advisors. The choice to have an abortion is typically an informed one. Passivity about the choice will likely result in significant change: the birth of a child. There is little debate about the result and the potential medical risks of abortion.[77] What produces huge debate is the morality of abortion.[78] Thus, this abortion choice is arguably complex because—while information is available—both action and forbearance result in significant consequences with moral implications.

Responsible sexual intimacy also arguably requires information about safety and consequences. One can find information about sexual safety through a variety of free services, including the public library and the Internet.[79] Information on consequences, however, other than pregnancy and sexually transmitted diseases, is harder to find. Where does one find out how sex will change a relationship? Where can a person find out how sex will affect his or her emotional well-being? How can a person know whether the experience will be "good" or worth potential risks?

Certainly, people can ask professionals—such as psychologists—for advice about sexual activity; however, accessing such professional information involves more effort than stopping by the public library and is often expensive. Additionally, many people do not feel comfortable talking about sex so they do not ask for advice about it. The survey information in chapter 3 supports these assertions about teenagers. Moreover, asking someone—even a professional—whether you will like sex with a particular partner is a bit like asking whether you will like spumoni ice cream. I have never tried spumoni, so I would be at a loss to advise you. And even if you were asking about vanilla, I would want to know whether you are trying it during a heat wave or in the middle of a blizzard. The circumstances might make a difference. Additionally, people often do not anticipate needing this information. My guess is that most people do not make an appointment to have sex for the first time with a new partner. I suspect that the ultimate decision to have sex is often more spontaneous and informal than even the choice to have an ice cream cone.

With sexual intimacy, the failure to participate does not disturb the status quo. Thus, no action means no change. However, as with abortion, morality colors the choice of whether to engage in sex—especially outside of marriage. Chapter 6 discusses the intersection of marriage and sex when it explores the socio-legal regulation of sex and the traditional view.

For now consider two decisions concerning abortion and sexual relations with an adolescent female as the decision maker. If she has the competence and, therefore, the capacity to make a legally valid choice, there is no problem. However, adult mentors often do not know and cannot tell whether she has the capacity to make the decision, to make a mature judgment. So they assume—perhaps wrongly—that she does not have capacity and consider whether she should make the choice anyway.[80] Several factors should influence policy makers as they decide whether the adolescent should have the right to make a choice: (1) the risk of her injury from no choice (no action at all), (2) the availability of assistance for a healthy choice if she has the right to choose, (3) available remedies if she changes her mind, and (4) the accuracy with which adult guardians can evaluate options for her or second-guess her choice.

First, if a pregnant teen has no right to choose abortion, her guardians will decide for her and she loses a valuable learning experience in the choice process. Those decision-making synapses are not exercised. Of course, a minor could choose to have an illegal abortion or to try to terminate the pregnancy herself. The risks of both those options are obvious. Her guardians may also require her to give birth to a child. Guardian choice necessarily leads to the birth of another child because the law does not permit guardians to force abortion on their unwilling minor charges. Adolescent childbearing is highly risky.[81] According to the United Nations Children's Fund, pregnancy is the leading cause of death for fifteen- to nineteen-year-old females worldwide.[82] The World Health Organization describes adolescent childbearing as "profoundly disempowering." It "cuts short her education, severely limits her income-earning capacity and impairs her ability to make well informed choices about life."[83] Thus, the risk of no choice is potentially high.

Second, if she has an abortion right, a teen will have medical professionals and probably other adults to advise her regarding her health and other consequences.[84] Moreover, the process of making the decision will be a learning experience. Even if the choice consists of two unattractive options, she may at least have the psychological satisfaction of choosing the option that she deems the lesser of two evils.

No remedy exists for a teen if she changes her mind once she has terminated a pregnancy. She cannot undo the procedure. Nor would society allow her to sue medical providers for damages—absent negligence or medical malpractice—because they acted to help her. The injury that the adolescent suffers comes not from the abortion procedure but from the undesired pregnancy (facilitated by someone else). The medical procedure was designed to terminate the injurious pregnancy. Thus, no good could come from permitting the withdrawal of consent to the abortion.

Finally, no matter which choice she makes, to either continue or terminate the pregnancy, few adults can say with absolute certainty that she made an incorrect or unwise choice. While some people view abortion as morally wrong, other intelligent and capable people disagree. Additionally, adults should not conflate the moral correctness of the choice with the more practical, factual considerations. The pregnant adolescent either gives birth to another child or endures an abortion. The statistics regarding the outcomes for teens and their children speak to the practical realities.[85] Who can say with absolute authority which outcome is morally worse: the handicapping of two lives or the termination of (the potential for) one.

With respect to the decision to have sex with an adult coworker or teacher, the first consideration is really a nonissue. Adult guardians cannot realistically control whether adolescents have sex. They can control access to safe, legal abortion services, but short of isolating every adolescent on a mountain peak or mandating modern chastity belts, guardians cannot completely control their access to sex.

If one removed the stigma concerning nonmarital sex and permitted it, teens might access more information about it. The problem remains, however, that sufficient information may be unavailable given the uniqueness and complexity of each circumstance and liaison. Thus, one should assume that inexperienced youths might not even be able to access sufficient information to make an informed choice about intimate sexual relations.

Are there available remedies if she changes her mind? If she realizes—within a reasonable time frame—that she did not have sufficient capacity to consent, can adults help her? Here is where the decision to have an abortion and the decision to have sex with an adult differ most prominently. While a teen cannot change her mind about abortion, she can about the advisability of her consent to sex. Obviously, teens cannot recapture their virginity and monetary damages will never make them "whole"; however, they can mitigate the negative consequences by suing for medical expenses, psychological counseling, and costs of lost opportunities. Society can and does prosecute adults for having sex with minors. Thus, the law could permit a teen to withdraw her consent, if she found that she made an uninformed or unwise choice, and sue her adult partner. Unlike the medical services provider, the adult sexual partner was probably acting on his own behalf, not (just) hers. Jurists assume that adults know the law and can conform to it. Jurists routinely hold adults responsible when they do not. Therefore, instead of imposing on the minor the costs of the detrimental choice, law can redirect those costs to the adult who should have known better—whether or not the act was illegal—and could have refrained from sex with the minor.

Finally, while adults might differ regarding the appropriateness of a pregnancy termination decision, fewer will argue with a teen who determines she should not have had sex with an adult coworker or teacher. Assuming no fraud, once a teen acknowledges an immature error, facilitated by a responsible adult, adults should assist her in remedying the problem. Some adults may blame the teen for bringing her injuries upon herself—or for not being more mentally mature when she looks physically mature. If behavior is truly the result of immaturity, however, a natural developmental condition, then there should be no associated blame. Society does not blame the blind for their inability to see, and adults should not blame youth for their inability to act maturely.

One might argue that a remedy in the form of money damages is not fair to the adult who relied on the consent or the employer who hired the seducer. The adult, however, was always free to refrain from the liaison that he knew could ultimately result in withdrawn consent. One might say that he assumed the risk. Additionally, the employer is able to monitor its workplace and select its agents. If it fails to do either, the principal rests in a better place to cover the damage costs otherwise borne by the employed minor.

THE FUTURE OF STATUTORY RAPE LAW IN LIGHT OF DISCOVERIES REGARDING ADOLESCENT CAPACITY. Professor Michelle Oberman offered a revised version of current statutory rape laws to account for adolescent autonomy while ensuring the protection of children.[86] Oberman opined, "[O]ne of the most powerful reasons for enforcing statutory rape laws is to set normative parameters around sex so that both boys and girls will learn to honor their own and others' sexual autonomy." Oberman suggested that the law is too harsh when it ignores the learning curve apparent in adolescent sexual encounters but said that "the failure to condemn 'mistakes' involving nonvoluntary sex with an underage partner is equally pernicious. Lenience in such cases only encourages girls to internalize a sexual script that fuses dominance and exploitation with sexual gratification." Oberman argued that statutory rape laws protect adolescents who are "coming of age."[87]

Rather than lowering the age of consent, Oberman recommended setting the minimum age for consent at no lower than sixteen and asking victims to direct whether the court should suspend the sentence of a first-time offender. (I would set the age at no lower than eighteen under this system and include minimum age differences for prosecution of the older party.) This scheme avoids the flaw that burdens the teenager with the decision of whether to prosecute. Under Oberman's plan, the prosecutor would retain prosecutorial discretion.[88] The victim would simply make a plea for a suspended sentence. All parties would understand that if the perpetrator completed a specified course of action, such as mandatory counseling and a sex education class, the court could dismiss the charges. If the victim declined to offer an opinion, the prosecutor, not the parents, could make the decision of whether to request a suspended sentence. Finally, Oberman suggested a set of statutorily defined exceptions that would indicate "per se violations." Statutory law would direct cases with facts suggesting coercion or behavior normatively reprehensible to full prosecution rather than a suspended sentence. In the list of exceptions, Oberman included cases involving incest, abuse of authority, repeat offenders, and multiple offenders.[89]

Oberman's envisioned changes to US statutory rape law acknowledge several public policy goals. First, they recognize society's determination that underage sex hurts children and that the law should punish and deter it. Second, they provide for full prosecution when the perpetrator uses a position of authority or manipulates a clear power disparity to coerce sexual conduct. Third, they reflect an awareness of the developing autonomy and capacity of teenagers to make decisions regarding sexual activity. They attempt to balance a protectionist, nurturance approach with the self-determinist philosophy that would afford adolescents more autonomy as their developing capacity permitted.[90] Under Oberman's plan, the sexual conduct remains illegal, but older adolescents with sufficient life experience may declare themselves ready for the activity and request the suspended sentence.

CAPACITY MATTERS IF IT EXISTS—BUT WHO KNOWS? By allowing a teen to withdraw consent in certain situations such as those involving contracts and sexual relations with adults, society might avoid some of the damage that results from assuming capacity where it does not exist. Moreover, while the law cannot completely prevent injury to those teens who consent to sexual relations, it can deter their prospective adult partners and later facilitate a remedy for any damage done to teens who realize that they lacked the capacity, power, or status to consent. The advantage of permitting consent in the context of access to medical services and treatment is that adults avoid violating the rights of those teens who, unbeknownst to us, have developed the threshold level of capacity to deliver meaningful consent.

Perhaps one day it will be possible for jurists to discover whether any given teen has developed the threshold level of competence and, therefore, the capacity to make legally binding, significant decisions. Until then adults should acknowledge their developing capacity and help them transition into adulthood and the myriad decisions that they will face. The transition process typically includes some kind of apprenticeship in the workforce. Adolescents need to develop a work ethic and job skills. Thus, adults should facilitate the development of these essential behaviors among teenagers as they transition into the labor force and into adult life more generally. Transition might include special legal treatment of adolescent consent.

Such facilitation might have helped Kati, who consented to sex with her supervisor. Chapter 7 reviews how federal courts have carefully examined acquiescence and consent in sexual harassment cases brought under Title VII of the CRA.[91] In 1998 in *Faragher v. City of Boca Raton*, the US Supreme Court emphasized that the "objectionable environment must be both objectively" offensive (the "reasonableness" standard) "and subjectively offensive" (the "unwelcomeness" requirement).[92] In sum, a complainant must find the harassing conduct personally offensive *and* the reasonable person must agree that the conduct is discriminatory or hostile. State fair employment practices statutes that prohibit sexual harassment also make unwelcomeness an element of the prima facie case.[93] Thus, in *Starbucks*, when Kati's consent gained legal attention, she risked losing her sexual harassment case because the conduct was not subjectively unwelcome under the law.[94] Consent similarly became an issue for all of the Does and Joe. Before one delves into sexual harassment law, however, one benefits from examining consent to sex and the historical roots of its legal treatment under civil law.

CHAPTER FIVE

The Development of Civil Law's Response to Worldly Women and Precocious Teenagers

Historical Wisdom or Oppressive Judgment?

Where criminal law often presumes a lack of capacity in juveniles, as chapter 4 detailed, civil law sometimes assumes full legal capacity. The civil system addresses personal injury, sexual exploitation, and consent, among other matters, through common law tort (personal injury) laws or more modern state statutory responses to human interactions. This chapter provides the civil law backdrop for the analysis of how adults, and especially jurists, might use the new information regarding adolescent development and psychosocial maturity. By comparing the varied traditional civil law approaches to juvenile behavior, sections I and II of this chapter reveal gross legal inconsistencies between criminal and civil law treatment of adolescent capacity and consent. Before one evaluates the efficacy of modern antidiscrimination statutes, most not designed to protect consenting teenagers, one should consider the development of civil common law rules that cover similar behavior. These common law claims highlight the importance of capacity and consent. They influenced the development of antidiscrimination law and, perhaps, reveal clues about how jurists exported some traditional and discriminatory attitudes to those new laws.

Historical Development of State Statutory and Common Law Personal Injury Claims

Historically, when sexual abuse targets decided to pursue personal civil law claims against the perpetrators, the victims looked to common law (nonstatutory) tort claims for relief. Typical common-law and civil code claims used in sexual harassment complaints include tortious interference with contractual relations, loss of consortium, intentional and negligent infliction of emotional distress, assault and battery, false imprisonment, invasion of privacy, defamation, and misrepresentation.[1] Other claims focus on the employer's failure to satisfy a particular duty. Those claims include negligent hiring and retention, negligent supervision, and breach of a duty of good faith and fair dealing.[2] However, most common-law intentional tort claims depended (and still depend) upon the plaintiff's subjective offense and an absence of consent,[3] under the maxim *volenti non fit injuria* ("a person is not wronged by that to which he or she consents").[4] Thus, a teenager's consent operates to weaken, if not extinguish, all these claims unless some statutory treatment of consent negates the default.

A Case Example: Barton v. Bee Line, Inc.

A 1933 New York Supreme Court case showcases how a minor's consent barred her personal injury claims. In *Barton v. Bee Line, Inc.*, the court held that fifteen-year-old Grace Barton, who allegedly consented to sex with a male bus driver, could not recover in a civil case for damages brought by Frank Barton, her guardian ad litem.[5] The court arrived at this conclusion even though New York had outlawed sex with a female under eighteen-years-old as a crime. Moreover, New York did not even allow her to sue directly, in her own name and without a named guardian, because she was a minor. Grace Barton claimed forcible rape, and the driver claimed that she consented to sex. The jury found for Grace in the amount of $3,000 (about $53,100 today).[6] However, "[t]he court set the verdict aside on the ground that, if plaintiff consented, the verdict was excessive."[7]

The appellate court ruled that Grace could not recover civilly, even though her seducer was criminally prosecuted "to protect the virtue of females and to save society from the ills of promiscuous intercourse."[8]

The court reasoned, "It is one thing to say that society will protect itself by punishing those who consort with females under the age of consent; it is another to hold that, knowing the nature of her act, such female shall be rewarded for her indiscretion." The court added,

> The very object of the statute will be frustrated if by a material return for her fall "we should unwarily put it in the power of the female sex to become seducers in their turn." Instead of incapacity to consent being a shield to save, it might be a sword to desecrate.[9]

Desecrate what, exactly? A society that righteously protects only "virtuous" (but still incapacitated) girls? This passage fosters gross stereotypes of young women as it anticipates that young women will use sex to extract money from unsuspecting consorts. The court's opinion highlights its moral disapproval of possibly sexually active, "promiscuous" young women. This case also demonstrates how Grace's consent carried no weight in the criminal action against her alleged rapist but carried controlling authority in her personal injury action against the bus line. The civil opinion also heralded the end of the age of consent for civil cases in New York.[10] Compare this case to Kati's against Starbucks. In seventy-five years, progress appears minimal.

This civil law evisceration of the age of consent is not unique to New York. Chapter 8 traces similar patterns in more modern jurisprudence across the nation, particularly in Illinois and California.[11] The *Bee Line* case, juxtaposed against the new neuroscience and psychosocial evidence of adolescent development, resurrects in New York and California the question of whether a minor should be permitted to recover civilly for alleged damages following a violation of criminal law. I argue that the law should permit such civil suits.

Consent as a Limiting Factor in Negligence Claims

For negligence-based tort claims, consent also triggers defenses, such as contributory negligence, comparative negligence, and assumption of risk.[12] Other legal doctrines, including the "rule of sevens"[13] and the "doctrine of misprision" intervene to thwart civil suits by abuse targets. A claim sometimes survives, however, if brought historically as a writ of seduction or, today, with help from the *Restatement (Second) of Torts.*

THE RULE OF SEVENS. Under this traditional rule, a minor under age seven cannot give consent, be held liable for negligent conduct, or formulate the requisite mental state to engage in criminal conduct. From ages seven to fourteen, the law presumes that a minor lacks capacity. Therefore, a claimant might rebut the presumption to hold a minor liable for some alleged tort but the default classifies the minor as incompetent. From fourteen to twenty-one (now eighteen), a rebuttable presumption declares that minors are competent to consent and responsible for criminal and negligent conduct.[14] Thus, in the context of a civil claim for damages and absent evidence to the contrary, this bright-line rule allows a trier-of-fact to presume that a child over fourteen can consent to sexual contact.[15]

Aaron Fisher, "Victim 1," was twelve in 2006 when Jerry Sandusky, a coach at Pennsylvania State University, started molesting him. "Fisher said fear, shame and confusion prevented him from seeking help and telling anyone about his tormentor. . . . 'Being a kid, you never know what to do, and you don't know who to tell because you don't know who you can trust.'" When he was fifteen, he finally told his mother about the abuse. School officials did not initially believe Aaron.[16] One told him to "go home and think about it."[17] Because of his age, fifteen, common law presumed Aaron capable of consent. However, a criminal court found Sandusky guilty of 45 counts of sex-related crimes.[18] Aaron settled his civil claims out of court in September 2013.[19] One sees from this example how irrational the common law appears in certain cases.

Another bright-line rule similar to the rule of sevens is the "mature minor" doctrine. Courts that apply this rule recognize that some mature minors may consent to conduct reserved for adults. Sometimes, for example, this doctrine permits a terminally ill older teenager to refuse continued medical intervention.[20] One can imagine how this common law doctrine might lead to irrational results similar to those stemming from application of the rule of sevens.

THE DOCTRINE OF MISPRISION. Another archaic rule that may relate to modern treatment of sexual harassment victims is the doctrine of misprision. Under this rule, a plaintiff risked criminal prosecution if she attempted to sue civilly for her physical injuries before first pressing criminal charges against her rapist or seducer.[21] The failure to file criminal charges effectively barred a civil suit. Criminal sanctions failed to compensate the victims for the damage to their reputations, medical expenses, and the expense of any child conceived. By funneling the redress for a rape or seduction into the public forum, the government minimized the damage to the victim, maximized the societal harm, and retained its exclusive control over vengeance and retribution.[22] This result has a parallel in modern jurisprudence, as embodied in the new affirmative defense to Title VII claims, discussed in chapter 7.

THE WRIT OF SEDUCTION. Common law was not historically without its remedies. Early American civil claims for sexual predation took the form of the writ of seduction.[23] This claim escaped the consent trap because the seduced young woman did not sue on her own behalf. Instead, a father sued for his lost honor, now besmirched by his daughter's damaged reputation, and possibly for his financial losses, tethered to her earning capacity if reduced by pregnancy and motherhood.[24] Consent was irrelevant to the seduction claim.[25]

Professor Lea VanderVelde suggested that two assumptions precluded women from recovering for themselves. First, VanderVelde explained that society assigned control of women to men so that women lacked the autonomy to prevent unwanted sexual activity. Second, she asserted that the law assumed from a woman's involvement in sexual activity that she consented to it and the resulting consequences: "The act of involvement in the event, even as a victim, spoke for the woman, denying her ability to recover against the man."[26]

Do these assumptions still apply to adolescents today? I think that they do. As to the first point, one could argue that current laws do not afford minors self-ownership. For example, the law gives parents the right to wages earned by their children.[27] Moreover, as discussed, teenagers do not enjoy many of the contractual and civil rights enjoyed by adults. They must emancipate themselves to enjoy full legal status.[28] As to the second point, current law, embodied in the rule of sevens, explicitly posits the capacity in most teenagers to consent.

A few states permitted seduction claims as late as 2003. That year, Professor Joanna Grossman commented on a seduction case filed in North Carolina by a young Duke University coed. She explained that most states had abolished the old torts, such as seduction, related to a property interest in someone's chastity. She noted, however, that an enlightened vision of female autonomy may not have been the prompting reason. Relying on work by Professor Janice Villiers, Grossman suggested that "the causes of action were abolished, instead, due to a concern that plaintiffs would use them to wrongfully extort money from defendants—in other words, a concern that unchaste women would lie to cover up their sexual indulgences."[29] One can evaluate in the chapters that follow whether that concern lives on in adult responses to sexual harassment suits by teenagers. I believe that it does.

Grossman predicted the complete extinction of the seduction claim even though it served in some states to compensate victims for sexual violation. Grossman emphasized that a seduction claim "reinforces disturbing stereotypes about women's vulnerability, need for protection, and lack of sexual autonomy."[30]

In her historical analysis of seduction, Professor Melissa Murray found additional negative stereotyping of women. She wrote, "Tainted with unchastity, the victim was corrupted and was now especially susceptible to the allure of vice and the prospect of future lapses."[31] She added, "Like male defendants, victims too required the deprivation of liberty and the imposition of discipline. Marriage was well-suited to accomplish these tasks, as the institution stripped women of certain liberties and imposed upon them the disciplined identity of 'wife.'"[32] This notion of the tainted victim persists. Recall the discussion of Dr. Sgroi's work on child abuse, discussed in chapter 3. Sgroi explained, "A sexually experienced child was viewed as an anomaly by most of the general public, who believed that youthful victims of sexual abuse had 'lost their innocence' and become contaminated in a way that made them seductive and dangerous."[33] This perspective may explain Judge Richard Posner's reference to a juvenile target, *Oberweis* Doe, as a "possible siren." Chapter 6 reviews the *Oberweis* case.

THE RESTATEMENTS (SECOND) OF TORTS AND CONSENT. Chapter 4 reviewed some guidance from the second restatements, *Torts* section 892A regarding the effect of consent and *Contracts* section 15 concerning mental illness or defect. Again, while not binding on courts, the restatements of the law offer legal guidance to assist a court in making a fair and just decision by summarizing common law precedent and juridical consensus. A section that chapter 4 did not review, the *Restatement (Second) of Torts* section 892C, offers hope for consenting adolescents who attempt to pursue tort claims. Subsection (2) states, "If conduct is made criminal in order to protect a certain class of persons irrespective of their consent, the consent of the members of that class to the conduct is not effective to bar a tort action."[34] This guidance suggests that in states with a high age of consent for statutory rape (eighteen), adolescent consent should not operate to bar tort recovery.[35]

Additionally, the *Restatement (Second) of Torts* section 892B addresses some of the special facts in Sara's case. Subsection (2) states,

> If the person consenting to the conduct of another is induced to consent by a substantial mistake concerning the nature of the invasion of his interests or the extent of the harm to be expected from it and the mistake is known to the other or is induced by the other's misrepresentation, the consent is not effective for the unexpected invasion or harm.[36]

This provision describes how fraud and misrepresentations can invalidate consent induced by such falsehoods. Recall the manager's profession of love for Sara, his lies about the brain tumor, and his failure to disclose his status as a registered sex offender. These assertions constituted multiple misrepresentations that vitiated her consent.[37] Because she never would have consented to have sex with him had she known the truth, and withdrew her consent once she understood the truth, the fraud paved the way for a sexual harassment suit. Whether a court would have followed this nonbinding legal guidance remains unclear.[38] Coming chapters revisit how misrepresentations taint consent and demonstrate disrespect. Suffice it to say here that true consent, as recognized under common law, requires informed understanding.

Public Policy and Civil Personal Injury Claims

While the goals of the criminal and civil systems overlap in some aspects, they remain distinct in others. The differences in motivating justifications for criminal and civil laws may explain the differing treatment of adolescent consent.

Professor Kenneth Abraham describes five functions served by the imposition of civil liability for accidental and intentional injuries. First, many people expect civil tort liability to compensate individuals for their injuries. Abraham reasons that compensation alone is not really a goal of the tort system, because then anyone injured could obtain compensation.[39] Second, Abraham instead focused on tortious conduct and other goals, including deterrence.[40] Like antidiscrimination laws, tort liability serves to deter bad acts and prevent future harm.[41] Third, Abraham mentions loss distribution. Rather than make the plaintiff bear the burden of any loss, tort law provides for a broader distribution. The tort system contemplates that insurers will pay damages incurred by policy holders and that those prospective defendants who can increase the costs of their goods and services to pay future judgments will do so.[42]

Fourth, Abraham suggests that corrective justice warrants civil liability in that it restores the moral balance between parties. For example, when one person intentionally injures another, basic fairness justifies the imposition of liability for damages on the bad actor. Corrective justice seems less appropriate when someone other than the actor, such as a corporate employer, must pay the damage award. In that situation, the disconnect between the intentional harm and the remedial compensation lessens the moral justification. The loss distribution function better justifies the imposition of tort liability in such a case—especially when the tortfeasor lacks deep pockets to pay for the damage caused.[43]

Fifth, Abraham reviewed the redress of social grievances through the tort system. Much like the function of antidiscrimination law, discussed in chapters 6 and 7, tort law arguably "is a populist mechanism that permits ordinary people to put authority on trial."[44] This conception of tort law envisions the amelioration of problems that affect society more broadly.

Taken together, the goals of the tort system harmonize nicely with the desire to protect adolescents. Arguably, society wants to deter sexual behavior that could harm these juveniles. By making adults responsible for their own conduct or employers liable for the acts of their agents, the system distributes the losses associated with teen injuries to the adults who can more easily cover those losses. Additionally, tort liability supports corrective justice by restoring the moral balance between adults and adolescents who may not have the experience or wisdom to recognize manipulative sexual advances. Tort law allows adolescents to challenge supervisors, teachers, and other adults. When tort law affords adolescent consent unmodified legal significance, it fails those teenagers and thwarts the goals of the system.

A Survey of Recent Personal Injury Cases

When I first began analyzing adolescent consent to sex with an adult via the Westlaw database, I found few cases and not one was a Title VII case. Therefore, I did a word search for civil cases involving adolescents, consent, and sex. Of eighteen tort cases involving teens with adult partners, seventeen split fairly evenly on whether they held consent relevant to the tort claims.[45] One found that fraud invalidated a minor's consent, but the court's reasoning suggested it might have credited the consent had the fraud not occurred.[46] Several of the cases that ruled consent relevant served as guiding precedent in Joe's case against Chris Abson and Mama Taori's Premium Pizza, discussed in chapter 7. Those nine cases that determined consent irrelevant employed reasoning consistent with each other, most adopting the home state's criminal law assessment of adolescent consent.

Consent as Irrelevant

In *Doe by Doe v. Greenville Hospital System*,[47] the court ruled that "Mary," a candy striper under sixteen-years-old and working in a hospital,[48] could not legally consent to sexual intercourse with a thirty-one-year-old hospital employee. The hospital argued that a criminal statute had no relevance to a battery (injurious touching) claim. The hospital further asserted that battery required nonconsensual touching. The court disagreed, finding that section 16–3-655(3) of the South Carolina Code[49] invalidated consent as a defense to a sexual battery of a minor. The court opined that this law applied in both criminal and civil contexts. The court explained, "As a matter of public policy, the General Assembly has determined a minor under the age of sixteen is not capable of voluntarily consenting to a sexual battery committed by an older person." Additionally, the court found that the criminal law applied to Mary Doe's negligent hiring and supervision claims against the hospital.[50]

The question understandably left unanswered by the *Greenville Hospital* decision is what the court would have done if Mary Doe had been sixteen, as Sara and Kati were. The *Greenville Hospital* court consistently applied the criminal law presumptions in a civil case, but this application is hardly shocking because the South Carolina Code defined the age of consent at sixteen. Mary Doe was under sixteen, so the criminal presumptions still applied in her case. The law might have forced the dismissal of Mary Doe's claims had she been only a few months older.[51] Again, one notices the relevance of the state-defined age of consent, which may or may not coincide with the age of majority, typically eighteen.

Other courts similarly found that the age of consent, as defined under criminal law, establishes a compelling public policy that underage youth lack the ability to consent to sexual conduct.[52] In *Bostic v. The Smyrna School District*, the court noted the public policy concerns and reasoned, "It would be a bizarre rule indeed that, for purposes of civil liability, would call a teenager's consent sufficient to make a relationship 'welcome' and thus not a basis for civil liability, when the very same relationship is rape under the exacting standards for criminal liability." Here, the *Bostic* court stressed the lack of logic in an inconsistent treatment of adolescent consent. The court added, "Bostic's sadly misguided participation in the affair is no shield from liability for the defendants."[53]

In *Robinson v. Moore*, the court focused on behavior that violates a statute that fixes the age of consent for intercourse. The court explained that under such a statute, "which has as its primary purpose the protection of a definite class of persons from their own immaturity of judgment, the plaintiff's consent is not a defense to a civil action."[54] This language tracks the reasoning of *Restatement (Second) of Torts* section 892C. Two other courts specifically cited or discussed this provision and the other torts restatement sections.[55]

Several cases did not make explicit the public policy rationale but held that consent could not constitute a defense under the circumstances alleged.[56] In *Doe v. City of Murietta*, Officer Derick Boyd engaged in sexual relations with two sixteen-year-old participants in the police department's Explorer Program. Boyd ultimately pled guilty to criminal unlawful sex with a minor under California law. Each juvenile filed civil tort claims against Boyd, the city, and the police department. In response to the consent defense, the *Murietta* court held, "But it is well documented that sexual abuse of minors causes significant emotional trauma to minors, with its related societal costs, and, no doubt, for this reason, such conduct constitutes a felony."[57] Without specifically ruling, the court failed to treat consent as a defense to the juveniles' personal injury claims.

Consent as Relevant

Other courts that found consent relevant to the discussion of civil liability based their determinations on several factors. First, the courts noted that criminal laws provide no private right of action.[58] As explained earlier, this reason does not clarify why courts should not apply the criminal law presumptions consistently for an existing civil private right of action. Additionally, the absence of a private right of action under a criminal statute fails to address irrationality of finding capacity in one system and a lack thereof in another.

Second, courts pointed to the different purposes of the criminal and civil systems.[59] The primary differences relate to the availability of damages and the influence of civil liberties afforded older adolescents. With respect to civil liberties, several courts reasoned that because minors engage in certain adult conduct, civil law should assign them full legal capacity. In *Cynthia M. v. Rodney E.*, the court listed the abortion right and the right to consent to other types of medical treatment.[60]

Relying on case precedent and statutory law, the *Cynthia M.* court ruled, "Capacity exits when the minor has the ability of the average person to understand and weigh the risks and benefits." The *Cynthia M.* court noted how law "is replete with examples of situations in which a child over the age of fourteen is deemed to have the mental capacity of an adult."[61] Again, these comments confuse a determination of adolescent capacity with other public policy reasons for granting minors the right to engage in these adult activities. As previously noted, just because laws permit an adolescent to obtain an abortion does not necessarily mean that society attributes to her the ability of the average adult to weigh the risks and benefits on a regular basis—or even in most circumstances.

Additionally, the Court decided *Cynthia M.* in 1991, eight years before Dr. Giedd published his groundbreaking research on adolescent brain development. As chapter 2 explains, most people understand now that average adults and average teenagers do not always think alike. The new research proves that teens do not weigh risks and benefits in the same manner that adults do.

The existence and assessment of damages appears to be the major concern of all of these courts. The damage calculus figures into not only the second factor concerning the different purposes of the criminal and civil systems, but also a third factor regarding unfairness. Specifically, courts that permitted consideration of adolescent consent emphasized the injustice of granting damages to a participant in a crime and of limiting evidence under those circumstances.

The restriction of evidence concerned many tribunals. For example, in *Doe by Roe v. Orangeburg County School District*, the South Carolina Supreme Court allowed admission of plaintiff's "willing participation" to the sex but only on the issue of damages, not the issue of liability. The court specifically distinguished the lower court's holding in *Greenville Hospital*, which found that a child under sixteen did not have the capacity to consent to sex. In *Orangeburg*, the plaintiff and her parents sued the school district and a teacher who failed to supervise students, during which time the alleged sexual assault occurred. A sixteen-year-old mentally handicapped student allegedly sexually assaulted a fourteen-year-old girl after the coach left them alone in the school gym.[62]

The *Orangeburg* court relied on *Barnes v. Barnes*,[63] a challenge to the Indiana Rape Shield Statute. Quoting *Barnes*, the *Orangeburg* court reasoned,

> Unlike the victim in a criminal case, the plaintiff in a civil damage action is 'on trial' in the sense that he or she is an actual party seeking affirmative relief from another party. Such plaintiff is a voluntary participant, with strong financial incentive to shape the evidence that determines the outcome. It is antithetical to principles of fair trial that one party may seek recovery from another based on evidence it selects while precluding opposing relevant evidence on grounds of prejudice.[64]

This passage highlights the court's focus on fairness. The court ignored, however, that prejudice regularly justifies the exclusion of probative evidence.[65] Additionally, the court missed the point of exclusion. The main reason for excluding the consent was not the prejudice potentially created, but the minor's incapacity that rendered the consent legally invalid. This court did not even hesitate to put the consenting minor "on trial."

The other concern pertaining to fairness focused on the minor's "willing participation" in the conduct.[66] Many of these cases invoked concepts of comparative fault, contributory negligence, or assumption of risk to deal with the victim's conduct.[67] Many took a moralistic stance, evaluating whether the victim was "innocent" or not.[68] The *Cynthia M.* court explained, "We have emphasized the word 'innocent' because we believe there is an important distinction between a party who is injured through no fault of his or her own and an injured party who willingly participated in the offense about which the complaint is made."[69]

Quoting a 1922 Louisiana Supreme Court decision, the *Cynthia M.* court reasoned, "[T]o recognize the asserted right to recover would be to permit plaintiff to profit by the wrong to which she voluntarily was a party."[70] The *Cynthia M.* court ignored the fact that a minor lacks the capacity to consent in the criminal context. The court missed the meaning of the statutory rape charge. The notion that a minor "profits" when she collects money for medical bills associated with a pregnancy, for psychotherapy, or for emotional and physical distress deserves no comment. *Cynthia M.* stands as another classic example in which adults blame the victim, this time a fourteen-year-old.

In *LK v. Reed*, a thirteen-year-old special education student, A.K., took the blame for her own injury, or at least a pro rata share of it. A.K., through her estate administrators, sued another student and the school board after A.K. allegedly agreed to engage in sex with an eighteen-year-old special education high school junior. The *LK* court criticized the trial court, pointing out that the original holding "necessarily entitles any carnal knowledge victim to civil damages." The *LK* court warned, "Under the trial court's holding, a girl could provoke a criminal prosecution against a sexual partner and recover damages from him, both as a result of her willful and voluntary actions in consenting to, or instigating, a sexual liaison."[71]

This cautionary augury conjures the specter of the young seductress, luring men to their financial demise. Anticipating partners outside of the special education environment, the *LK* court neglected to mention that any potential sexual partner of such a "Lolita"[72] remained free to reject her advances and spare himself criminal and potential civil liability. This notion of the child harlot, ready to entrap an unsuspecting adult partner, exemplifies the most dated, sexist notions of women (and girls) as avaricious temptresses.[73] The court's reduction of the fault percentage to even 5 percent seems odd in the context of a thirteen-year-old special education student with an IQ of between sixty-four and seventy-four.[74]

Despite its ultimate determination, the court explained other disturbing facts:

> [A]t the time of these events A.K. was a 13-year-old girl with minimal intellectual and social skills. She was shy and obedient and had never had a boyfriend. She had a history of seizures for which she took daily medication. Her family was poor in financial assets but rich in religious beliefs. In the year preceding these events, A.K.'s father was involved in an accident which rendered him a paraplegic, and A.K.'s mother donated a kidney to A.K.'s younger sister, a surgery requiring extended visits to New Orleans. A.K.'s family stress coupled with her age, intellect, and social skills, render her consent, from a legal standpoint, almost meaningless. Accordingly, we assess A.K.'s fault at 5% and reduce the damages awarded to her by that percentage.[75]

In this passage, the court justified the limit on its award reduction with the family's circumstances, not with the victim's conduct. This alternate explanation suggests that the court was sympathetic to A.K.'s family stress and its admirable religious character. Neither factor justified a reduction in the comparative negligence multiplier. The real question was whether A.K. was negligent at all.

In *McNamee v. A.J.W.*, the court suggested that the admissibility of the consent might hinge upon whether the sexual partner was also a minor. This suggestion again reflects an emphasis on comparative fault.[76] If neither party possesses the capacity to consent, why should society blame (in a comparative fault scheme) either? Such a policy makes no logical sense. While comparative fault seems inappropriate when applied to minors who lack capacity, the concept hints at a parallel concern—comparative power. The *McNamee* court was perhaps correct (but for the wrong reason) to emphasize the difference between teen-teen and teen-adult consensual sex.

From Comparative Fault to Comparative Power

Many of the tort cases that found adolescent consent relevant to a civil claim for damages favored comparative fault schemes. In contrast, those cases that found consent irrelevant emphasized the power disparity between teenagers and adult partners. Courts attributed enhanced power to factors such as older age and maturity, a position of authority, and a position of confidence or trust. For example, in *Angie M. v. Hiemstra*, a minor consented to sex with a forty-eight-year-old physician with whom she worked. The court found that he "took advantage of his position of authority and of Angie's confidence in him to cause her to develop a dependent relationship on him 'in much the manner of the phenomen[on] of "transference" between a patient and his or her psychotherapist.'"[77]

Similarly, in *Bohrer v. DeHart*, the court rejected a comparative fault instruction after a minister allegedly sexually abused a minor parishioner. The court determined that "dependence, transference and the resulting vulnerability do not cease merely because a child physically matures while sexual abuse in secrecy by an adult in a position of trust continues unabated." The *Bohrer* court determined that consent was inadmissible as a defense because of a power imbalance caused by the minor's sexual encounters with a religious counselor.[78]

Other teen-adult relationships, in addition to those involving doctors or ministers, resulted in power disparities acknowledged by courts. A teacher holds a position of authority that permits influence over and creates a power imbalance with an adolescent.[79] In *Bostic*, discussed above, the court explained that "Smith's affair with Bostic cannot be viewed as consensual, given the minority of the student and the relationship of trust and authority which the coach held over her."[80] Additionally, in *Orangeburg*, a case that found consent relevant to the issue of damages, the court referenced a South Carolina Code criminal provision that prohibited sexual conduct between a minor and an "actor [who] is in a position of familial, custodial, or official authority to coerce the victim to submit or is older than the victim."[81] Thus, both tort and criminal law recognize that a power imbalance creates a greater potential for influence and abuse of a minor. When adults recognize that power imbalances and inequality facilitate the sexual harassment and abuse of minors, they understand how public policy and the regulation of sexual activity influence adolescent experiences.

Conclusions Regarding Public Policy and Civil Personal Injury Law

This brief overview of the traditional legal responses and public policy demonstrates that statutory rape law and tort law share many similar functions and public policy goals. Each attempts to deter and prevent antisocial, harmful behavior. The sexual exploitation of minors conceivably falls into the set of antisocial behaviors under criminal and tort law. Each system holds actors who cause harm responsible, by punishing them with incarceration or by awarding damages against them. Each system operates to protect potential victims from harm through the deterrence and prevention mechanisms. The only function that the criminal system does not share with civil law is the redistribution of the costs of harm suffered. Typically, criminal laws do not compensate the victims for their losses. Tort laws provide for such compensation, however, with damage awards against either the tortfeasor or another responsible party, such as an employer or insurer.

The obvious next question is whether the civil compensation function explains why the criminal and civil systems treat adolescent consent so differently. The answer is not immediately apparent. If minors lack capacity to consent in the criminal arena, why might civil courts consider such consent in the redistribution of the costs of injury—especially at the minor's expense? A system that shifts the cost of injury resulting from sexual misconduct to the juveniles, who can least afford the expense or protect against those costs, appears irrational. It also validates Dr. Mike Males's concern regarding the scapegoating of powerless teenagers. This system seems even more irrational in light of the evidence regarding adolescent development and capacity. Another factor, already briefly explored, may explain the differences between criminal and civil treatment of consent—moral condemnation.

This review of criminal and civil law also reconfirms several truths. First, the law handles adolescent consent to sexual conduct inconsistently. The system (criminal or civil), the geographic region (or jurisdiction), and the particular claims alleged all influence the legal treatment of adolescent consent. A teenager in California can expect very different treatment than a teenager in Indiana, where the age of consent is two years younger. Second, common law claims may provide little or no relief to consenting teens. Courts may conclude that a minor appreciated the consequences of her consent to specific conduct. On the other hand, depending upon where the minor works, state criminal law may pave the way for tort recovery via *Restatement (Second) of Torts* section 892C(2). Third, statutory rape laws draw bright-line rules determining the age of consent and denying capacity below the set age. In sum, no national consensus exists regarding the age of consent or the treatment of adolescent consent to a broad variety of "adult" activities, including sex. Judicial response variance concerning the exact same consensual behavior begs the question why criminal and civil law handle consent so differently. Is the answer simply moral opprobrium? My conclusion, clear from the foregoing discussion, is yes.

CHAPTER SIX

Modern Worldly Wisdom?

The Theoretical Foundations of Antidiscrimination and Sexual Exploitation Law

The socio-legal regulation of sexual activity is not a new phenomenon; sex has been regulated since at least ancient times. Public policy and cultural perspectives concerning the regulation of sexuality evolved dramatically, however, over the twentieth century. Old and new perspectives provide guidance for exploring the foundational base of sexual harassment prohibitions and the redress of teen sexual harassment.

The Traditional View

Some scholars, including Professors Martha Chamallas and William Eskridge, analyze the regulation of sex not according to the system (i.e., civil or criminal), but according to historical, societal mores and values. In 1988 Chamallas distinguished between three dominant attitudes concerning sexual conduct: the traditional view, the liberal view, and the egalitarian view.[1] Chamallas explained that the traditional view relegated sexual conduct to the marriage bed. This view, dominant until World War II, promoted the marital family as the primary social institution. Embodied in law, this view focused concern not upon the sexual activity, but upon the status of the parties.[2] The traditional view established normative parameters around sex. This view rejected nonmarital sex and female sexual autonomy.[3] Needless to say, it also rejected the legitimacy of teen sexual exploration and autonomy.[4]

Statutory rape law fits neatly within this traditional approach. Criminalizing sex with unmarried young women works to discourage both premarital sex and female autonomy. Professor Lea VanderVelde discussed in her research on this subject how, historically, a rapist might avoid prosecution by marrying his victim.[5] In 1995 William Eskridge wrote that this was still the case in Virginia.[6] Chamallas noted that a promiscuous female adolescent could not sue for statutory rape.[7]

The G. W. Bush administration's funding of abstinence-only education and disapproval of premarital sex marked a renewed enthusiasm for this traditional approach.[8] What is unclear, however, is how a neo-traditional approach might influence sexual harassment law for teenagers. One might anticipate no reform. Those teens who can prove that they indicated the sexual harassment was unwelcome can file under Title VII or Title IX. Those who cannot prove their discomfort or those who consented deserve no relief under a traditional approach because those teens violated neo-traditional norms concerning appropriate teen sexual conduct. The result is similar to the denial of a rape claim by a promiscuous teenager.

Alternately, a neo-traditional reform might mandate the uniform treatment of adolescent consent in civil and criminal laws. Because the repeal of statutory rape laws would thwart neo-traditional control of nonmarital sexual expression, jurists would have to redraft civil law to match the dictates of criminal law regarding the legal validity of consent. Thus, we would end up with a variety of interpretations of adolescent *consent* under Title VII, depending on the respective state criminal designation of the age of consent. Under that reform, one might also anticipate the denial of money damages for those consenting underage plaintiffs because criminal law provides no financial compensation to the victim.

For a variety of reasons, including the limitations on female autonomy and the discriminatory distribution of marital benefits, some adults and parents do not share an enthusiasm for neo-traditionalism. They want their children to "know" their intended life partners well, in every way, including the biblical one, before they make an enduring commitment. This perspective does not mean, however, that these parents disfavor laws that protect adolescents from clever seducers and sexual pirates. Parents and guardians might prefer legal reforms that acknowledge adolescent autonomy and developing capacity. In other words, they might prefer legal reforms that focus on the alleged harasser's conduct and not on adolescent consent that may bear no resemblance to adult volitional affirmation.

The Liberal View and the *Oberweis* Doe Purported Siren

Associated with the sexual revolution that reached its height during the 1960s, the liberal view emphasizes consent, not marriage.[9] During the reign of sexual liberalism, the Supreme Court recognized the penumbral right to privacy, protecting citizens from governmental interference in matters pertaining to sexuality and procreation.[10] Only external harm to a third person justified legal intervention under this view. Chamallas noted that, because choice and consent legitimized much of what had been legally disapproved (nonmarital sex), the definition of *consent* became critically important.[11] Chamallas explained, "Consent is a devilishly malleable term which may describe a wide spectrum of responsive behavior, ranging from the mere failure to engage in active resistance, to active participation in and encouragement of another's initiatives." Chamallas suggested that how society classifies conduct as consensual or not "may mask value judgments implicit in the choice of definition. A determination of sexual consent may, for example, serve as a proxy for moral judgments about the behavior of the parties or as a shorthand method for classifying certain forms of sexual behavior as normal."[12]

Chamallas's discussion of consent prompts the idea that the criminal system's continuing denial of adolescent capacity reflects a value judgment that society, through its prosecutors, wants to control adolescent sexual conduct. Adults think that sex with a minor is abnormal.[13] Rather than punish the young for violating imposed parameters, jurists call them incompetent and punish, or attempt to deter, those who would thwart society's notion of what is acceptable sexual conduct for a minor.

Civil (legal) recognition of adolescent consent, where it exists, may indicate a liberal value judgment about adolescent sexuality. Perhaps the evolving societal liberalism influenced the civil system more quickly than it did the criminal system and, therefore, explains the civil system's treatment of adolescent sexuality. On the other hand, jurists still maintain control over adolescent conduct in the civil system by withholding access, thereby preventing adolescents, without representation by parents or guardians, from suing in court.[14]

At the same time, some civil courts deem restoration for sexual (mis)conduct against minors in the form of money damages abnormal, offensive, or at least suspect.[15] Former EEOC Acting Chair Paul Igasaki understood that money damages might seem inappropriate or confusing to older workers or observers. Igasaki noted that "one might ask how much is really 'lost' by a young person possibly working for a brief stint at a low-paying gig. . . . Viewed in this limited light, the loss of a presumably temporary, burger-flipping job may seem 'no big deal' or not worthy of significant damages." Igasaki also suggested, "Some may even suspect that complaints are a 'scam' to win big awards."[16] This reasoning parallels the scholars' proposed explanation for the elimination of the old seduction claim—fear that unchaste women were extorting money from unsuspecting lovers.

Do adults simply discount the value of a job at a burger joint (or movie theater or ice cream parlor)? Or do they also distrust sexually active youth?[17] The *Doe v. Oberweis Dairy* case helps to answer these questions.

Doe v. Oberweis Dairy

Like *Doe v. Starbucks, Inc.*, *Doe v. Oberweis Dairy* was a 2005 sexual harassment case involving a sixteen-year-old ice cream scooper and her twenty-something supervisor. The Illinois *Oberweis* federal district court decided that Doe had not complained of unwelcome conduct.[18] The district court also found the conduct was not severe or pervasive, another requirement of the legal sexual harassment case that chapter 2 noted. Suffice it to say here that the district court dismissed this case summarily because the judge did not find that the alleged facts reached the threshold level for a federal case. The court declared, "Here, it is undisputed that through Plaintiff's approximately eight-month employment with Defendant, Nayman [the supervisor] only touched Plaintiff on fifteen occasions." The court elaborated,

> [T]hese touches included squeezing Plaintiff's arm above her elbow, whereby Nayman would ask Plaintiff how she was doing, or giving Plaintiff non-sexual "side hugs." Once, Nayman gave Plaintiff a hug and kiss in an effort to make Plaintiff happy; and another time, Nayman gave Plaintiff a "happy-to-see-you type of hug" when she came to work. Nayman also "playfully" hit Plaintiff on the behind with a rag on one occasion. On a few occasions, Nayman

> made allegedly harassing remarks towards Plaintiff, but it is undisputed that Plaintiff found these remarks "flattering."

The court stressed that Doe "continued to visit with Nayman socially outside of work, even after Plaintiff's mother prohibited Plaintiff from visiting Nayman."[19] Therefore, the court concluded that there was no issue of material fact as to whether the sexual conduct was unwelcome.

In reversing the district court in 2006, the Seventh Circuit court described in much more detail how Nayman operated:

> Construing the evidence as favorably to her [Plaintiff] as the record permits, as we must, we assume that Nayman, the shift supervisor, regularly hit on the girls (most of the employees were teenage girls) and young women employed in the ice cream parlor. He would, as one witness explained, "grope," "kiss," "grab butts," "hug," and give "tittie twisters" to these employees, including the plaintiff. These things he did in the store, but he would also invite the girls to his apartment. He had sexual intercourse in the apartment with two of them, one of them a minor, before it was the plaintiff's turn. He was 25 when he had intercourse with her.[20]

This passage from the appellate decision highlights the importance of spin and the recitation of the facts in these cases. An unsympathetic judge can tell a very different account of adolescent sexual activity. For the district court, *Oberweis* Doe was a sneaky, conniving brat. To others, including the Seventh Circuit court, she was a sexually exploited minor.

The Liberal View and Oberweis *Doe*

Judge Richard Posner referred to *Oberweis* Doe, a sixteen-year-old ice cream scooper, as possibly a "siren" and "a part-time teenage worker—[who] would hardly have been considered a valued employee."[21] These quotes demonstrate that Igasaki was correct that some adults discount the value of a job at a burger joint and distrust sexually active youth.

Recall from chapter 5 how the South Carolina Supreme Court ruled that *Orangeburg* Doe's consent to sexual battery was admissible as to the issue of damages but not liability. The court put the plaintiff "on trial" because she was "a voluntary participant, with strong financial incentive to shape the evidence."[22] One might conclude that the court simply distrusted plaintiffs, but such a conclusion would not explain the inadmissibility of consent as to liability. The additional irony here is that *Orangeburg* Doe was not even the plaintiff. Her guardian was.[23]

The interpretation of consent, treated differently depending upon the context, may serve as a proxy for traditional moral judgments about adolescent sexuality. In *Oberweis*, Judge Posner commented that the law should permit Oberweis Dairy to put Nayman's "behavior into perspective. If Doe was sneaking around behind her mother's—and her employer's—back and thus facilitating Nayman's behavior [Doe's harassment and seduction], the employer may be able to show that the harm she suffered that was caused by its violation . . . was minimal."[24]

I would argue that a reading of the Illinois statutory rape law would put Nayman's conduct into perspective for any jury; he had sex with a minor under the age of consent. The federal civil court, however, would put *Oberweis* Doe on trial. The court focused on the possibility that Doe was sneaking around to facilitate Nayman's behavior—as if this supervisor,[25] the employer's agent, was incapable of resisting her sirenian charm. Clearly, the court saw her potentially as guilty as her supervisor, a man nine years her senior.[26] This reasoning also looks very much like a comparative negligence analysis.

Certainly, if Doe was "sneaking around" and deceiving her parents, she should not have been. However, one needs to look deeper. Why was she sneaking? Was she thinking clearly, anticipating the consequences of her actions? Had her neurological synapses formed sufficiently that she was even capable of fully anticipating the consequences? Was her conduct as culpable as Nayman's such that she deserved to be placed on trial for being a "siren"? And is *siren* just a more genteel substitute for *slut* or *ho*? Was the court concerned because she deceived her mother—because she defied adult authority and dominion to meet the man who professed to care for her? Is it possible that she was not defying adult authority but merely complying with Nayman's? Perspective is so important. Spin is everything. In *Romeo and Juliet*, William Shakespeare cautioned, "Virtue itself turns vice, being misapplied, / And vice sometime's by action dignified."[27]

As jurists craft legal defaults, society needs to consider a number of questions. For example, is it likely that nine girls out of ten will prove "Lolita," such that we need to protect unwary men and uninformed employers? Or is it more likely that nine out of ten girls will prove confused, misguided, foolishly duped—such that laws should protect them and put the adults on notice? And what about the tenth girl, the siren? How should the law deal with her? Rather than punish nine girls out of ten to catch her, perhaps society should, through operation of the law, admonish the supervisor or teacher to keep it zipped and the employer to select its agents more carefully. The law is a blunt knife and one that should not be turned against adolescent girls (or boys).

Conclusions from a Liberal Perspective

Whether the civil system's treatment of adolescent sexuality reflects a traditional or liberal perspective, the results are the same. An underage adolescent suffers the shame, humiliation, and trauma of a public trial, while she endures the prosecution of her abuser.[28] She may be constrained or completely preempted in her suit for damages and emotional distress because of her consent. A look at this ironic result raises two questions. First, why might one anticipate her shame and trauma in the criminal context? For example, would she suffer shame if someone stole her car or ran into her with one? Arguably, adults expect shame because of the lingering notion that a female attracts her rapist and the abuse she suffers. Similar attitudes prevail for boys who become sexually active with adult males. Traditional notions about homosexuality, premarital sex, the shame of unwed pregnancy, abortion, and welfare dependency contribute to the disapproval and therefore the shame.[29] If this is true, then one can answer a second question: Why does law deny civil damages to a sexually active minor? It does because adults believe that he or she is morally tainted and undeserving.

Another ironic fact results from the inconsistent treatment of consent: the convicted defendant faces incarceration and perpetual social stigma as a registered sex offender in the criminal arena. At the same time, the defendant enjoys potential immunity from prosecution for monetary damages for any emotional and physical injuries he caused the minor.[30] How is this logical? Again, one finds the adult male less culpable if the minor failed to say no, or if, heaven forbid, she said yes. American society may have experienced a sexual revolution but as with any revolution, one often returns to the starting point. Query whether society ever really abandoned the association between moral taint and the sexually active teen female or gay male.

Socio-legal Regulation of Sex

This chapter's discussion of the socio-legal regulation of sexual activity informs the review of historical perspectives concerning premarital and adolescent sexual conduct. More modern cultural norms influence public policy that provides the foundation for antidiscrimination and workplace sexual harassment law, particularly Title VII. Liberal views that elevate the importance of choice lead to an understanding of how context figures into the evaluation of the meaning of *consent* and its distinction from *acquiescence*. Twenty-first-century socio-legal perspectives also contribute to the debate on the modern regulation of adolescent consent to sexual activity.

The Egalitarian and Mutuality Perspectives

Professor Chamallas offered the egalitarian view as the feminist critical response to liberalism and the slippery definition of *consent*. The egalitarian perspective, a creation of the feminist movement of the 1970s, unveiled the fallacy of consent by females who were subordinated and disempowered in a male-dominated culture. This view questions whether women can truly consent in the face of threatened violence, economic coercion, and duplicitous misrepresentation. The negative answer prompted the reform of criminal rape laws, the advent of sexual harassment cases, and the first sexual deception tort actions.[31] Chamallas might distinguish the sexual deception claims from the traditional seduction claim in that the seduction claim typically hinged on a false promise to marry. Modern claims address other types of deception.

Thus, for Chamallas and feminist egalitarians, three inducements to consent—physical force, economic pressure, and deception—invalidate any consent procured by the more powerful, wealthier, or better-informed partner. These inducements also corrupt adolescent consent.

Physical Force

First, physical force certainly plays a role in the sexual harassment of adolescents by adults. Anecdotal evidence from teen sexual harassment charges confirms that supervisors use physical force to intimidate and harass teen workers. At one Burger King in Missouri, a male manager pinned young female workers against the wall in a walk-in freezer and grabbed their breasts.[32] A male manager at a California UltraStar Cinema assaulted a sixteen-year-old female worker, dislocating her shoulder.[33] A male manager at a Pennsylvania Mexican restaurant sexually assaulted a sixteen-year-old female worker.[34] Promising a ride home to a fourteen-year-old Kansas fast-food worker, a manager drove her to his house and sexually assaulted her.[35] These are just a few examples of how physical violence exacerbates the harassment of teenagers. These cases prompt another question for scientific investigation: whether youth workers disproportionately face more violence and aggression because of their physical and emotional immaturity and relative lack of power.

Duress and Teen Responses

Second, economic duress must figure prominently in an adolescent's choice to consent to sexual relations with workplace supervisors and managers. With adolescent unemployment so high and teen job skills so low, a supervisor can conceivably press sexual activity with just a verbal threat. One young female worker from a Missouri Burger King allegedly had sex with the manager after he threatened her job.[36] Why didn't this teen complain?

Chapter 2 related how the AACAP opined that some adolescents conceal sexual harassment and may never reveal their trauma. Chapter 3 covered the AACAP statistics that support this opinion. Paul Igasaki agreed that teens "may be reluctant to talk about the problem with adults. When the problem touches on sex, teenagers may not feel comfortable discussing the topic even with their own parents." He also emphasized that "young people are taught to respect their elders, and despite modern cautions that no one can touch you against your will, it is always difficult to take the risk of coming forward."[37]

Other experts hold similar views. One practitioner, Michael Blickman, believes that "[y]ounger employees are definitely more vulnerable to sexual harassment. . . . Because they have less experience in the workplace, they tend not to know their rights." This lawyer suggested that even if they do know their rights, fear of retaliation or termination inhibit their complaints and reporting. Harassers exploit those fears and become emboldened to engage in further abuse.[38]

How much of such sexual duress goes unreported because of the factors noted above? That question is hard to answer. Survey research and anecdotal observations indicate that teens underreport their abuse. In the Missouri case, family members conducted their own investigation to explain their adolescents' unusual, withdrawn, and moody behavior. A journalist reported,

> [One teen's] older sister figured something at work was the culprit. So the older sister went undercover—getting hired at the same restaurant—to find the truth. On the older sister's second day on the job, the boss began doing the same [sexually harassing] things to her. He would rub up against her while she was at a cash register and make sexual comments.
>
> The mother of another victim took a tape recorder into the Burger King to gather evidence. She asked people what they had seen. Her daughter had been too afraid to come forward, fearing she would lose her job as part of a school Work Study program and be unable to graduate.[39]

These anecdotes confirm expert experience regarding teen response to sexual harassment. The second also highlights a manipulation tool unique to student workers who work for scholastic credit. While harassers coerce adult workers with the loss of tangible economic benefits, predators can often coerce student workers with the loss of both economic and academic benefits.[40]

Deception and Teen Perception

Third, deception may also play an increased role in securing workplace adolescent consent or sexual favors. Inexperience and naiveté lead some adolescents to accept as true the most seemingly obvious misrepresentations. Naomi C. Earp, former vice chairwoman of the EEOC, commented, "As long as humans have a dark spot, you can find a more sophisticated co-worker who takes advantage of someone more naïve." Jocelyn Samuels, former vice president for education and employment with the National Women's Law Center said, "Teens are particularly vulnerable because they are new to the workplace, they are impressionable and are more likely than not at the bottom rung. . . . They feel less authorized to complain, and they may not know that procedures are available to them." Adele Rappaport, who served as a regional attorney for the EEOC in Detroit, explained that teens accept taunting and even touching as part of the work culture or as not serious enough to report. Rappaport suggested, "A very small percentage of women complain. That's part of the issue with teens. . . . They are not sophisticated enough to know how to use those kinds of resources to report it."[41]

At fifteen years old, Sara initially rebuffed her forty-year-old manager's sexual advances. Later, she believed him when he lied to her, saying that he had a brain tumor and would live only a few months. He said that he loved her and that they should consummate "their love" while he could. When she was sixteen, she finally consented and was soon pregnant.[42] This case provides just one example of youthful gullibility and predatory deception. The influence of coyote confidants highlights adolescent vulnerability.

Finally, adolescents may view their adult supervisors and coworkers as parental authority figures or as role models for whom compliance and obedience is expected. Recall the ABA's admonition that "[sexual abuse] offenders achieve compliance through the abuse of adult authority"[43] and Igasaki's comment that children are taught to respect their elders.[44] Both statements support this contention that adults can exploit their authority and respected positions. In one school sexual harassment case, the court noted, "[a] teenaged student's susceptibility to coercion by an adult role model inherently contains the elements of 'quid pro quo' activity which, under the current Title VII standards, invokes strict liability."[45] In *State v. Holm*, a 2006 criminal bigamy and sexual abuse of a minor case, the Utah Supreme Court relied on precedent "that young people should be protected from sexual exploitation by older, more experienced persons until they reach the legal age of consent and can more maturely comprehend and appreciate the consequences of their sexual acts."[46] Adult female workers might feel obliged to respect managerial authority, but unlike teen workers, they do not suffer the added servility of youth.

These complicating perfidies persuaded Professor Chamallas that equality and mutuality, and not just consent, are the keys to legitimate sexual activity. Chamallas acknowledged that her analysis of these corrupting connivances first found expression in contract law. The law voided contracts compelled by force and made voidable those contracts induced by economic duress or misrepresentations. She noted that the inducements "are novel, however, in their application to the sexual encounter, a relationship the law seldom treats as contractual."[47] *Sexual Exploitation of Teenagers* returns to the value of contract law to this discussion later in chapter 10's conclusion.

Status and Condemned Behaviors

Professor William Eskridge also wrote of modern law's "movement from status to contract, from a medieval, collectivist understanding of human relations to a liberal, individual rights one."[48] Like Chamallas, Eskridge believed that several factors invalidated consent to sexual contact. In addition to physical force, economic duress, and deception, Eskridge suggested that the form of the activity and the status of the parties, such as marital status and sexual orientation, continue to play important roles. For example, Eskridge emphasized that sodomy and sadomasochism (S&M) were (at the time he wrote) illegal in many jurisdictions despite the consent of the parties.[49] In 2003 the US Supreme Court invalidated a Texas criminal law that prohibited consensual, adult, homosexual sodomy, thereby removing one barrier to which Eskridge referred. [50] However, the Court specifically noted that its opinion addressed only adult conduct. It cautioned, "The present case does not involve minors. It does not involve persons who might be injured or coerced or who are situated in relationships where consent might not easily be refused."[51]

Professor Eskridge explained the continuing importance of consent in relation to status for the regulation of sexuality: "Liberal consent-based regimes of legal regulation do not spring full-grown from the brow of Zeus. They accrete over time, gradually displacing traditional status-based regimes." Eskridge argued that culture evolves slowly and inconsistently and that our current regime "reflects a mixture of consent-based and status-based rules. The ubiquitous language of consent is just a rhetorical device for discussing the issue, but a device masking the more complex reality."[52]

Eskridge discussed not only marital status but also familial status and incest. He identified pedophilia, bestiality, and mental disability as conditions or behaviors that negated consent. For this last trio of factors, Eskridge concluded that incapacity (of the child, animal, or disabled) ostensibly justified the negation of consent.[53] Eskridge challenged the inclusion of adolescents in this last trio with the contention that fourteen- and fifteen-year-olds engage in sexual behavior. He pondered whether they might actually have the capacity to make that choice.[54]

Accepting Eskridge's mixed-regime perspective, one might conclude that criminal statutory rape laws rely on the old status-based regime under which an adolescent's consent matters only to classify the level of the crime. Civil laws reflect the more modern liberal view and highlight the transition from a status-based regime to a consent-based one. Finally, sexual harassment law, embodied in Title VII and state fair employment practices statutes, results from the egalitarian, feminist response to the liberal view. Sexual harassment law addresses the economic coercion or the power differential between the perpetrator and the consenting employee. Perhaps the *Oberweis* case, involving the "sneaking around" ice cream clerk, showcases the gradual transition to a more liberal regime, if not a completely feminist one.

Mutuality also attracted Eskridge's attention, but he approached it from a slightly different angle than did Chamallas. He relied upon gay experience and gay theory to explore the regulation of sexuality. Agreeing with feminist theorists, Eskridge rejected marriage as the legitimizing force for sexuality. That rejection stemmed in part from the then complete ban on gay marriage. However, he went beyond some feminists to embrace the diversity of sexuality represented in S&M and bondage and domination (B&D). Eskridge explained that "[t]he B&D literature suggests both procedural and substantive methods by which to achieve the feminist goal of mutual benefit from sex in a society of diverse sexual preferences."[55]

Eskridge also addressed sex with minors. He noted, "What has been missing in the American hysteria about sex with children has been fact-based theorizing about children's sexual development and the effects of sex with older people on that development." Eskridge acknowledged, however, that HIV changed concerns about teen-adult sexual activity, when he wrote, "The HIV virus has infected the adolescent population through adolescent sex with older infected people who take advantage of adolescent immaturity to induce unsafe practices."[56] Eskridge's discussion of adolescent sexuality displays a frustration with the lack of fact-based knowledge about adolescent sexual development as well as an acknowledgement of teen vulnerability caused by immaturity. Teen ignorance and inexperience may also contribute to their vulnerability.[57]

In sum, scholars such as Chamallas and Eskridge view the treatment of consent to sex as only part of a regulatory regime. When procreative marriage is the goal, consent to nonmarital sex validates little. When individual power and autonomy are the valued conditions, consent validates much sexual conduct but also leads to asymmetrical relations and thereby taints consent. When society emphasizes equality and mutuality, the quality of the consent and the capacity of the one consenting receive greater scrutiny. The negative inducements—physical force, economic duress, and deception—invalidate apparent consent.

A Pansexual Perspective

A pansexual perspective provides yet another useful view of consent as part of a regulatory scheme. About fifteen years ago, I introduced the idea of pansexuality as a tool that "deconstructs the stereotypical interrelation [of] biological sex and sexual behavior."[58] I suggested, "Pansexuality encompasses all kinds of sexuality. It differs, however, from pansexualism, a perspective that declares 'all desire and interest are derived from the sex instinct.' Pansexuality includes heterosexuality, homosexuality, bisexuality, and sexual behavior that does not necessarily involve a coupling. It includes, for example, masturbation, celibacy, fetishism, and fantasy." Pansexuality also includes sexual aggression, sometimes mislabeled as horseplay, as well as true heteroerotic and homoerotic play. I still believe that all people are all pansexual, whether or not they act out in diverse ways.[59] For example, a priest may be celibate but fantasize about sexual activity. He is therefore pansexual. Other sources may give a variety of definitions to the term *pansexuality* and similar descriptors such as *unisexuality* and *omnisexuality*. I remain committed to the term *pansexuality*, however, because *pan* refers to "all" and *sexuality* is "associated with sex or the sexes."[60]

While some people might feel uncomfortable being classified with a less-favored group, this perspective is consistent with Eskridge's concern about status and highlights certain pigeonholes and the resulting status hierarchies. (Title VII has yet to protect on the basis of sexual orientation or transsexual status.) Thus, while people might not mind being identified with celibates and fantasizers, they may face their biases as they consider their commonality with fetishists and transsexuals in the greater pansexual community.

Pansexuality also encompasses the sexuality of children. When people think of sexuality, most people automatically think of adult activity. This automatic response reflects stereotyped thinking, the notion that only adults can (or should) engage in sexual conduct. A pansexual perspective is one that attempts to unveil stereotypical interconnections that hinder us in exploring biological sex, gender, and sexuality.[61] This perspective also facilitates the deconstruction of the stereotypical interrelation of age and sexual behavior. Experts agree that children are born sexual beings. As they mature, their sexuality develops. A pansexual perspective acknowledges this development and its nuanced expression. Chapter 2's statistics regarding teen sexuality reinforce the validity of a pansexual perspective.

Because the pansexual perspective eschews stereotypical interconnections and emphasizes the panorama of human potential, it encourages an approach to adolescent sexuality that steps beyond bright-line demarcations. For example, some parents might argue that if teens are finding adult sexual partners at work, society should toughen the statutory rape and other child molestation laws. Such an approach denies developing capacity and, more particularly, teen sexual development and autonomy. Researchers who recommend education concerning Internet sexual predation of adolescents suggest, "Important points to touch upon include the inequality of power and experience between youths and adults, the immaturity of teens and their lack of readiness for intimate relationships with adults, and the potential negative impact on victims in terms of healthy sexual development and other consequences." Experts recommend, "Even young adolescents should be given basic information about the inappropriateness of romantic advances from adults. This information should include reassurances that it is normal to have strong sexual feelings but wrong for adults to provoke or exploit these feelings."[62]

A pansexual perspective acknowledges that teens are sexual beings who need opportunities to develop sexually in age-appropriate, safe ways. This view is consistent with an emphasis on equality and mutuality. Such an approach rules out most teen-adult sexual relationships because such liaisons may compromise both equality and mutuality for teens. A pansexual perspective, combined with notions of mutuality and equality, holds promise for the legal regulation of adolescent sexuality and teen-adult sexual relations.

Sexual Harassment Legal Theory

While socio-legal analysis offers guidance for the theoretical justification of sexual harassment prohibitions, theorists have created a library of work that addresses the problem directly. Because federal law did not explicitly prohibit the sexual harassment of women, feminist legal theorists first worked to prove why sexual harassment constituted discrimination "because of . . . sex" under Title VII of the CRA. As noted, Professor MacKinnon introduced her subordination theory in 1979. She suggested that the male demand for sexual favors from female workers reinforces their subordination to men. She explained,

> Sexual harassment perpetuates the interlocked structure by which women have been kept sexually in thrall to men and at the bottom of the labor market. Two forces of American society converge: men's control over women's sexuality and capital's control over employees' work lives. . . .
>
> . . . A guarantee of equal access to job training, education, and skills has little substance if a requirement of equality in hiring, promotion, and pay can legally be withheld if a woman refuses to grant sexual favors.[63]

Certainly this reasoning applies to female teens as well as to adult women. However, it does not translate, without explanation, to support prohibitions for harassed teen males.

Beyond the Subordination of Women

The subordination theory depends on the exploitation of the association between sexuality and biological sex to sustain power roles, particularly heterosexual male power.[64] MacKinnon reasoned, "From an inequality perspective, too, the vulnerability of gays is analogous to that of women."[65] One might similarly argue that the vulnerability of minors is analogous to that of women. Males have traditionally exercised phenomenal power over children. Early Roman law even permitted infanticide by fathers.[66] Thus, one could argue that male domination finds expression in the sexual subordination of younger, less powerful males and females.

Prisons provide numerous examples of exactly this type of male subjection. Analyzing same-sex sexual harassment in male prisons, Professor James E. Robertson explained that sexual aggression in prison affirms the aggressor's heterosexuality. The aggressor's comments feminize targets who find the behavior offensive. Robertson wrote, "[A]ttributes that mark inmates as effeminate or weak make them likely targets of sexual harassment. . . . Being of slight stature or being a young, non-Hispanic white male also stigmatizes one as both effeminate and weak and thus prime sexual fodder."[67] Not only do physical attributes of targets correlate with the feminization of young inmates, labels such as "kid" and "punk" that are assigned to targets infantilize them and symbolically highlight the subordination of youth.[68] One wonders whether this explanation also applies in the context of military sexual assault and rape, described in chapter 2.

GENDER POLICING. Professor Katherine Franke further explored same-sex harassment, sexuality, and sex-role stereotypes in her discussion of the "technology of sexism." She suggested that sexual harassment produces "gendered bodies" and enforces the hetero-feminization of women and the hetero-masculinization of men. She resisted the notion that the harassment of non-masculine males meant their subordination as feminine objects. Instead, she insisted that legal theory acknowledges that men might be harassed "as a way of policing masculinity, which may or may not have the collateral damage of vilifying femininity."[69] MacKinnon also discussed gender identity, sex roles, and sex-role enforcement in her subordination theory.[70] No matter which angle one takes, a perspective that focuses on gender traits (often giving meaning to notions of masculinity and femininity), and not simply on biological sex, has value.

Franke did not, however, immediately equate same-sex male sexual horseplay and "bagging" (when the aggressor grabs the testicles of a co-worker or feints such action) as having a gendered disciplinary or regulating function. This practice of bagging came under court scrutiny in *Quick v. Donaldson Co.*: "Quick allege[d] that at least twelve different male co-workers bagged him on some 100 occasions," and that when he complained of this behavior, his employer "told him that the next time somebody bagged him 'to turn around and bag the shit out of them.'"[71] If not explicitly endorsing the characterization, Franke repeated the description of such behavior as "unnecessary juvenile behavior by aggressive male co-workers."[72] If it does not exemplify gender policing (and I think it does), this conduct arguably resembles the male self-assertive reinforcement of heterosexuality and power in prisons noted by Robertson.

The *Quick* case description of bagging also specifically labels this reinforcement as juvenile. Why? My guess is that people think of sexual bullying and horseplay as a socializing and stratifying behavior common to adolescent boys. In *Oncale v. Sundowner Offshore Services Inc.*, the Court equated male-on-male horseplay with "ordinary socializing."[73] Some people also minimize the harm of sexual harassment by calling it horseplay. In *Parker v. General Extrusions, Inc.*, the court noted that following a sexual harassment complaint the perpetrator "was not ultimately punished for sexual harassment, but instead was written up for the *relatively minor offense* of 'horseplay.'"[74] In another case, a company defended a complaint, claiming that the alleged behavior was "no more than childish or adolescent behavior and was not sexual harassment."[75]

It is possible that such socializing during adolescence, in fact, marks the establishment of a gendered hierarchy and the policing of gender norms, a socialization process that begins during adolescence. I hope social anthropologists will investigate this question. What becomes clear in this discussion, though, is that harassment may constitute not only the subordination of the disfavored sex (females) and sexual minorities (anyone other than heterosexuals), but also that of individuals who exhibit or are assigned untraditional gender traits and adolescents. Specific behaviors (such as calling a high school male a "flaming faggot") highlight the intersectional nature of sexual harassment. An intersectional approach acknowledges that race, class, gender, and other characteristics operate independently and in the aggregate to change the nature and meaning of discrimination and oppression.[76] Therefore, an intersectional perspective acknowledges the difference that age can make in the subordination of individual targets. This is a complex topic, worthy of much more analysis that is beyond the scope of this book. However, I raise the issue for further discussion and investigation by others.

SUBORDINATION IN CONTEXT. Both Vicki Schultz and Kathryn Abrams contributed to the evolution of sexual harassment legal theory by integrating gender discrimination and sex-based subordination.[77] Focusing on gender enforcement and the masculine hierarchy of the workplace, Abrams discussed how sexual harassment robs women of new work opportunities and undermines agency for both nonconforming men and women. Professor Abrams saw that the sexually charged workplace evidences an authorization of male sexual initiative, masculine norms, and male hierarchical dominance. Operating within the framework of Title VII, Abrams made a strong point about not losing sight of the context.[78]

Professor Schultz emphasized not the sexual nature of sexual harassment, but its sex-based, or gendered, nature. She suggested, "Indeed, many of the most prevalent forms of harassment are actions that are designed to maintain work—particularly the more highly rewarded lines of work—as bastions of masculine competence and authority." Schultz recommended that people acknowledge "conduct that consigns people to gendered work roles that do not further their own aspirations or advantage."[79] One might also take this emphasis on gendered roles and venue and focus not on the entry of women into male-dominated workplaces but on the entry of adolescents into adult-dominated workplaces.

SUBORDINATION, SOCIALIZATION, OR BOTH. Studies shed light on teen experiences as these adolescents enter into gender-policed and sexualized workplaces. In 2006 Robert Bozick published his findings regarding the relationship between employment and first sexual intercourse for young teens. He wanted to know whether work influenced teen sexual development. He tested two hypotheses: the opportunity-cost hypothesis[80] and the precocious development hypothesis. He hypothesized,

> In the precocious development hypothesis, involvement in an adult role at an early age may lead adolescents to prematurely view themselves as adults, resulting in early experimentation with other adult behaviors. Participation in the workforce, therefore, should be associated with an increased likelihood of early sexual behavior. Additionally, teens who hold jobs in adult environments, such as restaurants and retail stores, where they have less parental supervision and greater exposure to older teens and adults, should have higher odds of early first sexual intercourse than teens who hold jobs normative for their age, such as babysitting or mowing lawns.[81]

While nuanced details of his fascinating study are beyond the scope of this chapter, Bozick found that work experiences significantly influence twelve- to fourteen-year-olds. Specifically, young adolescents who work eleven to twenty hours per week engage in early sexual intercourse at a rate 71 percent higher than nonworkers. Young adolescents working at adult jobs engage in sexual intercourse at a rate 79 percent higher than nonworkers. Bozick determined, "Working in a youth job [such as babysitting] has no bearing on the odds of engaging in sexual intercourse in the early teen years." He concluded that the data supported the premise of the precocious development hypothesis.[82] Stunned? Consider next that few of these children had reached the age of consent (for sexual intercourse with an adult).

Of course, Bozick's study does not address several concerns important to the issue of adolescent sexual harassment. The sex Bozick studied might have been completely *welcome* for these teenagers. If sex is consensual (i.e., desired but still unlawful) one can distinguish it from conduct complained of by harassed adult workers who find sexual conduct unwelcome. With that thought, however, one also returns to the question of whether a twelve-year-old has the capacity or power to consent.[83] If not, the conduct might be equated at law with adult sexual harassment.

Second, the data does not reveal with whom these children are having sex, whether with their peers, adult coworkers, or others. One cannot evaluate the mutuality of that sex.[84] I am reminded of Professors Fineran and Gruber's finding that a "large majority of the perpetrators were older than the girls, with nearly half (46%) described as older than 30."[85] While one should not link the information from that study with Bozick's, I suggest again that this problem begs for research.

One might hypothesize that many sexual partners are male adult coworkers or supervisors. Abrams's concerns then resurface: adult coworkers may socialize these teens to the validity of male sexual initiative, masculine norms, and male hierarchical dominance. Moreover, one must reconsider Chamallas's discussion of equality and mutuality and question how equal a fourteen-year-old fast-food restaurant worker and her adult supervisor really are. How mutually beneficial is their sexual encounter? MacKinnon also spoke to socialization. She explained that perpetrators need not ask permission to engage in harassment: "Since communicated resistance means that the woman ceases to fill the implicit job qualifications, women learn, with their socialization to perform wifelike tasks, ways to avoid the open refusals that anger men and produce repercussions."[86]

Are adolescent girls learning wife-like tasks? Are their brains being hardwired with those lessons? One might infer the affirmative with the precocious development hypothesis. However, more research regarding the details of teen sexual activity, teen employment, and adolescent sexual harassment will answer some of these questions.

BEYOND SUBORDINATION THEORY. During the last two decades, sexual harassment theory has evolved beyond MacKinnon's subordination theory. Summarizing what she saw as the problem, Professor Linda Kelly wrote, "Yet despite feminism's hegemonic strength, feminist theory is on the brink of self-annihilation. After waves of liberal, radical, and cultural feminism, we are now riding a 'third wave' of feminism that risks crashing into nothingness." Kelly suggested that "to truly recognize the freedom of women and men, the ubiquity of patriarchy cannot be presumed."[87] Kelly emphasized a focus on the abominable conduct rather than on the motivation behind it.

In her review essay, Elizabeth Anderson recognized equality theory—

including sexual equality, economic equality, and formal equality—but also described two alternative approaches that provide relief when equality theory may not. She suggested that equality theory best addresses injuries among social groups.[88] About the alternatives, she explained,

> Sexual autonomy theories view sexual harassment as an oppressive enforcement of conventional sexist and homophobic norms of gender and sexuality. It forces people to conform to these norms, and punishes anyone who deviates. . . . These theories seek to protect individual freedom of sexual expression.
>
> Dignity theories abstract from the possibly sexist or homophobic intent and effects of harassing behavior, locating the wrong instead in the means harassers use to achieve their objectives. . . . Dignity theories uphold conventional norms of respect for individuals, rather than challenging conventional norms of gender and sexuality.[89]

Both of these theories, imported to remedy sexual harassment, serve without insisting on a challenge to a perceived patriarchal order.

One can immediately envision the utility of both sexual autonomy theory and dignity theory in a comprehensive theoretical scheme designed to bolster the prohibition of sexual harassment of teen workers. The pansexual perspective acknowledges that teens are sexual beings. A theory of sexual autonomy underscores the importance of permitting an adolescent to explore her sexuality in a safe, age-appropriate manner, without moralistic repression. A theory of dignity secures for her a basic level of respect as an individual. If combined with both a subordination theory and the notion that adolescents belong to one or more subordinated groups, these approaches could produce a robust theoretical base for legal protection of working teenagers.

Socio-Legal Regulation for the Twenty-First-Century Adolescent

New developments in the socio-legal regulatory regime that stress equality and mutuality must address the unique position of adolescents. Three factors complicate efforts to protect them. First, the law has never treated adolescents as fully equal to adults. The notion of adolescent-adult equality and mutuality contradicts historical and current social conditions as well as legal reality. Statutory rape laws discussed in chapter 4 provide one example of how the law treats adolescent sexual conduct differently than it does consensual adult conduct. Because children under the age of consent do not have the capacity to give legal consent, statutory rape laws demonstrate that the law invalidates adolescent consent under certain circumstances.

Second, minors are not simply young adults. As chapter 3 reviewed, teenagers exhibit psychosocial, physical, and neurological traits different from those of most adults. New research confirms that adolescent brain development extends into the twenties, beyond the age of consent set in every state. Impulse control, emotional regulation, planning, decision making, and organization capabilities may not fully mature until the third decade of life. In addition, youth experiences may influence the winnowing and reorganization of brain gray matter during adolescence. Thus, new scientific research proves that adolescents are human works in progress. If society values equality and mutuality, then jurists should never assume, as they do with the rule of sevens discussed in chapter 5, that an adolescent has the *legal* capacity to consent to sex with an adult. Whether or not she has cognitive function equivalent to an adult, she may lack the fortitude and power to refuse an adult solicitation of a sexual relationship. Her lack of equality alone makes any consent potentially suspect and dictates against a presumption of legal capacity.

Recognition of the unique nature and status of adolescence clarifies a third complicating factor: adolescent consent may signify something different than adult consent and may, therefore, justify unique treatment under the law. Because adult consent (as opposed to mere tolerance or acquiescence) provides a complete defense to allegations of sexual harassment, one must carefully consider adolescent consent in the analysis of the theoretical and ethical basis for sexual harassment prohibitions.

Kantian Ethics, Socio-Legal Theory, and Adolescent Consent

While Drs. Onora O'Neill and R. George Wright analyzed adult consent in the context of Kantian philosophy, their comments find application for consenting teenagers.[90] With "the formula of the end in itself," Immanuel Kant proposed treating humanity always as an end and "never merely as a means" to an end.[91] An actor uses another person as a tool, as a mere means to an end, when his proposed activity reflects an underlying principle to which the other could not consent.[92] Clearly, rational and informed consent matters in this maxim. Starting from this maxim,

O'Neill focused on the treatment of "others as persons."[93] Wright explored "[h]uman dignity."[94] They each discussed the notion of capacity and probed "morally significant" or "genuine" consent.[95]

Morally significant consent must be informed and match the activities it legitimates. One who is less than fully informed of the intentions of another, even when she consents to those intentions that are clear, consents nonetheless to other intentions to which she might choose to dissent if she could only be aware of the full range of those intentions. When the possibility of dissent does not exist, neither does significant consent. Coercion, though more subtle, nevertheless treats its subject as a mere means preventing a full range of consent/dissent possibilities.[96]

O'Neill argued that to treat "others as persons" one "must view them not abstractly as possibly consenting adults, but as particular men and women with limited and determinate capacities to understand or to consent to proposals for action." For O'Neill, consent is obviously inauthentic in several circumstances. For example, true consent may not exist "when there is ignorance, duress, misrepresentation, pressure, or the like."[97] This view is reminiscent of Chamallas's and Eskridge's discussion of mutuality and equality.

Wright added that noncoercive factors can also influence a person's consent that "has social antecedents." He explained:

> We do not have pure personalities apart from the social formation of our preferences, including our preferences to consent or refuse to consent. . . .
>
> . . . .
>
> But not all processes of the social formation of preferences are equal in the degree to which they respect freedom and dignity. There is a real difference . . . between a broad education and brainwashing.[98]

One might argue that the socialization to male sexual initiative, masculine norms, and male hierarchical dominance that Abrams noted, and to wife-like tasks that MacKinnon identified, are examples of socialization processes that do not respect individual freedom and dignity. Arguably, teens are socialized when the president of Harvard University opines that that girls don't succeed in math and science because of "issues of intrinsic aptitude."[99] They receive additional messages when a Montana judge announces that a fourteen-year-old student, seduced by her fifty-four-year-old teacher, was "as much in control of the situation as was the defendant" and sentences him to only 30 days in a rape case.[100] Perhaps the public outcry following such events counteracts the original message but we all recognize the underlying fear: these powerful men actually believe what they say and so will our children.

Commercial advertising provides another example of a noncoercive influence on consent, beyond even the inclination to consent to a purchase. Aspirational advertising specifically appeals to people through images that portray them as they wish to be. As discussed in chapter 2, the aspirational age in our culture is young—teenage or young adult. While philosophical purists might argue that twenty-first-century American advertising has nothing to do with Kantian ethical discourse, others will disagree. Wright suggested, "The imperatives of a commercial society based on consumption tend to close our eyes to legal enforcement of transactions based on insufficient knowledge and freedom."[101] O'Neill suggested, "A planned seduction of someone less experienced treats him or her as means even when charmingly done."[102] The seducer entices the seduced into a wrongful, foolish, or unintended action. The seduced does not consent because she does not have the experience to understand the action itself, its probable consequences, or both. She does not know to what she might be consenting.

O'Neill said that sexual intimacy, commonly understood, conveys affection, openness, trust, and "a commitment which goes beyond a momentary clinging." When "gestures of intimacy are not used to convey what they standardly convey, miscommunication is peculiarly likely."[103] O'Neill discussed two important results from intimate conduct:

> First, those who are intimate acquire deep and detailed (but incomplete) knowledge of one another's life, character, and desires. Secondly, each forms some desires which incorporate or refer to the other's desires, and consequently finds his or her happiness in some ways contingent upon the fulfillment of the other's desires. Intimacy is not a merely cognitive relationship, but one where special possibilities for respecting and sharing (alternatively for disrespecting and frustrating) another's ends and desires develop. It is in intimate relationships that we are most able to treat others as persons—and most able to fail to do so.[104]

If one considers this reasoning in the context of an adult's sexual advances toward a teen, one sees how the teen might misconstrue the communication. The teen might see affection and commitment where the adult desires only sexual intercourse or other sexual gratification. Assume that O'Neill is correct and intimacy is not merely a cognitive relationship. Then, adolescents, who demonstrate less temperance, perspective, responsibility, and who are generally less sexually experienced, are even less likely than adults to recognize manipulative or exploitative gestures. Adolescents may consent, having formed a desire that incorporates the other's desire for sexual gratification.

Professor Robin West anticipated a similar response from adult women when she contemplated a liberal, gender-neutral perspective regarding consent and sexual engagement. West wrote,

> [I]f women "consent" to transactions not to increase our own welfare, but to increase the welfare of others—if women are "different" in this psychological way—then the liberal's ethic of consent, with its presumption of an essentially selfish human (male) actor and an essentially selfish consensual act, when even-handedly applied to both genders, will have disastrous implications for women.[105]

If women do think differently from men, and if teens, because of their developing capacities, think differently from adults, then teen females may need adults to anticipate their particular adolescent capabilities, especially when addressing teen sexual harassment.

Adolescent Power, Rights, Consent, and Sexual Harassment Theory

Professor Katherine Federle understood the problematic nature of children's capacity and emphasized power in her discussion of juvenile civil rights.[106] Her historical and theoretical review of wisdom concerning juvenile capacity and civil rights adds significantly to this discussion of the socio-legal regulation of adolescents. Federle explained,

> We must reconstruct rights talk about children in terms of power, and only when we make explicit the role of capacity is a new theory of rights for children possible. . . .
>
> . . . .
>
> My point here is that an adequate rights theory must account for power. Power is the obverse of social oppression and political inequality, for it licenses hierarchy and status. Rights, however, mitigate the exclusionary effects of power by allowing the powerless to access existing political and legal structures in order to make claims. Permitting these types of rights claims

> also has the salutary effect of redistributing power and altering hierarchies. Herein lies the real value of rights, for rights require that we respect the marginalized, empower the powerless, and strengthen the weak.[107]

From this elucidation of the importance of children's power and rights, Federle demonstrated that the focus on children's capacity, and one might argue the developing capacity of adolescents, is misguided. Such a focus leads to the disabling of children in the name of their own protection. Federle argued that children need rights to access existing political and legal structures.[108]

Most people will agree that, vis-à-vis adults, children lack political, economic, and legal power. Translate this lack to MacKinnon's definition of sexual harassment:

> Sexual harassment, most broadly defined, refers to the unwanted imposition of sexual requirements in the context of a relationship of unequal power [between males and females]. Central to the concept is the use of power derived from one social sphere [employment] to lever benefits or impose deprivations in another [sexual relations].[109]

My revision of her definition reads,

> Sexual harassment, most broadly defined, refers to the unwanted imposition of sexual requirements in the context of a relationship of unequal power [between adults and teens]. Central to the concept is the use of power derived from [one every] social sphere [employment] to lever benefits or impose deprivations in another [sexual relations often deemed illegal].

The sexual harassment of minors is unique. At least women now enjoy the right to vote, file suit in court, and serve on juries. So when we refer to their discriminatory abuse, we know that women nevertheless wield at least some political and legal authority. Minors, as noted, wield little to none. Often their power—if it can be called that—rests in the hands of the adults who purport to care for them but who may have conflicting interests. From this discussion of socio-legal theory, capacity, and rights, one sees another unique justification for the prohibition of sexual harassment against minors. Specifically, they enjoy even less political and legal power than do women, nonwhite adults, and adults with untraditional sexual orientation or gender traits.

CHAPTER SEVEN

Wising Up in the Workplace

Modern Antidiscrimination Law and Its Application

With the background of knowledge reviewed in chapters 1 through 6, one can now fully appreciate and evaluate the efficacy of modern antidiscrimination law. This law, originally implemented to foster equality, now must redress the intersectional biases, power imbalances, and corrupting manipulations of adults who target teenagers. This chapter examines Title VII, public policy, and the application of workplace antidiscrimination law. Chapter 8 traces the evolution of Title VII through its broader application to juveniles, and chapter 9 addresses Title IX. Combined, these chapters provide the information to assess whether current law adequately protects American teenagers from sexual harassment and exploitation by adults, at least at work and at school.

Modern Antidiscrimination Law

Neither specific criminal charges nor individual personal injury claims reviewed in chapters 4 and 5, respectively, adequately address systemic discrimination and the subordination of women and other target populations. Criminal charges and personal injury complaints fail to deal with pernicious but subtle stereotypes and particular class harms. While courts borrow from tort law in the interpretation of Title VII of the CRA,[1] Professor Catharine MacKinnon argued against treating sexual harassment as a tort. She argued that such treatment "rips injuries to women's sexuality out of the context of women's social circumstances as a whole." She suggested that sexual harassment "is a group-defined injury which occurs to many different individuals regardless of unique qualities or circumstances. . . . Such an injury is *in essence* a group injury."[2] Twentieth-century feminist attempts to secure protection for women through the Equal Rights Amendment failed. However, piecemeal antidiscrimination legislation, including Title VII and Title IX of the 1972 Education Amendments,[3] passed to protect workers and students, respectively, from sex-based abuse and discrimination.

Title VII and State Fair Employment Practices Statutes

Title VII prohibits discrimination against any individual "with respect to his compensation, terms, conditions, or privileges of employment because of such individual's race, color, religion, sex, or national origin."[4] Almost every state has passed legislation that, in many aspects, mirrors Title VII. They are referred to as state fair employment practices statutes (FEPS). In the 1986 *Meritor Savings Bank v. Vinson* decision, the US Supreme Court held that severe or pervasive sexual harassment violates Title VII when it alters the worker's conditions of employment and creates an abusive working environment.[5] The requirement of severe or pervasive conduct prevents many cases of less serious but still offensive behavior from becoming federal cases (figuratively and literally). Seven years before *Meritor*, Professor MacKinnon had defined sexual harassment as "the unwanted imposition of sexual requirements in the context of a relationship of unequal power. Central to the concept is the use of power derived from one social sphere to lever benefits or impose deprivations in another."[6] Courts assess the working environment by "'looking at all the circumstances,' including the 'frequency of the discriminatory conduct; its severity; whether it is physically threatening or humiliating, or a mere offensive utterance; and whether it unreasonably interferes with an employee's work performance.'"[7] Practitioners refer to this as the "totality of the circumstances" test.

In order to bring a case of hostile work environment sexual harassment against an employer under Title VII, a plaintiff must show (1) membership in a protected class (Title VII protects both men and women),[8] (2) unwelcome sexual harassment, (3) harassment based on sex, (4) an effect on the terms or conditions of employment (from severe or pervasive conduct), and (5) direct or indirect employer liability.[9]

No claim against individual perpetrators exists under Title VII.[10] However, some state FEPS permit sexual harassment damage claims against individual perpetrators.[11] Employers are strictly liable for quid pro quo sexual harassment. Courts distinguish quid pro quo harassment—from hostile work harassment—when sex-based abuse by supervisors results in a tangible economic detriment for the target. Thus, if a boss retracts a salary increase because the worker refuses sexual advances, the principal is strictly liable. For coworker harassment, the employer is liable only if it knew or should have known of the harassment and failed to take immediate and appropriate corrective action.[12] This standard tracks the basic standard of care in common negligence claims brought under tort law.

In *Faragher v. City of Boca Raton* (1998), the US Supreme Court elaborated on the requirements for the prima facie case. It emphasized that the "objectionable environment must be both objectively and subjectively offensive, one that a reasonable person would find hostile or abusive, and one that the victim in fact did perceive to be so."[13] Jurists refer to the objective component as the "reasonableness" standard and to the subjective element as the unwelcomeness requirement.[14] Every state FEPS that similarly prohibits sex discrimination and sexual harassment also makes unwelcomeness an element of the prima facie case.[15]

The *Meritor* Court specifically addressed the issue of volition in its discussion of unwelcomeness. The Court acknowledged that credibility determinations complicate the evaluation of whether the conduct was unwelcome. The *Meritor* Court held that "the District Court in this case erroneously focused on the 'voluntariness' of respondent's participation in the claimed sexual episodes. The correct inquiry is whether respondent by her conduct indicated that the alleged sexual advances were unwelcome, not whether her actual participation in sexual intercourse was voluntary."[16]

Thus, acquiescence to sex is not consent. The plaintiff must prove only that she somehow indicated that the sexual behavior was unwelcome.[17] One can imagine how the unwelcomeness requirement, absent invocation of Federal Rule of Evidence 412 (or a similar state statute in combination with a FEPS claim), could lead to the trial of the plaintiff's conduct. A judge might allow introduction of prior sexual conduct and history if he deems that the probative value of the evidence, concerning whether the target found the alleged conduct unwelcome, outweighs any prejudice to the plaintiff. During pretrial discovery, attorneys have great latitude to explore topics that might lead to admissible evidence. Professor Deborah Rhode explained,

> [Pretrial,] attorneys . . . can often grill victims about their sex lives, birth control practices, and counseling histories. If a plaintiff alleges physical or psychological damage resulting from harassment, opposing attorneys can explore possible alternative causes for her distress—everything from closeted lesbian experiences to intimate marital difficulties. As a result, defendants' lawyers can discredit or deter a harassment complaint with harassing tactics of their own.[18]

Some lawyers and judges declare how easily plaintiffs can bring sexual harassment claims and how difficult those claims are to defend. These jurists ignore the realities summarized by Professor Rhode.

An Affirmative Defense to Modern Sexual Harassment Claims

In 1998 the US Supreme Court added an affirmative defense to a Title VII claim. In *Faragher v. City of Boca Raton* and *Burlington Industries, Inc. v. Ellerth*, the Court examined a victim's unreasonable failure to avail herself of an employer's preventive or corrective procedures. The Court determined that, unless the sexual harassment results in a tangible employment detriment, such a failure insulates the employer from liability for supervisor harassment. The *Ellerth* Court explained, "The defense comprises two necessary elements: (a) that the employer exercised reasonable care to prevent and correct promptly any sexually harassing behavior, and (b) that the plaintiff employee unreasonably failed to take advantage of any preventive or corrective opportunities provided by the employer or to avoid harm otherwise."[19] Thus, if the employer adopts a complaint procedure that a target "unreasonably" fails to follow, the *Faragher* and *Ellerth* decisions effectively bar her from pursuing a sexual harassment claim for a supervisor's conduct. This affirmative defense finds no application in coworker harassment cases because the negligence standard applies in those. Specifically, in such cases, the plaintiff must show the employer knew or should have known of the abusive conduct and failed to take immediate and appropriate action in order for a court to hold the employer liable.

The rationale behind the new affirmative defense centers on motivating employers to adopt preventive and corrective procedures regarding its agents' conduct.[20] The Court's *Faragher* and *Ellerth* decisions encourage targets to complain and employers to cure hostile work environments. However, a complaint procedure and corrective action cannot remedy the damage already done by a harasser. Moreover, by completely insulating the employer from liability for past harassment, the Court has ultimately charged the cost of this incentive system to the injured victim. For example, in *Ashton v. Okosun*, a minor complained the day after she left work because her manager allegedly touched her on her buttocks and attempted to hug her. The court found that she had unreasonably failed to avail herself of all complaint procedures when she refused to return to work after an investigating manager declared her allegations unfounded but offered to transfer her to another shift to avoid the accused.[21]

Compare this affirmative defense with the doctrine of misprision discussed in chapter 5. As noted, the doctrine of misprision subjected a plaintiff to possible criminal prosecution if she attempted to sue civilly for her physical injuries before first pressing criminal charges against her rapist or seducer.[22] The government thereby minimized the damage to the victim, emphasized the societal harm, and retained its exclusive control over vengeance and retribution.[23] With the modern Title VII affirmative defense, the government (the judiciary) minimizes the harm to the victim, emphasizes the harm (discrimination) to society, and gives almost exclusive control over vengeance and retribution to the employer.

Working Youth and Title VII

So, can Sara successfully sue for sexual harassment under federal antidiscrimination laws? The real question is whether she can prove that her manager's sexual attention was unwelcome. At first glance, she cannot. She consented to sex after initially rebuffing her manager's advances. Does her initial rebuff negate ultimate consent? Maybe not.[24] She continued to write to her lover while he was in jail.[25] Not until she learned that he had lied to her and was a registered sex offender did she again declare his attention unwelcome.[26] Not until her parents discovered the underlying facts could they assist her in remedying the situation. Even if Sara had not consented, however, if a court determined that she unreasonably failed to avail herself of employer complaint procedures, she might still have faced a bar to her claims. Defense counsel surely would have activated Title VII's affirmative defense to challenge her case. So, the question remains how best to support adolescent agency and autonomy and protect them with the law.

Title VII and state FEPS make clear that legislators either neglected adolescent workers when they drafted these laws or knowingly created a glaring conflict between state criminal statutory rape laws and civil antidiscrimination laws. In most states, fifteen-year-old workers lack the capacity in a criminal context to consent to sexual intercourse with a twenty-one-year-old supervisor, but Title VII and state FEPS assume that capacity by making no mention of adolescents. How did this blatant inconsistency pass inspection? A review of the legislative history of Title VII reveals no mention of adolescents. This book examines the public policy motivating these laws, but it's quite possible that legislators simply forgot adolescent workers.[27]

Public Policy Behind Civil Antidiscrimination Law

Like criminal law, antidiscrimination law addresses harms to individuals as well as to society. Professor MacKinnon described the class harm of sexual harassment: "Sexual harassment exemplifies and promotes employment practices which disadvantage women in work (especially occupational segregation) and sexual practices which intimately degrade and objectify women."[28] MacKinnon focused on the subordination of women to explain why sexual harassment constitutes sex discrimination in employment. MacKinnon listed three reasons for her view: "first, the exchange of sex for survival has historically assured women's economic dependence and inferiority as well as sexual availability to men. Second, sexual harassment expresses the male sex-role pattern of coercive sexual initiation toward women." MacKinnon concluded, "Third, women's sexuality largely defines women as women in this society, so violations of it are abuses of women as women."[29]

Other feminist legal theorists have added to an understanding of why workplace sexual harassment constitutes a civil rights violation.[30] Professor Rhode described the social harms specifically and more generally:

> For individual victims, harassment often results in economic and psychological injuries, including job dismissals, transfers, coworker hostility, anxiety, depression, and other stress-related conditions. For women as a group,

> harassment perpetuates sexist stereotypes and discourages gender integration of male-dominated workplaces. For employers and society as a whole, the price includes decreased productivity and increased job turnover. The estimated cost of harassment for a Fortune 500 company averages $8 million a year.[31]

In this passage, Rhode untangled the consequential threads of sexual harassment for the individual target, for women, and for society. An $8 million price tag in 1997 translates to between $11 million and $15 million today.[32]

Antidiscrimination laws respond to each level of injury. "For example, Title VII is designed to encourage the creation of antiharassment policies and effective grievance mechanisms."[33] "Although Title VII seeks 'to make persons whole for injuries suffered on account of unlawful employment discrimination,' . . . its 'primary objective,' like that of any statute meant to influence primary conduct, is not to provide redress but to avoid harm."[34] The US Supreme Court noted that Title VII compensates individuals for their damages but emphasized Title VII's prevention goal and deterrent effect.

If Title VII serves primarily to prevent abusive sex-based conduct, then legal tolerance of the consent defense as applied to adolescents interferes with Title VII's deterrence effect.[35] To avoid Title VII's purview, sexual predators will manipulate their vulnerable adolescent targets to consent. Without an incentive to prevent consensual adolescent sexual exploitation, employers will not create effective policies or warn adolescent workers about coercive or subtly manipulative managers. Obviously, this concern over prevention premises the undesirability of all adolescent workplace sexual conduct, including consensual behavior. Over 90 percent of parents think that adolescents should not engage in sexual relations until after high school.[36] Thirty-two states define the age of consent at eighteen under special circumstances.[37] Therefore, this presumption concerning the undesirability of consensual adolescent sexual conduct in the workplace seems reasonable.

Modern Antidiscrimination Law Applied

By the beginning of the twenty-first century, courts had accepted the illegality of sexual harassment as sex discrimination under Title VII and state FEPS. In 1998 the US Supreme Court established that even same-sex sexual harassment violates Title VII.[38] Most states similarly interpreted their antidiscrimination FEPS. Although sexual harassment law and the underlying public policy have evolved, several cases involving minors demonstrate how these antidiscrimination statutes failed (and still fail) to protect minors adequately. One of the first opinions to explore the claims of a minor was *Doe v. Mama Taori's Premium Pizza*, a sexual harassment case brought under the Tennessee FEPS.[39]

FEPS: Doe v. Mama Taori's Premium Pizza

In the 2001 *Mama Taori's* case, a sixteen-year-old male, "Joe," and his parents brought suit against a male adult coworker and the restaurant owner. In addition to the FEPS sexual harassment claim, Joe and his parents made claims under the Tennessee Human Rights Act as well as intentional tort and negligence claims.[40] Joe claimed he engaged in sexual acts in the restaurant bathroom with thirty-two-year-old coworker Christopher Abson, who had given him a "marijuana cigarette [that] contained a 'knock out drug' that caused [him] . . . to become incapacitated." The parents alleged that Abson had two prior rape convictions, one for raping a child. Abson pled guilty to two counts of the statutory rape of Joe. He also pled guilty to contributing to the delinquency of a minor.[41]

In the civil case, the restaurant denied liability. It asserted that Joe had contributed to his own injury by consenting to the sexual acts with Abson. The restaurant also alleged that Joe's parents were comparatively at fault. Joe and his parents moved to strike those defenses, a motion that that trial court denied. Via an interlocutory appeal in the civil case, Joe and his parents challenged the trial court's refusal to strike the restaurant owner's affirmative defenses based on the minor's consent and comparative fault. In sum, the plaintiffs challenged the court's use of traditional tort law defenses to thwart Joe's FEPS and personal injury claims. The appellate court granted the interlocutory appeal and then affirmed the trial court's denial of plaintiffs' motion to strike the restaurant's defenses.[42]

CONSENT—A CIVIL DEFENSE? Joe and his parents first argued that consent should not constitute a defense to a civil action for damages when it fails as a defense to a criminal statutory rape charge. The court disagreed, classifying the sexual behavior as a battery—a tort. Referring to well-established principles of common law, the court held that a plaintiff who "consents" cannot later complain of the behavior. One sees reasoning similar to this in the 1933 New York *Barton v. Bee Line* case discussed in chapter 5. Citing the *Restatement (Second) of Torts* sections 892A(2) and 892B, the *Mama Taori's* court acknowledged that consent lacks defensive significance "if (1) the person giving consent lacked the necessary capacity, (2) the consent was coerced, (3) the person giving the consent was mistaken about the nature and quality of the act, or (4) the nature of the act was such that no person could consent to it."[43] The court also explained, "Incapacity to give consent may arise from age, intoxication or mental incompetence."[44] However, the court declined to rule, as a matter of law, that Joe lacked capacity simply because he was under eighteen. Joe's capacity and the quality of his consent remained triable issues of fact.[45]

In discussing the capacity of minors to consent, the court relied upon a medical consent case, *Cardwell v. Bechtol*. Quoting *Cardwell*, the court found "that maturity is now reached at earlier stages of growth than at the time the common law recognized the age of majority at 21 years."[46] The court listed the *Cardwell* factors that determine a mature minor's capacity: "age, ability, experience, education, training, degree of maturity or judgment, [and] . . . the minor's conduct and demeanor at the time of the incident."[47] However, the *Mama Taori's* court avoided a detailed evaluation of the nuanced indicia of maturity and training. The *Mama Taori's* court endorsed the rule of sevens, used in *Cardwell*, as guidance for determining whether a minor has the capacity to give consent. Thus, the *Mama Taori's* court found Joe presumptively capable of giving consent and thereby presumptively insulated his coworker (and the restaurant owner) from liability.[48]

The *Mama Taori's* court bolstered its conclusion that minors develop the capacity to consent before age eighteen by reviewing the post-*Cardwell* mature minors doctrine and the Tennessee law that affords minors legal decision-making capacity in a variety of contexts. First, the court discussed consent to medical treatment such as abortion, birth control information and supplies, and treatment for drug abuse.[49] With respect to a minor's capacity to consent to abortion, the court ignored the fact that a minor must typically have a parent's permission or be adjudged competent by a court to make that decision *before* obtaining an abortion.[50] Surely the *Mama Taori's* court was not suggesting that a minor should seek judicial bypass for a capacity determination prior to consenting to sexual relations at the workplace.

With respect to contraception and drug abuse treatment, the *Mama Taori's* court failed to address the public policy rationale for these provisions. Laws permit minors to obtain contraceptives and seek treatment for drug abuse and sexually transmitted diseases but not because society considers those minors necessarily competent to make medical decisions without parental involvement. To the contrary, adults can figure that many of these minors need medical treatment because they made immature, unwise, or uninformed decisions to have unprotected sex, thus demonstrating their lack of competence to make consistently well-reasoned decisions regarding sexuality. Rather, as a matter of public policy, society has determined that medical assistance is so important, and the potential negative consequences of no treatment are so devastating, that it will facilitate the medical treatment of minors, despite their immaturity.

Professor Elizabeth Scott explained the reasoning that the *Mama Taori's* court might have considered. Scott argued that no one thinks minors should be treated like adults because minors are mature: "Rather, the focus is on the harm of requiring parental consent. The targeted treatments all involve situations in which the traditional assumption—that parents can be counted on to respond to their children's medical needs in a way that promotes the child's interest—simply might not hold."[51] Scott gave the example that some parents might become angry if they discovered that their child used drugs or engaged in sex. Scott also noted that a teenager, who correctly or mistakenly anticipates a parent's negative reaction, might not seek help if she has to inform that parent about her problem. Scott reasoned that affording teenagers the right to consent "encourages adolescents to seek treatment that may be critically important to their health." Scott concluded that society also benefits from the reduction in "the incidence of sexually transmitted diseases, substance abuse, mental illness, and teenage pregnancy. Together, these social benefits largely explain why lawmakers shift the boundary of childhood for the purpose of encouraging treatment of these conditions."[52] The *Mama Taori's* court never addressed any of this reasoning.

The *Mama Taori's* court also noted that Tennessee law criminalizes sex with teenagers over the age of thirteen only if their partners are more than four years their senior.[53] However, Tennessee's failure to criminalize sex between two fourteen-year-olds does not necessarily mean that the Tennessee legislature has judged these minors to be emotionally, psychologically, and physically mature. The permissive stance concerning young teens, associated with the required age differential for prosecution, results more likely from Tennessee's focus on predation by mature adults. Tennessee can avoid penalizing young Romeos and Juliets by emphasizing the age gaps between teens and adults.

When neither teen has the capacity to consent to sex, why prosecute one (or both)? In *Allstate Ins. Co. v. Patterson*, an insurance coverage case, the court stressed that children who "cannot fully appreciate the consequences of sexual activity, should not be held to an adult standard as a perpetrator. Noting that minors lack the experience to give meaningful consent to sex, the *Allstate* court explained that "courts cannot seek to protect naïve fourteen-year-old[s] . . . on the one hand, while inferring the most degrading and unnatural [intentions] on the other hand."[54] Moreover, laws pertaining to underage sex may not deter those adolescents who lack the capacity to appreciate the ramifications of their sexual behavior. When the threat of death, from AIDS or other sexually transmitted diseases, fails to inhibit teen sexual exploration, one cannot expect that statutory rape laws will do so.

In addition, age difference requirements in statutory rape laws say little about the ability of adolescents to consent at the workplace. Even if the *Mama Taori's* court properly used this age differential element to demonstrate that a sixteen-year-old has the capacity to consent to sex with peers away from the workplace, one cannot conclude that the same youth possesses the capacity to consent to sex with a thirty-two-year-old coworker. The logic simply fails. If anything, the age difference requirement and its associated concern for power disparities are even more relevant at the workplace. At work, a manager or an adult with more work experience enjoys a position of greater status, power, or seniority, and can more easily seduce an inexperienced minor.

The *Mama Taori's* court equated the capacity of adolescents to consent to teen-adult sex with their ability to engage in a broad variety of activities: lease safe-deposit boxes, work part-time, obtain a driver's license, execute a durable power of attorney for health care, and consent to sex with a peer.[55] The court drew completely inapposite analogies. Bright-line age demarcations account crudely for the fact that adolescent capacity varies by individual and, more particularly, by specific situation. The suggestion that an adolescent worker has the capacity to consent to oral sex at the workplace with an adult coworker because Tennessee law allows him to lease a safe-deposit box is potentially devastating. The court repeatedly failed to recognize the more plausible motivating reasons for permitting minors certain liberties normally reserved for adults. For example, the law allows minors to surrender their children for adoption,[56] not because jurists think those minors are sufficiently competent to make the adoption decision, but because adults consider them unprepared to raise children.

The *Mama Taori's* court found that the mature minors rule as well as the rule of sevens governed this case and presumptively determined that Joe's consent carried legal weight.[57] In sum, the court placed the burden of proof on Joe, requiring him to overcome the presumption of capacity. The court's further discussion of the "totality of the circumstances" and the *Cardwell* factors was irrelevant because the court never engaged in a detailed analysis of Joe's maturity.[58] Chapter 10 addresses the advisability of engaging in such analysis. Suffice it to say here, with a reference back to the Texas *Hernandez* case, that a serious concern arises. Any sexual harassment case could devolve into a trial of the minor's maturity and morality rather than of the perpetrator's culpability and the principal's liability. The question arises whether adults really want their children on trial as these children seek remedy for sexual abuses.

CONSENT'S ADMISSIBILITY. The *Mama Taori's* court also rejected the plaintiffs' reliance on criminal law to prevent the jury from considering Joe's consent. The court suggested that barring consideration of consent "would permit any victim of statutory rape to recover civil damages notwithstanding the circumstances."[59] The court listed three reasons for its rejection of the plaintiffs' argument. The courts that previously declined to adopt this per se liability rule have recognized that (1) the statutory rape laws do not explicitly create a private right of action for damages, (2) criminal and civil proceedings have different purposes, and (3) it is fundamentally unfair to permit a civil litigant to obtain money damages while preventing the trier of fact from considering relevant evidence regarding damages and credibility.[60]

In this analysis, the court found first that statutory rape laws create no private civil claim. However, they do enforce a public consensus that adolescents lack the capacity to consent to sexual intercourse and, at certain ages, to sexual contact of any kind. Statutory rape laws also reflect society's determination that underage sex hurts children. The *Mama Taori's* court deflected attention from the relevance of the consent defense by focusing on the availability of civil damages in a private civil claim. The court did not explain how the availability of damages transforms the nature of capacity to consent. More particularly, the court neglected to explain why the lack of a private claim in the criminal statute precludes, in a civil claim, treatment of adolescent consent consistent with the criminal law's approach.

Second, the court noted the different purposes of criminal and civil law with regard to the admissibility of consent. However, our recent review of the public policy goals suggests that criminal and civil law functions are more similar than they are different. Statutory rape laws have a threefold purpose: to protect children (individuals subordinated because of their immaturity) from sexual predators, to punish perpetrators, and to deter predators. Civil rights claims such as Title VII and FEPS serve similar purposes: to protect those workers (subordinated because of their weaker status) who experience discrimination (often in the form of sexual predation) and to punish and deter those employers who permit employees (or agents) to prey upon subordinated individuals.[61] The primary difference relates to the availability of damages, intended to make the person whole in the civil case. The civil system compensates victims for their injuries and influences employers with the threat of a financial penalty.

Thus, the different purposes of the civil and criminal systems, and the second reason for the court's treatment of Joe's consent, boils down to the availability of damages to compensate the victim in the civil system. The *Mama Taori's* court referred to the difference in the right to damages as the first reason for a rejection of a per se liability rule. The second of the court's reasons collapses into the first and is therefore similarly highly questionable. The court again failed to explain why the lack of a private claim for damages in the criminal statute precludes, in a civil claim, treatment of adolescent consent consistent with the criminal law's approach.

The third reason reveals the court's motivating concerns: credibility and damages. This reason centers on the alleged unfairness of permitting the recovery of money damages absent a hearing of all relevant evidence, including consent, which may provide guidance on the evaluation of credibility and the calculation of damages. It also highlights several problems with the court's treatment of adolescent consent. If a sixteen-year-old lacks the capacity to consent to teen-adult sex in Tennessee under criminal law, how does this same consent miraculously shed light on either credibility or damages under civil law? If the minor lacks the capacity to consent, then credibility is not relevant as long as the sex occurred. The sex constitutes an offense no matter what the adolescent said at the time of the incident or says later in court. It qualifies as an offense because society (the legislature) has determined that teen-adult sex is offensive and injurious.

Was the court in this case misguided? Is teen-adult sex inoffensive? Because the *Mama Taori's* case was civil and not criminal, the court did not consider whether Abson "hurt" society by having sex with Joe. Because this case was not a criminal prosecution, it lacked the underlying criminal public policy concern for "society." Abson may have outraged those adults who learned of the behavior, but "society" did not change. The reality is that Joe suffered the brunt of whatever injury Abson caused. Moreover, society (via the prosecutor) did not sue for its own damages. Nor did society sue on behalf of Joe. His parents did. Here rest the problems.

The credibility determination for the *Mama Taori's* court contemplates not whether the sex occurred, but the severity, and even existence, of consequential damages. The *Mama Taori's* court wanted to ensure that the jurors had the opportunity to evaluate Joe's credibility regarding his personal offense and damages. Society's determination that teen-adult sex is criminally offensive in Tennessee was irrelevant to the *Mama Taori's* civil court. Society's determination evaporated, and the court started from a clean civil slate, demanding that Joe prove his personal offense and damages. This civil court equated consent with immunity from damage (*volenti non fit injuria*) and did not equate societal harm with individual harm. The judge and jurors may have felt outraged about the homosexual "rape," but their offense was not Joe's, and the judge wanted the jurors to evaluate Joe's personal offense and damages.

Joe's consent fostered the judge's skepticism about Joe's damages and outrage. Why? Because jurors might find that Joe was morally culpable, an accomplice in an illicit act. The court even noted in the recitation of the facts that, prior to the alleged sexual encounter, when Mama Taori's transferred Abson to another restaurant, Joe sought a transfer to the same location. When Mama Taori's denied Joe the transfer, he threatened to quit and reapply at the other location.[62]

These facts are irrelevant to the issue of capacity for several reasons. First, just because Joe may have admired or even adored Abson does not prove that Joe had the cognitive and psychosocial ability to formulate legally significant consent to sex. Second, Tennessee statutory rape law that sets the age of consent at eighteen indicates the legislature's determination that someone Joe's age does not have capacity. Third, reliance on these facts risks the importation of a defense similar to the chastity and promiscuity defenses. Recall that in *Hernandez* the court ruled that consent to sex elevates a minor's capacity to one of legal significance.[63] As noted previously, the choice to engage in sex is not a scientific indicator of maturity and capacity. Neither is the choice to follow a worker to another employment site. These facts paint Joe as a willing accomplice and foreshadow the court's true concerns—moral culpability and legal responsibility. Ultimately, the court conflated the two and found Joe (potentially) legally responsible because he was (possibly) morally culpable.

DEVELOPMENTAL CAPACITY APPLIED TO *MAMA TAORI'S*. I distinguish between legal responsibility and moral culpability or blameworthiness. If I accidentally break a glass, I am responsible but not morally culpable because I did not smash the glass purposefully. With the rule of sevens and the infancy defense, the law shields young children from legal responsibility for their criminal and negligent behavior because jurists adjudge them incapable of understanding or avoiding criminal and tortious conduct. They do not have legal capacity and therefore have no moral culpability or legal responsibility. Society believes them innocent, morally blameless.[64]

Consider this distinction step by step as it relates to *Mama Taori's*. Begin with the notion that no capacity equates with no fault. That idea makes sense. Graduate to the concept that teenagers have some capacity. What level of fault should one associate with developing capacity? No fault hardly seems fair because the teenager has some capacity. Logically, one could equate the quantum of fault with the level of maturing capacity. Thus, one sees how a comparative fault scheme might appear attractive to a court attempting to associate fault with capacity. This reasoning is seriously flawed, however.

Full legal capacity means just that in a legal context—complete capacity. One can distinguish diminished capacity and developing capacity from full legal capacity. Full legal capacity is an all-or-nothing proposition. Liability attaches *only* if an actor has full legal capacity. If an actor has full legal capacity the level of actual legal responsibility for the harm influences the comparative level of fault-based liability. Chapter 3's discussion confirms that adolescents have not reached developmental maturity. If they are not adults, they have not arrived at that adult legal threshold. Even in the criminal system, jurists try adolescents in juvenile court as children or in adult court as adults. Jurists do not try them in adult court as mature children. When one considers a sliding scale such as a comparative fault scheme seriously, one sees the fallacy of such an idea for children. How can society justify holding someone morally culpable and then fully legally liable when that person is incapable of manifesting full adult reasoning and decision-making abilities because of transitioning developmental maturity?

I realize that this stance necessarily leaves intact an inconsistency between the criminal and civil systems. The law holds juvenile offenders criminally responsible once convicted (as juveniles) even if they do not have full legal capacity. Because of the need to protect society from crimes committed by adolescents, I endorse Professors Elizabeth Scott and Laurence Steinberg's proposal that the juvenile justice system recognize adolescent "diminished responsibility" due to diminished culpability.[65] However, I reassert that adolescents—even adolescent criminal offenders—lack full adult legal capacity. Moreover, I do not suggest a diminished culpability or diminished responsibility parallel for the civil system because my focus is the protection of youth, and their developing capacity, from sexual exploitation by adults. I would still shield adolescents from legal responsibility for their immature choices because adult exploitation causes their injury. The need to protect society (and individual victims) from crimes committed by adolescents, however, justifies the different treatment in the criminal system of adolescent developing capacity and the different level of legal responsibility (and culpability) attributed to adolescent criminal offenders. However, I cannot recommend the treatment of adolescents as adults—even within the criminal system.

Consider another example using a younger child and compare it to the *Mama Taori's* case. A stranger in a car offers candy to a six-year-old on the street. If the child consents to enter the car, does the law hold the child legally responsible for his damages that result? No. First, the child lacks the experience and knowledge to comprehend that he should not follow the stranger for the candy. The child lacks capacity—the ability to make a well-reasoned decision in the given circumstances. Second, the damage results not from the child's choice nor from his entering the car. The damage results when the adult molests or abducts that child.

One might argue that a sixteen-year-old should know better than to enter a car with a stranger. Should the teenager know better than to follow a caring workplace mentor to another pizzeria however? Society often gives children (including adolescents) the benefit of the development doubt until they reach the age of eighteen. They are innocent until adjudged mature. Tennessee criminal law considers Joe incapable of consenting to sex. Why would this same law credit him capable of foretelling his own abuse? And, just as with the younger child, Joe's damages resulted neither from his requested (and denied) transfer to another location nor from his consent. They resulted from Abson's abuse and exploitation of Joe's immaturity.

Given this discussion of capacity and the distinction between culpability and responsibility, the most likely explanation for the *Mama Taori's* holding is that the judge did not credit Joe's lack of capacity. One without capacity remains faultless, morally innocent and legally shielded. From the perspective of a strict moralist, Joe's consent destroyed his credibility and negated his subjective offense. Shades of *Barton v. Bee Line.* The Tennessee court's treatment of Joe resembles the 1933 New York court's treatment of Grace Barton. In the courts' perspective, both teens behaved immorally and negated their entitlement to damages. Because the judge deemed Joe morally culpable, the judge was willing to let a jury find him legally responsible. One wonders whether Joe's status, created by his homosexual involvement with another man, contributed to the court's determination. Professor Eskridge might argue it would have.

COMPARATIVE FAULT IN *MAMA TAORI'S*. The *Mama Taori's* court revealed its fault-based, moralistic perspective as it dealt with *Restatement (Second) of Torts* section 892C. The court explained,

> As we construe this provision, it eliminates consent as a complete defense to a civil action for damages. It does not, however, prevent the trier-of-fact from considering evidence of consent when it is allocating fault or determining the existence and extent of the plaintiff's damages.
>
> Deterrence and punishment for illegal acts should be left to the criminal law. The public's interests are sufficiently protected by the imposition of criminal sanctions. Thus, civil actions for damages should be left to proceed under ordinary tort law principles.[66]

The court completely sidestepped the provisions of *Restatement (Second) of Torts* section 892C. If this subsection eliminates consent as a complete defense, because the legislature intended to protect minors from underage sex, how did the court justify removing that shield with respect to damages? The court ignored the shared purposes of both criminal and civil laws. It ignored that criminal law generally protects potential individual victims as well as society. Additionally, the court ignored the deterrent and punitive effects of tort law.

Rather than accept Tennessee's judgment regarding teen capacity, the court reverted to "ordinary tort law principles" and redirected the litigation into a comparative fault paradigm. The court reasoned, "Consistent with the doctrine of comparative fault, one of these principles is that a mature minor's conduct, like an adult's conduct, is relevant with regard to fault and damages."[67]

A moralistic perspective also explains the court's suggestion that Joe's consent could negate consequential damages. However, consent does not disprove damage. It merely releases the tortfeasor from liability, civil legal responsibility. If Abson had offered to punch Joe, and Joe had consented, his consent would not have erased the resulting bloody nose. It would have simply insulated Abson from liability for the broken nose and resulting medical bills. The damage would still exist.

If the *Mama Taori's* court had been truly worried about the extent or even existence of damage, it could have directed the litigation in other ways. Defense counsel could have impeached Joe's testimony regarding his damages by pointing to a lack of corroborating medical or other physical evidence. Defense counsel could have introduced evidence of Joe's ability to function in other contexts during that same time period. Evidence of persistently good academic evaluations, excellence on an athletic team, and the ability to maintain other friendships might all speak to his good adjustment and the lack of negative impact by the alleged sexual encounter.

If consent has relevance, one might argue that Joe's consent exacerbated his trauma. The knowledge that he consented to homosexual activity and a sexual predator who duped him might enhance his sense of shame and humiliation. One expert reminds us, "If the victim knows the perpetrator, the maltreatment is not only the act of maltreatment itself (e.g., sexual abuse) but also a dysfunctional and traumatized interpersonal relationship. . . . An interpersonal stressor likely involves the maltreated child losing faith and trust in a parent or an authority figure."[68]

However, the introduction of that evidence will inevitably raise prejudices regarding sexuality and morality: good children do not engage in sex. That notion raises again the *Hernandez* morality: children who have sex do not deserve protection or compensation for their injuries.[69]

Conclusions for Mama Taori's

The ultimate issue addressed in the interlocutory appeal opinion by the *Mama Taori's* court was whether the defense could use Joe's consent as a legal defense to the FEPS and tort claims. Instead of protecting Joe, the *Mama Taori's* court effectively arranged for the trial of Joe. With the harassment trial, he risked what rape victims often experience—a trial of his character and the accusation, "He asked for it!"

Professor Susan Estrich argued against the unwelcomeness requirement in sexual harassment Title VII cases and commented upon the relevance of adult consent (or failure to resist adequately):

> The [rape] consent standard—and the corresponding inquiries into what a woman did or said, how she "led the man on," or how she failed adequately to signal her nonconsent—have, at least until recently, made successful prosecution of acquaintance rape all but impossible. Where the relationship is "appropriate," at least to the court's eyes, judges tend to see sex, not rape. Similarly, in Title VII cases they see sex, not sexual harassment. In both types of cases, they are often wrong. That a certain relationship might be appropriate does not necessarily mean that the man's behavior has been.
>
> The strongest justification for the welcomeness doctrine is that the rule ensures that consensual workplace sex does not provide the basis for a civil action. The more radical response to this argument is that there is no such thing as truly "welcome" sex between a male boss and a female employee who needs her job. And if there is, then the women who welcome it will not be bringing lawsuits in any event.[70]

Estrich's comments prove even more poignant with respect to consenting teens. One could argue (and the Tennessee legislature, among others, has decided) that there is no such thing as truly welcome sex between adults and minors below the age of consent. Employment only worsens the calculus. If a mature (but subordinated) woman who needs her job has difficulty refusing a man, think of the trouble an immature teen will experience in trying to refuse the same man.

Estrich concluded that the unwelcomeness requirement serves, in part, to discourage women from filing suit. She noted the empirical studies concerning the prevalence of workplace sexual harassment and pointed to the dearth of lawsuits.[71] One returns to the stark reality that teenagers also underreport their abuse.

The *Mama Taori's* court's justifications for considering Joe's consent cannot withstand scrutiny. In many cases, what the court referred to as the mature minor rule is a misnomer. The rule of sevens pretends to mark accurately the development of adolescent maturity. In reality, it is an archaic bright-line rule designed to avoid the onerous and inexact task of evaluating the maturity of a minor at a given point in time that has long since passed.[72] The court sidestepped the *Restatement's* guidance in section 892C and ignored underlying public policy reasons that justify both criminal and civil law. To add insult to injury, the court charged Joe and his parents with the costs of the appeal.[73]

The *Mama Taori's* decision stands in a line of cases that will have a chilling effect on future sexual harassment cases by minors. It also demonstrates that a court, struggling with a new issue, might presume Sara capable of consenting. Such a presumption could thwart a successful sexual harassment suit under Title VII, state FEPS, relevant tort law, or even Title IX. Chapter 8 traces the migration of legal precedent concerning the capacity of California teenagers from Kati's Title VII case to the case of *Willits* Doe, discussed in chapter 9.

CHAPTER EIGHT

The Evolution of Conflicting Law in California and Perhaps Beyond

One could persuasively argue that a dozen tort cases and a Tennessee FEPS sexual harassment case do not prove that American personal injury and sexual harassment law consistently fails to protect consenting teenagers. Some jurists might conclude that the Tennessee court's decision to permit the restaurant's defenses against Joe and his parents was appropriate. Joe presumably learned a lesson even if his case did not survive the preliminary motion phase. However, do most consenting teens resemble Joe? And, might future Does and Joes learn their lessons without the heavy burdens of protracted discovery, a lengthy court case, and a trial of the minor's moral and legal culpability? Is there a way to prevent the harm in the first place? This chapter consolidates the information from prior chapters to examine the evolution of current law in California cases involving consenting teenagers. By examining the *Starbucks* case and the decisions that preceded and followed it, chapter 8 highlights an evolutionary path that may be occurring in other states. It demonstrates how the American common-law system preserves legal mutations that may disadvantage vulnerable teenagers. This chapter reveals that the reasoning in individual Title VII, FEPS, and tort cases involving consenting teenagers creates new jurisprudential systems that will fail to protect other adolescents. This chapter also shows how legal precedent from Title VII cases spills over into the Title IX jurisprudence discussed in chapter 9.

Starbucks through Another Filter

In 2009 a California federal district court explored whether Kati Moore, first introduced in chapter 4, could assert a sexual harassment claim against Starbucks and her supervisor, Tim Horton. At issue was whether she had consented to the alleged offensive sexual conduct when she was sixteen.[1] One might reasonably guess that, because the age of consent in California is eighteen, the district court ultimately rejected consideration of Kati's (Doe's) consent. However, one would be wrong. Just as happened in Joe's case, the *Starbucks* court granted preliminary motions against Kati that credited her consent and gutted her case.

In support of its decision, the *Starbucks* court cited *People v. Tobias*. *Tobias*, discussed below, is a 2001 California Supreme Court criminal incest case. *Tobias* is relevant for other states because the US Supreme Court decision in *Michael M. v. Superior Court* (1981) addressed issues raised in *Tobias*. Thus, that US Supreme Court decision has precedential value for sister states. *Tobias* was extended to civil cases in *Donaldson v. Dep't of Real Estate*, also discussed below, the matter involving *Donaldson* Doe and her brother-in-law, Robert Donaldson.[2] As previously noted, state sex crime statutes that specifically prohibit sexual conduct with minors complicate sexual harassment and sex-based tort cases. Typically, a criminally accused adult may not assert consent as a defense.[3] So what happens when criminal and civil claims stem from the same conduct? Chapter 7 described the outcome of Joe's FEPS case. A review of recent California criminal and civil cases shows that conflicts between civil and criminal law have led to disparate results in several jurisdictions. Currently, thirteen states treat adolescent consent to sexual activity with an adult inconsistently in civil and criminal cases.[4] *Tobias*, *Donaldson*, and *Starbucks* mark changes in California law that may have legal implications across the nation.

California Criminal Law—People v. Tobias

In 2001, the year before Sara's case settled out of court, the California Supreme Court decided *People v. Tobias*. *Tobias* addressed the question of whether a minor who gives consent to an incestuous relationship is an accomplice under California Penal Code section 285. The court held that a child under the age of eighteen who engages in a "sexual relationship with an adult is a *victim*, not a perpetrator," regardless of the child's consent. The court concluded that the adult, not the minor, bears the burden of refraining from a sexual relationship.[5]

The *Tobias* court relied on prior cases, including *People v. Stratton* and *People v. Stoll* to support its conclusion.[6] Specifically, the *Tobias* court pointed to the *Stratton* court's conclusion that, because minors are unable legally to consent to sexual intercourse, they cannot be criminally liable for incest.[7] However, *Stratton* and its successor cases preceded significant changes in the California forcible rape statute, California Penal Code section 261. Therefore, the *Tobias* court felt compelled to address, in dictum, the passage of California Penal Code section 261.5, which prohibits unlawful sex with a minor. Section 261.5(a) makes sex with a minor who is not the partner's spouse unlawful. The code states, "For the purposes of this section, a 'minor' is a person under the age of 18 years and an 'adult' is a person who is at least 18 years of age."[8]

Later subsections of section 261.5 detail age differences between the juvenile and adult, levels of offense, and penalties.[9] This provision did not exist prior to 1970. Before then, unlawful sex with a minor had been codified in section 261, which defined *rape*, in part, as "an act of sexual intercourse, accomplished with a female not the wife of the perpetrator . . . [w]here the female is under the age of eighteen years."[10] Although the two statutes appear almost identical, they are unique because section 261 fell within the forcible rape statute. The post-1970 version, section 261.5, stands alone and prescribes variations in the offenses and penalties.

The *Tobias* court suggested that the statutory reforms of 1970 marked the California legislature's implicit rejection of incapacity among minors. Moreover, the *Tobias* court implied that these legislative reforms undermined the incest cases, including *Stratton* and *Stoll*, which rejected the notion that consenting minors were accomplices. According to the *Tobias* court, "the Legislature created the crime of unlawful sexual intercourse with a minor ([section] 261.5) and amended the rape statute ([section] 261) so that it no longer included sex with a minor in the definition of rape."[11] Consequently, the court posited that when a minor "knowingly and voluntarily" engages in a sexual act, the conduct may not equate to rape but, instead, a less serious crime. Although the *Tobias* court noted that a minor may still be found incapable of providing legal consent, the court concluded that by making this change, the California legislature "implicitly acknowledged that, *in some cases at least, a minor may be capable of giving legal consent to sexual relations*."[12] The *Tobias* court failed to consider or rejected the notion that the legislature had merely separated two offenses: (1) the crime of unresisted sexual activity between adults and juveniles incapable of consent and (2) the crime of forcible rape. It is also possible that the *Tobias* court misconstrued the legislature's isolated treatment of *actual* consent by minors to signify the legislature's rejection of juvenile *legal* incapacity.

The *Tobias* court focused on behavior committed "knowingly and voluntarily," arguably terms that closely track assent or acquiescence. The *Tobias* court referred explicitly to legal consent, however, leaving no doubt that it did not mean assent or acquiescence.[13] This reasoning, later quoted in *Starbucks* and *Donaldson*, announced a new determination that contradicts more than one hundred years of criminal court precedent finding that girls under a specified age are unable to give consent as a matter of law, regardless of their actual consent.[14] One can see how such a misunderstanding regarding *actual* and *legal* consent, assuming it is one, might occur in other states that must address willing juvenile sexual behavior.

Acquiescence, Legal Consent, and Legal Capacity—The Impact of Tobias

Perplexingly, neither section 261.5 nor section 261 refers to a minor acting "knowingly and voluntarily." One can distinguish these terms from legally binding consent, however, which presumes emotional, intellectual, and developmental capacity, or essentially, legal capacity. In 2003 in *People v. Hillhouse*, a California appeals court evaluated this issue in the context of an adult's defense to an oral copulation charge involving a minor. The *Hillhouse* court explained that "legal consent presupposes an intelligence capable of understanding the act, its nature, and possible consequences."[15] This explanation mirrors section 892A of the *Restatement (Second) of Torts* regarding consent, which specifies that, in order to extinguish liability, consent must be "by one who has the capacity to consent." As previously noted, comment 2(b) of this section explains that consent of a child "may still be effective *if* [the child] is capable of appreciating the nature, extent and probable consequences of the conduct consented to."[16] Thus, the restatement implicitly starts with the notion that most minors are not capable of giving legal consent.

The emphasis on capacity by both criminal and civil law stands at odds with the *Tobias* concept of juvenile consent in California criminal and civil law. We must consider whether the *Tobias* court also conflated volitional acquiescence with legal consent. Did the court simply follow California's legislative lead and obscure the relation between legally binding consent and legal capacity? Confusion concerning these similar but distinct concepts is common. As noted in the last chapter, the *Meritor* Court examined volition in its discussion of unwelcomeness. To clear up confusion in the lower courts, the Supreme Court reasoned that acquiescence is not legal consent. Moreover, the *Meritor* Court refuted the district court's opinion because it focused on the *voluntariness* of the plaintiff's participation in the alleged sexual acts. Rather, the appropriate inquiry is whether or not the plaintiff indicated that the sexual advances were *unwelcome*.[17] If an adult's knowledge of and voluntary participation in sexual conduct do not necessarily equate with consent, then surely juvenile acquiescence and consent deserve special regard.

"COMMUNAL EXPERIENCE" OF ADOLESCENCE. The *Hillhouse* court did not need the new neuroscience literature to explain "communal experience" regarding adolescent capacity. The court stated, "It is teenagers' judgment and impulse control, not his or her knowledge or intelligence, which tend to be problematic."[18] The court added, "Adolescents are more vulnerable, more impulsive, and less self-disciplined than adults, and are without the same capacity to control their conduct and to think in long-range terms." The court concluded that a minor's consent to sexual contact is irrelevant given the "communal experience" that adolescents are less mature and responsible than adults.[19]

The *Hillhouse* court confirmed one hundred years of common sense and observation that teenagers are not always emotionally and developmentally mature enough to make wise choices about sexual activity. Accordingly, adolescent sexual initiative with an adult deserves special treatment. Thus, the *Tobias* court's implication that adolescents might be ready for consensual sexual activity with an adult in the civil context, at the workplace for example, but not under criminal law, challenges logic.

CHILD ABUSE AND THE CORRUPTION OF CONSENT. As noted in chapter 3, another factor to consider in a discussion of adolescent consent is the sexual victimization of children and teenagers. Sexual predators may manipulate children of all ages to extract consent or compliant cooperation. Many courts recognize the need for expert testimony regarding the methods employed by child molesters and the behavior of targeted victims. In *Jones v. United States*, the court explained "that the behavioral characteristics and psychological dynamics of child molestation victims are beyond the ken of the average juror."[20]

In *Jones*, the court considered whether the admission of expert testimony in a case against a high school counselor and teacher accused of sexually assaulting three female students was a reversible error. The expert, FBI Special Agent Kenneth Lanning, had twenty years of experience in the FBI's Behavioral Science Unit, which focuses on sexual exploitation of minors. Lanning explained that at one end of the spectrum are "situational offenders" who have no clear preferred target but opportunistically exploit children. At the other end of the spectrum, "preferential" predators target children consistently.[21]

The court recapped Lanning's conclusions that "preferential" child molesters manipulate and "groom" their victims, who may eventually comply with the molesters' advances. The court noted that, according to Lanning, immature victims often delay reporting the abuse and provide inconsistent accounts of the abuse because their acquiescence produces shame and guilt.[22]

Lanning's testimony demonstrates that teenage acquiescence may result from predatory abuse. Lanning testified that most child molesters do not force themselves on children but bond with young victims in order to psychologically manipulate them. You might find that this kind of abuse is worse than forcible rape. In these cases, the perpetrator uses the teenager to facilitate her own abuse. The adult leaves the teenager not only physically violated, but also emotionally and psychologically traumatized.[23]

The *Jones* court detailed the grooming process presented by Lanning. The court explained that the abuser identifies and attempts to fill a child's needs, and in some cases, molesters employ severe, unsavory tactics to coerce victims. The court noted that molesters coerce, "for example by listening sympathetically to the child, complementing [sic] her on her looks, giving her hugs, and buying her things she needs," and in some instances, molesters will "expos[e] children to pornography, supply[] them with drugs and alcohol, blackmail[] them, and coerc[e] their silence by threats of suicide." In particular, teenagers from dysfunctional households are most susceptible to the grooming process.[24]

Lanning's testimony sounds surprisingly similar to Sara's case, in which the forty-year-old manager of a movie theater allegedly befriended teenage employees, provided them with alcohol, gave them free theater tickets, and even offered to teach sixteen-year-old Sara to drive. This manager encouraged Sara "to speak with him about her problems, how her parents did not understand her, and about things that mattered to her, a teenage girl." The manager gave Sara expensive gifts, took her to nice dinners, and gave her cash. Sara had no idea that her manager was a registered sex offender, convicted of molesting his twelve-year-old niece.[25]

The manager lied to Sara after repeatedly soliciting sexual favors from her. He told Sara that he was suffering from a potentially inoperable brain tumor and shortly thereafter suggested they go to a hotel to have sexual intercourse. Convinced that she loved her "desperately ill" manager, Sara eventually acquiesced.[26]

Sara became the compliant victim that Lanning described. The *Jones* court recounted Lanning's testimony, noting, "The grooming process results in . . . 'compliant victims'–children who cooperate in their victimization. Their non-resistance may seem to indicate consent . . . ; indeed, the children may return to their abusers and even enjoy the sexual activity."[27] In Lanning's testimony, he noted that "compliant victims suffer a lifetime of shame, embarrassment, and guilt because their victimization does not fit society's understanding that children do not willingly acquiesce in abuse."[28] The court stated, "According to Lanning, those feelings help explain why victimized children fail to disclose or delay disclosure of their abuse, and why their disclosures often contain 'incomplete,' 'inaccurate,' 'distorted,' or 'contradictory' information." Lanning's testimony in *Jones* clarified that although nonresistance may appear to indicate consent, in reality, it may indicate abuse and manipulation.[29]

This summary of Lanning's testimony is consistent with information covered in chapter 2 from the AACAP and other experts. Recall the AACAP policy statement. It explained that children and adolescent victims of sexual harassment commonly conceal the perpetrator's offenses based on feelings of shame, fear, humiliation, and vulnerability. Children and adolescents may even believe that their behavior precipitated the sexual abuse.[30] In *Doe v. Taylor Indep. Sch. Dist.*, the court found, "Doe explained that she had kept the [sexual conduct with a teacher] a secret because she feared the repercussions of disclosure."[31] In *Leach v. Evansville-Vanderburgh Sch. Corp.*, the court held that that a student failed to report sexual harassment because she felt ashamed, was afraid to tell her mother for fear of upsetting her, and was afraid that no one would believe that her teacher was sexually fondling her.[32]

Often, the abuse is not revealed for years, if ever. In *Doe v. Estes*, the court explained that minor victims may not reveal "invasions of their bodily integrity. They may fear reprisals by their attackers, they may harbor doubts that their attackers' fellow grownups will display sympathy or willingly credit their accounts, and they all too frequently are paralyzed by the shame that attends subjection to sexual abuse."[33] Tragically, these children often correctly anticipate the response of adults in their lives. Recall Aaron Fisher who accused Jerry Sandusky of sexual abuse. Initially, school officials did not believe Aaron.[34] Such responses confirm Lanning's conclusion that in "the United States, society's historical attitude about the sexual victimization of children can generally be summed up in one word: denial."[35]

Lanning's testimony in *Jones*, coupled with the AACAP policy statement, highlights how a manipulated teenager might respond to sexual abuse and harassment with acquiescence and later with shame, humiliation, or worse. After being kissed by her manager, Sara "remember[ed] feeling 'numb' at first. Everything was moving so quickly. Everything was a blur to her."[36] When Sara's brother, also a theater employee, observed the manager kissing his sister in a storage room, the manager again lied, stating that Sara had forced herself on him. Sara felt ashamed and was concerned about how her brother thought of her. Later, the manager began calling Sara a whore and a slut. When Sara and the manager argued, he threatened to tell her parents about their relationship. Sara was ashamed and fearful of how her parents would respond to her conduct with the manager. So she kept their relationship a secret. She did not realize that as the adult her manager was responsible for the abuse.[37] Ultimately, the manager was convicted criminally for abusing Sara.[38]

Sara's conduct in response to her manager's manipulations supports the *Jones* court's findings. Sara concealed her manager's abuse and the resulting trauma from her parents.[39] She reported feeling humiliation and shame.[40] Had the manager not continued to telephone her from jail following an unrelated larceny conviction, Sara's parents might never have discovered the cause of her plummeting grades and bizarre behavior.[41] Lanning's profile of a sexually abused or manipulated teenager like Sara helps us understand why adolescent consent demands special treatment under the law.

The Tobias *Irony*

Despite the *Tobias* court's finding that minors may "knowingly and voluntarily" participate in sexual relations, it distinguished incest. The court explained that incest differs from other sex crimes because "the act itself is unlawful," regardless of the minor's involvement or consent. An important purpose of the incest law is the protection of minors, and the court found it inconceivable that a minor in an incest case would be criminally liable as an accomplice to the incest rather than a victim.[42]

The irony is that the *Tobias* court supported its reasoning concerning the nature of the incest crime with reference to section 261.5. According to the *Tobias* court, the legislature intended section 261.5 to protect minors by making sexual intercourse with minors a strict liability offense. At the same time, the court stated that the California legislature "implicitly acknowledged that, in some cases at least, a minor may be capable of giving legal consent to sexual relations." How could the 1970 legislative initiative implicitly mark the abandonment of the age of consent and the legislature's rejection of a minor's incapacity? If anything, section 261.5 confirms eighteen as the age of consent and, standing alone, reinforces that minors lack capacity to consent to sex with adults.[43] The *Tobias* majority opinion is internally inconsistent on this issue.

OFFENDING MINORS. Another analytical snarl discussed in *Tobias* and other criminal cases becomes apparent when one considers that minors commit sex crimes against other children. Jurists may readily agree that adults should carry the burden of resisting criminal sexual temptation when contemplating adult-child sexual conduct. However, what if all of the actors are children? Do criminally offending minors have legal capacity? This may be the wrong question to ask in the context of the criminal prosecution of a minor for offenses committed against another child. Rather, the more appropriate question is whether the law is designed to protect the *offending* minor.

Legislatures draft sex crime statutes to protect minors from abuse by adults who wield more power and authority than the minor. The law protects those who cannot protect themselves. When a minor wields power over another child and sexually abuses the child, the sex crime law does not protect the offending minor who is not the contemplated innocent target. Thus, whether or not an offending minor possesses what one might call legal capacity, one can choose to prosecute offending minors in order to protect the less powerful and less sophisticated child victim. Whether one prosecutes the offending minor the same way that one would prosecute and punish an adult is a separate question. Especially in the area of sex crimes, teenagers' lack of sophistication and knowledge can lead to devastating results. Sexting is just one example of how the consequences (life-time assignment to a sex offender registry) may not fit the crime.[44]

In *Renguette v. Board of School Trustees ex rel. Brownsburg*, D.A.V., a fourteen-year-old freshman, and J.R., a twelve-year-old seventh-grader, engaged in consensual sexual activity on a school bus. D.A.V. was initially charged with one juvenile count of child molesting. That charge was dropped, and D.A.V. pled guilty to one juvenile count of public indecency. J.R.'s mother sued D.A.V.'s mother under the Indiana parental liability statute. Judge Sarah Evans Barker ruled, "[W]e cannot conclude, based on uncontroverted evidence or as a matter of law, that the sexual conduct between J.R. and D.A.V. was consensual."[45] The court confirmed that the key issues were whether a twelve-year-old could legally consent to sex with another minor and whether a factual inquiry regarding "welcomeness" was required. Because these issues arose on a motion for summary judgment, the court properly denied the motion, preserving these issues for trial.[46] I suggest here that a welcomeness inquiry, borrowed from Title VII and *Meritor* does not work for minors. Developing teenagers are grappling with their own transformational changes and may not be clear about whether they "welcome" sexual attention. They may feel numb, confused, and ashamed, and these emotions could mask any sense of unwelcomeness in any event.

Finally, what about the Romeo and Juliet example where two minors engage in consensual sexual intercourse, thereby becoming victims of the other's crime? Common sense should determine that case. If both children are victims, there is no classic offender to prosecute. In 1998 in *People v. T.A.J.*, the court opined that section 261.5 may criminalize conduct between minors.[47] California Penal Code section 261.5(b) states, "Any person who engages in an act of unlawful sexual intercourse with a minor who is not more than three years older or three years younger than the perpetrator, is guilty of a misdemeanor." The *T.A.J.* court explained that the decision to prosecute a minor for violating section 261.5 is an exercise of prosecutorial discretion.[48] One can only hope that common sense will prevail.[49] The odd dictum in *Tobias* and news of other

Romeo and Juliet prosecutions suggest, however, that section 261.5 may not stand as a beacon of judicious use of prosecutorial discretion.[50]

A VOICE OF REASON: CHIEF JUSTICE GEORGE'S *TOBIAS* CONCURRENCE. In a *Tobias* concurring opinion, then Chief Justice Ronald M. George expressed concern. He disputed the *Tobias* majority's reasoning regarding the legislative intent of the 1970 rape statute revision. After reviewing case law and historical acknowledgement of juvenile incapacity, Chief Justice George distinguished the revised section 261 from section 261.5 pertaining to minors. He offered that section 261 (rape) involves a victim incapable of consenting because of a mental disability or one who was challenged by violence or force. Chief Justice George noted that a minor's consent might be relevant to the prosecution of section 261. He argued that the California legislature did not intend to establish that a minor is capable of legally consenting to sexual relations. Instead, Chief Justice George contended that in section 261.5 the legislature merely recodified the preexisting principle in section 261 that provided that a minor's consent to sexual intercourse with an adult does not relieve the adult of criminal responsibility. In turn, by amending section 261, the legislature enhanced the criminal severity of raping a minor, requiring that it be accomplished by additional circumstances specified in the statute.[51]

Chief Justice George's concurrence causes one to wonder whether the legislature would have acted differently if it had heard Special Agent Lanning's testimony regarding nonresistance. Would it have left criminal sexual intercourse as part of the forcible rape statute? Chief Justice George provided an explanation of the statutory revisions that differentiate the elements of section 261 from the elements of section 261.5, while preserving the traditional view that minors lack the legal capacity to consent to sex.

A final point by Chief Justice George in his concurrence detailed that the *Tobias* majority's analysis conflicts with section 261.6. Section 261.6 reads,

> In prosecutions under Section 261, 262, 286, 288a, or 289, in which consent is at issue, "consent" shall be defined to mean positive cooperation in act or attitude pursuant to an exercise of free will. The person must act freely and voluntarily and have knowledge of the nature of the act or transaction involved.

Note that section 261.6 does *not* list section 261.5, arguably because consent is not at issue, as minors cannot *legally* consent. Chief Justice George drew from *People v. Young*, a case that "recognized that a defendant might violate section 261.5 without also violating section 261." *Young* clarified "that, although a minor cannot give *legal* consent to sexual intercourse, he or she voluntarily and willingly can participate in the act, and thus *actually* consent within the meaning of section 261.6."[52] Chief Justice George asserted that the *Young* court accurately determined that the concept of "*actual* consent," defined in section 261.6, is distinct from "*legal* consent."[53]

So what was the actual intent of the 1970 California legislature? In *Michael M. v. Superior Court*, the US Supreme Court addressed this very question.

The Intent of Section 261.5: *Michael M. v. Superior Court*

In *Michael M. v. Superior Court*, the US Supreme Court heard an Equal Protection Clause challenge to California Penal Code section 261.5. Originally, section 261.5 criminalized sexual intercourse only with minor girls but not with boys. Thus, only males faced criminal liability under the statute. In evaluating whether the statute constituted invidious sex discrimination, the Court reviewed the legislature's intent. The Court cautioned that questioning the legislative intent of statutes is troublesome and often elusive. For example, the Court noted that, in passing section 261.5, some legislators may have been interested in protecting young females from the loss of chastity or physical injury, while other legislators may have been espousing moral or religious views.[54]

Theorizing about chastity and physical injury, the *Michael M.* plurality hypothesized about the possible intentions of legislators. Significantly, the plurality made no mention of juvenile legal incapacity or of traditional ages of consent. Ultimately, the plurality deferred to California's expressed goal of preventing "illegitimate teenage pregnancies." The Court stated that California has a strong interest in preventing such pregnancies.[55]

However, the expressed goal, affirmed in the plurality, makes sense for only menarchal teenage females. The statute prohibited sexual intercourse with all minor girls, not just those who may become pregnant.[56] The statute was grossly over inclusive, calling into doubt whether the officially stated goal was the primary motivator. Now that the statute applies to protect minor boys and girls, the pregnancy prevention justification makes even less sense. Given that this legislation came on the heels of the "Summer of Love" (1967) and Woodstock (1969), the more likely legislative intent in 1970 was the prevention of sexual activity with all of California's daughters.[57]

An Alternative Interpretation: Justice Brennan's Michael M. *Dissent*

In his *Michael M.* dissent, Justice William J. Brennan Jr. strongly contested the legislative intent adopted by the plurality. Justice Brennan noted that California courts and commentators had only recently advanced the theory that the legislature intended the California statutory rape law to safeguard against pregnancy in young women. Justice Brennan traced the historical development of section 261.5 concluding that legislators initially promulgated the statute because society considered young women incapable of legally consenting to sex. Legislators, who valued the chastity of young women, assumed the young women to be particularly in need of protection from the state. Conversely, society deemed young men capable of making such decisions and thus not in need of special legal protection. Justice Brennan's analysis highlights the stereotypes traditionally enforced with respect to juvenile capacity to consent to sex.[58]

Justice Brennan elaborated in several footnotes, tracing the legislative history and statutory precursors to section 261.5. Justice Brennan explained, "The only legislative history available, the draftsmen's notes to the Penal Code of 1872, supports the view that the purpose of California's statutory rape law was to protect those who were too young to give consent." Later revisions of the statute postponed the age of consent, ultimately to the age of majority—eighteen.[59]

In a separate footnote, Justice Brennan analyzed case law interpreting statutory rape. Quoting *People v. Hernandez*, a 1964 California Supreme Court decision (*not* the Texas case discussed in chapter 4), Justice Brennan explained that a minor female was "presumed too innocent and naive to understand the implications and nature of her act."[60] Thus, Justice Brennan stated that the law of statutory rape may be explained in part by a popular conception of the moral, social, and personal values preserved by a young woman's sexual abstinence. In *Hernandez*, the court further held, "An unwise disposition of her sexual favor is deemed to do harm both to herself and the social mores by which the community's conduct patterns are established. Hence the law of statutory rape intervenes in an effort to avoid such a disposition."[61]

Justice Brennan's emphasis on the historical and stereotypically gendered motivation for California's section 261.5 is consistent with my lay understanding of statutory rape in California when I was a teenager there in the 1970s. Who knew, but a handful of lawmakers and jurists, that section 261.5 would later be billed as "The Teenage Pregnancy Prevention Act of 1995"? How many Californians today know there is no California "statutory rape law"? Do they know that sexual intercourse with a minor is illegal but that the victim may not be able to recover civilly if he or she consents? How many people know the statutory rape laws of their own respective states?

Michael M.: *The California Supreme Court Opinion*

The earlier *Michael M. v. Superior Court* California State Supreme Court decision also contributes to an understanding of the conclusions reached in *People v. Tobias*. The defendant, Michael M., argued that a validation of section 261.5 would necessarily signal California's disrespect for the autonomy and independence of girls. In upholding the constitutionality of section 261.5, the *Michael M.* court used familiar language, rejecting the assertion that upholding the constitutionality of section 261.5 "creates adverse inferences concerning the capacity of minor females to make *intelligent and volitional* decisions." The court further stated that the legislature's adoption of section 261.5 indicates the "obvious truism that minor females are fully capable of *freely and voluntarily* consenting to sexual relations." The court concluded that if this were not so, then the charge in such cases would be forcible rape.[62]

In *Michael M.*, the court walked a fine line between dismissing or infantilizing minor females and attributing to them legal status and capacity, which they had not held before under California law. As explained, the *Tobias* California Supreme Court majority revisited this discussion of when a minor "knowingly and voluntarily" engages in the sexual act.[63]

However, in his *Tobias* concurrence, Chief Justice George argued that *Michael M.* referred to a girl's voluntary behavior rather than her legal consent or capacity. Recall the discussion of "voluntariness" by the majority opinion in *Meritor Savings Bank v. Vinson*. The US Supreme Court found that voluntary participation did not equate with legally significant consent. Also, recall Special Agent Lanning's discussion of acquiescence and how it only *seemed* to indicate consent. In *Tobias*, Chief Justice George explained that a minor may "voluntarily" engage in sexual relations but cannot "legally consent" to such acts. Chief Justice George contended that *Michael M.* concerned *actual* consent, not *legal* consent, and thus lent no support to the *Tobias* majority's reasoning.[64]

The remaining discussion by the California majority in *Michael M.* foreshadows Chief Justice George's interpretation in *Tobias*. The court in *Michael M.* noted that section 261.5 does not address a young woman's ability to consent. Rather, the statute simply prohibits sexual intercourse with underage females, thereby rejecting consent as a defense. According to the *Michael M.* court, "In this regard section 261.5 is no different than a variety of other statutes which prohibit minors from engaging in certain activities of much less consequence to the minor, *no matter how well informed, how knowledgeable and how willing or consenting the minor might be*." *Michael M.* clarified that section 261.5 was not a radical shift by the California legislature but rather, another treatment of juvenile *legal* incapacity.[65]

Civil Law Adoption of Criminal Case Dictum

Whether or not the California Supreme Court accurately interpreted the intent of the California legislature in *People v. Tobias*, California criminal courts continually sanction adults who engage in sex with minors. However, when California civil courts began relying on the *Tobias* dictum, protections for minors against sexual abuse eroded. In 2005 the California Appeals Court in *Donaldson v. Dep't of Real Estate* created a slippery slope.[66]

The Slippery Slope: Donaldson v. Dep't of Real Estate

The *Donaldson* case involved not a suit by a minor but an appeal of the withdrawal of a real estate license. While Robert Donaldson's wife was away on a business trip, her sixteen-year-old sister took care of the Donaldson children one evening. During his wife's absence, thirty-year-old Donaldson gave his sister-in-law marijuana and the two engaged in sexual activities. Later, Donaldson was charged with two counts of furnishing marijuana to a minor and unlawful sex with a minor, a violation of section 261.5 of the California Penal Code. A court ultimately dismissed the marijuana charges. The judge suspended the sentence on the felony sex conviction and placed Donaldson on three years' probation.[67]

At an administrative hearing following the disciplinary charges, the administrative law judge (ALJ) asked, "[D]o you understand that because you are an older man in a position of power that [the minor] did not consent to the act that followed or do you think she consented?" Donaldson responded, "I think I had consensual—she consented, and in every sort of the way."[68] The ALJ concluded that Donaldson could retain his realtor license on a restricted basis because the sexual misconduct was an isolated incident.[69]

The appellate decision does not indicate whether any of the reviewing *Donaldson* tribunals received expert testimony. The ALJ's determination, however, sounds like a finding that Donaldson was, what Special Agent Lanning described, a "situational offender."[70] Still, facts in this case reveal that Donaldson gave his minor sister-in-law marijuana.[71] That conduct may be more consistent with grooming behavior. Special Agent Lanning suggested, in *Jones v. United States*, that once an abuser cultivates a relationship of trust and dependence with a victim, the abuser may manipulate the victim's feelings, encouraging the child to overcome her sexual inhibitions.[72] Perhaps the real estate commissioner felt that Donaldson had behaved in this manner with his sister-in-law.

The real estate commissioner issued her own decision, contrary to that of the ALJ. She relied on the victim's statements in investigative reports to find that the intercourse was rape. The commissioner asserted that circumstantial evidence and the police report indicated that the minor felt "paralyzed" and "forced" to participate in the sexual activity. The commissioner noted that, although Donaldson subsequently realized that his sister-in-law was not old enough to consent legally and that he betrayed a position of trust, Donaldson failed to recognize that his sister-in-law did not consent to the act. Rather, the commissioner noted, Donaldson believed the act was consensual, denied that he raped his sister-in-law, and did not seem to appreciate that his position of trust and physical size may have been coercive. She found that these intimidating factors led to the minor's feelings of paralysis.[73]

In revoking Donaldson's real estate license, the California real estate commissioner construed his actions to be "[s]exually related conduct causing physical harm or emotional distress to a . . . non-consenting participant in the conduct."[74] The commissioner's assessment focuses much more on Doe's perspective and leaves the reader confused about what actually happened. One wonders whether an expert ever interviewed *Donaldson* Doe or whether the jurists involved received any training or education regarding the effects of incest and sexual abuse/involvement.

The reviewing district court found that the police reports constituted hearsay and were admissible only to support or explain other unidentified, circumstantial evidence. In response to the petition for the writ of mandamus (a special request for a court order), the district court held that the available admissible evidence did not support the commissioner's decision and remanded it for further consideration. With a new decision omitting any discussion of actual consent, the commissioner again found against Donaldson. The district court denied a subsequent petition.[75] Donaldson appealed.

Relying on *Tobias*, the California appellate court reversed the revocation. Summarizing the *Tobias* holding, the *Donaldson* court concluded that the commissioner had incorrectly relied on the offense of statutory rape, which according to the court, the legislature abolished thirty-five years prior. Accordingly, the *Donaldson* court stated that the California Supreme Court in *Tobias* had authoritatively disavowed the presumption of nonconsent solely based on the minor's age.[76] Through this professional discipline case, the *Tobias* dictum made its way into California civil law precedent.

THE *DONALDSON* APPELLATE DECISION. When reviewing the second Real Estate Commission decision against Donaldson, the appellate court analyzed the legislature's passage of section 261.5, the meaning of nonconsent and the age of consent, and the function of the Real Estate Commission. The court reasoned that section 261.5 effectively restored rape "to its traditional outlines." It explained that the California legislature abolished the crime of statutory rape, thereby implicitly foreclosing the presumption of juvenile nonconsent. The *Donaldson* court recommended referring to conduct prohibited under section 261.5 as "criminal intercourse" to avoid confusion.[77] The court offered no support other than the *Tobias* dictum for its interpretation of the 1970 legislative amendments to section 261 and the passage of section 261.5.

The *Donaldson* court also considered the "age of legal consent." The court explained, "This phrase, like 'statutory rape,' has passed into lay usage and been incorporated into folk law." The court explored the activity and the age to which the phrase referred. In a detailed discussion, citing both civil code sections and case law, the court concluded that the phrase was used primarily in the context of consent to marriage—even with respect to the former "*tort* of seduction of a person under the age of legal consent."[78] It meant the age at which consent to marriage would garner legal authority. Acknowledging, however, that many courts have used the phrase in reference to sexual relations, the *Donaldson* court held that the legislature abolished statutory rape as a crime and, with it, the age of consent.[79]

How many people know that there is no age of consent in the state of California? One sees how this outcome, if not the exact sequence of legal maneuvers, might be replicated in another state. Few people follow the evolutionary paths of such nuanced legal reasoning and so might not realize what's evolving in their own proverbial legal backyards. Do residents of Mississippi, New York, Tennessee, Virginia, and Wisconsin (to name just a few states) know that their laws treat adolescent consent inconsistently?

Neither court—*Donaldson* nor *Tobias*—concluded that the California legislature intended merely to simplify the forcible rape statute (section 261) and to classify more precisely criminal (but perhaps unresisted) sex with a minor (section 261.5). Such reorganization actually permitted the legislature to confirm what had been implied in the so-called statutory rape provisions of the former penal code: that minors are *legally incapable* of consenting.[80]

DONALDSON'S FLAWS. As noted, many jurists suggest that the California legislature intended to abandon the notion of nonconsent. Rejecting Chief Justice George's *Tobias* concurrence, the *Donaldson* court stated that the concurrence merely established "an artificial distinction between 'legal' and 'actual' consent." Continuing, the court explained that although this distinction provided a mechanism for preserving the presumption of nonconsent, which preceded the 1970 legislation, Chief Justice George failed to provide a legal reason for doing so.[81]

Several problems surface in the *Donaldson* court's line of reasoning. First, one wonders why the court thought the notion of nonconsent advocated for in the *Tobias* concurrence was unsound.[82] Did the court really think that all minors have the capacity to consent? Did the *Donaldson* court really believe that the civil law should afford sixteen-year-old girls the opportunity to consent to sex with an adult boss, teacher, or brother-in-law?

Second, why did the court disfavor the "artificial distinction" between legal and actual consent? The law often makes such "artificial distinctions" to protect consenting people. For example, would the *Donaldson* court have erased the artificial distinction between legal and actual consent of the mentally challenged and the disoriented elderly? Would the court have repealed "cooling off" periods for the revocation of adult consent given in door-to-door sales?[83] Such artificial distinctions protect minors and others from savvy operators who extract actual consent using unscrupulous methods. The *Donaldson* court could have embraced the distinction between legal and actual consent to interpret the real estate regulation at issue. Had the court read the regulation to require actual nonconsent, as opposed to legal nonconsent, it might have ruled in favor of the licensee, Donaldson. In other words, the court could have read the regulations to require elements similar to those of only section 261 (rape) rather than including those of section 261.5 (unlawful sex with a minor).

Third, the discussion in the majority's *Tobias* opinion was nonbinding dictum. Section 261.5 was not at issue in *Tobias*. The *Donaldson* court was not obligated to follow the *Tobias* majority's dictum.

Fourth, the *Donaldson* court should have accepted section 261.5 as the prescriptive rule of law and the reason for confirming a minor's nonconsent. Instead, the court stated that the presumption asserting a minor's inability to consent to sexual relationships was inferred from statutory law that was abandoned by the California legislature. The court noted, "That consent is *not* a defense to section 261.5 means only that for reasons of policy, the legislature has chosen to treat sexual intercourse with a minor as a criminal act *notwithstanding that the minor consented to it*." The *Donaldson* court concluded that such a law, regardless of how widely it is accepted, cannot remain established when the legislature elects to change course.[84]

This fourth reason raises several more issues. Concerning legal definitions, the court casually labeled nonconsent a presumption. Presumptions may be refuted; no refutation appears possible in the scheme handed down in *Donaldson*. If the minor consents, the *Donaldson* court gave no explain for how she might rebut the presumption of capacity. Certainly the court gave *Donaldson* Doe no such opportunity to assert her incapacity. Furthermore, the court offered no evidence that minors have the capacity to give legal consent.[85] The court fell into the same pit that entraps so many: the pit of conflation concerning actual consent and legal consent. The court ignored the requirement of legal capacity.

The *Donaldson* court also referred to "reasons of policy," which undergirded the legislature's decision not to permit consent as a defense in a section 261.5 action.[86] What policy? Isn't a determination of juvenile incapacity the logical basis of a legislative policy judgment that teenagers cannot legally consent to sex? Why else would the legislature choose to criminalize sex with minors if it thought that their consent was meaningful, advised, appropriate, and so on? Just to prevent pregnancy? If minors have (legal) capacity, then surely they can plan against pregnancy. The truth is that adults know teenagers take risks that other adults do not take. Did the legislature pass section 261.5 simply because it was politically expedient? How is it expedient to criminalize the conduct and then allow courts to credit the associated consent in the civil trial? Maybe something else motivated the *Donaldson* decision.

DONALDSON'S FOOTNOTE 10. In a footnote, the *Donaldson* court revealed important additional information that influences this discussion.[87] The court explained that although it felt Donaldson's conduct was "troubling," it did not "ha[ve] any bearing on his or her qualifications as a real estate professional under prescribed criteria." Essentially, the court thought that Donaldson had been punished enough by the felony conviction for seducing his sixteen-year-old sister-in-law and that he was still qualified to work in the real estate business. The court did not think that a felony conviction for criminal intercourse with a minor should interfere with his ability to pursue his profession.[88] Of course, this reasoning has nothing to do with whether the minor had actual or legal capacity to consent to sex with her brother-in-law.

Another interesting aspect of this footnote is the court's characterization of Donaldson's conduct as "troubling." Why was it troubling to the court if the conduct was consensual and the minor possessed legal capacity? And, why was the liaison just troubling and not "outrageous," "despicable," "predatory," "contemptuous," or another stronger adjective? After all, the crime is a felony. Donaldson seduced his wife's minor sister while his wife was out of town and when her sister was caring for their children. No matter the *Donaldson* court's true motivation, one can now trace its adoption of the *Tobias* dictum to the *Doe v. Starbucks* case.

The Tobias *Legacy:* Doe v. Starbucks

As previously noted, Kati Moore was sixteen years old in July 2005 when she began working at Starbucks. Timothy Horton, who was then twenty-four years old, supervised and worked closely with Kati. She reported that Horton repeatedly asked her out and that she initially spurned his advances.[89] In pleadings, Kati claimed that, while at work and in front of coworkers, Horton made "perhaps hundreds" of profane, sexually explicit remarks concerning his sexual interest in her.[90] Eventually, Kati acquiesced to Horton's advances in the hopes that he would stop.[91] In November or December 2005, they allegedly engaged in sexual activity.[92] Kati stated,

> [Horton] demanded that I perform oral sex on him, which I did. I felt like I had to—that I had no choice. . . . I felt that, because he had given me marijuana and I had smoked it with him, I had to do what he said, because he was my Supervisor and I didn't want to lose my job.[93]

Kati and Horton engaged in sexual activities regularly through June 2006.[94] In addition to "vaginal intercourse and oral copulation" at work and offsite, "[t]hey exchanged explicit sexual comments and text messages at work."[95] Horton insisted that Kati not disclose their relationship to anyone.[96] This insistence on secrecy suggests that Horton knew his relationship with Kati was wrong.

Starbucks management and employees suspected that Horton was having an "extracurricular" relationship with Kati. An assistant manager reminded Horton of Starbucks's policy, which prohibited him from dating Kati. Horton denied any relationship. Kati did not deny their involvement when a shift leader asked about her offsite relationship with Horton. When Horton found out about the exchange, he shouted at Kati. Both Kati and Horton subsequently denied their involvement when other Starbucks employees confronted them. Store Manager Lina Nobel contacted Sarah Kelly, Starbucks's human resources director, about her concerns regarding Horton and Kati. However, no one fully investigated the matter.[97]

Kati informed her mother about her sexual relationship with Horton in February 2006. Kati's mother requested that Starbucks take steps to protect her daughter and conduct an investigation of the allegedly illicit relationship. Nobel agreed to ensure that Kati and Horton would not have contact until she completed an investigation.[98] Nobel questioned Kati, who admitted that she was sexually involved with Horton. Horton continued to deny anything other than a professional relationship with Kati. Nobel felt like she was not in a position to question Horton about a sexual relationship. Moreover, she did not make a credibility determination because she did not believe it was her place to pass judgment.[99] Nobel was concerned that terminating Horton would lead to a wrongful termination claim.[100] Starbucks did not otherwise formally investigate.

Although Starbucks initially failed to take action against Horton, others interceded for Kati. Kati's mother eventually learned from Nobel that Horton had denied Kati's allegations of wrongdoing.[101] Presumably at her mother's urging, Kati requested a "transfer[] to a different Starbucks store because she 'felt like she had to.'"[102]

According to the district court, Kati left her job in 2006 to enroll in a mental health treatment facility.[103] A news report clarified that Kati left Horton "when her mother called Integrity House, a home in Utah for troubled teens. Counselors from Integrity House 'abducted' Moore with her parents' consent, shoving her into a car and driving her to their facility, where she lived for the next year."[104] Such was Horton's grip on Kati that her parents felt compelled to take drastic measures to separate them. Ultimately, state authorities charged Horton with criminal unlawful sexual intercourse with a minor for his conduct with Kati, to which he pled guilty. In a 2009 civil action, Kati, by then an adult under the law and able to file in her own name, alleged sexual harassment and torts claims against Starbucks and Horton.[105]

In response to Starbucks's Motion for Summary Judgment, the court analyzed Kati's capacity to consent and whether she consented to Horton's advances. The *Starbucks* court explained that resolution of the arguments concerning Kati's capacity influenced several claims at issue, including Kati's sexual harassment claim.[106]

First, the court evaluated California Penal Code section 261.5, which Kati argued confirmed her incapacity to consent to sexual contact. The *Starbucks* court disagreed, quoting the relevant *Tobias* dictum that "in some cases at least, a minor may be capable of giving legal consent to sexual relations."[107] The court failed to explain why, if some minors are capable of giving legal consent, section 261.5 is a strict liability offense for which the minor's consent means nothing. The court acknowledged that *Tobias* was a criminal case but held that *Donaldson* had extended its rule to civil cases.[108]

Second, in support of her contention that minors lack the capacity to consent to sexual intercourse with adults, Kati's counsel cited *Doe v. Oberweis Dairy*, a 2006 case decided by the US Court of Appeals for the Seventh Circuit and one discussed in chapter 6.[109] The court determined that *Oberweis* had "little persuasive effect" because it was a Seventh Circuit case, did not consider California law, and controverted the precedent established by *Tobias*.[110] A closer examination of *Oberweis*, however, demonstrates that it may have had more to offer in the *Starbucks* sexual harassment case than the California federal district court concluded.

Doe v. Oberweis Dairy*: An Alternate View*

As introduced earlier, *Oberweis* involved the sexual harassment of a sixteen-year-old ice cream scooper by her twenty-five-year-old supervisor. The Illinois federal district court decided that Doe had not complained of unwelcome conduct.[111] The district court also found the conduct was not severe or pervasive, another requirement in the sexual harassment legal case. The court declared, "[I]t is undisputed that through Plaintiff's approximately eight-month employment with Defendant, Nayman [the supervisor] only touched Plaintiff on fifteen occasions." The court stressed that Doe "continued to visit with Nayman socially outside of work, even after Plaintiff's mother prohibited Plaintiff from visiting Nayman."[112] Therefore, the court concluded that there was no issue of material fact as to whether the sexual conduct was unwelcome.

In reversing the district court in 2006, the Seventh Circuit in *Oberweis* described in more detail how Nayman operated. As noted previously, Nayman would "'grope,' 'kiss,' 'grab butts,' 'hug,' and give 'tittie twisters' to these employees, including the plaintiff." The court specified that Nayman engaged in this conduct both in the store and at his apartment, to which he invited his subordinates. The court found, "He had sexual intercourse in the apartment with two of them, one of them a minor, before it was the plaintiff's turn. He was 25 when he had intercourse with her."[113] This summary of the suit from the appellate decision highlights facts omitted in the district court's rendition of the case.

The appellate court portrayed Nayman as what Special Agent Lanning referred to as a situational offender, opportunistically exploiting young subordinates.[114]

Emphasizing the age disparity between Nayman and Doe, the Seventh Circuit court found that, although Nayman had not committed forcible rape, he had committed statutory rape.[115] The court reasoned that statutory rape is a crime because minors may be unable to make responsible decisions about whether to engage in sex. The court noted that in Illinois, as elsewhere, the severity of the crime increases with the age disparity between the parties.

The court explained the graduated crimes with the theory that minors are likely to have difficulty resisting the flatteries of adults. In this case, *Oberweis* Doe was nine years younger than Nayman. Thus, the *Oberweis* appellate court implicitly recognized the "communal experience" regarding teenage capacity that the California appellate court, in *People v. Hillhouse*, had identified and labeled three years prior.[116]

Acknowledging the unwelcomeness requirement under Title VII *and* understanding that minors may not always make responsible decisions about sex, the *Oberweis* appellate court devised a plan for dealing with adolescent consent to sex. Writing for the court, Judge Posner explained that the court wanted to avoid reclassifying sex, which a state deems to be nonconsensual, as consensual. Posner avoided "intractable inquiries into maturity that legislatures invariably pretermit by basing entitlements to public benefits (right to vote, right to drive, right to drink, right to own a gun, etc.) on specified ages rather than on a standard of maturity."[117] He suggested that, in reference to Title VII, courts should defer to the state's age of consent, which reflects the judgment of average maturity for sexual matters. Judge Posner cautioned against an effort to determine whether a minor was able to welcome the sexual overtures of an adult. Thus, the court concluded that, for Title VII cases, the age of consent should be the rule of decision.[118]

However, a serious flaw in Judge Posner's plan is evident. Judge Posner acknowledged that the protection afforded to teenage employees by Title VII varies by jurisdiction because the age of consent differs between states. However, the court mistakenly calculated that the variance would be limited to a "fairly narrow band."[119] For states with no age of consent, such as California, adolescent consent garners legal significance: whether or not the minor has legal capacity in the criminal context. The Seventh Circuit likely did not know that only a few months earlier the *Donaldson* California state district court declared the end of the age of consent in California civil cases. Thus, the Seventh Circuit offered the nation a logical but seriously flawed formula for responding to adolescent consent in sexual harassment and sexual abuse cases. In states such as California and New York, where state criminal and civil law conflict, this formula provides no clear guidance on how to treat adolescent nonresistance or consent.

The Hidden Conflicts Regarding the Age of Consent

A Google search of "ages of consent" fails to warn that state civil law may conflict with "ages of consent" designated for criminal prosecution in any given jurisdiction. I found at least twelve states with civil case law precedent that conflicted in some way with the statutory age of consent.[120] In *Sex and the Workplace: "Consenting" Adolescents and a Conflict of Laws*, I reviewed the conflicting laws across the United States and evaluated the chances that a sixteen-year-old such as Sara (or her guardian who would sue on her behalf) might have in pursuing a sexual harassment or other related tort case. I determined that the outcome depended upon the jurisdiction where the alleged conduct took place, the court in which she sued, and which claims she brought.[121] Today Sara probably could not win a case in fifteen states where the age of consent is sixteen or lower. That number of states would certainly be higher if courts rejected some of the aggravating circumstances of her case. Finally, that number increases to twenty-three states because of inconsistencies between civil and criminal laws. Those eight additional states would treat Sara as a consenting adult and bar most claims or significantly reduce the damage award.[122]

California, Sara's home state, should be on the list of states where Sara's chances for success in civil court are quite unlikely. Because California rejected *Oberweis*, one may anticipate that more jurisdictions will follow suit in actions by acquiescing teenagers against employers. The trend at the approach of the twenty-first century was to punish teenagers for their lack of resistance and failure to abstain. That punishing result becomes literal if an underage male fathers a child via illicit sexual intercourse with an adult female. For example, in 1996 in *San Luis Obispo v. Nathaniel J.*, a fifteen-year-old described sex with his thirty-four-year-old consort as "a mutually agreeable act."[123] Therefore, the California appellate court refused to release the boy from liability for child support, finding that the adolescent plaintiff was not an innocent victim of the adult's criminal acts.[124]

This discussion of legislative intent and case law interpretation shows even more inconsistencies that are problematic.

Misguided Confusion?

Does misguided confusion—or paternalistic judgment—concerning sexually active teenagers explain the current state of affairs for adolescents? The *Tobias* court was not reviewing Penal Code section 261.5 nor a civil sexual harassment claim when it determined that in some situations California minors might give legal consent to sex.[125] With its 2001 pronouncement, *Tobias* set California civil law and criminal law completely at odds. Neither the California legislature nor the California Supreme Court responded in almost fifteen years to ameliorate the resulting situation. As precedent expands, scholars will find it less plausible to attribute the resulting conflicts between civil and criminal law to continuing misunderstanding or confusion.

Fortunately for Sara Doe, her case settled in 2002 before *Donaldson* extended the *Tobias* dictum to the civil context.[126] Kati Moore was not so lucky. Relying on the *Tobias* dictum, the *Starbucks* court determined that the issue of Kati's actual consent was a triable fact. The case then settled out of court.[127] Had the case not settled, Kati could have anticipated an invasive trial, similar to what Joe might have expected in his Tennessee case. Kati may not have made it to trial, based on her maturity and consent under the unwelcomeness standard of the California FEPS, even though Tim Horton was convicted under section 261.5. Other teenagers should anticipate (if they are that forward thinking) that defense attorneys will use the *Starbucks* summary judgment opinion to defend sexual harassment and other civil rights and tort claims, brought by their parents, across the country. At least one judge has already cited *Starbucks* outside the employment context in a Title IX claim of abuse against a schoolteacher. Chapter 9 discusses that *Willits* case next.

CHAPTER NINE

Students Who "Lov'd Not Wisely but Too Well" and the Biases That Influence Adults in Judgment

. . . I pray you, in your letters,
When you shall these unlucky deeds relate,
Speak of me as I am; nothing extenuate,
Nor set down aught in malice. Then must you speak
Of one that lov'd not wisely but too well;
. . . .
Perplex'd in the extreme. . . .

—William Shakespeare, *Othello*

When I think of the Does and Joes, I am reminded of Shakespeare's treatment of Othello. Angry-mad in love and in a jealous rage, Othello behaves heinously, immorally. Crazy mad in love, teenagers behave foolishly, immorally. Perplexed in the extreme like Othello, these adolescents often profess deep love for the adults that abuse and exploit them. Iago, the consummate manipulator who orchestrated Othello's downfall, asserted,

> If the balance of our lives had not one scale of reason to poise another of sensuality, the blood and baseness of our natures would conduct us to most preposterous conclusions: but we have reason to cool our raging motions, our carnal stings, our unbitted lusts, whereof I take this that you call love to be a sect or scion.[1]

Iago concluded that reason cools "raging motions" and redirects lives from the "most preposterous conclusions." Ironically, reason did not save Othello from himself or Desdemona from her jealously mad husband. How poignant that the prefrontal cortex, the area of sober second thought, is only just developing in adolescence. Without the balancing influence of the prefrontal cortex, adolescents follow predatory manipulators to the most preposterous conclusions because of their teenage love.

Having shown how courts treat adolescents at work, *Sexual Exploitation of Teenagers* returns in this chapter to students, certain teens who "lov'd not wisely but too well." This chapter explores how Title VII and FEPS precedent has infiltrated the treatment of adult harassment and sexual abuse of teenagers at school. Beyond the schoolyard, though, this chapter also examines how the law, science, and various contexts really influence teen lives. What extenuations does one discover? What malice and bias affect the outcomes? Who are the critics of these "perplex'd" youth? What will become of future Does and Joes? What work is left undone regarding "these unlucky deeds"?

From Title VII and FEPS to Title IX and Section 1983—Sexual Harassment Law at Schools

Adolescents face harassment at school, a fact documented in chapter 2 and in the first US Supreme Court decision to rule on the issue, *Gebser v. Lago Vista Indep. Sch. Dist.* The *Gebser* Court reconfirmed that Title IX of the Education Amendments of 1972 prohibits discrimination in education, including sexual harassment, and applies to all federally funded schools.[2] States have similar antidiscrimination code provisions that apply to schools.[3] A number of cases address teen-adult sexual conduct in the context of Title IX or 42 U.S.C. § 1983.[4] Lawyers typically add the section 1983 claim against a public school employee to pursue a violation of the student's Fourteenth Amendment substantive due process liberty interest right to bodily integrity.[5]

Title IX and section 1983 cases raise some of the same issues as the more traditional tort claims but borrow heavily from Title VII jurisprudence. The *Gebser* Court affirmed, in a case involving harassment of a student by a teacher, that Title IX provides for a private right of action, but it also distinguished Title IX from Title VII. *Gebser* specifically created a new, more onerous proof for finding the responsible party liable. This chapter discusses the details of the *Gebser* changes to the Title VII standard. *Davis v. Monroe County Board of Education* also addressed the application of Title IX but in the context of peer sexual harassment. In *Davis*, the Court further refined the standard of proof in school sexual harassment cases. The Court explained that "a plaintiff must show harassment that is so *severe, pervasive, and objectively offensive*, and that so undermines and detracts from the victims' educational experience, that the victims are effectively denied equal access to an institution's resources and opportunities."[6] The standards of proof for liability delineated in both *Gebser* and *Davis* demonstrate that the law affords much more protection to working adults than it does to captive children at school. I acknowledge *Davis*'s use of Title VII precedent but do not review it in this discussion of adult-teen exploitation.

Gebser v. Lago Vista Independent School District

Alida Star Gebser (Jane Doe) was an eighth grader when she joined Frank Waldrop's high school book discussion group in the spring of 1991.[7] Neither the Supreme Court nor the Fifth Circuit court opinions mention Waldrop's age. However, a journalist reported that Waldrop was a fifty-year-old teacher at Lago Vista's high school.[8] (To put Waldrop's age in context, I note that he was six years younger than Justices Antonin Scalia and Anthony Kennedy, who dissented, and six years older than Justice Thomas, who joined Justice Sandra Day O'Connor and Chief Justice William Rehnquist in the majority opinion.)[9] The Fifth Circuit court opinion relates that Waldrop's wife was Alida's eighth-grade honors class teacher and referred Alida, then thirteen, to her husband's book group. They believed Alida needed more academic challenge.[10]

CRITICAL *GEBSER* FACTS. When Alida started high school later in 1992, Frank Waldrop became her ninth-grade social studies teacher. The Fifth Circuit court noted, "Waldrop went out of his way to flatter Doe [Alida] and spend time alone with her, and Doe enjoyed receiving attention from her instructor."[11] Was Waldrop "grooming" Alida? Were they falling in love? Given that Waldrop was thirty-seven years older than Alida, I would not characterize this relationship as one based on mutuality and equality. The courts' failure to mention Waldrop's age in their opinions as they recounted Alida's is surprising.

The Fifth Circuit court conveys the facts this way:

> Waldrop initiated sexual contact with her at her home in the spring of 1992. Knowing she would be alone, he visited under the pretext of returning a book and proceeded to fondle her breasts and unzip her pants. During the summer, Waldrop had sex on a regular basis with Doe, who was by then fifteen years old. None of the encounters took place on school property. The relationship ended in January of 1993, when a Lago Vista police officer happened to discover Waldrop and Doe having sex.[12]

Neither the Supreme Court nor the Fifth Circuit court opinion detailed that "Waldrop was given a 10-year suspended jail sentence after pleading no-contest to attempted sexual assault."[13] A suspended sentence? For *attempted* sexual assault? A criminal court handed down this sentence after police found Waldrop naked in the woods with Alida.[14] As we learned in our discussion of the Texas *Hernandez* case in chapter 4, however, Texas abandoned its promiscuity defense only in 1993, the same year that police found Waldrop naked with Alida in the woods. While these details may not be critical to an analysis of Title IX, they add to a complete understanding of the situation and case brought before the federal civil courts.

THE *GEBSER* NOTICE REQUIREMENT. Alida admitted that she told no one about the abuse, and her failure figured critically with the reviewing courts. The Lago Vista principal had received complaints from the parents and guardian of two other female students that Waldrop had made inappropriate comments to those young women. Waldrop denied the allegations and the principal did not inform the district superintendent.[15] Waldrop's reported behavior with these two other students did not make a difference in Alida's case. Both the Fifth Circuit court and the Supreme Court stressed that Lago Vista did not know of Waldrop's conduct with Alida. The Supreme Court held, "[W]e conclude that it would 'frustrate the purposes' of Title IX to permit a damages recovery against a school district for a teacher's sexual harassment of a student based on principles of *respondeat superior* [Latin for "let the master answer" (for the misdeeds of the employee servant)] or constructive notice, *i.e.*, without actual notice to a school district official." Thus, because Alida did not complain or report Waldrop's abuse, the Court opined that she could not recover for her injuries under Title IX.

By making Alida's failurc to report a major factor in its decision, the *Gebser* Court appears to blame the victim. If by issuing its opinion the Court meant to motivate youth to complain about harassment and discrimination, it probably failed in this endeavor. It is simply unrealistic to expect, or assume, that other thirteen-year-olds now know about the Court's *Gebser* holding. Moreover, even if a few teenagers have heard of it, it's unlikely that many would have the fortitude, emotional maturity, and synaptic function to reject or report the breast fondling and jeans unzipping of a respected high school honors teacher.

Is anyone surprised that Alida told no one? Apparently, the *Gebser* dissent was not. It reviewed the *Gebser* facts this way:

> Waldrop first sexually abused Gebser when he visited her house on the pretense of giving her a book that she needed for a school project. See App. 54a (deposition of Alida Star Gebser). Gebser, then a high school freshman, stated that she "was terrified": "He was the main teacher at the school with whom I had discussions, and I didn't know what to do." *Id.*, at 56a. Gebser was the only student to attend Waldrop's summer advanced placement course, and the two often had sexual intercourse during the time allotted for the class. See *id.*, at 60a. Gebser stated that she declined to report the sexual relationship because "if I was to blow the whistle on that, then I wouldn't be able to have this person as a teacher anymore." *Id.*, at 62a. She also stated that Waldrop "was the person in Lago administration . . . who I most trusted, and he was the one that I would have been making the complaint against." *Id.*, at 63a.[16]

I leave the citations in this dissent passage to share my conclusion that Alida Gebser was on trial for *her* failure to report her own abuse to school officials. The dissent drew its rendition of the *Gebser* facts from Alida's deposition, presumably because that source provided the most sympathetic recitation of the facts. However, it also clarifies that this teenager faced intense public scrutiny. In this *Gebser* dissent, one comes to understand how Waldrop cultivated the trust of this young student from a rural Texas town.

PROTECTION NOT DAMAGES? Shortly after Waldrop's arrest in the woods, Lago Vista fired Waldrop and the Texas Education Agency revoked his teaching license. Alida's mother filed suit on behalf of her daughter, alleging violations of Title IX, section 1983, and state personal injury claims against the school district and Waldrop. A federal district court granted a summary judgment motion against Alida and her mother, and they appealed only the Title IX decision.[17]

The Fifth Circuit court also ruled against Alida and her mother, and the US Supreme Court affirmed in a five-to-four decision. As noted, both appellate courts declined to impose strict liability under Title IX against the school district.[18] In particular, these courts wanted to avoid holding school districts, which are ignorant of the harassing and discriminating conduct of their rogue teachers, liable for money damages that might exceed their amount of federal funding. The *Gebser* Court distinguished Title VII and declared, "[W]hereas Title VII aims centrally to compensate victims of discrimination, Title IX focuses more on 'protecting' individuals from discriminatory practices carried out by recipients of federal funds."[19] This statement seems incongruous with the Court's *Faragher* and *Ellerth* decisions of that same year—1998.

When the *Faragher* Court crafted the affirmative defense for employers under Title VII, the Court stressed, "Although Title VII seeks 'to make persons whole for injuries suffered on account of unlawful employment discrimination,' its 'primary objective,' like that of any statute meant to influence primary conduct, is not to provide redress but to avoid harm."[20] This sentence contradicts the *Gebser* holding concerning Title VII's central purpose. Unfortunately for workers, the Court justifies Title VII's affirmative defense by suggesting that Title VII's central purpose is the *avoidance* of harm. Unfortunately for students, when the Court distinguishes Title IX, Title VII's central focus becomes *compensation,* and Title IX's central focus on protection of individuals from discrimination is distinguished. So much for consistency.

Moreover, the *Gebser* Court did not explain why the imposition of money damages under a strict liability approach against Lago Vista would be inconsistent with Title IX's goal of protecting individuals from discriminatory practices by federally funded schools and their employee agents. The *Gebser* dissent noted as much when it reviewed Waldrop's abuse of his authority over Alida, conferred by the school district. The dissent explained,

> The reason why the common law imposes liability on the principal [for the acts of its employee agents] in such circumstances is the same as the reason why Congress included the prohibition against discrimination on the basis of sex in Title IX: to induce school boards to adopt and enforce practices that

> will minimize the danger that vulnerable students will be exposed to such odious behavior. The rule that the Court has crafted creates the opposite incentive.[21]

One would think that a compensatory money judgment might just provide the motivating inducement for school districts to better screen and supervise their employees. True, Lago Vista could not have anticipated Waldrop's abuse of Alida Gebser. Presumably, however, the school and its insurers were better positioned to pay for Alida's damages than she (or her mother) was.

DELIBERATE INDIFFERENCE TO ABUSE AND THE BURDEN OF INJURIES. The *Gebser* majority elaborated on the requirement that an official, empowered to remedy the problem, have actual knowledge of the abuse. The Court further held that an informed school official must demonstrate "deliberate indifference to discrimination" for a damage claim to lie. The Court concluded, "Until Congress speaks directly on the subject, however, we will not hold a school district liable in damages under Title IX for a teacher's sexual harassment of a student absent actual notice and deliberate indifference."[22] This standard sets a very high legal threshold for traumatized children to satisfy. Moreover, given what we now know—that sexually abused youth often hide their abuse and shame—this standard is one that most victims will not meet. The *Gebser* dissent forecasted the predicament this way: "Presumably, few Title IX plaintiffs who have been victims of intentional discrimination will be able to recover damages under this exceedingly high standard. The Court fails to recognize that its holding will virtually 'render inutile causes of action authorized by Congress through a decision that *no* remedy is available.'"[23]

Finally, the *Gebser* dissent criticized the majority for its focus on the price of injuries that might exceed federal funding. The dissent first noted that courts have the power to order a *remittitur* (a reduction in damages awarded) should a verdict amount exceed federal funding of any given school.[24] Second, the dissent emphasized that, unlike the abused student, a school district could insure itself against such a risk of harm. Third, Justice John Stevens suggested, "As a matter of policy, the Court [majority] ranks protection of the school district's purse above the protection of immature high school students." Justice Stevens concluded, "Because those students are members of the class for whose special benefit Congress enacted Title IX, that policy choice is not faithful to the intent of the policymaking branch of our Government."[25]

Beyond Gebser—*Consent at School*

Gebser remains only guidance from the Supreme Court concerning adult-teen sexual relations under Title IX. Because Alida's consent to Waldrop's sexual solicitations were not at issue in *Gebser*, lower courts struggle with not only "deliberate indifference" and the nature of notice appropriate for a federally funded recipient, but also the legal meaning of consent following the *Gebser* decision.

For example, in *Benefield v. Board of Trustees of the University of Alabama*, the federal trial court in Alabama considered whether a fifteen-year-old college student could sue her university under Title IX for sexual harassment by classmates. The *Benefield* court ultimately ruled, "To constitute sexual harassment, the behavior in question must be unwelcome."[26] Because the court conflated acquiescence and consent, and did not consider capacity at all, it ruled that Benefield's consent constituted a complete defense. The *Benefield* court distinguished college students from elementary and secondary school students, however.[27] The court rejected Benefield's claim, holding that the university did not stand *in loco parentis*,[28] which *Black's Law Dictionary* defines as "[a]cting as a temporary guardian of a child." When an adult acts *in loco parentis*, typically the law will impose upon that person a higher duty of care for the child supervised. Ironically, when defining the noun, *Black's* refers to "[s]upervision of a young adult by an administrative body such as a university."[29] Possibly, *because* Benefield sued as a college student, the court interpreted Title IX more strictly. Other cases reveal that court treatment of juvenile consent under Title IX has been inconsistent and has not ultimately resulted in greater protection for youth.

MARY M. V. NORTH LAWRENCE COMMUNITY SCHOOL CORP. In *Mary M. v. North Lawrence Community School Corp.*, the Seventh Circuit court adopted a resolution different from the one accepted by the Alabama *Benefield* trial court. The *Mary M.* court reviewed a Title IX claim by a thirteen-year-old eighth-grader, Diane M., against a twenty-one-year-old cafeteria worker, Andrew Fields. Chief Judge Sarah Evans Barker had allowed evidence at trial concerning Diane's responses to Fields's sexual advances and whether Diane welcomed his attention. In 1997 the district court also permitted a jury instruction regarding whether Diane found the conduct unwelcome.[30] The instruction read,

> In order to find in favor of the Plaintiff, you must find first that the alleged sexual advances and/or abuses occurred, and if it did, that the advances and/or abuses were unwelcome by her. Conduct is unwelcome if Diane M. did not solicit or incite it, and if she regarded the conduct as undesirable or offensive. In determining whether the conduct was unwelcome, you should consider such things as Diane M.'s receptiveness to the alleged sexual advances and/or abuse in light of her words, acts and demeanor; her emotional predisposition, if any; the age disparity between her and Andrew Fields; any power disparity between them due to Diane M.'s status as a student and Andrew Field's status as a school employee.[31]

This instruction tracks the unwelcomeness requirement established for Title VII cases. And, consistent with the ED's OCR definition, this instruction also acknowledges the potential power disparity between an adult school worker and a minor.

THE *MARY M.* APPELLATE COURT DECISION. The appellate court "decline[d] to extend the [Title VII welcomeness] inquiry to Title IX cases when elementary students are involved." The court determined "that sexual harassment in the workplace is vastly different from sexual harassment in a school setting."[32] The court rejected the instruction and noted that in Indiana, where the harassment occurred, elementary school extends through the eighth grade (unlike other jurisdictions where junior high school starts with the eighth grade). The court added, "We decline to opine, however, on whether secondary school students can welcome sexual advances in harassment claims arising under Title IX."[33]

Despite the differences between school and work and the Seventh Circuit court's indecision regarding high school students, the *Mary M.* appellate court listed six reasons why sexual harassment at school deserves a special analysis. First, the court noted the greater ability of teachers and school officials to control behavior in the classroom, suggesting that "students look to their teachers for guidance as well as for protection." Second, the court explained that school harassment leaves a "longer lasting impact on its younger victims and institutionalizes sexual harassment as accepted behavior." Third, the court reasoned that while adults can leave a hostile work environment, children can rarely leave school. Fourth, the court emphasized that children need a nondiscriminatory environment in which to maximize their intellectual growth. The court stated, "A sexually abusive environment inhibits, if not prevents, the harassed student from developing her full intellectual potential and receiving the most from the academic program." Fifth, the court admonished that schools act *in loco parentis* while employers do not. Sixth, the court concluded that "employees are older and (presumably) know how to say no to unwelcome advances, while children may not even understand that they are being harassed."[34]

The third and sixth reasons reveal that the *Mary M.* appellate court assumed a workplace populated by adult workers. If one reviews the court's reasoning and substitutes adolescent workers for the adults, the court's analysis weakens, and the two environments (school and work) appear less distinct. For example, one might argue that sexual harassment at work leaves a lasting impact on young workers just as it does on young students. Additionally, as noted previously, many adolescent workers may not understand they are experiencing sexual harassment. Arguably, the court should have distinguished two different types of sexual harassment—harassment of children and harassment of adults—rather than two different environments. In other words, the unwelcomeness requirement may be appropriate as applied to adults (although many other feminists and I would dispute this assertion) but not as applied to minors, whether they are at school or at work.

MARY M.'S RELIANCE ON CRIMINAL LAW. Like many of the tort cases, the *Mary M.* case also raised the relevance of the criminal law's definition of the age of consent. Rejecting the idea of setting criminal and civil law at odds, the *Mary M.* court concluded,

> An opposite holding would defeat the purposes of Title IX and make children claiming sexual discrimination under Title IX subject to intense scrutiny. . . . If welcomeness were properly an issue for the jury in cases involving elementary students, the very children bringing the suits would be subject to intense scrutiny regarding their responses to their alleged abusers. Trial transcripts would be replete with insinuations that a child dressed or acted in such a manner as to ask for the very conduct she or he is seeking to redress. . . . We decline to allow the inference that an elementary school student is presumed to have not consented to molestation by a twenty-one year old in a criminal case, but welcomed the same conduct in a civil case.[35]

In this passage, the court acknowledged the inconsistency of a failure to apply a criminal law presumption in a civil case. More important, the *Mary M.* court understood that once a child's consent comes into evidence, the child goes on trial. Unlike the *Orangeburg* court, the *Mary M.* court eschewed the notion of putting a child on trial.[36] The *Mary M.* court "refused to transfer the onus on the child to prove that in fact she or he did not welcome the complained-of advances."[37]

Decided in 1997, *Mary M.* came before *Gebser* and more recent court treatment of adolescents working in the shadow of Title VII. More recent Title IX case law has been much less protective of students than *Mary M.*

CHANCELLOR V. POTTSGROVE SCHOOL DISTRICT. *Chancellor* was a 2007 Title IX and section 1983 case involving a seventeen-year-old student, Jeanette Chancellor, and her twenty-nine-year-old band teacher, Christian Oakes.[38] In addition to noting her age, the Chancellor court added, "From an early age, Plaintiff [Jeanette] struggled with depression, anorexia, and bulimia."[39] Presumably, the court added this information to indicate Jeanette's fragile condition and to alert the reader that Jeanette may not have had the fortitude to resist an adult seducer. Jeanette and Oakes engaged in sex on more than forty-five occasions during band camp, in the band room closet at school, in Oakes's car, and at a hotel during a band school trip. Allegedly, Oakes had sex with a second female student, A.P., in 2004. A.P.'s mother reported her suspicions to police officers, who investigated and interviewed Jeanette. Police later arrested Oakes who pled guilty to two counts of corruption of a minor. "Following Oakes's arrest, Plaintiff attempted suicide and was repeatedly hospitalized for psychiatric reasons, including major depressive disorder."[40] The *Chancellor* court ultimately ruled for the plaintiff, finding that Jeanette did not have the capacity to consent and that the principal's alleged conduct had been outrageous.[41]

THE *CHANCELLOR* ANALOGS. The *Chancellor* court focused on "two helpful analogs in determining whether Plaintiff had the capacity to consent to sex with Oakes." First, the court identified the custodial nature of the adult-teen relationship. The court suggested that the adult "by virtue of his position of custody or authority over" the minor renders her "incapable of offering her effective consent." To support this analog, the court offered the example of "a prisoner [who] lacks the capacity to consent to sex with her prison guard."[42] This analog applies directly in cases of sexual harassment of youth in prisons by adults that chapter 2 noted.

"The second helpful analog is the premise of statutory rape (or statutory sexual assault) and ages of consent. A minor under a certain age is legally unable to offer her consent . . . even if the sexual conduct was free of coercion or duress."[43] The *Chancellor* court announced, "Pottsgrove, however, conflates the question of whether Plaintiff 'consented' to Oakes's sexual advances with the question of whether Plaintiff (a high school student in Oakes's class) had the legal capacity to consent to the sex. If Plaintiff lacked the capacity to consent, of course, she did not have the capacity to 'welcome' Oakes's sexual advances."[44] The *Chancellor* court continued, "[M]any states have 'corruption of minors' laws, [prohibiting] sexual conduct with sixteen- and seventeen-year-olds—minors who are above the age of consent for statutory rape purposes. . . . In other words, at least in the corruption of minors context, a minor lacks the capacity to consent to sex with an adult."[45]

The criminal offense label "corruption of minors," to which the *Chancellor* court referred, suggests that society views sexually active older teenagers as "tainted" and "corrupted." Chapter 3 noted this view in its discussion of Dr. Suzanne M. Sgroi and sexual abuse. In finding for Jeanette, the *Chancellor* court also rejected guidance from the ED's OCR.

CHANCELLOR'S CRITIQUE OF OCR GUIDANCE. The *Chancellor* court acknowledged that the OCR, the US agency charged with oversight of Title IX, takes a stance different from the one adopted in *Chancellor*. OCR presumes that secondary students may consent to sex with a teacher in some cases and "lists a number of factors to be considered in determining whether the conduct could be considered 'welcome.' Age, relationship of the student and teacher, and disability, according to the [ED], should be considered in the totality-of-the-circumstances test."[46] These factors were also embedded in the jury instructions that Judge Sarah Evans Barker logically permitted in *Mary M.*, which were later rejected by the Seventh Circuit *Mary M.* court.

Chancellor critiqued the OCR's guidance for three reasons. First, *Chancellor* accused ED of "conflat[ing] consent with the capacity to consent," the same error committed by the Pottsgrove School District. The *Chancellor* court emphasized that *actual* consent is not the same as *legal* consent and may not signal legal capacity to consent. This reasoning mirrors that of Chief Justice George's *Tobias* concurrence, discussed in chapter 8. Second, the *Chancellor* court stressed that OCR imported the "totality of the circumstances" test from Title VII jurisprudence. The *Chancellor* court reasoned that *capacity* to welcome a supervisor's conduct or advances is not part of the Title VII inquiry. Rather, the question under Title VII centers on whether the target actually welcomed the conduct. Therefore, Title VII does not work for an evaluation focused on juveniles. Finally, the *Chancellor* court rejected the OCR guidance as unworkable, practically speaking. The court explained that under the OCR's guidance, a high school teacher might violate Title IX with one student but not with another in the same class because "they [the students] are of a different age or mental capacity or the sex occurs under slightly different circumstances. . . . In this situation, a murky line is worse than a bright one."[47] In this passage, one reads the court's frustration with line-drawing-based factors such as chronological age.

DOE V. WILLITS UNIFIED SCHOOL DISTRICT. The 2010 California *Willits* case considered both the *Mary M.* and *Chancellor* cases but found against the minor plaintiff. The *Willits* case adumbrates potential issues under Title IX for teenagers across the country. *Willits* Doe, a fifteen-year-old student, "agreed" to have sexual relations with her thirty-eight-year-old teacher, Clint Smith.[48] Few details came to light about the case from the *Willits* trial court opinion because the court made no summary disposition of the lawsuit and merely decided a discovery dispute before the case settled out of court. Specifically, the court responded to a controversy over whether defense counsel could explore *Willits* Doe's past sexual activity. The court explained that because Doe sought damages, in part, for a torn hymen allegedly caused by Smith, the defense should be permitted to question her about it. The court suggested that questions might include those concerning nonsexual activity and "whether she [Doe] engaged in any sexual activity, other than intercourse with Smith, that *may have caused* the torn hymen. If, and only if, plaintiff responds in the affirmative, defendants may ask follow-up questions to learn the basic (but not explicit) details of the particular sexual activity."[49]

Thus, the court sanctioned discovery during the continuation of Doe's deposition of *any* related sexual activity with anyone, including a peer. Because of the nature of Doe's injury (the loss of her virginity), rules of evidence and discovery that normally prohibit exploration of a victim's sexual history did not protect Doe. If Doe had engaged in related sexual activity with another person, by pursuing her lawsuit and revealing this prior activity, she also risked her prior partner's prosecution as a possible sex offender. At the very least she risked embarrassing herself and that other partner in front of her parents, the court, and the greater community. Then again, if she was not a virgin, Smith had a right to defend himself, despite the fact that he was Doe's teacher and twenty-three years older than she was. Smith's guilty plea in the criminal court to one count of unlawful sex with a minor under sixteen and receipt of a six-month county jail sentence with thirty-six months of probation may not have made a difference in the civil case.[50]

The *Willits* court acknowledged that other Ninth Circuit courts had incorporated Title VII's unwelcomeness requirement but had not specifically addressed whether the unwelcomeness requirement is properly considered in cases in which a minor alleges sexual harassment at an educational institution.[51] The court found that cases outside the Ninth Circuit had explored whether consent is an element of a Title IX case. In each of those cases, consent was not at issue and did not constitute a defense. The *Willits* court discussed both *Mary M.* and *Chancellor v. Pottsgrove Sch. Dist.*

WILLITS AFTER *MARY M.* AND *CHANCELLOR*. The *Willits* court discerned from both *Mary M.* and *Chancellor* that it should not conflate welcomeness or consent with capacity to consent. Moreover, when capacity is absent, the court concluded that any evidence of welcomeness or consent is irrelevant as a matter of law.[52] This analysis demonstrates that the *Willits* court recognized the complexity of the issue. The court evinced the distinction between "voluntary and willing participation" and capacity to consent, which may produce actual, legally significant consent. The *Willits* court seemed persuaded by the reasoning from other courts regarding the issues of capacity to consent and adolescent consent to sexual activity with an adult.[53]

In a footnote, however, the *Willits* court explained that California case law is unsettled regarding the relevance of consent, citing *Tobias* and *Donaldson*.[54] The court then ruled on the discovery of Doe's consent, finding that cases have resolutely held that consent and welcomeness are not elements of a Title IX claim. Still, because the *Willits* court refused to define the elements for the cause of action, it held that questions on the issue of welcomeness and consent with regard to the minor's sexual relationship with an adult constituted permissible discovery.[55]

This compromise and acknowledgement of the *Tobias* dictum, next adopted in *Donaldson*, essentially ensured that Doe would face invasive, humiliating, and perhaps traumatizing inquiries by defense counsel during the continuation of her deposition. One could expect that defense counsel would focus on whether Doe set limits with her thirty-eight-year-old teacher, thus casting *Willits* Doe as the "responsible" actor.

News articles, not referenced in the *Willits* court opinion, gave more details about the Doe-Smith liaison, details that the defense counsel could also use. For example, the district attorney suggested that Doe at least acquiesced to the sexual conduct. One news article reported, "The relationship, believed to have taken place over several months, was not forced, [Mendocino County District Attorney Meredith] Lintott said. But a 15-year-old cannot legally consent to a sexual relationship with a 38-year-old, she said." Despite what the district attorney believed, the *Willits* civil judge left it open as to whether Doe could legally consent and ruled to allow discovery on the matter. Smith's guilty plea to one count of unlawful sex with a minor under sixteen (Penal Code section 261.5) and receipt of a six-month county jail sentence with thirty-six months of probation may not have made a difference in the civil case.[56]

The *Willits* discovery ruling highlights how the conflicts in California put American teenagers at risk. It also threatens to chill future reporting of sexual exploitation. A teenager, who understands that she may have to endure rigorous examination in front of her parents and strangers on whether she "came-on" to an adult teacher, may opt not to report offensive conduct at all. Because the *Willits* case began as a Title IX filing, it could serve as guidance in other federal Title IX cases across the nation. Critics might argue that other states will not follow California into the legal tangle created by *Tobias* and the inconsistent treatment of adolescent consent. Still, do parents really want to take that chance with their teenage children? Appendix 2 makes clear that conflicts between state criminal and civil law already exist in a number of states across the nation.

One might argue that inconsistent treatments do not always result in illogical results. For example, people can understand that a criminal jury might acquit O. J. Simpson of the murder of his wife and that a civil jury might convict him. Those outcomes are inconsistent, but they are not illogical. The burden of proof for criminal conviction, proof "beyond a reasonable doubt," is much more rigorous than that for civil liability, proof by "a preponderance of the evidence."[57] The O. J. criminal trial jury apparently did not have enough evidence to convict on the higher standard. If the burdens are stricter in a criminal case, however, the adult respondent who engages in sexual intercourse with a teenager should more likely face liability in civil court. Since 2001 that outcome does not necessarily follow in California if the teenager consented. Now California's criminal laws function much more restrictively than do the civil laws regarding the same episode. An adult who has sex with a minor might go to jail for unlawful sex with a minor who consented to his sexual advances. He cannot use her consent as a legal defense. However, that same consent might bar the teenager from civil damages recovery under Title VII, Title IX, and common law. It operates as a complete defense for the civil respondent. One wonders whether there is any other area of law in which civil liability attaches much less readily than criminal guilt. And, if not, one wonders why. I suggest here that bias against sexually active youth, and particularly teenage girls, explains the difference.

Sexual Harassment: From the Court of Law to the Court of Public Opinion

The incongruence of criminal and civil laws makes no sense and penalizes consenting youth who, arguably, have been sexually exploited. The state exacts its retribution on the perpetrator, but the juvenile cannot seek recompense for her injuries. Some jurists might argue that the new California case law marks a liberated, if misguided, appreciation of adolescent autonomy and maturity.[58] Others might insist that it reflects a latent misogyny against "promiscuous" teenage girls. One argument suggests that consenting girls are "bad" girls who should not collect "awards." Therefore, the judiciary credits their consent as legally significant in the suit for civil damages. The young women are, thereby, barred from "reward" for their licentious conduct. However, this reasoning and associated approach is incongruent with the current scientific neuroscience findings discussed in chapter 3.

Professor Tom Lininger's Study of Rape Victims' Civil Suits

This treatment of consenting teenagers may remind some scholars of a study by Professor Tom Lininger. He looked at the incidents of rape victim impeachments following the accuser's pursuit of civil tort claims against the rapist. Lininger emphasized that criminal court judges permit the harsh impeachment of accusers who bring civil claims. Lininger explained, "Criminal defense attorneys tell juries that accusers forfeit their credibility when they file civil suits." He referenced many recent examples of this defense strategy and noted appellate reversals of judges who quashed the tactic. Lininger suggested, "The judiciary seems more suspicious of rape suits than of suits seeking damages for other crimes. While lawsuits by victims of automobile accidents can proceed without objection alongside criminal prosecutions for the same conduct, rape suits bespeak corrupt motives that undermine criminal prosecutions."[59] Lininger concluded that society sees rape victims who sue for civil damages as "corrupt"—and perhaps even consenting. His review of this judicial backlash against civilly assertive rape victims lends support for the hypothesis that society has not abandoned the old stereotypes that valued "abstinence from sexual indulgence on the part of a young woman."[60]

Lininger also explained that "jurors generally distrust accusers in rape prosecutions. In particular, jurors' cognition seems prone to an ulteriority heuristic: confronted with fact patterns in which one or more parties appear to have acted irrationally, jurors too readily accept the explanation that the accuser has lied or exaggerated to serve selfish goals." He equated juror "instinctive prejudice" prompted by the accuser's parallel civil litigation to the prejudice inflamed by evidence of the accuser's prior sexual history.[61] All this discussion of inflamed prejudice leads one to question how jurors, and even judges, respond to teenagers who consent to sexual intercourse.

Cultural Attitudes and Willits

Polling highlights some cultural attitudes. According to one health journalist, European and American attitudes concerning teenage sexuality differ significantly, but the views of researchers in both regions reflect European attitudes. Researchers "agree that the mixed message America sends to teens about sex—authorities say 'don't' while mass media screams 'What are you waiting for?'—endanger our children."[62] Recall Dr. Sgroi's comment that people commonly "believed that youthful victims of sexual abuse had 'lost their innocence' and become contaminated in a way that made them seductive and dangerous."[63] This comment echoes the notion of corruption and contamination that Professor Lininger described as associated with rape survivors who sue civilly. Again, one must evaluate whether American society sees consenting youth, particularly girls, as morally corrupt and undeserving, not only of damage awards but also of society's sympathy and protection.

Another problem is that many parents do not realize that their teens are sexually active. Chapter 3 reviewed studies regarding teen-parent communication about sex. A question arises concerning the significance of parental ignorance, when parents do not associate their children with early sexual activity. More specifically, one wonders whether parents (including judges and jurors) disassociate their "good," sexually inactive children from "bad," sexually active ones, ignorant of the fact that most teens have had sex by the time they are 18.[64]

The *Willits* case and the underlying criminal prosecution against Clint Smith support the need to scrutinize cases for underlying motivations, including this type of bias and latent misogyny. About Clint Smith's criminal case, one commentator wrote,

> All the nice people standing [at the sentencing hearing] in silent support of their hero, the fallen physics teacher, seemed to regard Smith as the victim of the 15-year-old, Jezebel the sophomore. Or, if not her victim, just a guy who was too darn nice to turn down the gift of young flesh.[65]

Interpreting the crowd's sentiment, the observer, Bruce Anderson, referred to Doe as a Jezebel. In the *Bible*, Jezebel represents the powerful, evil prostitute who leads men to their ruin.

In the *Book of Revelation*, God said about Jezebel,

> You tolerate that woman Jezebel, who calls herself a prophetess. By her teaching she misleads my servants into sexual immorality and the eating of food sacrificed to idols. I have given her time to repent of her immorality, but she is unwilling. So I will cast her on a bed of suffering, and I will make those who commit adultery with her suffer intensely, unless they repent of her ways.[66]

This biblical verse not only condemns Jezebel and her adulterous partners, it also disapproves God's "servants" who "tolerate" Jezebel and her immoral ways. One can imagine how a devout community might feel the need to excise the Jezebels who lead their otherwise righteous teachers to their moral demise.

Anderson's interpretation of crowd sentiment and metaphoric description of a fifteen-year-old high school coed recasts Doe as a danger in the community and as one who must repent. She carries the responsibility for corrupting men who would commit adultery with her. Clearly, Anderson was disturbed by the Smith-allied crowd's attitude toward *Willits* Doe.

Just as one might question the *Donaldson* court's characterization of Donaldson's seduction of his sister-in-law as "troubling,"[67] Anderson questioned the crowd's loyal support of Smith:

> One has to wonder if all the people standing for Smith, who included Smith's father-in-law, Roger Hearn, would have remained standing if they'd seen the videos Smith had sent his young love, those charming little movies Smith made of himself masturbating. Smith sent his 15-year-old lots of those, dispatched them so heedlessly that the 15-year-old's 12-year-old sister saw them too, a premature lesson for the younger child of the joys awaiting her at the Willits Charter School.[68]

This quote emphasizes the particularly graphic and disturbing nature of Smith's conduct. Anderson's satiric description of the "joys awaiting . . . at the Willits Charter School" reinforces that such predators threaten not just older teenagers but younger children too.

Community attitudes reflect not only the views of devout Christians who believe in God's teaching about Jezebel, but also views of a broader cross section, including judges and jurors. Chapter 7 reviewed Professor Susan Estrich's comparisons between the rape consent standard and the sexual harassment unwelcomeness standard. Recall that Estrich focused on judges who "tend to see sex, not rape. Similarly, in Title VII cases they see sex, not sexual harassment. In both types of cases, they are often wrong. That a certain relationship might be appropriate does not necessarily mean that the man's behavior has been."[69]

Estrich highlights the role of judges in the interpretation of female acquiescence. Their beliefs, Estrich suggests, taint their decisions. Her arguments, extended for teenagers dealing with sexual harassment or adult sexual advances, are even more compelling.[70] Even if lawmakers decline to eliminate the unwelcomeness requirement for adults, they might do so for adolescents and still justify the inconsistent treatment of consent.

Judicial Bias and the New Legal Process Theory

The *Willits* case also raises the question of judicial bias. Bruce Anderson was particularly concerned about it:

> All the other charges against Smith had been dropped by Judge Brennan, the loosest judge in Mendocino County, maybe the loosest judge anywhere. Those charges included lewd and lascivious acts with a child; oral copulation with a child under the age of 16; sexual penetration with a foreign object; sexual intercourse with a minor; and providing harmful matter to a minor with the intent of seduction.

Anderson calls Judge Brennan "the loosest judge in Mendocino County." Ironically, loose is also a term used to describe wanton women.[71] However, here the term refers to the judge's lax principles and freedom from moral restraint. Did the judge also think of *Willits* Doe as a Jezebel?

A few judicial opinions reflect the attitude that sexually active teenagers are morally corrupt, tainted, and perhaps even dangerous. Professors Edward Rubin and Malcolm Feeley have commented on the influences that affect judicial reasoning. In 1996 Rubin and Feeley published their conclusions about how personal beliefs influence judicial decision making and legal policy.[72] Concerning their New Legal Process Theory, Rubin and Feeley suggested that phenomenology explains judicial decision making. Rubin and Feeley wrote, "Phenomenology focuses on the lived experience of human beings, and on their desire to create meaning for themselves out of the disparate forces that act upon them."

Rubin and Feeley next defined "new institutionalism" as "the functional and dysfunctional elements of institutional structure . . . created by and embedded in complex social environments." Melding phenomenology and the new institutionalism, Rubin and Feeley advocated for "a microanalysis of institutions that links the conceptual behavior of individuals to the output of institutional structures." They noted, "It is a linkage that has already been developed by both economists and sociologists; applied to law, it becomes a tool for analyzing the previously impenetrable process of judicial lawmaking." In their work, Rubin and Feeley examined "the factors that motivate individual judges when they create new legal doctrine." Rubin and Feeley characterized the factors "as existing doctrine, personal belief or attitude, and the desire to integrate the two.[73] At the core of Rubin and Feeley's theory rests the notion that judges' beliefs and biases, as well as legal doctrine and court precedent, will influence judicial decisions.

Rubin and Feeley posited that when political actors such as legislators and executives fail to remedy chronic or glaring social problems, judges often provide remedies through legal decisions and, in the process, create public policy.[74] Professors Rubin and Feeley acknowledged that such judicial response might constitute "a second best solution."[75] However, they argued, "There is no reason why the courts should decline to carry out this task, at least where a moral imperative for doing so exists."[76] They also suggested that legal scholarship directed at judges factors in political realities, as well as public-oriented considerations, to make recommendations for judge-sponsored legal reform.[77]

The inconsistent legal treatment of adolescent consent across the nation and within the criminal and civil law systems may exist in part because of judicial activism and beliefs about teenage sex. Rubin and Feeley expressed great confidence that judges can make sound public policy when their approach is "pragmatic, cautious, and incremental."[78] However, as recently as 2003, Rubin and Feeley conceded, "The revived legal process school acknowledges self-interested and ideological motivations [of decision-makers]."[79] No matter the reason for the current conflict of laws regarding teenage consent, legislatures have not acted to cure the problem. Thus, legal scholarship should consider judicial ideological perspectives and offer advice for legal reform.

JUDICIAL BIAS IN CASE PRECEDENT. Given the statistics concerning adolescent sexual activity, one might readily agree that some judges, even as teenagers, may have had "consensual relations" with underage girls. Such illicit activity might make sitting judges generally sympathetic, consciously or not, to adult consorts like Donaldson (the realtor) and Nayman (the ice creamery manager). Additionally, some judges may view particular girls as sexually irresistible and therefore dangerous. Support for such hypotheses exists in judicial opinions.

In 1999 the South Carolina Supreme Court ruled in *Doe by Roe v. Orangeburg County School District* that a fourteen-year-old's consent to sexual battery was admissible as to the issue of damages but not as to liability.[80] Quoting *Barnes v. Barnes*, a challenge to the Indiana Rape Shield Statute, the *Orangeburg* court reasoned that "the plaintiff in a civil damage action is 'on trial' in the sense that he or she is an actual party seeking affirmative relief from another party. Such plaintiff is a voluntary participant, with strong financial incentive to shape the evidence that determines the outcome."[81] This holding suggests that both the South Carolina and Indiana courts were prone to Professor Lininger's ulteriority heuristic. Ironically, the *Orangeburg* plaintiff was not "on trial" because the target victim was not old enough to sue in her own name. Roe sued for Doe. According to court records, Roe was the "voluntary participant," not the fourteen-year-old child.

One sees similar concerns by a court in *LK v. Reed*, the case of a thirteen-year-old special education student who "agreed" to have sex with an eighteen-year-old special education high school junior. The *LK* court worried that "a girl could provoke a criminal prosecution against a sexual partner *and* recover damages from him, both as a result of her willful and voluntary actions in consenting to, or instigating, a sexual liaison."[82] Whether or not damages were appropriate in the *LK* case, this court ignored the fact that most adult men are not mentally challenged and can "Just Say No" to a "naughty" teenager.[83] Liability avoidance in all of these cases is not expensive for the adult "victim" respondent.[84]

JUDICIAL BIAS REGARDING DOES AND JOE. Even when the court appears to understand the complexities of adolescent behavior, bias or stereotypes may influence a decision. As previously noted, in *Doe v. Oberweis Dairy*, Judge Richard Posner referred to Doe as possibly a "siren."[85] Here one finds yet another literary reference to a woman who lures men to their demise. How ironic that the logo for Starbucks coffee is a siren.[86] Posner also commented, "Nor are American teenage girls such blushing violets that sexual badinage is harassment per se."[87] These references to Doe and American teenage girls appear somewhat cynical—perhaps even cynically hostile. "[S]exual badinage," playful banter,[88] is an odd turn of phrase to describe conduct from a supervisor who would "'grope,' 'kiss,' 'grab butts,' 'hug,' and give 'tittie twisters' to these employees, including the plaintiff."[89]

The *Oberweis* appellate court also distinguished this case from other sexual harassment cases and suggested, "If Doe was sneaking around behind her mother's—and her employer's—back and thus facilitating Nayman's behavior, the employer may be able to show that the harm she suffered that was caused by its violation of Title VII (if such a violation is found on remand), rather than by Nayman, was minimal."[90] This passage portrays Doe as possibly corrupt, engaging in covert activity. But was this behavior really covert? Maybe her mother did not know, but certainly most of the ice-cream shop employees did.[91] The same can be said for much of the conduct involving *Starbucks*'s Doe. Judge Posner's characterization makes *Oberweis* Doe an accomplice in her own exploitation, something that even the *Tobias* court held is not an appropriate casting for minor victims of incest. Do minor victims of predatory workplace supervisors deserve less protection?

Additionally, the *Oberweis* appellate court found,

> The district judge ruled that the plaintiff was not harassed, because she welcomed Nayman's advances. In so ruling, however, the judge stepped out of the proper role of a judge asked to decide a motion for summary judgment and made findings on contested factual issues relating to the plaintiff's dealings with Nayman, as when the judge said that "once, Nayman gave Plaintiff a hug and kiss in an effort to make Plaintiff happy," or that "Nayman also 'playfully' hit Plaintiff on the behind with a rag on one occasion."[92]

District court judge John Darrah's minimization of the rampant sexual conduct was perhaps not the only problem. One might argue that his treatment of the facts reflected more pervasive adult male bias. Professors Rubin and Feeley might consider Judge Darrah's conclusions emblematic of the phenomenology of judicial decision making. The question is how Judge Darrah could rule that plaintiff "welcomed" Nayman's advances, at legal issue in the prima facie case, if she did not have *legal capacity* to consent under Illinois law.

Even after criticizing Judge Darrah's summary conclusions, the *Oberweis* appellate court adopted, in dicta, his treatment of Doe's consent for the damages phase of the case. Specifically, the appellate court ruled that while underage consent is no defense at the liability phase, it is admissible at the damages phase of trial. The *Oberweis* appellate court relied on an analog to make its point, "In a negligence case brought by an exchange student against the company that had placed her with a couple and the husband raped her, we said that it would have been error to instruct the jury that because Kristin was below the age of consent her comparative fault must be reckoned at zero. That would have given too much force to the criminal statute in this civil case." The court added that the legislature's creation of criminal sex offense "cannot be considered a legislative judgment that minors are utterly incapable of avoiding becoming ensnared in sexual relationships."[93] This reasoning takes us back to a comparative negligence perspective and completely misses the fact that legal capacity is an all-or-nothing test. Does society really want to penalize people who are developing capacity?

This reasoning is completely consistent with the findings in *Donaldson* and *Starbucks* and is therefore inconsistent with state criminal law treatment of adolescent consent. In this dictum regarding damages, the *Oberweis* appellate court negated Illinois statutory rape law and, arguably, placed the burden on the minor to "avoid[] becoming ensnared in sexual relationships."[94] Thus, within federal civil law, adolescent consent receives inconsistent legal treatment at the liability and damage phases. The age of consent takes another hit. Some scholars, and most parents, may wonder what "moral imperative" justifies this type of judicial legal policy making.[95]

Nature and Developing Capacity vs. Nurture and Social Conditioning

If teenagers are developing capacity, then treating them with full legal capacity makes little sense. Moreover, comparative negligence penalizes teenagers for a natural stage of development—adolescence. But what if "adolescence" does not exist? What if the court of public opinion and popular culture are the schoolyards that form and inform our teenagers? Dr. Robert Epstein suggested that adolescence does not exist. Scientists and other scholars might readily dismiss Epstein's views, but I would be remiss in not covering his alternative perspective.

Epstein argued, "Claims of a teen brain constitute scientific fraud, in my view."[96] Epstein asserted that "it is dangerous to presume that snapshots of activity in certain regions of the brain necessarily provide useful information about the causes of thought, feeling and behavior."[97] Epstein claims that any unique features of the teen behavior that researchers attribute to adolescent brain development result from social influences and that adolescent developmental changes do not cause "teen turmoil." He suggests that if the "teen brain" were a developmental phenomenon, we would see "teen turmoil" around the world and we do not. Epstein maintains that US culture has created the "artificial extension of childhood[,]" infantilizing young adults.[98] Noting studies by Giedd, Sowell, Luna, and others, Epstein stresses, "I have not been able to find even a single study that establishes a *causal* relation between the properties of the brain being examined and the problems we see in teens. [I]maging studies are correlational, showing simply that activity in the brain is associated with certain behavior or emotion."[99] Many researchers might agree with Epstein on this last point.

Epstein's argument is that teens "are extraordinarily competent, even if they do not normally express that competence." Epstein's explanation for teen misbehavior is cultural insistence on their infantilization. He reasons that because "teens [are] trapped in the frivolous world of peer culture, they learn virtually everything they know from one another rather than from the people they are about to become."[100] I agree that teenagers can display great discipline, talent, and maturity.

However, I think Epstein oversimplifies the explanation for teen turmoil. Moreover, he offers no robust scientific evidence to support his claims. Teens learn not just from each other. As chapter 2 noted and as demonstrated by each of the Does and Joes, teenagers also learn from adults. From savvy adult marketing agents to 50 Cent to the Clint Smiths and Tim Hortons of the world, teenagers learn about fashion, sex, and ultimately, sexual exploitation. One cannot simply blame teenagers for their poor indoctrination of each other.

Epstein also hypothesized that teenagers "act out" in adult ways because we have isolated and "wrongly treated [them] like children. . . . Almost without exception, the reckless and irresponsible behavior we see is the teen's way of declaring his or her adulthood or, through pregnancy or the commission of serious crime, of instantly becoming an adult under the law."[101] Again Epstein oversimplified the problem. Adults treat teenagers inconsistently, sometimes like adults and sometimes like children. For example, some public school boards responsible for school curriculums consider sexual activity exclusively for married adults and decline to offer teenagers comprehensive sex education. Our nation might see fewer pregnancies and cases of STIs if all of our children received comprehensive sex education.[102] At the same time, some adults expect teenagers to "avoid[] becoming ensnared in sexual relationships" that these same adults might have difficulty avoiding. The law should not treat teenagers like adults when adults have not prepared them to assume adult responsibilities. For example, transfer of teenagers to adult criminal courts hardly prepares them for the literal trials that follow. The MacArthur Study evidence, noted in chapter 3, supports this assertion.

Epstein concluded, "Fortunately, we also know from extensive research both in the U.S. and elsewhere that when we treat teens like adults, they almost immediately rise to the challenge."[103] When jurists try teenagers as adults, society often finds that they (the teenagers) do not "rise to the challenge," especially in adult prisons where they are most likely to be the victims of rape and sexual assault. It is not that teenagers are incapable of rising to the challenge. They simply need time and training. Time and training, growth and experimentation contribute to developing capacity.

Epstein's focus takes one back to the historic nature versus nurture debate. Are people who they are because of their genes, brains, and biology? Or do social influences explain conduct? This is one debate that society won't solve any time soon. And, it really does not matter from where the teenage predisposition to take great risks derives. As confirmed in chapter 3, they do, and they sometimes suffer for it. American society should play it safe and strike a balance: call adolescent development both nature and nurture. Having taught and raised teenagers, I find this compromise more logical anyway. Adults can then take Epstein's concerns and harmonize his views with the research of adolescent neurological and psychosocial maturation. Jurists can reform law to account for developing capacity *and* treat teenagers like the adults they are about to (but have not yet) become.

Righting Wrongs

Why, the wrong is but a wrong i' th' world; and having the world for your labour, 'tis a wrong in your own world, and you might quickly make it right.

—*Othello*, act 4, scene 3, 78–79 (Emilia to Desdemona)

As one contemplates that US culture contributes to teen turmoil (and trauma), one must acknowledge that such a wrong in the world is ours to make right. As a few adults initiate, perpetuate, and fail to cure the sexual abuse of teenagers, all adults must accept that, currently, only adults have the power to change laws and create rights. A response to corrupted US culture, inconsistent laws, and sexual exploitation starts with responsible adults. We need to get wiser as we deal with adolescents and their developing capacities. If teenagers "love not wisely but too well," then how can we expect them to be wise if we do not model that trait ourselves and if we fail to teach them well?

Wisdom comes from experience and reflection on that experience. Wisdom is difficult, therefore, to transfer. The poet and philosopher Kahlil Gibran advised, "The teacher who is indeed wise does not bid you to enter the house of his wisdom but rather leads you to the threshold of your mind."[104] I suggest that we follow Gibran's advice and lead American teenagers to the threshold of their minds (and brains).

CHAPTER TEN

Becoming Wiser

Public Policy, Developing Capacity, the Law, and Legal Assent

Wisdom is knowing what to do next; virtue is doing it.

—David Starr Jordan, president of Indiana University, 1884–1891; president of Stanford University, 1891–1913

Becoming Wiser

Sexual Exploitation of Teenagers has examined the cases of six profiled teenagers and numerous more in the process of exploring three questions. First, this book has explored whether teenagers face more sexual harassment than do adults. Second, it has investigated whether they are developmentally different than adults and, if so, whether these differences influence how they deal with sexual abuse by adults. Third, it has analyzed whether civil law, as opposed to criminal law, is congruent with adolescent developing capacity. In other words, *Sexual Exploitation of Teenagers* has evaluated whether current sexual harassment law adequately protects teenagers who are responding to sexual advances by adults.

The scientific evidence and legal information that this book has offered provide clear answers to those questions. First, chapter 2 confirms that, in some contexts, teenagers do encounter more sexual harassment at work and at school than adults do. I suspect teenagers face much more in many other arenas as well. One just cannot know because adults do not monitor these environments sufficiently or keep adequate records.

Second, chapter 3's discussion of neuroscience and psychosocial studies indicates that teenagers are not mini-adults but are developmentally different from fully mature adults. Teenagers are developing capacity with unique and changing traits and developmental needs. Therefore, one should not assume that, as a population, teens make decisions and act as the law expects and anticipates adults will. Third, chapters 4 through 9 have reviewed US criminal and civil law and the law's treatment of teenagers. State and federal laws vary and are sometimes inconsistent in their treatment of adolescent acquiescence and "consent." Does the law adequately protect teenagers? My response is an emphatic *no*. The stories of the six profiled teenagers demonstrate that the law does not. I hope you now agree that American personal injury and sexual harassment laws need reform.

The inconsistency in the treatment of adolescent consent by the civil and criminal systems poses a jurisprudential puzzle. If the inconsistency offered some truly constructive advantage, one might argue for the maintenance of the status quo. The arguments offered to explain it, however, range from unconvincing to outright silly. They lead one to conclude that no such advantage exists and that the systems have simply evolved inconsistently and incongruently.

One stated explanation for affording adolescent consent legal significance, seen in the civil case law, centers on the need in civil cases to evaluate the existence and extent of a plaintiff's damages. As the discussion of *Mama Taori's* demonstrated, however, consent does not measure or even indicate damages. Alternative avenues for the exploration of a plaintiff's injuries exist. Thus, the critical evaluation of the plaintiff's injuries cannot justify treatment of adolescent consent that is inconsistent with the criminal statutory rape scheme or with conclusions based on scientific evidence regarding adolescent neurological and psychosocial development.

A second proposed justification for the inconsistent treatment of adolescent consent relates to the protection of adults who extracted that consent. Those who "counted on" the "yes." However, does society really want to protect adults who are already in violation of criminal law, and at the expense of teenagers, from responsibility in the civil context? Does society really want to protect those adults who have used our children as merely a means to a particular end? If society does not allow the consent to protect these offenders from jail time, why does society protect abusive adults from civil damages? Society should expect these adults to know (and behave!) better when dealing with teenagers. I suggest that these adults should owe a moral and legal duty to treat these teens not simply as mere means.

As *Sexual Exploitation of Teenagers* shows, the law's consent scheme is a poor, all-or-nothing framework within which jurists address adult-teen sexual relations. It ignores that juveniles may lack full legal capacity. It conflates *actual* consent and *legal* consent. Public policy concerning the treatment of adolescent consent deserves attention and revision. Scientific evidence and social science studies (as far as they can) should inform the revision to secure for minors a legal standard that properly accounts for their constitutional liberties as well as their developmental abilities and needs.

A Synthesis for a Future Approach

If wisdom involves lessons from the past and knowledge applied for the future, then jurists need to come up with a wiser approach. Adults need to better protect maturing children. Society should not endorse the maintenance of the status quo. It is simply too illogical and provides too little or inconsistent protection for developing teenagers. Moreover, it perpetuates outdated moral judgments concerning nonmarital and homosexual sex, as well as stereotypical attitudes about "good" girls and boys.

State Statutory Rape Laws and the Rule of Sevens

State statutory rape laws also fail to provide adequate direction for the treatment of adolescent consent. The first problem with reliance on statutory rape laws rests on the fact that the age of consent varies from state to state and from statute to statute within states. While states' rights advocates argue that individual states should enjoy the right to set the age of consent as local judgment dictates, scientific evidence does not suggest that minors in Indiana develop physically, emotionally, and mentally any earlier than do those in California or New York. In setting age thresholds, adults establish the age at which they think a subset of minors can handle the challenges posed by certain conduct. Jurists determine *legal* capacity for *legal* consent. Therefore, jurists should focus on adolescent developmental capacity, not moral judgments concerning sex or local attitudes about "deviant" sexual behavior when reviewing the age of consent.

MORALITY CODES. If society continues to endorse dated moral judgments concerning sex and codify local attitudes about "deviant" sexual behavior then jurists should responsively highlight constitutional privacy rights. In *Planned Parenthood of Southeastern Pennsylvania v. Casey* (1992), the US Supreme Court considered state law limits on access to abortion. In reaffirming the privacy interest in the right not to procreate, the Court emphasized, "Our obligation is to define the liberty of all, not to mandate our own moral code."[1] The Court has more than once declined to validate morality legislation and quoted this passage from *Casey* in its 2003 *Lawrence v. Texas* opinion that invalidated a Texas criminal sodomy statute.[2]

However, both *Casey* and *Lawrence* distinguished cases involving minors. The *Lawrence* Court explained, "The present case does not involve minors. It does not involve persons who might be injured or coerced or who are situated in relationships where consent might not easily be refused."[3] In *Casey*, the Court held, "This conclusion is in no way inconsistent with our decisions upholding parental notification or [parental] consent requirements. Those enactments, and our judgment that they are constitutional, are based on the quite reasonable assumption that minors will benefit from consultation with their parents and that children will often not realize that their parents have their best interests at heart."[4]

Rather than legislate morality or enforce it in civil case law precedent, politicians and jurists should leave it to parents and guardians to decide how to monitor their respective children and teenagers when they consent to sex. Judicial bypass exceptions that further protect the civil rights of teens (and currently ensure judicial review of access to abortion and other medical services) could ensure that teenagers with abusive or neglectful parents might avail themselves of their constitutional rights.

ARCHAIC RULES AND LAW. Second, it is unlikely that state legislatures passed statutory rape laws in reliance on medical research regarding adolescent developmental capabilities. Many of these laws have been on the books for decades. American adults could invest the resources necessary to complete scientific research regarding adolescent capabilities and then seek to implement an appropriate national standard based upon reliable scientific evidence. If states want to choose an age of consent higher than that indicated by scientific evidence, then let the states' rights versus individual rights debate ensue.

The same reliance on science prompts us to question the archaic rule of sevens and the mature minor doctrine. Until adults know that fourteen-year-olds possess the same ability as adults to make reasoned decisions and judgments in unfamiliar circumstances or when under stress, jurists should not presume *legal* capacity. Society should protect children from sexual abuse. If jurists must adopt a bright line for an age of consent, because society has no sure measure of individual cognitive, neurological, and psychosocial maturity, the age of majority (currently eighteen in most states) better serves everyone—at least for the formulation of criminal law pertaining to *adults* engaging in sex with minors. Society can expect adults to be responsible for their actions independent of the consent they may have persuaded a minor to give.

Such a solution is not, however, similarly appropriate for regulating the rights and behavior of other juveniles. The same limits that make the consent vulnerable to critique can impair the ability to understand those limits on the other side of the interaction. Below I advocate for the reinstitution of twenty-one for the age of majority along with the adoption of my legal assent proposal.

Solutions Regarding the Age of Consent

When one focuses on developmental capacity, emerging scientific discoveries guide the direction one takes with American youth. It makes no logical sense to permit multiple and inconsistent legal determinations of any given adolescent's *actual* capacity absent some accurate maturity test. Without the ability to determine actual capacity, jurists should not assume *legal* capacity for legally binding consent.

At first glance, the synchronization of the age of consent with the age of majority at eighteen appears more sensible than the current patchwork of conflicting approaches and ages. Specifically, jurists might deny juvenile *legal* capacity until eighteen even though adults may agree that some minors demonstrate sufficient maturity to constitute legal capacity before that age. Several reasons support this move, although ultimately it is ill advised. First, efficient administration justifies the drawing of a bright line. The Twenty-Sixth Amendment to the US Constitution sets the voting age at eighteen, so why not mark eighteen as the age for legal capacity and the age of consent in all states? While adults might disagree about where to draw the line (at sixteen, eighteen, or twenty-one), few will dispute that rules are easier to enforce than maturity evaluations are to conduct.

Second, many adults would rather err on the side of protecting all teenagers, even the relatively mature ones, than risk traumatizing or sacrificing the immature ones. The point of the law is to protect those who need the protection the most, not to sacrifice those immature youth because society is concerned about protecting a few who do not really need protection.

However, a rule that eighteen marks the beginning of adulthood, such as most states have adopted, makes little sense given the neuroscience of late adolescent development. This bright-line rule ignores the nuances of adolescent neurological and psychosocial development. According to Dr. Ruben Gur, the brain continues to mature into the early twenties for those sectors "that govern impulsivity, judgment, planning for the future, foresight of consequences, and other characteristics that make people morally culpable." He added, "Additionally, since brain development in the relevant areas goes in phases that vary in rate and is usually not complete before the early to mid-20s, there is no way to state with any scientific reliability that an individual 17-year-old has a fully matured brain. . . . Indeed, age 21 or 22 would be closer to the "biological" age of maturity."[5]

His comments make clear that maturation continues beyond the point adults have assumed (age eighteen, since the 1971 passage of the Twenty-Sixth Amendment). Maturation happens in phases with maturity being hard to pinpoint. What one really sees is an emerging capacity rather than a bright line. And the development of that capacity, paradoxically, requires that adolescents have opportunities to test themselves, in buffered and protected contexts, against the realities of life—realities that include sexual intimacy. Finally, the scientific data relate to adolescent populations, not individuals. Population trends do not say anything about the maturity or capacity of a given teenager.

Therefore, I join opponents of bright-line demarcations for the reservation of most rights because American children need maturing experiences. They need to experiment in age-appropriate ways sexually too. By setting the age of consent at a particular age below twenty-one, society denies younger teenagers many of the experiences that will lead to their neurological and psychosocial development. Society also denies them important rights to which they are entitled and which they may need, such as the right to procreate or not. If adults infantilize children until they are eighteen or twenty-one, society may harm the very young people it would hope to protect. In the same vein, a failure to monitor adult predators who exploit these developing teenagers is also unacceptable. How does one resolve this contradiction?

The task is to design a different responsive network. Together adults might craft a variety of solutions to address the concern that adolescent consent is not a replica of adult consent. However, the design should be thoughtful. The following proposals deserve examination but may not be adequate or nuanced enough.

ELIMINATE THE AGE OF CONSENT? The *Tobias* dictum, for instance, which eliminates the age of consent in the context of civil liability, creates more problems than it solves and appears inconsistent with what adults know from expert scientists regarding adolescent development and psychosocial maturity. This book's review of conflicting laws and US Supreme Court acceptance of the developmental differences between adults and teenagers suggests that the elimination of the age of the consent in civil law, without a replacement regime of adult responsibility in its place, would put teenagers at risk—of sexual predation, at least.

CREATE NEW MULTIFACTOR STANDARDS FOR LEGAL CONSENT? Another approach involves a tripartite or multifaceted scheme. First, society might use particular age requirements in certain contexts or for particular privileges, such as smoking or gaming, as the law does now. Second, where juveniles have less familiarity with the activity, where power imbalances exist, and where more serious consequences (than, for example, a financial loss on a lottery ticket) might result for a teenager, the law might set a higher age requirement tied to an objective criterion. Professor R. George Wright notes that a focus on the age of consent might simply be a distraction. He suggests that, where no discernible disparity in power or subtle coercion complicates a relationship or situation, one might eliminate age requirements.[6] This third approach certainly empowers youth in certain contexts.

The risk of mandated maturity evaluations still poses a problem under this tripartite approach. As the Doe cases demonstrate, when jurists set fixed age barriers, judges make exceptions, sometimes to remain consistent with other legal doctrines. One should not presume legal capacity and tie the age of consent to sexual activity with an adult to the age at which one can, for example, rent a safe-deposit box. And, as noted, science does not yet provide definitive, comprehensive guidance on any given adolescent's maturity. Additionally, evaluator bias can skew results of psychosocial evaluations. Lawmakers have the power to eliminate age of consent requirements to the detriment of youth, as was done in *Tobias*.

Moreover, not all adolescent consent requires formal legal analysis. As previously noted, when a six-year-old steals a kiss from a classmate, the child needs adult supervision and age-appropriate parenting guidance, not legal intervention. Arguably, Romeo and Juliet (or Romeo and Romeo) need similar and age-appropriate adult supervision and parenting guidance. By relying on responsible parenting and other informal strategies (such as peer counseling and mentoring by qualified youth leaders, teachers, and coaches), one can sidestep formal legal intervention to avoid the misplaced application of law regarding the age of consent. The wholesale elimination of these rules does more harm than good, however. In New York, California, and across the nation, legal reform must remedy haphazard and misguided treatment of adolescent consent when power imbalances, adult-teen sexual predation, and more serious forms of youth exploitation put adolescents at risk of injury and trauma.

Teenagers on Trial

One alternative to the bright-line drawing, accomplished by ages of consent, would involve the case-by-case evaluation of the plaintiff's maturity. Presumptions, either for or against capacity, also inevitably devolve into such an analysis because the side disadvantaged by the presumption will try to challenge it. Either way, the evaluation puts the teen on trial. One should emphatically reject trial by "ordeal."

Such an inquisition concerning a teenager's maturity raises several serious concerns. First, the evaluation typically will occur months (if not years) after the teenager consented. Therefore, no objective test can accurately evaluate the teenager's maturity as it existed at the time of the consent. Everyone has been a teenager and thus knows that adolescents mature and grow with astonishing rapidity. A teenager who consents in April may demonstrate a very different level of maturity than he will in December, let alone years later. Fairness dictates that jurists not use the level of maturity that he exhibits during trial or discovery to judge capacity at the time of alleged injurious events.

Second, the indicators that one uses to gauge teenager maturity may subject that teenager to humiliating, prejudicial, and perhaps even unconstitutional scrutiny. For example, the defense may attempt to introduce evidence of prior sexual activity to demonstrate a teenager's maturity. While federal sexual harassment law and rules of evidence regulate the use of the plaintiff's sexual history, exceptions allow introduction of that evidence when the plaintiff places the issue in controversy or for other reasons during civil trials. Defense counsel may argue that the claim of incapacity places the plaintiff's maturity, and therefore her sexual history, in controversy. Conceivably, a court could allow the introduction of the plaintiff's history of sexual abuse or incest survival to demonstrate that the plaintiff was aware of the difference between consensual and offensive or coerced sex. Even the threat of such admission or discovery of such evidence will deter some teenagers, and their parents, from prosecuting civil claims.

Third, juveniles risk that judges and jurors will blame them for not being more mentally mature when they look physically mature or for bringing injuries upon themselves with their immaturity. One might argue that jurors can resist the temptation to blame the victim. Think about how many times, however, you have thought to yourself, as a phrase of condemnation, Oh, that is so immature! If behavior is truly the product of immaturity, there should be no associated blame. Young people cannot help their immaturity. Immaturity is a natural stage of development. Society does not shame and condemn the mentally challenged for their failure to comprehend. Similarly, one should not blame the immature for their failure to act maturely. However, adults do blame teenagers, regularly.

Associated with this argument concerning blame, one might suggest that even though people should not censure adolescents for their immaturity, neither should adults protect them from the consequences of their behavior. How else are people to learn if they do not suffer the consequences of their behavior? I offer two responses to this question. First, teenagers do not consent to what we would otherwise label sexual harassment in isolation. The controversial conduct always involves another person. If the sexual partner is another adolescent, I would deny recovery because neither teenager has acquired the *legal* capacity to consent. Both would bear their own costs, unless, for example, an employer knew or should have known of the conduct. In that case, I would hold the employer liable under a negligence standard for failing to prevent and cure sexual harassment. Similarly, if the second adolescent is a supervisor, I would impose liability on the employer because the employer has made an adolescent its supervising agent. In that case, the employer should bear the burden of that decision and pay for the resulting damages caused by its agent. If the second person is an adult, that adult has the power to prevent the harm by refusing to become sexually involved with the minor. But for the willing assistance of the adult, the harm would not occur. Thus, I would hold the adult responsible for the consequential damages.

My second response to the imposition of consequences borrows from common parenting wisdom. When a child reaches for the hot pot and burns himself, parents do not refuse to treat the burn so that the child will learn a lesson and refrain from grabbing pots on the stove. The pain of the moment should deter the child in the future. Neither do parents consider a bandage and dressing a reward for bad behavior. Additionally, parents would not hesitate to scream "Stop!" at the child to prevent the injury in the first place. Finally, society would sanction an adult who knowingly encouraged the child to touch the pot. Take this simple example and apply it to teen-adult sexual activity. When a teenager suffers injury from teen-adult sex, society should not hesitate to compensate for the injury. The teenager is injured through no fault of his own because he did not have capacity to consent. One should not view the compensatory monetary payment to be a reward for bad behavior. The money is not an "award," even if jurists use that term in legal parlance. Nor should adults hesitate to yell, "Stop!" to prevent teen-adult sex that traumatizes and injures adolescent workers, students, athletes, and other children. Finally, society should hold adults who persuade youth into harmful sexual relations responsible for their adult actions in exposing teenagers to a harmful "learning experience."

Finally, who knows how to do an effective maturity evaluation? No such foolproof test exists or every department of motor vehicles might use it before issuing a driver's license to a teenager. As noted previously, in *Graham v. Florida* the Supreme Court confirmed that psychological evaluations to link behavior and maturity may not produce robust results. Until American society's maturity metering improves, society needs another solution.

Strict Liability—Law Reform and Legal Regulation

The best way to prevent workplace sexual harassment of teenagers involves the implementation of both regulatory mechanisms and statutory reform. First, sexual harassment of minors by adults must become a strict liability offense for which consent is no defense. Lawmakers should amend Title VII, state FEPS, Title IX, and tort law to account for adolescents in all environments, their developmental abilities, and the phenomenon of their sexual exploitation. Research evidence regarding adolescent development and sexual harassment of minors should inform and guide statutory reform.

STRICT LIABILITY. Strict liability serves many of the public policy concerns explored in this book. By strict liability, I mean that if the conduct occurred and the minor has withdrawn any consent extracted, the adult is automatically liable under the law and cannot raise consent as a defense. I recognize the moral hazard of affording adolescents the opportunity to withdraw consent in the context of teen-adult sexual conduct. However, most adolescents, who are not informed regarding the nuances of sexual harassment law, will not be influenced by a reform that provides them more protection. Second, because adolescents tend to focus on the short-term aspects of their conduct, I doubt many will engage in a long-term strategy to disadvantage their adult employers, teachers, coaches, or other adult mentors. And third, the proper person at risk should be the adult, who is the person in the position to know better and act accordingly.

If jurists invalidate consent at the liability phase and admit evidence of consent at the damages phase of any trial, they treat consent inconsistently and use teens merely as a means to their end of eradicating sexual harassment. They also give consent more value than it is worth. Professor R. George Wright suggested,

> The crucial point remains that the proper scope or value of consent—even free and knowledgeable consent—depends on other considerations and finally on an ultimate value, human dignity. An act of consent or refusal to consent that genuinely and substantially undermines human dignity, in the person of the chooser or others, is on shaky grounds at best, however much that choice may promote utility.[7]

The notion of allowing even adults to withdraw consent is not a new one. As previously noted, consumers often have the right to rescind agreements made with door-to-door salespeople within three days without penalty or obligation. Wright explained, "In the door-to-door sales case, the salesperson may use manipulative or high-pressure sales techniques that create a merely temporary desire for the product. The cooling-off period gives the buyer time to reflect on whether the perceived need is authentic."[8] Wright also gave the example of a consumer credit transaction in which the creditor acquires a security interest in the consumer's home. The consumer also has the right to rescind that contract within three days. This right reduces the chance that a consumer might lose "one of his most precious possessions" after making an ill-considered deal.[9]

Arguably, this reasoning applies to adolescents who might succumb to manipulative or high-pressure requests for sexual favors that create merely a temporary desire to experience sex. The rescission period, extended through minority, to account for developing capacity would give the adolescent time to reflect on whether the relationship was equal and mutual.

One might argue that consumers do not typically proceed to sue the employers of high-pressure salespeople after withdrawal of consent and rescission of the agreement; however, consumers need not do so. Consumers can return to their pre-bargain position typically by providing written notice of rescission. Youth who consent typically cannot return to their "pre-consent" position; therefore, they should be allowed to sue for the value of what was lost in the corrupt transaction or for their damages.

Wright concluded that "there is no deep Kantian reason why the Kantian duty of respect should not be legally enforced even in cases in which the target did not, for some reason, perceive her situation to be one of harassment."[10] When she does perceive conduct as harassment within a reasonable period thereafter, the law should respect her and protect her dignity.

If a minor had successfully sued for injuries on a prior occasion, I would consider making evidence of consent admissible in any similar second (or successive) trial for money damages from a different perpetrator. Such a rule should satisfy those skeptics who will argue that an adolescent "siren" will win her fortune from multiple unsuspecting Humberts (the adult pedophile in *Lolita*) and other ephebophiliacs. Additionally, once an injured adolescent has received her recovery and "learned the lesson," she should not need the same protection, funded by an employer or school district, as one who has never been involved in a civil court case.

I would also consider making evidence of consent admissible during the review of a preliminary motion by the "adult" younger than twenty-one, if the adult is truly a peer of the target teenager. Consider, for example, that Romeo Montague (19) and Juliet Capulet (17) begin a romance. She is a high school senior, and he is a university student. They first met in high school. Their parents, the Montagues and Capulets, are furious when they discover that their children have become lovers. As guardians for Juliet, the Capulets sue Romeo for civil corruption of a minor and raise other tort claims. They cannot sue under Titles VII and IX because Juliet is neither his student nor his employee. In the civil case and per my unaltered strict liability scheme, Juliet's consent would be inadmissible.

However, this outcome that places the financial burden for Juliet's "corruption" on Romeo hardly seems fair. Romeo is different from Michael Cosio, the forty-year-old movie theater supervisor; Clint Smith, the thirty-six-year-old math teacher; and Robert Donaldson, the thirty-year-old brother-in-law. Romeo did not exploit Juliet in the sense that theirs was a relationship of unequal bargaining power. Theirs appears to be a natural romance between two immature but willing teenagers. It's possible that Romeo's prefrontal cortex was not fully mature and that he, like Juliet, was still developing capacity. Therefore, the law should not penalize him for his consent any more than it should Juliet for hers. However, because Romeo has reached the legal age of majority, the law will presume that he has the *legal* capacity to consent. The law will hold him liable for tortious injuries he causes. I would allow Romeo the opportunity to rebut this presumption in a preliminary motion. Only for the purposes of this motion, he might submit evidence of Juliet's consent. The discussion of *legal assent* below offers another response to this Romeo and Juliet scenario.

For mature adults who exploit teenagers, strict liability ensures the development of appropriate policies and procedures by employers, school districts, and others to prevent and cure the sexual predation of adolescents. Strict liability and the necessarily related exclusion of consent evidence also lead to cost redistribution. Strict liability lifts the financial burden of sexual harassment injuries from minors and their parents. Sexual predators responsible for the injuries should bear the costs.

Any employer, school superintendent, and governing principal, who regulates teen environments, reaps the rewards of adolescent labor, or carries responsibility for teen welfare, will share in covering costs resulting from adult sexual misconduct. Moreover, employers and other principals can purchase liability insurance to spread the cost burden further. Strict tort and antidiscrimination law liability will redress the social grievance of the subordination of this nation's youth. Such laws will attack the treatment of adolescents as fungible, a problem discussed in chapter 2.

EDUCATION, LEGAL REGULATIONS, AND STRICT LIABILITY. In addition to law reform, education and regulatory mechanisms might address this problem of teen sexual harassment. Professor Wright explained, "Education is closely linked to rational development, the exercise of autonomy, and the fullest expression of human dignity. Treating all persons as ends in themselves requires the provision of educational opportunities, at public expense if necessary. . . . Kant regards education as of central importance."[11] Thus, education may help in the case of teen sexual harassment.

Some adults and organizations have already implemented education and regulatory solutions. For example, in 2004 the EEOC launched its website and educational campaign, Youth@Work.[12] Some states subsidize the employment of young workers.[13] State employment departments and the ED could mandate that, in exchange for tax breaks, funding, or other benefits received, businesses and institutions provide special training for adolescents regarding their rights and sexual harassment. Courts occasionally mandate such educational outreach in the resolution of sexual harassment suits. In an unpublished consent decree, Judge Sarah Evans Barker of the US District Court for the Southern District of Indiana ordered Taco Bell to adopt and implement a special training program.[14] Judge Barker ruled, "This training shall cover unlawful employment practices under Title VII . . . with particular emphasis on the awareness of discrimination issues that may affect youth, and especially minors, at work."[15] I suggest that American adults also need to educate explicitly and by example. Adults must model appropriate conduct for adolescents whether they are at work, at school, on the playing field, or in correctional custody.

Will education cure the problem? As Professors Cauffman and Steinberg noted, increasing knowledge may not always lead to better decision making. For example, they warned that "while adolescents are largely aware of the relationships between condom use and the probability of HIV infection, two-thirds of sexually active sixteen to nineteen year olds surveyed in a recent study reported engaging in sexual intercourse without using a condom."[16] Thus, the law needs to anticipate that until adolescents have sufficient experience and maturity, some will consent to sex solicited by an adult.

Regulation might anticipate some of the gaps that educational training fails to fill. States might require that, to obtain a permit to work, adolescent applicants must complete a sexual harassment training seminar. State education departments might also mandate sexual harassment curricula in their health and business administration classes. These are just a few of the possible regulatory approaches.

A strict liability scheme and regulatory mechanisms are compatible with affording adolescents some measure of autonomy and self-determination. An adolescent might still choose to engage in sex with an adult, who would still run the risk of civil and criminal liability. In essence, this scheme operates like adolescent consent to a contract. The sex "contract" is voidable by the adolescent but not void. The adolescent can retract the consent if she realizes during her minority (or shortly thereafter but subject to a limited period) that her adult partner took advantage of her developing capacity at the workplace.

One might worry that if law imposed strict liability on employers for the sexual harassment of adolescent workers by supervisors, employers would simply stop hiring adolescents. Teenagers would face even higher unemployment rates. I challenge that criticism. Employers can pay adolescent workers less money for the same work performed by adults.[17] Often employers avoid providing part-time adolescent employees benefits that adult workers receive. It makes good business sense to hire young, seasonal, or part-time workers. I doubt that the cost of sexual harassment judgments and training would exceed the financial advantages employers enjoy by employing adolescents—if those employers implemented age-appropriate policies and proper training. If the law held employers strictly liable for the sexual exploitation of their minor workers, jurists would not shut down the markets of this nation. Moreover, when society excuses employers from liability, it simply pushes the costs of such harms onto teenagers, the most vulnerable in the interaction. Society also provides no incentive for the *most adult* actor and best harm avoider to seek means to minimize such harms.

Strict liability provides solutions to a number of our concerns, but potential refinements could improve it further; one such approach is what I call *legal assent*.

Legal Assent: Beyond Consent, Bias, and Moral Prejudice

In addition to a simple strict liability solution that extends contract law's voidability principle to the context of sexual relations between a juvenile and an adult, *Sexual Exploitation of Teenagers* offers a more refined approach to adolescent consent. Specifically, the law should credit adolescent consent not as legal consent but as *legal assent*. Unlike medical assent, discussed in chapter 1, legal assent requires no associated parental consent or permission. Unlike legal consent, it carries *no associated threshold level of legal capacity*. Legal assent remains agnostic on the existence of any given juvenile's maturity. Similar to consent by a minor under contract law, legal assent is voidable by the minor. However, legal assent operates somewhat differently from traditional, voidable contract consent by a minor.

Legal assent works in the following way. If a minor gives legal assent, that consent is legally binding unless the minor voids her assent during her minority, or during a reasonable time thereafter. Parents cannot void a minor's assent for her. The voiding or revocation is not automatically effective, however. As explained more fully below, the court will make a "best interests" analysis in deciding whether to validate the revocation. If a minor successfully voids her assent, a court will not admit it into evidence at the trial on the merits or permit further discovery on the matter. A criminal prosecutor might still prosecute an adult who has sex with an assenting minor, however, because the legal assent operates *only for the benefit of the minor*. Voters, legislators, and district attorneys might still act in society's best interests. Additionally, parents would still have the authority to discipline and regulate their children. However, the adult consort in the situation would now be the one bearing the risk of harm for any juvenile who might not have fully understood a situation or responded in a self-protective manner.

Legal Assent, Willits *Doe, and Another Joe, Vili Fualaau*

Imagine a few examples. Suppose the minor, such as *Willits* Doe, agrees to sex with her teacher. The district attorney can prosecute Clint Smith for statutory rape or, in California, unlawful sex with a minor. A successful case results in a vindication for a society that does not want its teachers having sex with minor students. If Doe reaffirms her assent, there is no parallel civil case; the legal controversy ends. Of course, Doe's parents can act domestically to comfort, guide, or discipline their daughter as they see fit.

If, on the other hand, Doe determines that she was duped, coerced, or made a mistake in assenting, she can void her legal assent and bring a sexual harassment action against the school district that employed Smith or a tort claim (via an adult) against her teacher to recover for her damages. The reviewing civil court then engages in a *two-step response* to Doe's abrogation of legal assent.

First, the court analyzes whether or not Doe's original decision (to have sex with her teacher) was in Doe's best interests. I cannot imagine a scenario in which a court would find the decision in her best interests, but let's walk through the analysis. Legal assent borrows from traditional family law for an incorporation of a "best interests" analysis. Most definitions of the "best interests of a child" examine custody determinations and emphasize the maximization of the child's welfare with respect to the court's selection of a parental caretaker. In the context of child custody, a court focuses on "the child's needs rather than on parental rights. . . . [T]he cases make it clear that conduct that is harmful to the child or that reflects what may be deemed 'unfitness' will be weighed in the determination of what constitutes the child's best interests."[18]

In the case of legal assent, a jurist evaluates whether the teen's consent in any given context promoted his best interests by advancing his welfare, education, and mental, physical, and psychosocial well-being and maturation. Similar to the custody context, in a legal assent analysis, the court must focus on the teen's welfare and not on what may be best for the involved adults. Additionally, courts may reject conduct that is at odds with teens' healthy growth, maturation, and development and is not in their best interests. In that instance, the court invalidates the consent extracted and validates the juvenile's later retraction of consent.

Sexual intercourse with Clint Smith (or Tim Horton or Robert Donaldson) was not in Doe's best interests. Criminal sanctions for adults clearly suggest that particular activities are not in a minor's best interests. Thus, a violation of California Penal Code section 261.5 would suggest that the original decision was not in Doe's best interests. One might argue that a best interests evaluation focused on criminal conviction based on age collapses the response back into an age-based bright line. The distinction here is that criminal conviction serves as just one factor in a best interests analysis once *the juvenile* has abrogated her assent.

A court must consider numerous other factors in evaluating *Willits* Doe's best interests. Key in the inquiry must be why *Willits* Doe voided her assent. Did Smith lie to her? Did he cause her to believe that he loved her, that they would marry, and that they would live happily ever after, when in fact he was only interested in sex? Did they have unsafe sex? Was she pregnant, dealing with an STI, or otherwise physically injured? Did she void her assent simply because her parents discovered the affair and were angry? Even if she thought she still loved Smith and was afraid of parental rebuke, a judge might still accept her revocation as in her best interests. However, outside pressure could corrupt the revocation.

One wonders whether such pressures influenced the Mary Kay Letourneau case. Letourneau, a married mother (then 34) of four children, spent more than seven years in prison for seducing a twelve-year-old former student, Vili Fualaau.[19] In 2002, however, while Letourneau was still in prison, Fualaau (then 18) and his mother sued the Highline School District and the city of Des Moines. According to a news report, "Their lawsuit claims both should have protected Fualaau from the advances of his now-notorious former teacher."[20]

If one looks at this case using the lens of legal assent, the lawsuit indicates an abrogation by Fualaau of his assent. Apparently "Fualaau testified during the trial about his continued conflicting emotions regarding Letourneau. 'I loved her. At least I thought I loved her,'" Fualaau said.[21] This qualification suggests an awareness that his love was not real. One might conclude that Fualaau understood that Letourneau abused him. In 2005, however, Fualaau married Letourneau.[22]

This case highlights that human emotions are complex. One cannot know with certainty whether Letourneau, his mother, or anyone else manipulated Fualaau. The circumstances do raise suspicions, however. Ultimately, the Fualaau jury returned a verdict that denied any recovery.[23] The jury's determination that neither the school district nor city was liable was not a victory for Letourneau. Fualaau and his mother did not sue her. Fualaau's conflicted feelings about her and her status as the mother of his two children may indicate why they did not. Moreover, she was in prison at the time and presumably had no assets.

The Letourneau case demonstrates the need for judicial review of the best interests of the child. There is no question in my mind that Letourneau abused Fualaau. Their age difference was too great. Theirs was not a relationship built on mutuality and equality. They did not have safe sex (as evidenced by her two pregnancies) and Fualaau was left as a single, teenage parent of two children while Letourneau was in prison. They could have waited until Fualaau matured to confirm that he still loved Letourneau. If I were a judge asked to affirm the revocation of assent, I would have validated Fualaau's abrogation. His relationship with his former teacher when he was twelve was not in his best interests. She was not a peer. Similarly, and based on the available facts, I would accept *Willits* Doe's abrogation of her assent to Smith. That relationship was not in her best interests either.

Once a court determines whether to validate or overturn Doe's abrogation of assent, it proceeds to the next legal determination. In the next phase, *if the court has validated an abrogation, the court must then deny any discovery, and exclude admission, of evidence regarding the Doe's assent* if Smith raises it as a civil defense. Society allows Doe to void her assent and expects that teachers will take warning and stay away from teenage girls and boys. The difference between this system and a strict liability approach is that jurists cannot automatically discount the *assent.* The minor must abrogate it, and the judge must affirm that abrogation using a best interests analysis. Then by default the assent becomes undiscoverable and inadmissible at every phase of the trial.

Legal Assent and Medical Treatment

This approach to legal assent also works in other contexts, such as when a minor seeks medical treatment. Imagine next that Doe assents not to sex with an adult but to treatment for an STI and then voids her assent in refusing to pay for treatment. The clinic then sues for payment. Note that this matter goes to a court *only if* Doe assents, revokes her assent, and then someone protests the abrogation with legal action. Under this theory of legal assent and in the context described, a court might issue an injunction prohibiting Doe from voiding her assent if the *original decision* (not the results, but the original decision) was in her best interests. Almost all of us would agree that medical treatments are in a minor's best interests (although this consensus may be taxed in some communities if the procedure is an abortion). If Doe's parents agree, the court would give credit to their support of her original decision. A discussion below covers when parents do not agree. In this first case, the court rejects Doe's abrogation and makes her original assent binding.

Rhinoplasty and breast augmentation are more debatable examples. Arguably, those medical procedures are elective and not necessary for a happy, healthy teenager. If Doe voids her consent after nose surgery, a court might validate her abrogation if the surgeon sues for payment. Again, the court should consider the opinions of Doe's parents. If her parents conclude that nose surgery was not in Doe's best interests, the court again has additional support for the validation of her revocation. If the parents disagree and think that nose surgery was in her best interests, the court can weigh this appropriately in deciding whether to invalidate Doe's revocation. If it enjoins Doe from voiding her assent, the court might hold the ratifying parents liable for payment to the surgeon who performed the rhinoplasty for their daughter. Doe's parents can then deal with Doe at home.

Alternately, the court might support Doe's abrogation—even if her parents disapprove of that abrogation—because the court finds that the original decision was not in her best interests and the revocation is. Plastic surgeons will then be more cautious before cutting or augmenting teenagers. They might require parental permission or a co-consenter (cosigner). Such a method works in same way for service providers, vendors, employers, and the like.

Romeo's Consent and Juliet's Legal Assent

One might argue that legal assent works well in very narrow circumstances, such as in the context of sexual abuse of a teenager by an adult or in the context of sensible medical treatment. However, one might question the efficacy of this solution to consent in the more difficult case involving Romeo and Juliet. Let us return to Shakespeare's star-crossed lovers. The Capulets have filed a personal injury case against Romeo for injuries they claim Juliet suffered. Note that the Capulets should have no influence over whether the local district attorney prosecutes Romeo under any applicable criminal laws. I would hope that the prosecutor opts against pursuing Romeo and recognizes that the teenage romance was not exploitative. Evidence of any exploitative conduct might change that perspective; however, let us assume that Romeo and Juliet are in love. If Juliet refuses to revoke her assent, the Capulets' case ends. Juliet's assent operates as a complete defense for Romeo against the personal injury claims brought on her behalf.

Suppose, however, that the Capulets pressure Juliet to abrogate her assent. Fearful that her parents will reject her, kick her out on the street, or otherwise discipline her, Juliet abrogates her assent. Therefore, the court must first analyze whether or not Juliet's original decision (to have sex with Romeo) was in her best interests. Given adult attitudes about sexually active teenagers, I do not envision a judge concluding that Juliet's assent was in her best interests. I suppose that if the two young lovers were mature in making their decision, communicated about it, used birth control, and engaged with each other respectfully and safely, a judge might find such a liaison in Juliet's best interests and invalidate the abrogation. Still, I find that result unlikely.

What I would prefer to see is an in camera (in a chamber, or in private) review of Juliet's abrogation. The Capulet parents would not be invited to participate in this review. The judge (and perhaps a court-appointed social worker or psychologist) should ascertain the true reasons for the abrogation. Why is she revoking her assent? Does Juliet feel that Romeo exploited her? Did he lie to her about a brain tumor (as Cosio did with Sara)? Did he offer her intoxicants (as Donaldson and Horton gave marijuana to their Does)? Or was Juliet simply embarrassed by her parents' discovery of the affair? Hopefully, the judge will discover that Juliet loves Romeo but fears her parents' wrath. At that point, the judge should summarily reject Juliet's abrogation. No judge should give legal effect to coercive manipulations, even those by well-meaning parents. By coercing a revocation from their daughter, the Capulets threaten Romeo's financial welfare and social reputation. They also perpetrate a fraud upon the court. No court should countenance such a maneuver.

If a judge affirms the abrogation of Juliet's assent for any reason, however, Romeo has a serious problem. The law will presume that he has legal capacity because of his age. As I noted above, I do not think it just to hold Romeo liable for Juliet's "corruption" and injuries in this case. When crafting the legal scaffold of *assent*, I contemplated allowing the "adult" Romeo a chance to prove that he lacked *legal capacity*. I considered allowing the proof of his incapacity only if Romeo were under the age of twenty-one. While the neuroscience and psychosocial evidence suggests that males may be developing capacity beyond this age, I acknowledge the need to draw a line somewhere to distinguish adults from juveniles. Twenty-one is another legal dividing line and is closer than eighteen to the age of adult maturity indicated by current neurobiological and social science indicators. However, this safety mechanism carries the same flaw that an evaluation of any consenting teen raises. Maturity evaluations are difficult, if not impossible, to perform and especially so months or years after the relevant events.

Therefore, in promoting the adoption of legal assent for teenagers, I also urge a restoration of twenty-one as the age of majority and full adulthood. At least until the science indicates a more appropriate dividing line, the law should not presume adult traits, which have not finished developing, in an eighteen-year-old. I understand that the implementation of this proposal would necessitate broad legal reform. Such a discussion is beyond the scope of this book. Chapter 3 makes clear, however, that the biological and psychosocial transition to adulthood is gradual. The transition to full legal and political participation (in all respects including drinking, driving, voting, etc.) should be just as gradual. The emerging science of adolescent development currently supports such reform. American adults might better nurture and protect teenagers by affording teenagers opportunities to exercise, or spread, their proverbial legal wings under circumstances that protect them.

Certainly Romeo should have known that Juliet was a minor and that he risked legal sanction for pursuing a sexual relationship with Juliet. Even twelve-year-old Fualaau understood that his relationship with Letourneau was problematic. During his civil case against the city of Des Moines, he remarked, "I thought we were lucky that she didn't go to jail" [after police discovered them together in a van early one morning at the Des Moines Marina in 1996].[24] "Adult" Romeo may still have been developing capacity, however. Focusing on short-term consequences and his love for Juliet, Romeo might not have engaged in a decision-making process that replicated a more mature analysis. Counting on her assent and not completely considering that the Capulets, not Juliet, could pursue him under the law, Romeo might have made an immature and foolish decision to have sex with Juliet. He might not have thought of any of these factors at all. Therefore, I would allow Romeo to avoid legal liability for Juliet's seduction. As with Juliet, however, he gets only one bite of the apple of knowledge. If he engages sexually again with another Doe, he faces potential liability if that Doe revokes her assent.

Note that I would not make this defense available for employers or school districts. Business and educational organizations need to hire mature, responsible supervisors and managers to educate children, supervise employees, and represent the principal to the public. If an organization hires an immature "adult," the organization should pay for any damage caused. Finally, an elevation of the age of majority back to twenty-one would have had no effect on the profiled Does and their adult consorts who were all older than twenty-one.

Legal Assent, Capacity, and Moral Imperatives

Thus, Doe makes the first and second choices to assent and whether to void her assent. Society permits her the second choice to protect her from the bad choices that it anticipates she might make *and to facilitate her own correction of her mistake.* Jurists hold her to her assent if she errs in the revocation of assent. At that point, however, if someone challenges the abrogation, the court evaluation focuses not on the moral purity or maturity of the minor but upon whether the original assent was in her best interests. It considers the reasoning behind the revocation. The evaluation focuses on the circumstances, not on the individual minor's character and chastity. Additionally, this theory does not interfere with the allocation of other rights and duties. For example, if the surgeon commits malpractice when performing Doe's rhinoplasty, Doe need not void her assent but can simply sue for medical malpractice.

DOES AND JOES. Under this approach, all our Does, including *Orangeburg* Doe, could have voided their assent. The *Orangeburg* court could not have allowed evidence of Doe's assent at a subsequent civil trial of the school unless it first determined that it was in the fourteen-year-old Doe's best interests to assent to sex with her sixteen-year-old classmate while the coach was gone. Absent that determination, the court would have had to validate Doe's abrogation of assent and allowed Roe to pursue the case without the prejudice of Doe's proffered consent.

And what about Sara, with whom we began this investigation concerning adolescent sexual harassment, capacity, and consent? Had the law characterized Sara's consent as assent, she might have more easily dealt with legal hurdles in challenging her forty-year-old manager and the theater. Sara could have withdrawn her assent. Presumably, a court would have sustained her abrogation, finding it not in her best interests to have sex (and especially unprotected sex) with her boss. The court could have supported its determination, citing to his conviction under California Penal Code section 261.5 in the best interests analysis. Then,

Sara could have sued her manager and the theater that entrusted him without the risk of a trial of her moral purity and maturity. Presumably, the case would have settled but with less controversy. Moreover, it is possible that Sara would not have even needed to file the complaint. Once Sara's lawyer notified the defendants of the impending litigation, the prospective defendants might have chosen to enter into settlement negotiations to compensate Sara for her injuries. To avoid a filing and adverse publicity about the allegations, defense counsel will often advise clients to settle before a case is even filed.

This theory of legal assent is also consistent with what we know about adolescent development. Teenagers need maturing experiences and opportunities to practice their skills. They may not have the capacity to make every decision, but this approach permits teenagers to make some and perhaps void some of those that they later believe were unwise, foolish, or mistaken. Legal assent gives teenagers the opportunity to practice good decision making while the law protects them in their development and full transition into the adult world.

Judges, politicians, and legal scholars all have the ability to influence decision making and policy formulation. A moral imperative to protect children while they are still maturing justifies bias-free, reasoned intervention. Arguably, New York and other states are moving in the wrong direction in their civil legal treatment of juveniles. Additionally, California civil decisions compounded problems with criminal law case precedent. The existing conflicts between criminal and civil law treatment of adolescent consent leave teenagers vulnerable, especially to sexual predators.

LEGAL ASSENT FOR ELDERS AND OTHERS. Court conflation of acquiescence, consent, and capacity, discussed in chapter 1, highlights the need for legal reform and intervention. Rather than eliminate default guidance or attempt to implement myriad separate rules for the regulation of adolescent activities and consent across the nation, society should give adolescent consent more coherent and effective legal significance. Legal assent allows adults to provide more wisely for the best interests of American adolescent children.

The fact that legal assent might work for other populations as well as juveniles lends support for its adoption and implementation. When one considers that *adult* legal capacity is often posed as an all-or-nothing proposition, one wonders whether adults who are legally compromised in their respective capacities might also benefit from the ability to offer legal assent. For example, shift the focus from developing capacity to "declining capacity." Consider the other end of the aging spectrum, the elderly. New neuroscientific and social science evidence indicates that many elders develop dementia or cognitive dysfunction that may not immediately affect decision making or cognitive processing in all situations. However, this dysfunction increases over time as elderly people age and can manifest in particular types of circumstances. Jurists may not be able to identify a point in time when an elder loses *legal* capacity. Scientific documentation of "sundowning" suggests that some elders lose clarity and cognitive function only after the sun goes down, literally, as they tire from a day of activity. Legal assent might work to protect this population, affording elders the right to make legally binding decisions until they discover that they have been duped or taken advantage of.

Suppose that an unscrupulous salesperson targets elderly people who live alone. Suppose further that Granny Doe consents to a new $40,000 roof that her home really does not need. Granny might revoke her assent and refuse to pay for the new (unneeded) roof. The unscrupulous roofer might challenge that revocation of assent and sue on the $40,000 contract. A court might apply my rule of legal assent and validate Granny Doe's revocation of her assent because the original decision was not in her best interests. Granny Doe's house did not need a new roof. Granny Doe does not have to endure a trial of her competence or business acumen. Her assent to the contract would not be admissible at trial because the original decision was not in her best interests. Such a legal determination would protect Granny Doe and would put unscrupulous salespeople on alert that they cannot target and disadvantage the elderly. Responsible roofers who work with elderly clients will document the legitimate need for a new roof or get a cosigner or some other surety on the contract. The roofer needs to evaluate the *needs* of the buyer, and not her *vulnerability* to persuasion.

As American elders age and live longer, one can anticipate greater trouble in dealing with their legal capacity. Legal assent offers a workable solution, short of conservatorships and guardianships, that affords elders dignity, autonomy, and continued independence for as long as practicable. While a fuller exploration of legal assent for populations in addition to adolescents is outside the scope of this book, it is worth noting that adolescents are not the only group that needs attention and protection. Legal assent may prove quite useful in a variety of contexts.

Conclusion

Sara spoke with me during the fall of 2013, coincidentally on the thirteenth anniversary of the filing of her lawsuit. Full of enthusiasm and joy, she reported, "Life is surprisingly good now." She explained that, with the help of her family and "strong women role models," she used education to deal with her experiences. She first earned an associate of arts degree in criminal justice and then a bachelor of arts degree in psychology. Finally, she settled on how she really wanted to help others. In 2012 Sara graduated with a bachelor of science degree from California State University's nursing program and recently moved across the country with her husband of three years. Sara's son turned two-years-old that Thanksgiving and she exclaimed to me, "He is amazing! He makes everything better!" In a quieter voice, however, she told me, "I am one of the lucky ones, though."

I asked Sara what she thought might have made a difference in her case. Looking back, she noted that the movie theater should have done a simple and inexpensive criminal background check on any adult it intended to hire to supervise the teenage workers. She said, "No sex offender should ever be able to work with underage workers, with children." How true. I told Sara about the *Tobias* case and the changes in California law since her employment experience. She was surprised. When I then introduced to her the idea of *legal assent*, she said, "Now, that makes sense!"

I asked Sara what advice she would give a teenage worker or student today. Her answer was immediate, "Tell someone. Tell an adult you trust." She said that telling a friend who might not understand the situation or who might feel conflicted only puts pressure on another teenager. She added, "If you are not ready to tell an adult, put it in writing as I did—in poetry. Write it out. Begin to open up and get it off your conscience." Moments later, she suggested that a teen might "accidentally" leave the note or writing for a parent or teacher or trusted person to discover. She also suggested that schools should educate teenagers about sexual harassment and the dangers of manipulation by sexual predators, including supervisors and teachers. As Sara contemplated her life in a new city with her new family, she reflected, "I turned my life into something amazing." In listening to Sara, I was so impressed. I heard the voice of a wise woman.

Sara and the other Does and Joes of this nation deserve protection as they transition to adulthood. These minors mature and develop full capacity in part through work and other life experiences. They need to practice good decision making as the law protects them from the unwise choices that we anticipate they will make.

As teenagers mature, the law should continue to shield them from the humiliating and devastating trauma of sexual exploitation in the workplace, at school, and at play. At the same time, parents and supervising adults need to promote their maturation and developing capacities. American tort and sexual harassment laws fail our nation's youth, leaving them vulnerable to adult sexual predators, harassers, and seducers. American adults need to get wise to the worldly problems that many of this nation's teenagers encounter. We must reform the law to ensure their safe and healthy transition into the adult world. When we reform law and implement a rational program that includes legal assent, we foster for our children an inheritance of worldly wisdom.

Postscript

In November 2014, after I completed this manuscript, I spoke with Karen Foshay, a news reporter who was covering a case involving a California middle school student.[25] Los Angeles School District lawyers used the girl's consent to sex with her teacher to defend a civil action filed by her family. Then, after Arun Rath interviewed me on ALL THINGS CONSIDERED, I received calls from several California legislative aides regarding possible changes to California civil law.[26] In July 2015, Governor Jerry Brown signed S.B. 14, effective January 1, 2016. This bill creates California Civil Code section 1708.5.5, which will prohibit the use of a minor's consent in a civil action against an adult in a position of authority.[27] It is not clear how this law will affect California civil cases involving adults who do not occupy positions of authority. Additionally, one cannot tell how this new state law will affect federal cases, and particularly those filed under Titles IX and VII. However, this postscript demonstrates that one person can make a difference. You can make a difference.

Acknowledgments

I received real-world wisdom, practical advice, and guidance for this book from special mentors and experts. First, I thank "Sara" who shared her reflections with me so that I could share them with you. She is brave, generous, and wise beyond her years. I also sincerely thank my friend and colleague, Professor Oliver Goodenough, who believed in this project and me. He made introductions, offered advice, listened, and gave serious encouragement when needed. Professor June Carbone has also given invaluable advice over the years—especially during a four-hour drive to a Gruter Institute Conference. Thanks, June.

Others who contributed support and expert assistance and whom I thank include my colleagues: Professor Cynthia Baker, Dr. Kathy Beck-Coon, Professor Shawn Boyne, Dr. Tracy Gunter, Dr. Leslie Hulvershorn, Dean Andrew R. Klein, Vice Dean Antony Page, (former) Dean Gary Roberts, Professor Lahny Silva, and especially Professor R. George Wright who read much of my draft work. I also appreciate the assistance I received on prior drafts from Bridget Drobac, M.A., Martin Drobac, Esq., Julia Hill, Esq., Dina Hoffman, Esq., and Dr. Michal McDowell.

Several presentations of draft portions of this book resulted in wonderful comments and suggestions from conference participants including Professors Susan Frelich Appleton, Abigail Baird, Carl Bergstrom, Beth Burkstrand-Reid, Mary Anne Case, Monika Gruter Cheney, Susan Fineran, David Faigman, Lisa Faigman, Barbara Glesner Fines, Brittany Fletcher, Erik Girvan, James Gruber, Leslie Harris, Mary Kay Kisthardt, Rana Lehr-Lehnardt, Nancy Levit, Jody Madeira, Erin O'Hara O'Connor, Laura Rosenbury, Julie Seaman, Deborah B. Smith, Merle Weiner, Kelly Weisberg, Robert Weisberg, and Lois Weithorn. Additional comments from Drs. Drew Altman, Diane Rowland, and Alina Salganicoff and from Tina Hoff were also quite helpful. Thanks to you all.

I am grateful for editorial and publication advice from Jenni Fry, Monica Oakley, David Pervin, Kristin Raddatz, Christopher Rhodes, Jillian Tsui, Whitney Ward, Shenyun Wu, and the two anonymous Chicago Press reviewers. Under the able leadership of (now) Director of the Ruth Lily Library Miriam Murphy and Research Librarian Susan deMaine, numerous students contributed research and editing assistance for this book, including Alex Cunny, Greg Gentry, Jordan Heitman, Houston Hum, Michael Hooker, Rosa Kim, Melinda Mains, Stephanie Marshall, Kristi McMains, Jeremy Musgrave, Landon Scott, Eric Schronce, Megan Smith, Augustus Tabor, Joshua Trockman, Audrey Wessel, Adam Willfond, and James Wu. Administrative assistants including Wendy Fisk, LuAnn Holman, and Sylvia Regalado also deserve thanks.

Legal reform has already occurred thanks to dedicated jurists and journalists, including Karen Foshay and Arun Rath. I also thank the California legislators and Governor Jerry Brown, who recently implemented legal reform in California.

A project of this duration comes to fruition only with the help of close friends and numerous others whom I thank here. Finally, but no less sincerely, I thank the teenage Does and Joes who have shared their stories. With courage and perseverance, they have alerted us to the sexual exploitation faced by too many teenagers and to the inadequacies of American law. I am grateful for the opportunity to share their message and thankful that readers, such as you, will be the ones to make our world safer for them.

Appendix 1: Common Forms of Sexual Harassment

The American Association of University Women (AAUW) surveyed for the following behaviors:

In Person

- Having someone make unwelcome sexual comments, jokes, or gestures to or about you
- Being called gay or lesbian in a negative way
- Being touched in an unwelcome sexual way
- Having someone flash or expose themself to you
- Being shown sexy or sexual pictures that you didn't want to see
- Being physically intimidated in a sexual way
- Being forced to do something sexual

Through Text, E-Mail, Facebook, or Other Electronic Means

- Being sent unwelcome sexual comments, jokes, or pictures or having someone post them about or of you
- Having someone spread unwelcome sexual rumors about you
- Being called gay or lesbian in a negative way[1]

To this list of AAUW-identified behaviors, I would add the following from the University of California at Santa Cruz (UCSC) definition of sexual harassment. While there is some overlap, there is enough that is different to make the two lists useful and complementary:

- verbal, nonverbal, and physical sexual behaviors
- coerced sex
- remarks about a person's body
- turning discussions inappropriately to sexual topics
- whistling or cat calls [or other noises made in a sexual manner or to intimidate]
- ["elevator eyes," or] looking a person up and down or staring in a sexually suggestive manner
- invading someone's personal space or blocking her/his path
- sexually explicit visuals such as pin-ups
- suggestions of sexual intimacy
- repeated requests for dates
- unwanted letters, electronic mail, or other computer communications
- unwanted gifts
- touching, hugging, massaging, and other gestures or sounds that a reasonable person of the same sex as the recipient would find offensive
- unwelcome sexual advances or requests for sexual favors
- unwelcome physical, verbal, or nonverbal behavior of a sexual nature or based on sex
- uninvited, unwanted, and/or unsolicited attention/conversations
- terms of endearment
- sabotaging a person's work or academic standing
- withholding information
- exclusion from informal meetings/social events
- sexual jokes, comments, or innuendoes
- cartoons or visuals that ridicule or denigrate a person's gender
- employment or academic decisions that are based solely or partially on a person's gender
- sexual assault and/or rape[2]

Appendix 2: Summary of State Juvenile Sex Crime Statutes

State[a]	Code	Comment
Alabama 16 Consistent? Gaither v. Meacham, 108 So. 2 (Ala. 1926); *but see* Benefield v. Bd. of Trs. of the Univ. of Ala., 214 F. Supp. 2d 1212 (N.D. Ala. 2002) (crediting consent of a 15-yr.-old college student).	ALA. CODE § 13A-6–61 Rape, 1st degree	Gender neutral, but must be with member of opposite sex. Perpetrator (Perp): 16 or older; Target (Targ): under 12.
	ALA. CODE § 13A-6–62 Rape, 2nd degree	Gender neutral, but must be with member of opposite sex. Perp: 16 or older; Targ: 12–15 plus 2 yr. age diff.
	ALA. CODE § 13A-6–63 Sodomy, 1st degree	Gender neutral. Perp: 16 or older; Targ: under 12.
	ALA. CODE § 13A-6–64 Sodomy, 2nd degree	Gender neutral. Perp: 16 or older; Targ: 12–15.
	ALA. CODE § 13A-6–65 Sexual misconduct	Gender neutral, but must be with member of opposite sex. No age specified. (This is the statutory rape section.)
	ALA. CODE § 13A-6–67 Sexual abuse, 2nd degree	Male perp only. Perp: 19 or older; Targ: 13–15.
Alaska 16/18 No inconsistency found.	ALASKA STAT. § 11.41.434 Sexual abuse of a minor, 1st degree	Gender neutral. Perp: 16 or older; Targ: under 13. Perp: 18 or older; Targ: under 18 plus perp is parent or guardian. Perp: 18 or older; Targ: under 16 plus perp in position of authority.
	ALASKA STAT. § 11.41.436 Sexual abuse of a minor, 2nd degree	Gender neutral. Perp: 17 or older; Targ: 13–15 plus 4 yr. age diff. Perp: 16 or older; Targ: under 13. Perp: 18 or older; Targ: under 18 plus family relationship. Perp: 18 or older; Targ: under 16 plus perp in position of authority. Perp: 18 or older; Targ: 16–17 plus 3 yr. age diff. and perp in position of authority. Perp: under 16; Targ: under 13 plus 3 yr. age diff.

(*continued*)

State[a]	Code	Comment
	ALASKA STAT. § 11.41.438 Sexual abuse of a minor, 3rd degree	Gender neutral. Perp: 17 or older; Targ: 13–15 plus 3 yr. age diff.
	ALASKA STAT. § 11.41.440 Sexual abuse of a minor, 4th degree	Gender neutral. Perp: under 16; Targ: under 13 plus 3 yr. age diff. Perp: 18 or older; Targ: 16–17 plus 3 yr. age diff. and perp in position of authority.
	ALASKA STAT. § 11.41.455 Unlawful exploitation of a minor	Gender neutral. Targ: under 18.
Arizona 18 No inconsistency found.	ARIZ. REV. STAT. § 13–1404 Sexual abuse	Gender neutral. Targ: 15 or older without consent or under 15 if only female breast involved.
	ARIZ. REV. STAT. § 13–1405 Sexual conduct with a minor	Gender neutral. Targ: under 18.
	ARIZ. REV. STAT. § 13–1409 Unlawful sexual conduct	Gender neutral. Variations in level of punishment according to age of target. Targ: under 18.
Arkansas 15/18/21 Consistent Hamm v. Office of Child Support Enforcement, 985 S.W.2d 742 (Ark. 1999) (father (13) found liable for support of child conceived despite statutory rape by mother (15)).	ARK. CODE ANN. § 5–14–103 Rape	Gender neutral. Targ: under 14 plus 3 yr. age diff. Targ: under 18 plus family relation and 3 yr. age diff.
	ARK. CODE ANN. § 5–14–110 Sexual indecency with a child	Gender neutral. Perp: 18 or older; Targ: under 15 plus 3 yr. age diff.
	ARK. CODE ANN. § 5–14–124 Sexual assault, 1st degree	Gender neutral. Targ: under 18 plus perp in position of authority and 3 yr. age diff. Targ: under 21 plus perp is personnel at target's school.
	ARK. CODE ANN. § 5–14–125 Sexual assault, 2nd degree	Gender neutral. Perp: 18 or older; Targ: under 14. Targ: under 18 plus perp in position of trust. Perp: under 18; Targ: under 12 plus 3 yr. age diff. Perp: under 18; Targ: 12–13 plus 4 yr. age diff. Targ: under 21 plus perp is personnel at target's school.
	ARK. CODE ANN. § 5–14–126 Sexual assault in the 3rd degree	Gender neutral. Perp: under 18; Targ: under 14 plus 3 yr. age diff.
	ARK. CODE ANN. § 5–14–127 Sexual assault in the 4th degree	Gender neutral. Perp: 20 or older; Targ: under 16. (This is the statutory rape code.)
California 18	CAL. PENAL CODE § 261.5 Unlawful sexual intercourse with person under 18	Gender neutral. Variations in level of punishment according to age of target. Targ: under 18.

State[a]	Code	Comment
Inconsistent: People v. Tobias, 106 Cal. Rptr. 2d 80 (2001), and Co. of San Luis Obispo v. Nathaniel J., 57 Cal. Rptr. 2d 843 (Cal. Ct. App. 1996).	CAL. PENAL CODE § 269 Aggravated sexual assault of a child	Gender neutral. Targ: under 14.
Colorado 15/18 Consistent? Bohrer v. DeHart, 943 P.2d 1220 (Colo. Ct. App. 1996); *but see* Schierenbeck v. Minor, 367 P.2d 333 (Colo. 1961) (finding father (16) may be liable for support of child conceived with mother (20)).	COLO. REV. STAT. § 18–3-402 Sexual assault	Gender neutral. Targ: under 15 plus 4 yr. age diff. Targ: 15–16 plus 10 yr. age diff.
	COLO. REV. STAT. § 18–3-404 Unlawful sexual contact	Gender neutral. Targ: under 18.
	COLO. REV. STAT. § 18–3-405 Sexual assault on a child	Gender neutral. Targ: under 15 plus 4 yr. age diff.
	COLO. REV. STAT. § 18–3-405.3 Sexual assault of a child by one in a position of trust	Gender neutral. Targ: under 18 plus perp in position of trust.
Connecticut 16/18 Consistent: Silva v. Warecke, 2004 WL 1925882 (not reported).	CONN. GEN. STAT. § 53a-70 Sexual assault in the 1st degree	Gender neutral. Targ: under 13 plus 2 yr. age diff.
	CONN. GEN. STAT. § 53a-71 Sexual assault in the 2nd degree	Gender neutral. Targ: 13–15 plus 3 yr. age diff. Targ: under 18 plus perp is target's guardian. Perp: 20 or older; Targ: under 18 plus perp in position of authority.
	CONN. GEN. STAT. § 53a-73a Sexual assault in the 4th degree	Gender neutral. Targ: under 13 plus 2 yr. age diff. Targ: 13–14 plus 3 yr. age diff. Targ: under 18 plus perp in position of authority or guardian.
	CONN. GEN. STAT. § 53a-90a Enticing a minor	Gender neutral. Targ: under 16.
Delaware 16/18 Consistent: Bostic v. Smyrna Sch. Dist., 2003 WL 723262 (not reported).	DEL. CODE ANN. tit. 11, § 223 Gender/Number	Masculine includes the feminine.

(*continued*)

State[a]	Code	Comment
	Del. Code Ann. tit. 11, § 761(k) Definitions	Targ: under 16 plus more than 4 yr. age diff. Targ: under 12 cannot consent.
	Del. Code Ann. tit. 11, § 762(b) Gender	Masculine includes the feminine.
	Del. Code Ann. tit. 11, § 768 Unlawful sexual contact, 2nd degree	Gender neutral. Targ: under 18.
	Del. Code Ann. tit. 11, § 769 Unlawful sexual contact, 1st degree	Gender neutral. Targ: under 13.
	Del. Code Ann. tit. 11, § 770 Rape in the 4th degree	Gender neutral. Targ: under 16. Perp: 30 and over; Targ: under 18.
	Del. Code Ann. tit. 11, § 771 Rape in the 3rd degree	Gender neutral. Targ: under 16 plus 10 yr. age diff. or perp causes physical injury or serious mental or emotional injury. Perp: 19 or older; Targ: under 14.
	Del. Code Ann. tit. 11, § 772 Rape, 2nd degree	Gender neutral. Targ: under 16 plus perp causes serious physical injury or uses deadly weapon or dangerous instrument. Perp: 18 or older; Targ: under 12.
	Del. Code Ann. tit. 11, § 773 Rape, 1st degree	Gender neutral. Perp: 18 older; Targ: under 12.
D.C. 16/18/20 No inconsistency found.	D.C. Code § 22–3001 Definitions	"'Child' means a person who has not yet attained the age of 16 years." "'Minor' means a person who has not yet attained the age of 18 years."
	D.C. Code § 22–3008 1st degree child sexual abuse	Gender neutral. Targ: under 16 plus 4 yr. age diff.
	D.C. Code § 22–3009 2nd degree child sexual abuse	Gender neutral. Targ: under 16 plus 4 yr. age diff.
	D.C. Code § 22–3009.01 1st degree minor sexual abuse	Gender neutral. Perp: 18 or older; Targ: 16–17.
	D.C. Code § 22–3009.02 2nd degree minor sexual abuse	Gender neutral. Perp: 18 or older; Targ: 16–17.
	D.C. Code § 22–3009.03 1st degree sexual abuse of secondary student	Gender neutral. Targ: under 20 plus personnel in target's school.
	D.C. Code § 22–3009.04 2nd degree sexual abuse of secondary student	Gender neutral. Targ: under 20 plus personnel in target's school.
	D.C. Code § 22–3010 Enticing a child	Gender neutral. Targ: under 16 plus 4 yr. age diff.

State[a]	Code	Comment
	D.C. Code § 22–3010.01 Misdemeanor sexual abuse of a minor or child	Gender neutral. Perp: 18 or older; Targ: under 18 plus 4 yr. age diff.
Florida 16/18 Consistent? Shaw v. Fletcher, 188 So. 135 (Fla. 1939); *but see* Dep't of Revenue on Behalf of Bennett v. Miller, 688 So. 2d 1024 (Fla. Dist. Ct. App. 1997) (finding father (15) liable for support of child conceived with mother (20)).	Fla. Stat. § 794.011 Sexual battery	Gender neutral. Perp: 18 or older; Targ: under 12 plus injury to sexual organs. Targ: 12 or older without consent.
	Fla. Stat. § 794.05 Unlawful sexual activity with certain minors	Gender neutral. Perp: 24 or older; Targ: 16 or 17.
	Fla. Stat. § 800.04 Lewd or lascivious offenses committed upon or in the presence of persons less than 16 years of age	Gender neutral. Diff. punishment if perp is under/over 18; Targ: under 12 or 12–15.
Georgia 16 Inconsistent: McNamee v. A.J.W., 519 S.E.2d 298 (Ga. Ct. App. 1999); *but see* Gaines v. Wolcott, 167 S.E.2d 366 (Ga. Ct. App. 1969).	Ga. Code Ann. § 16–6-1 Rape	For *rape*, perpetrator is only male and target is only female. Targ: under 10.
	Ga. Code Ann. § 16–6-2 Sodomy	Gender neutral. Targ: under 10.
	Ga. Code Ann. § 16–6-3 Statutory rape	Gender neutral. Diff. punishment if perp is under/over 21; Targ: under 16.
	Ga. Code Ann. § 16–6-4 Child molestation	Gender neutral. Targ: under 16.
	Ga. Code Ann. § 16–6-5 Enticing a child for indecent purposes	Gender neutral. Targ: under 16.
	Ga. Code Ann. § 16–6-22.1 Sexual battery	Gender neutral. Targ: under 16.
Hawaii 14/16 No inconsistency found.	Haw. Rev. Stat. § 707–730 Sexual assault, 1st degree	Gender neutral. Targ: under 14. Targ: 14–15 plus 5 yr. age diff.
	Haw. Rev. Stat. § 707–732 Sexual assault, 3rd degree	Gender neutral. Targ: under 14. Targ: 14–15 plus 5 yr. age diff.
	Haw. Rev. Stat. § 707–733.6 Continuous sexual assault of a minor	Gender neutral. Targ: under 14.
Idaho 16/18 No inconsistency found.	Idaho Code Ann. § 18–1506 Sex abuse of child under age 16	Gender neutral. Perp: 18 or older; Targ: under 16.
	Idaho Code Ann. § 18–1507 Sexual exploitation of a child	Gender neutral. Targ: under 18.

(*continued*)

State[a]	Code	Comment
	IDAHO CODE ANN. § 18–1508 Lewd conduct with a minor	Gender neutral. Targ: under 16.
	IDAHO CODE ANN. § 18–1508a Sexual battery of a minor	Gender neutral. Targ: 16–17 plus 5 yr. age diff.
	IDAHO CODE ANN. § 18–6101 Rape	This code section specifies that *rape* can only be committed by a male and only a female may be a target. Perp: 18 or older; Targ: under 16. Targ: 16–17 plus 3 yr. age diff.
	IDAHO CODE ANN. § 18–6108 Male Rape	For *male rape*, perpetrator is only male and target is only female. Perp: 18 or older; Targ: under 16. Targ: 16–17 plus 3 yr. age diff.
Illinois 17/18 Inconsistent: Doe v. Oberweis Dairy, 456 F.3d 704 (7th Cir. 2006) (finding that consent might limit damages).	720 ILL. COMP. STAT. 5/11–1.20 Criminal sexual assault	Gender neutral. Targ: under 18 plus perp is family member. Perp: 17 or older; Targ: 13–17 plus perp in position of authority.
	720 ILL. COMP. STAT. 5/11–1.30 Aggravated criminal sexual assault	Gender neutral. Perp: under 17; Targ: under 9. Targ: 9–12 plus use of force or threat of force.
	720 ILL. COMP. STAT. 5/11–1.40 Predatory criminal sexual assault of a child	Gender neutral. Perp: 17 or older; Targ: under 13.
	720 ILL. COMP. STAT. 5/11–1.50 Sexual abuse	Gender neutral. Perp: under 17; Targ: 9–16. Targ: 13–16 plus less than 5 yr. age diff.
	720 ILL. COMP. STAT. 5/11–1.60 Aggravated criminal sexual abuse	Gender neutral. Targ: under 18 plus perp is family member. Perp: 17 or older; Targ: under 13. Perp: 17 or older plus in position of authority, trust, etc.; Targ: 13–17. Perp: 17 or older plus used force or threat of force; Targ: 13–16. Perp: under 17; Targ: 13–16 plus 5 yr. age diff.; Targ: under 9. Perp: under 17 plus use of force or threat of use of force; Targ: 9–16.
	720 ILL. COMP. STAT. 5/11–6 Indecent solicitation of a child	Gender neutral. Perp: 17 or older; Targ: under 17.
Indiana 16/18 Consistent? Renguette v. Bd. of Trs. ex rel. Brownsburg Comty. Sch. Corp.,	IND. CODE § 35–42–4-1 Rape	Must be with "member of the opposite sex." No age specified.
	IND. CODE § 35–42–4-3 Child molesting	Gender neutral. Diff. punishment if perp is under/over 21; Targ: under 14.

State[a]	Code	Comment
2007 WL 1536841 (not published) (leaving open the question of whether minor had capacity to consent to sex).	IND. CODE § 35–42-4-5 Vicarious sexual gratification	Gender neutral. Perp: 18 or older; Targ: under 16.
	IND. CODE § 35–42-4-6 Child solicitation	Gender neutral. Perp: 18 or older; Targ: under 14. Perp: 21 or older; Targ: 14–15.
	IND. CODE § 35–42-4-7 Child seduction	Gender neutral. Perp: 18 or older; Targ: 16–17 plus 4 yr. age diff. and perp in various positions of trust or authority.
	IND. CODE § 35–42-4-9 Sexual misconduct with a minor	Gender neutral. Perp: 18 or older; Targ: 14–15.
Iowa 14/16/18 Consistent: Reutkemeier v. Nolte, 161 N.W. 290 (Iowa 1917).	IOWA CODE § 702.5 Definition of "Child"	Targ: under 14.
	IOWA CODE § 709.3 Sexual abuse, 2nd degree	Gender neutral. Targ: under 12.
	IOWA CODE § 709.4 Sexual abuse, 3rd degree	Gender neutral. Targ: 12–13. Targ: 14–15 plus family relationship, position of authority, or 4 yr. age diff.
	IOWA CODE § 709.8 Lascivious acts with a child	Gender neutral. Perp: 16 or older; Targ: under 14.
	IOWA CODE § 709.12 Indecent contact	Gender neutral. Perp: 18 or older or 16–17 plus 5 yr. age diff.; Targ: under 14.
	IOWA CODE § 709.14 Lascivious conduct with a minor	Gender neutral. Perp: over 18 plus in position of authority; Targ: under 18.
Kansas 16 Consistent? Herman v. Turner, 232 P. 864 (Kan. 1925); *but see* State ex rel. Hermesmann v. Seyer, 847 P.2d 1273 (Kan. 1993) (finding father (13) liable for support of child conceived with mother (16)).	KAN. STAT. ANN. § 21–5503 Rape	Gender neutral. Targ: under 14.
	KAN. STAT. ANN. § 21–5504 Criminal sodomy	Gender neutral. Targ: 14–15.
	KAN. STAT. ANN. § 21–5505 Sexual battery	Gender neutral. Targ: 16 or older without consent.
	KAN. STAT. ANN. § 21–5506 Indecent liberties with a child	Gender neutral. Targ: 14–15.
	KAN. STAT. ANN. § 21–5508 Indecent solicitation of a child	Gender neutral. Targ: 14–15.
	KAN. STAT. ANN. § 21–5510 Sexual exploitation of a child	Gender neutral. Targ: under 18.
	KAN. STAT. ANN. § 21–5512 Unlawful sexual relations	Gender neutral. Targ: 16 or older.
Kentucky 16/18 Consistent? Monahan v. Clemons, 279 S.W. 974 (Ky. Ct. App. 1926); *but see* Commonwealth	KY. REV. STAT. ANN. § 446.020 Gender & number	Use of the masculine includes the feminine unless otherwise indicated.
	KY. REV. STAT. ANN. § 510 References and Annotations	Explanation of legislative age choices (ages 12, 14, and 16). Age of full consent: 16.

(*continued*)

State[a]	Code	Comment
ex rel. Rush v. Hatfield, 929 S.W.2d 200 (Ky. Ct. App. 1996) (finding father (15) ultimately liable for support of child conceived with mother (over 21)).	KY. REV. STAT. ANN. § 510.020 Lack of consent	Gender neutral. Targ: incapable of consenting when under 16.
	KY. REV. STAT. ANN. § 510.040 Rape, 1st degree	Written in masculine but gender neutral due to Ky. Rev. Stat. Ann. § 446.020. Targ: under 12.
	KY. REV. STAT. ANN. § 510.050 Rape, 2nd degree	Written in masculine but gender neutral due to Ky. Rev. Stat. Ann. § 446.020. Perp: 18 or older; Targ: under 14.
	KY. REV. STAT. ANN. § 510.060 Rape, 3rd degree	Written in masculine but gender neutral due to Ky. Rev. Stat. Ann. § 446.020. Perp: 21 or older; Targ: under 16. Perp: 21 or older; Targ: under 18 plus perp in position of authority.
	KY. REV. STAT. ANN. § 510.070 Sodomy, 1st degree	Written in masculine but gender neutral due to Ky. Rev. Stat. Ann. § 446.020. Targ: under 12.
	KY. REV. STAT. ANN. § 510.080 Sodomy, 2nd degree	Written in masculine but gender neutral due to Ky. Rev. Stat. Ann. § 446.020. Perp: 18 or older; Targ: under 14.
	KY. REV. STAT. ANN. § 510.090 Sodomy, 3rd degree	Written in masculine but gender neutral due to Ky. Rev. Stat. Ann. § 446.020. Perp: 21 or older; Targ: under 16. Perp: 21 or older; Targ: under 18 plus perp in position of authority.
	KY. REV. STAT. ANN. § 510.110 Sexual abuse, 1st degree	Written in masculine, but gender neutral due to Ky. Rev. Stat. Ann. § 446.020. Targ: under 12. Perp: 21 or older; Targ: under 16. Perp: 18 or older; Targ: under 18 plus perp in position of authority.
	KY. REV. STAT. ANN. § 510.120 Sexual abuse, 2nd degree	Written in masculine but gender neutral due to Ky. Rev. Stat. Ann. § 446.020. Perp: 18–21; Targ: under 16.
	KY. REV. STAT. ANN. § 510.130 Sexual abuse, 3rd degree	Written in masculine but gender neutral due to Ky. Rev. Stat. Ann. § 446.020. Perp: 18 or older; Targ: under 14.
Louisiana 17/18 Inconsistent: Landreneau v. Fruge, 676 So. 2d 701 (La. Ct. App. 1996).	LA. REV. STAT. ANN. § 14:43.1 Sexual battery	Gender neutral. Targ: under 15 plus 3 yr. age diff. Perp: 17 or older; Targ: under 13.
	LA. REV. STAT. ANN. § 14:43.2 Sexual battery, 2nd degree	Gender neutral. Perp: 17 or older; Targ: under 13.
	LA. REV. STAT. ANN. § 14:43.3 Oral sexual battery	Gender neutral. Targ: under 15 plus 3 yr. age diff.
	LA. REV. STAT. ANN. § 14:80 Felony carnal knowledge of a juvenile	Gender neutral. Perp: 17 or older; Targ: 13–16 plus 4 yr. age diff.

State[a]	Code	Comment
	LA. REV. STAT. ANN. § 14:80.1 Misdemeanor carnal knowledge of a juvenile	Gender neutral. Perp: 17 or older; Targ: 13–17 plus 3 yr. age diff.
	LA. REV. STAT. ANN. § 14:81 Indecent behavior with a juvenile	Gender neutral. Targ: under 17 plus 2 yr. age diff.
	LA. REV. STAT. ANN. § 14:81.2 Molestation of a juvenile	Gender neutral. Perp: over 17; Targ: under 17 plus 3 yr. age diff. plus perp use of force, intimidation, or position of authority.
Maine 14/16/18 No inconsistency found.	ME. REV. STAT. 17-A § 253 Gross sexual assault	Gender neutral. Targ: under 14. Targ: 18 plus perp has supervisory or disciplinary control.
	ME. REV. STAT. 17-A § 254 Sexual abuse of minors	Gender neutral. Targ: 14–15 plus 5 yr. age diff. Perp: 21 or older; Targ: 16–17 plus perp is personnel in target's school.
	ME. REV. STAT. 17-A § 255-A Unlawful sexual contact	Gender neutral. Targ: under 14 plus 3 yr. age diff. Targ: 14–15 plus 10 yr. age diff. Targ: under 18 plus perp with certain familial relationship or is personnel in target's school.
	ME. REV. STAT. 17-A § 256 Visual sexual aggression against a child	Gender neutral. Perp: 18 or older; Targ: under 14.
	ME. REV. STAT. 17-A § 258 Sexual misconduct with a child	Gender neutral. Perp: 18 or older; Targ: under 14.
	ME. REV. STAT. 17-A § 259-A Solicitation of a child to commit a prohibited act	Gender neutral. Perp: 16 or older; Targ: under 14 plus 3 yr. age diff.
	ME. REV. STAT. 17-A § 260 Unlawful sexual touching	Gender neutral. Targ: under 14 plus 5 yr. age diff.; Targ: under 18 plus perp is personnel in target's school or guardian.
Maryland 14/16 Inconsistent: Tate v. Bd. of Edu., 843 A.2d 890 (Md. Ct. Spec. App. 2004).	MD. CODE ANN., CRIM. LAW § 3–303 Rape, 1st degree	Gender neutral but must involve a vagina. Perp: 18 or older; Targ: under 13.
	MD. CODE ANN., CRIM. LAW § 3–304 Rape, 2nd degree	Gender neutral but must involve a vagina. Targ: under 14 plus 4 yr. age diff.
	MD. CODE ANN., CRIM. LAW § 3–305 Sexual offense, 1st degree	Gender neutral. Perp: 18 or older; Targ: under 14.
	MD. CODE ANN., CRIM. LAW § 3–306 Sexual offense, 2nd degree	Gender neutral. Targ: under 14 plus 4 yr. age diff.

(*continued*)

State[a]	Code	Comment
	Md. Code Ann., Crim. Law § 3–307 Sexual offense, 3rd degree	Gender neutral. Targ: under 14 plus 4 yr. age diff. Perp: 21 or older; Targ: 14–15.
	Md. Code Ann., Crim. Law § 3–308 Sexual offense, 4th degree	Gender neutral. Perp: 21 or older; Targ: 14–15 plus 4 yr. age diff. and perp is personnel in target's school.
	Md. Code Ann., Crim. Law § 3–324 Sexual solicitation of minors	Gender neutral.
Massachusetts 16 Consistent: Glover v. Callahan, 12 N.E.2d 194 (Mass. 1937).	Mass. Gen. Laws ch. 265, § 22A Rape of a child	Gender neutral. Targ: under 16 plus force or threat used.
	Mass. Gen. Laws ch. 265, § 23 Rape and abuse of a child	Gender neutral. Targ: under 16.
	Mass. Gen. Laws ch. 265, § 24B Assault of child; intent to rape	Gender neutral. Targ: under 16.
	Mass. Gen. Laws ch. 272, § 4 Inducing persons under 18 to have sexual intercourse	Gender neutral. Targ: under 18 but must be of "chaste life." [I do not consider this a protective statute since it leaves the target open to a trial regarding her sexual history.]
Michigan 16/18 Consistent? L.M.E. v. A.R.S., 680 N.W.2d 902 (Mich. Ct. App. 2004) (finding father (14) liable for support of child conceived with mother (a married adult)).	Mich. Comp. Laws § 750.520b Criminal Sexual Conduct, 1st degree	Gender neutral. Targ: under 13. Targ: 13–15 plus perp in position of authority.
	Mich. Comp. Laws § 750.520c Criminal Sexual Conduct, 2nd degree	Gender neutral. Targ: under 13. Targ: 13–15 plus perp in position of authority.
	Mich. Comp. Laws § 750.520d Criminal Sexual Conduct, 3rd degree	Gender neutral. Targ: 13–15. Targ: 16–17 plus perp is personnel in target's school.
	Mich. Comp. Laws § 750.520e Criminal Sexual Conduct, 4th degree	Gender neutral. Targ: 13–15 plus 5 yr. age diff. Targ: 16–17 plus perp is personnel in target's school.

State[a]	Code	Comment
Minnesota 16/18 Consistent? Bjerke v. Johnson, 727 N.W.2d 183 (Minn. Ct. App. 2007); *but see* Jevning v. Cichos, 499 N.W.2d 515 (Minn. Ct. App. 1993) (finding father (15) liable for support of child conceived with mother (20)).	MINN. STAT. § 609.342 Criminal Sexual Conduct, 1st degree	Gender neutral. Targ: under 13 plus 36 mo. age diff. Targ: 13–15 plus 48 mo. age diff. plus perp in position of authority. Targ: under 16 plus perp has "significant relationship" to target and force or coercion used.
	MINN. STAT. § 609.343 Criminal Sexual Conduct, 2nd degree	Gender neutral. Targ: under 13 plus 36 mo. age diff. Targ: 13–15 plus 48 mo. age diff. and perp in position of authority. Targ: under 16 plus perp has "significant relationship" to target and force or coercion used.
	MINN. STAT. § 609.344 Criminal Sexual Conduct, 3rd degree	Gender neutral. Targ: under 13 plus 36 mo. age diff. Targ: 13–15 plus 24 mo. age diff. Targ: 16–17 plus 48 mo. age diff. and perp in position of authority. Targ: 16–17 plus "significant relationship" to perp.
	MINN. STAT. § 609.345 Criminal Sexual Conduct, 4th degree	Gender neutral. Targ: under 13 plus 36 mo. age diff. Targ: 13–15 plus 48 mo. age diff. or perp in position of authority. Targ: 16–17 plus 48 mo. age diff. and perp in position of authority. Targ: 16–17 plus "significant relationship" to perp.
	MINN. STAT. § 609.3451 Criminal Sexual Conduct, 5th degree	Gender neutral. Targ: under 16.
	MINN. STAT. § 609.352 Solicitation of Children to Engage in Sexual Conduct	Gender neutral. Perp: 18 or older; Targ: under 16.
Mississippi 14/16 **Inconsistent:** Miss. St. Fed. Colored Women's Club Housing v. L.R., 62 So. 3d 351 (Miss. 2010).	MISS. CODE ANN. § 97-3-65 Statutory Rape	Gender neutral. Perp: 17 or older; Targ: 14–15 plus 36 mo. age diff. Targ: under 14 plus 24 mo. age diff.
	MISS. CODE ANN. § 97-3-95 Sexual Battery	Gender neutral. Perp: 17 or older; Targ: 14–15 plus 36 mo. age diff. Targ: under 14 plus 24 mo. age diff.
Missouri 17 No inconsistency found.	MO. REV. STAT. § 566.032 Statutory Rape, 1st degree	Gender neutral. Targ: under 14.
	MO. REV. STAT. § 566.034 Statutory Rape, 2nd degree	Gender neutral. Perp: 21 or older; Targ: under 17.
	MO. REV. STAT. § 566.062 Statutory Sodomy, 1st degree	Gender neutral. Targ: under 14.

(*continued*)

State[a]	Code	Comment
	MO. REV. STAT. § 566.064 Statutory Sodomy, 2nd degree	Gender neutral. Perp: 21 or older; Targ: under 17.
	MO. REV. STAT. § 566.067 Child molestation, 1st degree	Gender neutral. Targ: under 14.
	MO. REV. STAT. § 566.068 Child molestation, 2nd degree	Gender neutral. Targ: under 17.
	MO. REV. STAT. § 566.083 Sexual misconduct involving child	Gender neutral. Targ: under 15.
	MO. REV. STAT. § 566.151 Enticement of a child	Gender neutral. Perp: 21 or older; Targ: under 15.
Montana 13/16 No inconsistency found.	MONT. CODE ANN. § 45–5-501 Definitions	Gender neutral. Targ: under 16.
	MONT. CODE ANN. § 45–5-502 Sexual assault	Gender neutral. Targ: under 16 plus 3 yr. age diff.
	MONT. CODE ANN. § 45–5-503 Sexual intercourse without consent	Gender neutral. Perp: 18 or older; Targ: under 13. Targ: under 16 plus 4 yr. age diff.
Nebraska 16/17 Consistent: Bishop v. Liston, 199 N.W. 825 (Neb. 1924).	NEB. REV. STAT. § 28–319 Sexual assault, 1st degree	Gender neutral. Perp: 19 or older; Targ: 12–15.
	NEB. REV. STAT. § 28–319.01 Sexual assault of a child, 1st degree	Gender neutral. Perp: 19 or older; Targ: under 12. Perp: 25 or older; Targ: 12–15.
	NEB. REV. STAT. § 28–320 Sexual assault, 2nd or 3rd degree	Gender neutral. No age specified.
	NEB. REV. STAT. § 28–320.01 Sexual assault of a child, 2nd or 3rd degree	Gender neutral. Perp: 19 or older; Targ: 14 and under.
	NEB. REV. STAT. § 28–805 Debauching a minor	Gender neutral. Perp: 18 or older; Targ: under 17.
Nevada 16 No inconsistency found.	NEV. REV. STAT. 200.364 Definitions	Gender neutral. Perp: 18 or older; Targ: under 16.
	NEV. REV. STAT. 200.368 Statutory sexual seduction: Penalties	Gender neutral. Specifies age of perpetrator.
New Hampshire 16/18 Inconsistent: Kravitz v. Beech Hill Hosp., 808 A.2d 34 (N.H. 2002).	N.H. REV. STAT. ANN. § 632-A:2 Aggravated felonious sexual assault	Gender neutral. Targ: under 13. Targ: 13–15 plus perp lives in same household or family relation. Targ: 13–17 plus perp in position of authority.
	N.H. REV. STAT. ANN. § 632-A:3 Felonious sexual assault	Gender neutral. Targ: 13–15 plus 4 yr. age diff., penetration. Targ: under 13, contact only.

State[a]	Code	Comment
	N.H. Rev. Stat. Ann. § 632-A:4 Sexual assault	Gender neutral. Targ: 13 and over. Targ: 13–15 plus 5 yr. age diff., contact only. Targ: 13–15 plus age diff. of 4 yrs. or less, penetration.
New Jersey 16/18 No inconsistency found.	N.J. Stat. Ann. § 2C:14–1 Definitions	Gender neutral. No age specified.
	N.J. Stat. Ann. § 2C:14–2 Sexual assault	Gender neutral. Targ: under 13. Targ: 13–15 plus family relation or perp in position of authority or 4 yr. age diff. Targ: 16–17 plus family relation or perp in position of authority.
	N.J. Stat. Ann. § 2C:14–4 Lewdness (exposure)	Gender neutral. Targ: under 13 plus 4 yr. age diff.
New Mexico 14/19 No inconsistency found.	N.M. Stat. Ann. § 30–9-11 Criminal sexual penetration	Gender neutral. Targ: under 13. Targ: 13–18 plus perp in position of authority. Perp: 18 or older; Targ: 13–16 plus 4 yr. age diff. Targ: 13–18 plus perp is personnel in target's school.
	N.M. Stat. Ann. § 30–9-12 Criminal sexual contact	Gender neutral. Targ: 18 and over plus no consent.
	N.M. Stat. Ann. § 30–9-13 Criminal sexual contact with a minor	Gender neutral. Targ: under 13. Targ: 13–18 plus perp in position of authority.
New York 17 Inconsistent: Barton v. Bee Line, 265 N.Y.S. 284 (1933).	N.Y. Penal Law § 130.05 Sexual offense: lack of consent	Gender neutral. Targ: under 17.
	N.Y. Penal Law § 130.25 Rape, 3rd degree	Gender neutral. Perp: 21 or older; Targ: under 17.
	N.Y. Penal Law § 130.30 Rape, 2nd degree	Gender neutral. Perp: 18 or older; Targ: under 15 and 4 yr. age diff.
	N.Y. Penal Law § 130.35 Rape, 1st degree	Gender neutral. Targ: under 11. Perp: 18 or older; Targ: under 13.
	N.Y. Penal Law § 130.40 Criminal sex act, 3rd degree	Gender neutral. Perp: 21 or older; Targ: under 17.
	N.Y. Penal Law § 130.45 Criminal sex act, 2nd degree	Gender neutral. Perp: 18 or older; Targ: under 15 plus 4 yr. age diff.
	N.Y. Penal Law § 130.50 Criminal sex act, 1st degree	Gender neutral. Targ: under 11. Perp: 18 or older; Targ: under 13.
	N.Y. Penal Law § 130.55 Sexual abuse, 3rd degree	Gender neutral. Targ: under 14 plus 5 yr. age diff.
	N.Y. Penal Law § 130.60 Sexual abuse, 2nd degree	Gender neutral. Targ: under 14.
	N.Y. Penal Law § 130.65 Sexual abuse, 1st degree	Gender neutral. Targ: under 11.

(continued)

State[a]	Code	Comment
	N.Y. PENAL LAW § 130.66 Aggravated sexual abuse, 3rd degree	Gender neutral. Targ: under 11.
	N.Y. PENAL LAW § 130.67 Aggravated sexual abuse, 2nd degree	Gender neutral. Targ: under 11.
	N.Y. PENAL LAW § 130.70 Aggravated sexual abuse, 1st degree	Gender neutral. Targ: under 11.
North Carolina 13/16 No inconsistency found.	N.C. GEN. STAT. § 14–27.2 Rape, 1st degree	Gender neutral. Perp: 12 or older; Targ: under 13 plus 4 yr. age diff.
	N.C. GEN. STAT. § 14–27.2A Rape of a child	Gender neutral. Perp: 18 or older; Targ: under 13.
	N.C. GEN. STAT. § 14–27.4 Sexual offense, 1st degree	Gender neutral. Perp: 12 or older; Targ: under 13 plus 4 yr. age diff.
	N.C. GEN. STAT. § 14–27.4A Sexual offense with a child	Gender neutral. Perp: 18 or older; Targ: under 13.
	N.C. GEN. STAT. § 14–27.7A Statutory rape or sexual offense	Gender neutral. Targ: 13–15 plus 6 yr. age diff.
North Dakota 18 Inconsistent: Braun v. Heidrich, 241 N.W. 599 (N.D. 1932).	N.D. CENT. CODE § 12.1–20–03 Gross sexual imposition	Gender neutral. Targ: under 15.
	N.D. CENT. CODE § 12.1–20–03.1 Continuous sexual abuse of child	Gender neutral. Targ: under 15.
	N.D. CENT. CODE § 12.1–20–05 Corruption or solicitation of minor	Gender neutral. Perp: 18 or older; Targ: 15–17. Perp: 18 or older; Targ: under 15. Perp: 22 or older; Targ: 15–17.
	N.D. CENT. CODE § 12.1–20–07 Sexual assault	Gender neutral. Perp: 18 or older; Targ: 15–17.
Ohio 16/18 No inconsistency found.	OHIO REV. CODE ANN. § 2907.01 Definitions	*Minor* and *juvenile* are under 18.
	OHIO REV. CODE ANN. § 2907.03 Sexual battery	Gender neutral. Targ: under 18 plus perp in position of authority, guardian, or other certain relationships.
	OHIO REV. CODE ANN. § 2907.04 Unlawful sexual conduct with a minor	Gender neutral. Perp: 18 or older; Targ: 13–15.
	OHIO REV. CODE ANN. § 2907.05 Gross sexual imposition	Gender neutral. Targ: under 13.
	OHIO REV. CODE ANN. § 2907.06 Sexual imposition	Gender neutral. Perp: 18 or older; Targ: 13–15 plus 4 yr. age diff.

State[a]	Code	Comment
Oklahoma 14/16 Consistent? Priboth v. Haveron, 139 P. 973 (Okla. 1914); *but see* In the Matter of the Paternity of K.B. v. Dep't of Human Serv., ex rel. Baker, 104 P.2d 1132 (Okla. Civ. App. 2004) (finding father (15) liable for support of child conceived with mother (19)).	OKLA. STAT. tit. 21 § 888 Forcible Sodomy	Gender neutral. Perp: 19 or older; Targ: under 16.
	OKLA. STAT. tit. 21 § 1111 Definitions	Gender neutral rape. Targ: under 16. Targ: 16–19 plus perp is personnel in target's school.
	OKLA. STAT. tit. 21 § 1114 Rape, 1st degree & 2nd degree	Gender neutral. Perp: 18 or older; Targ: under 14.
	OKLA. STAT. tit. 21 § 1123 Lewd or indecent propositions or acts to a child	Gender neutral. Targ: under 16.
Oregon 12/16/18 Consistent: Wilson v. Tobiassen, 777 P.2d 1379 (Or. Ct. App. 1989); Hough v. Iderhoff, 139 P. 931 (Or. 1914).	OR. REV. STAT. § 163.315 Incapacity to consent	Gender neutral. Targ: under 18.
	OR. REV. STAT. § 163.355 Rape, 3rd degree	Gender neutral. Targ: under 16.
	OR. REV. STAT. § 163.365 Rape, 2nd degree	Gender neutral. Targ: under 14.
	OR. REV. STAT. § 163.375 Rape, 1st degree	Gender neutral. Targ: under 12. Targ: under 16 plus certain family relationships.
	OR. REV. STAT. § 163.385 Sodomy, 3rd degree	Gender neutral. Targ: under 16.
	OR. REV. STAT. § 163.395 Sodomy, 2nd degree	Gender neutral. Targ: under 14.
	OR. REV. STAT. § 163.405 Sodomy, 1st degree	Gender neutral. Targ: under 12. Targ: under 16 plus certain family relationships.
	OR. REV. STAT. § 163.408 Unlawful sex. Penetration, 2nd degree	Gender neutral. Targ: under 14.
	OR. REV. STAT. § 163.411 Unlawful sex. Penetration, 1st degree	Gender neutral. Targ: under 12.
	OR. REV. STAT. § 163.415 Sexual abuse, 3rd degree	Gender neutral. Targ: under 18.
	OR. REV. STAT. § 163.427 Sexual abuse, 1st degree	Gender neutral. Targ: under 14.
	OR. REV. STAT. § 163.435 Contributing to the sexual delinquency of a minor	"Opposite sex" requirement. Perp: 18 or older; Targ: under 18.
	OR. REV. STAT. § 163.445 Sexual misconduct	Gender neutral. Targ: under 18.

(*continued*)

State[a]	Code	Comment
Pennsylvania 16/18 Consistent: C.C.H. v. Philadelphia Phillies, 940 A.2d 336 (Pa. 2008).	18 Pa. Cons. Stat. § 3121 Rape of a child	Gender neutral. Targ: under 13.
	18 Pa. Cons. Stat. § 3122.1 Statutory sexual assault	Gender neutral. Targ: under 16 plus 4 yr. age diff.
	18 Pa. Cons. Stat. § 3123 Involuntary deviate sexual intercourse	Gender neutral. Targ: under 18.
	18 Pa. Cons. Stat. § 3125 Aggravated indecent assault	Gender neutral. Targ: under 13. Targ: under 16 plus 4 yr. age diff.
	18 Pa. Cons. Stat. § 3126 Indecent assault	Gender neutral. Targ: under 13. Targ: under 16 plus 4 yr. age diff.
Rhode Island 15/18 No inconsistency found.	R.I. Gen. Laws § 11–37–6 Sexual assault 3rd degree	Gender neutral. Targ: 14–15.
	R.I. Gen. Laws § 11–37–8.1 Child molestation 1st degree	Gender neutral. Targ: under 15.
	R.I. Gen. Laws § 11–37–8.3 Child molestation 2nd degree	Gender neutral. Targ: under 15.
	R.I. Gen. Laws § 11–37–8.8 Indecent solicitation of a child	Gender neutral. Targ: under 18.
South Carolina 11/15/16 Inconsistent (damages): Roe by Doe v. Orangeburg County Sch. Dist., 518 S.E.2d 259 (S.C. 1999).	S.C. Code Ann. § 16–3-655 Criminal sexual conduct with minors	Gender neutral. Targ: under 11. Targ: 11–14. Targ: 14–15 plus perp in position of familial, custodial, or official authority.
South Dakota 16 Consistent: Huempfner v. Bailly, 156 N.W. 78 (S.D. 1916).	S.D. Codified Laws § 22–22–1 Rape defined	Gender neutral. Targ: under 13. Targ: 13–15 plus 3 yr. age diff.
	S.D. Codified Laws § 22–22–7 Sexual contact with a child	Gender neutral. Perp: 16 or older; Targ: under 16.
	S.D. Codified Laws § 22–22–7.3 Sexual contact with a child, misdemeanor	Gender neutral. Perp: 16 or under; Targ: under 16.
	S.D. Codified Laws § 22–24A-5 Solicitation of a minor	Gender neutral. Perp: 18 or older; Targ: under 16.
Tennessee 13/18 Inconsistent: Doe v. Mama Taori's Prem. Pizza, 2001 WL 327906 (not reported).	Tenn. Code. Ann. § 39–13–504 Aggravated sexual battery	Gender neutral. Targ: under 13.
	Tenn. Code. Ann. § 39–13–506 Statutory rape	Gender neutral. Targ: age 13–17 plus 4 yr. age diff.

State[a]	Code	Comment
	TENN. CODE. ANN. § 39–13–522 Rape of a child	Gender neutral. Targ: 4–13.
	TENN. CODE. ANN. § 39–13–527 Authority figure, sexual battery	Gender neutral. Targ: age 13–17 plus perp in supervisory or disciplinary position.
	TENN. CODE. ANN. § 39–13–531 Aggravated rape of a child	Gender Neutral. Targ: under 4.
Texas 17 Consistent: Altman v. Eckermann, 132 S.W. 523 (Tex. Civ. App. 1910); Robinson v. Moore 408 S.W.2d 582 (Tx. Civ. App. 1966).	TEX. PENAL CODE ANN. § 21.01 Definitions	Gender neutral. No age.
	TEX. PENAL CODE ANN. § 21.11 Indecency with a child	Gender neutral. Targ: under 17 plus 4 yr. age diff.
	TEX. PENAL CODE ANN. § 22.011 Sexual assault	Gender neutral. Targ: under 17.
	TEX. PENAL CODE ANN. § 22.021 Aggravated sexual assault	Gender neutral. Targ: under 17.
Utah 14/16/18 Consistent: Elkington v. Foust, 618 P.2d 37 (Utah 1980).	UTAH CODE ANN. § 76–5-401 Unlawful sex activity with a minor	Gender neutral. Targ: 14–15 plus 4 yr. age diff.
	UTAH CODE ANN. § 76–5-401.1 Sexual abuse of a minor	Gender neutral. Targ: 14–15 plus 7 yr. age diff.
	UTAH CODE ANN. § 76–5-401.2 Unlawful sexual conduct with a 16- or 17-yr.-old	Gender neutral. Targ: 16–17 plus 7 yr. age diff.
	UTAH CODE ANN. § 76–5-402 Rape	Gender neutral. No age specified.
	UTAH CODE ANN. § 76–5-402.1 Rape of a child	Gender neutral. Targ: under 14.
	UTAH CODE ANN. § 76–5-402.3 Object rape of a child	Gender neutral. Targ: under 14.
	UTAH CODE ANN. § 76–5-403 Forcible sodomy	Gender neutral. Targ: 14 and over.
	UTAH CODE ANN. § 76–5-403.1 Sodomy on a child	Gender neutral. Targ: under 14.
	UTAH CODE ANN. § 76–5-404 Forcible sexual abuse	Gender neutral. Targ: 14 and over.

(*continued*)

State[a]	Code	Comment
	UTAH CODE ANN. § 76–5-404.1 Sexual abuse of a child, aggravated	Gender neutral. Targ: under 14.
	UTAH CODE ANN. § 76–5-406 Sexual offense without consent	Gender neutral. Targ: under 14. Targ: under 18 plus certain family relationships. Targ: 14–17 plus 3 yr. age diff.
Vermont 16/18 No inconsistency found.	VT. STAT. ANN. tit. 13 § 3252 Sexual assault	Gender neutral. Targ: under 16. Targ: under 18 plus certain family relationships.
	VT. STAT. ANN. tit. 13 § 3253 Aggravated sexual assault	Gender neutral. Perp: 18 and older; Targ: under 13.
	VT. STAT. ANN. tit. 13 § 3253a Aggravated sexual assault of a child	Gender neutral. Perp: 18 or older; Targ: under 16.
	VT. STAT. ANN. tit. 13 § 3258 Sexual exploitation of a minor	Gender neutral. Perp: 18 or older; Targ: no age specified but 4 yr. age diff.
Virginia 13/15/18 Inconsistent (damages): Parsons v. Parker, 170 S.E. 1 (Va. 1933).	VA. CODE ANN. § 18.2–61 Rape	Gender neutral. Targ: under 13.
	VA. CODE ANN. § 18.2–63 Carnal knowledge of a child	Gender neutral. Targ: 13–14.
	VA. CODE ANN. § 18.2–67.1 Forcible sodomy	Gender neutral. Targ: under 13.
	VA. CODE ANN. § 18.2–67.2 Object sexual penetration	Gender neutral. Targ: under 13.
	VA. CODE ANN. § 18.2–67.3 Aggravated sexual battery	Gender neutral. Targ: under 13. Targ: 13–14 plus use of force or threat. Targ: 13–17 plus perp in certain familial relationship.
	VA. CODE ANN. § 18.2–67.4:2 Sexual abuse of a child	Gender neutral. Targ: 13–14.
	VA. CODE ANN. § 18.2–370.1 Taking indecent liberties with a child	Gender neutral. Perp: 18 or older; Targ: under 18 plus perp in supervisory position.
	VA. CODE ANN. § 18.2–371 Causing or encouraging acts rendering children delinquent, abused, etc.; penalty; abandoned infant	Gender neutral. Perp: 18 or older; Targ: "child" 15 or older.

State[a]	Code	Comment
Washington 16/18/21 Consistent: Christensen v. Royal Sch. Dist., 124 P.3d 283 (Wash. 2005).	WASH. REV. CODE § 9A.44.073 Rape of a child, 1st degree	Gender neutral. Targ: under 12 plus 24 mo. age diff.
	WASH. REV. CODE § 9A.44.076 Rape of a child, 2nd degree	Gender neutral. Targ: age 12–13 plus 36 mo. age diff.
	WASH. REV. CODE § 9A.44.079 Rape of a child, 3rd degree	Gender neutral. Targ: age 14–15 plus 48 mo. age diff.
	WASH. REV. CODE § 9A.44.083 Child molestation, 1st degree	Gender neutral. Targ: under 12 plus 36 mo. age diff.
	WASH. REV. CODE § 9A.44.086 Child molestation, 2nd degree	Gender neutral. Targ: 12–13 plus 36 mo. age diff.
	WASH. REV. CODE § 9A.44.089 Child molestation, 3rd degree	Gender neutral. Targ: 14–15 plus 48 mo. age diff.
	WASH. REV. CODE § 9A.44.093 Sexual misconduct with a minor, 1st degree	Gender neutral. Targ: 16–17 plus 60 mo. age diff., perp in significant relationship with target, and perp in supervisory position over target. Targ: 16–21 plus perp is personnel in target's school and 60 mo. age diff. Targ: 16 or older plus perp is foster parent.
	WASH. REV. CODE § 9A.44.096 Sexual misconduct with a minor, 2nd degree	Gender neutral. Targ: 16–17. Targ: 16–21 plus perp is personnel in target's school and 60 mo. age diff. Targ: 16 or older plus perp is foster parent.
West Virginia 16 No inconsistency found.	W. VA. CODE § 61–8B-2 Lack of consent	Gender neutral. Targ: under 16.
	W. VA. CODE § 61–8B-3 Sexual assault, 1st degree	Gender neutral. Perp: 14 or older; Targ: 11 and under.
	W. VA. CODE § 61–8B-5 Sexual assault, 3rd degree	Gender neutral. Perp: 16 or older; Targ: under 16 plus 4 yr. age diff.
	W. VA. CODE § 61–8B-7 Sexual abuse, 1st degree	Gender neutral. Perp: 14 or older; Targ: 11 and under.
	W. VA. CODE § 61–8B-9 Sexual abuse, 3rd degree	Gender neutral. Perp: 16 or older; Targ: under 16 plus 4 yr. age diff.
Wisconsin 18 Inconsistent: Michelle T. by Sumpter v. Crozier, 495 N.W.2d 327 (Wisc. 1993).	WIS. STAT. § 948.02 Sexual assault of a child	Gender neutral. Targ: under 13; Targ: under 16.
	WIS. STAT. § 948.05 Sexual exploitation of a child	Gender Neutral. Targ: under 18.
	WIS. STAT. § 948.09 Sexual intercourse with a child	Gender neutral. Targ: 16 and over.

(*continued*)

State[a]	Code	Comment
Wyoming 13/16/18 No inconsistency found.	WYO. STAT. ANN. § 6–2-308 Criminality of conduct; Victim's age	Gender neutral. Targ: age varies with degree of crime.
	WYO. STAT. ANN. § 6–2-314 Sexual abuse of minor, 1st degree	Gender neutral. Perp: 16 or older; Targ: under 13. Perp: 18 or older; Targ: under 18 plus perp in certain familial relationship. Perp: 18 or older; Targ: under 16 plus perp in position of authority.
	WYO. STAT. ANN. § 6–2-315 Sexual abuse of minor, 2nd degree	Gender neutral. Perp: 17 or older; Targ: 13–15 plus 4 yr. age diff. Perp: 16 or older; Targ: under 13. Perp: 18 or older; Targ: under 18 plus perp in certain familial relationship. Perp: 18 or older; Targ: under 16 plus perp in position of authority.
	WYO. STAT. ANN. § 6–2-316 Sexual abuse of minor, 3rd degree	Gender neutral. Perp: 17 or older; Targ: under 13 plus 4 yr. age diff. Perp: 20 or older; Targ: 16–17 plus perp in position of authority and 4 yr. age diff. Perp: under 16; Targ: under 13 plus 3 yr. age diff. Perp: 17 or older; Targ: under 17 plus 4 yr. age diff.
	WYO. STAT. ANN. § 6–2-317 Sexual abuse of minor, 4th degree	Gender neutral. Perp: under 16; Targ: under 13 plus 3 yr. age diff. Perp: 20 or older; Targ: 16–17 plus perp in position of authority and 4 yr. age diff.
	WYO. STAT. ANN. § 6–2-318 Soliciting to engage in illicit sexual relations	Gender neutral. Perp: 18 or older; Targ: under 14.

Source: Jennifer Ann Drobac & Leslie A. Hulvershorn, *The Neurobiology of Decision-Making in High Risk Youth & The Law of Consent to Sex*, 17 NEW CRIM. L. REV. 502, 527–551 (Summer 2014). I again thank Landon Scott for his excellent research and work on updating this table, originally created with the assistance of Sandie McCarthy Brown in 2004. Every effort was made to make this chart current to the date of press submission. Because of the difficulty in locating cases that indicate inconsistencies between state civil law and criminal statutory rape law, I offer the conflicts noted here merely as examples. I invite comments, updates, and corrections for this chart from all readers. Please send notes to jdrobac@iu.edu.

[a] The "State" column also includes some conclusions about ages of consent, criminal code consistency with civil law, and citations to authority for those associations.

Notes

Chapter One

This chapter draws from Jennifer Ann Drobac, *Consent, Teenagers, and (un)Civil(ized) Consequences*, *in* CHILDREN, SEXUALITY AND THE LAW (M. Coupet & Ellen Marrus eds., NYU Press, 2015); Jennifer Ann Drobac & Leslie A. Hulvershorn, *The Neurobiology of Decision-Making in High Risk Youth & The Law of Consent to Sex*, 17 NEW CRIM. L. REV. 502 (Summer 2014); Jennifer Ann Drobac, *Wake Up and Smell the Starbucks Coffee: How* Doe v. Starbucks *Confirms the End of the "Age of Consent" in California and Perhaps Beyond*, 33 B.C. J.L. & SOC. JUST. 1 (2013); Jennifer Ann Drobac, *A* Bee Line *in the Wrong Direction: Science, Teenagers, and the Sting to "The Age of Consent,"* 20 J.L. & POL'Y 63 (2011); Jennifer Ann Drobac, *I Can't to I Kant: The Sexual Harassment of Working Adolescents, Competing Theories, and Ethical Dilemmas*, 70 ALBANY L. REV. 675 (2007); Jennifer Ann Drobac, *"Developing Capacity": Adolescent "Consent" at Work, at Law and in the Sciences of the Mind*, 10 UC DAVIS J. JUVENILE L. & POL'Y 1 (2006); and Jennifer Ann Drobac, *Sex and the Workplace: "Consenting" Adolescents and a Conflict of Laws*, 79 WASH. L. REV. 471 (2004), and supporting citations in these texts.

1. Complaint at 2–9, Sara Doe [alias] v. Culver Theaters, Inc., No. 139513 (Cal. Super. Ct. Oct. 27, 2000). I note that I was personally involved in the preparation and filing of Sara Doe's case while I was still in private practice. I did not, however, negotiate her case's resolution, as it was handled by independent counsel.

2. *Id.* at 6–8.

3. *Id.*

4. *Id.* at 9–10; *see* Minute Order Entering Guilty Plea, People v. Cosio, No. S9-09852 (Cal. Super. Ct. Nov. 29, 1999) (order entering defendant-manager's guilty plea to count one for unlawful sexual intercourse with Sara).

5. Doe v. Willits Unified School District, No. C-09–03655-JSW (DMR), 2010 WL 2524587 (N.D. Cal. June 23, 2010); Doe v. Starbucks, Inc., No. SACV 08–0582 AG (CWx), 2009 WL 5183773 (C.D. Cal. Dec. 18, 2009); Doe v. Oberweis Dairy, No. 03 C 4774, 2005 WL 782709 (N.D. Ill. Apr. 6, 2005), *rev'd*, 456 F.3d 704 (7th Cir. 2006); Donaldson v. Department of Real Estate, 36 Cal. Rptr. 3d 577 (Cal. Ct. App. 2005); Doe v. Mama Taori's Premium Pizza, No. M1998–00992-COA-R9-CV, 2001 WL 327906 (Tenn. Ct. App. Apr. 5, 2001).

6. 86 Stat. 373, as amended, 20 U.S.C. § 1681 *et seq.* (Title IX).

7. Ind. Code 22–9-1–16 (specifying "both the respondent and the complainant must agree in writing to have the claims decided in a court of law").

8. Sandra Grauschopf, *Age of Majority by State—What is the Age of Majority in My State?*, ABOUT.COM. (updated Sept. 21, 2012), http://contests.about.com/od/sweepstakes101/a/agemajoristate.htm (last accessed Nov. 4, 2014).

9. THE NEW OXFORD AMERICAN DICTIONARY 365 (Elizabeth J. Jewell & Frank Abate eds., 2001).

10. *Id.* at 94.

11. *Id.* at 14.

12. *See* RESTATEMENT (SECOND) OF TORTS § 892A(2) (1979), § 892A cmt. b.

13. *Id.* § 892A(2)(a).

14. *Id.* § 892A cmt. b.

15. *See* RESTATEMENT (SECOND) OF CONTRACTS § 12(2)(a) (1981).

16. *See, e.g.*, Jones v. Dressel, 623 P.2d 370, 373 (Colo. 1981); JEFF FERRIELL, UNDERSTANDING CONTRACTS 603–04 (2d ed. 2009).

17. RESTATEMENT (SECOND) OF CONTRACTS § 15(1).

18. *Id.* § 15 cmt. b.

19. *Id.*

20. *See, e.g.*, Kathryn Lynn Modecki, *"It's a Rush": Psychosocial Content of Antisocial Decision Making*, 33 LAW & HUM. BEHAV. 183, 183–84 (2009).

21. *See, e.g.*, Elizabeth S. Scott & Laurence Steinberg, *Blaming Youth*, 81 TEX. L. REV. 799, 829–36 (2003). Because of the need to protect society from crimes committed by adolescents, I endorse Professors Elizabeth Scott and Laurence Steinberg's proposal that the juvenile justice system recognize adolescent "diminished responsibility" due to diminished culpability. However, I reassert that adolescents—even adolescent criminal offenders—lack full adult legal capacity. Moreover, I do not suggest a "diminished culpability" or "diminished responsibility" parallel for the civil system because my focus is the protection of youth, and their developing capacity, from exploitation by adults. I would still shield adolescents from legal responsibility for their immature choices because adult exploitation causes their injury. The need to protect society (and individual victims) from crimes committed by adolescents, however, justifies the different treatment in the criminal system of adolescent "developing capacity" and the

different level of legal responsibility (and culpability) attributed to adolescent criminal offenders.

22. 45 C.F.R. § 46.404 (2010).

23. § 46.408(a).

24. § 46.408(c).

25. Elizabeth Cauffman & Laurence Steinberg, *The Cognitive and Affective Influences on Adolescent Decision Making*, 68 TEMP. L. REV. 1763, 1766 (1995).

26. I would, however, permit high school students, who have successfully completed a high school US government or civics class and who have passed a basic knowledge test (similar to a written driver's license test), to participate in elections by voting.

27. *See, e.g.*, People v. Hillhouse, 1 Cal. Rptr. 3d 261, 268 (Ct. App. 2003) (explaining that "we would not assume—nor would we infer a legislative presumption—that the average 14 year old in our current society does not possess the intelligence capable of understanding the nature and consequences of a sexual act").

28. R. George Wright, *Consenting Adults: The Problem of Enhancing Human Dignity Non-Coercively*, 75 B.U. L. REV. 1397, 1435 (1995) [hereinafter Wright, *Consenting Adults*].

29. Katherine Hunt Federle, *On the Road to Reconceiving Rights for Children: A Postfeminist Analysis of the Capacity Principle*, 42 DEPAUL L. REV. 983, 985–86 (1993).

Chapter Two

This chapter draws from Jennifer Ann Drobac, *Consent, Teenagers, and (un)Civil(ized) Consequences*, *in* CHILDREN, SEXUALITY AND THE LAW (Sacha M. Coupet & Ellen Marrus eds., NYU Press, 2015); Jennifer Ann Drobac & Leslie A. Hulvershorn, *The Neurobiology of Decision-Making in High Risk Youth & The Law of Consent to Sex*, 17 NEW CRIM. L. REV. 502 (Summer 2014); Jennifer Ann Drobac, *Wake Up and Smell the Starbucks Coffee: How* Doe v. Starbucks *Confirms the End of the "Age of Consent" in California and Perhaps Beyond*, 33 B.C. J.L. & SOC. JUST. 1 (2013); Jennifer Ann Drobac, *A* Bee Line *in the Wrong Direction: Science, Teenagers, and the Sting to "The Age of Consent,"* 20 J.L. & POL'Y 63 (2011); Jennifer Ann Drobac, *I Can't to I Kant: The Sexual Harassment of Working Adolescents, Competing Theories, and Ethical Dilemmas*, 70 ALBANY L. REV. 675 (2007); Jennifer Ann Drobac, *"Developing Capacity": Adolescent "Consent" at Work, at Law and in the Sciences of the Mind*, 10 UC DAVIS J. JUVENILE L. & POL'Y 1 (2006); and Jennifer Ann Drobac, *Sex and the Workplace: "Consenting" Adolescents and a Conflict of Laws*, 79 WASH. L. REV. 471 (2004), and supporting citations in these texts.

1. The National Center for Missing and Exploited Children offers services and a tip line for children exploited primarily through pornography and sex trafficking. Its work is very important, but this organization cannot mandate reporting by clubs, schools, churches, etc. *See* www.missingkids.com/AnnualReport (last accessed Nov. 4, 2014).

2. Melissa Brodowski, HHS, Children's Bureau, *Child Maltreatment 2011* 22 (2011), *available at* www.acf.hhs.gov/sites/default/files/cb/cm11.pdf#page=57 (last accessed Nov. 4, 2014); *see also* American Academy of Child & Adolescent Psychiatry [hereinafter AACAP], *Child Sexual Abuse*, Facts for Families No. 9, Mar. 2011, *available at* www.aacap.org/App_Themes/AACAP/docs/facts_for_families/09_child_sexual_abuse.pdf (last accessed Nov. 4, 2014) at 1; MARCI A. HAMILTON, JUSTICE DENIED: WHAT AMERICA MUST DO TO PROTECT ITS CHILDREN 4 and 129–30 n.2 (2008) (finding that 25% of girls and 20% of boys are sexually abused during their childhood).

3. David Finkelhor et al., *Violence, Crime, and Abuse Exposure in a National Sample of Children and Youth*, JAMA PEDIATRICS, published online May 13, 2013, at E3.

4. AACAP, *supra* note 2; HAMILTON, *supra* note 2, at 4.

5. 42 U.S.C.A. § 2000e(2)(a)(1) (2013).

6. 29 C.F.R. § 1604.11(a) (2013). The full definition reads:

> Unwelcome sexual advances, requests for sexual favors, and other verbal or physical conduct of a sexual nature constitute sexual harassment when (1) submission to such conduct is made either explicitly or implicitly a term or condition of an individual's employment; (2) submission to or rejection of such conduct by an individual is used as the basis for employment decisions affecting such individual or (3) such conduct has the purpose or effect of unreasonably interfering with an individual's work performance or creating an intimidating, hostile or offensive work environment.

Id.

7. Meritor Savings Bank v. Vinson, 477 U.S. 57, 67 (1986). Professor Catharine MacKinnon defined *sexual harassment* as "the unwanted imposition of sexual requirements in the context of a relationship of unequal power. Central to the concept is the use of power derived from one social sphere to lever benefits or impose deprivations in another." CATHARINE A. MACKINNON, SEXUAL HARASSMENT OF WORKING WOMEN 1 (1979).

8. Harris v. Forklift Systems, Inc., 510 U.S. 17, 23 (1993).

9. 20 U.S.C. § 1681 et seq. (2013).

10. Revised Sexual Harassment Guidance: Harassment Of Students By School Employees, Other Students, Or Third Parties, 66 F.R. 5512–01 (2001);

see also US Dep't of Educ. [hereinafter ED], Office for Civil Rights [hereinafter OCR], *Sexual Harassment: It's Not Academic* 3 (2008), *available at* www2.ed.gov/about/offices/list/ocr/docs/ocrshpam.pdf (last accessed Nov. 4, 2014). The full definition reads:

> Sexual harassment is conduct that:
> 1) is sexual in nature;
> 2) is unwelcome; and
> 3) denies or limits a student's ability to participate in or benefit from a school's education program.
>
> Sexual harassment can take different forms depending on the harasser and the nature of the harassment. The conduct can be carried out by school employees, other students, and non-employee third parties, such as a visiting speaker. Both male and female students can be victims of sexual harassment, and the harasser and the victim can be of the same sex.
>
> The conduct can occur in any school program or activity and can take place in school facilities, on a school bus, or at other off-campus locations, such as a school-sponsored field trip or a training program at another location. The conduct can be verbal, nonverbal, or physical.
>
> The judgment and common sense of teachers and school administrators are very important elements in determining whether sexual harassment has occurred and in determining an appropriate response, especially when dealing with young children.

Id.

11. *See, e.g.*, Tamar Lewin, *After Harvard Controversy, Conditions Change but Reputation Lingers*, N.Y. Times, Mar. 5, 2010, *available at* www.nytimes.com/2010/03/06/education/06iht-ffharvard.html?scp=3&sq=harvard&st=cse (last accessed March 7, 2015).

12. *See, e.g.*, Doe v. Willits Unified Sch. Dist, No. C-09–03655-JSW (DMR), 2010 WL 2524587 (N.D. Cal June 23 2010) (involving a thirty-eight-year-old physics and math teacher who was charged with lewd acts, oral copulation, and sexual penetration of his fifteen-year-old student); *see also* Glenda Anderson, *Jail term for former Willits teacher who had sex with student*, Press Democrat (Santa Rosa, Cal.), Aug. 4, 2009, *available at* www.pressdemocrat.com/article/20090804/articles/908049914?template=printart (last accessed Nov. 4, 2014).

13. OCR, *supra* note 10, at 5 (italics added).

14. *See, e.g.*, US Figure Skating, *U.S. Figure Skating Harassment and Abuse Policy—Revised (November 2013)* 1, *available at* www.usfigureskating.org/content/Sexual%20Harassment%20Policy.pdf (last accessed Nov. 4, 2014);

see also Charol Shakeshaft, ED, Office of the Under Secretary, Educator Sexual Misconduct: A Synthesis of Existing Literature [hereinafter Shakeshaft, Educator Sexual Misconduct] 2 (2004), *available at* www2.ed.gov/rschstat/research/pubs/misconductreview/report.pdf (last accessed Nov. 4, 2014) (referring to Canada's Ontario College of Teachers definition). The Ontario College of Teachers refers to child sexual abuse by teachers as "educator sexual misconduct" because that phrase emphasizes the conduct of the responsible adult. Its list of abusive conduct is not limited to unwelcome behaviors but includes, for example, "[a]ny activity directed toward establishing a sexual relationship such as sending intimate letters; engaging in sexualized dialogue in person, via the Internet, in writing or by phone; making suggestive comments; dating a student." Shakeshaft, Educator Sexual Misconduct (paraphrasing Ontario College of Teachers, Professional Advisory on Professional Misconduct Related to Sexual Abuse and Sexual Misconduct 2–3 (2002)).

15. Rotary International, Abuse and Harassment Prevention Training Manual and Leader's Guide 2 (2002). The Rotarians define sexual harassment as "[s]exual advances, requests for sexual favors, or verbal or physical conduct of a sexual nature. In some cases, sexual harassment precedes sexual abuse and is a technique used by sexual predators to desensitize or groom their victims."

16. AAUW, Hostile Hallways: Bullying, Teasing, and Sexual Harassment in School 4, 32 (2001).

17. Catherine Hill and Holly Kearl, AAUW, Crossing the Line: Sexual Harassment at School 3, 11 (2011).

18. ED, National Center for Education Statistics [hereinafter NCES], *Digest of Education Statistics, 2011* Table A (2012), *available at* http://nces.ed.gov/programs/digest/d11/ch_1.asp (last accessed Nov. 4, 2014).

19. App. 1, *supra* pp. 241–42.

20. *See, e.g.*, Amy M. Young et al, *Adolescents' Experiences of Sexual Assault by Peers: Prevalence and Victimization Occurring within and Outside of School*, 38 J. of Youth & Adolescence 1072 (2008) (finding about 50 percent of high school girls reported being sexually assaulted), *available at* www.ccasa.org/wp-content/uploads/2014/01/adolescents-experiences-of-sexual-assault-by-peers.pdf (last accessed Nov. 4, 2014).

21. Campbell Leaper & Christia Spears Brown, *Perceived Experiences with Sexism Among Adolescent Girls*, 79 Child Development 685 (2008), *available at* http://faculty.weber.edu/tlday/HUMAN.DEVELOPMENT/RealStudy/CultureStudy.pdf (last accessed Nov. 4, 2014).

22. *See* Jennifer Ann Drobac, *The* Oncale *Opinion: A Pansexual Response*, 30 McGeorge L. Rev. 1269, 1287–88 (1999) (reviewing Oncale v. Sundowner Offshore Serv. Inc., 523 U.S. 75, 81–82 (1998), and discussing the stereotypical

assumptions in Justice Scalia's classification of butt smacking on a playing field as not sexual harassment).

23. URBAN DICTIONARY, *biatch*, www.urbandictionary.com/define.php?term=biatch (last accessed Nov. 4, 2014).

24. *Id.*

25. HILL, *supra* note 17, at 3.

26. *See, e.g.*, Adam Nossiter, *Six Year Old's Sex Crime: Innocent Peck on the Cheek*, N.Y. TIMES (Sept. 27, 1996) (reporting on a six-year-old boy who was charged with sexual harassment for kissing a classmate on the cheek), *available at* www.nytimes.com/1996/09/27/us/6-year-old-s-sex-crime-innocent-peck-on-cheek.html?pagewanted=all&src=pm (last accessed Nov. 4, 2014).

27. WILLIAM SHAKESPEARE, ROMEO AND JULIET act 1, sc. 2 (specifying through Lady Capulet that "[s]he [Juliet] hath not seen the change of fourteen years"). Shakespeare did not specify how old Romeo was, but scholars believe that he was from sixteen to nineteen years old. *See, e.g.*, Steve James, *Romeo and Juliet Were Sex Offenders: An Analysis of the Age of Consent and a Call for Reform*, 78 UMKC L. REV. 241 (2009–2010).

28. SHAKESHAFT, EDUCATOR SEXUAL MISCONDUCT, *supra* note 14, at 3, 51.

29. *Id.* at 17–18 (citing Charol Shakeshaft, *Educator Sexual Abuse* [hereinafter Shakeshaft, *Educator Sexual Abuse*], HOFSTRA HORIZONS, Spring 2003, at 10–13).

30. *Id.* at 22, 48.

31. *Id.* at 36.

32. *Id.* at 18 (emphasis added) (relying on Shakeshaft, *Educator Sexual Abuse*, *supra* note 29). I conducted an intensive literature search to find more recent statistics concerning educator sexual misconduct. Citations continue to point to Shakeshaft's 2003 and 2004 work.

33. For more information on sexual harassment in schools, see SUSAN L. STRAUSS, SEXUAL HARASSMENT AND BULLYING (2012).

34. Bureau of Labor Statistics, *Labor Force Statistics from the Current Population Survey, Household Data Seasonally Adjusted*, Table A-8. Employed persons by age, sex, marital status, multiple job holding status, and self-employment, seasonally adjusted *available at* www.bls.gov/web/empsit/cpseea08.htm (last accessed Nov. 4, 2014).

35. EEOC, *Sexual Harassment Charges FY 2010–FY 2012*, *available at* www.eeoc.gov/eeoc/statistics/enforcement/harassment_new.cfm (last accessed Nov. 4, 2014).

36. Email from Rebecca Short, EEOC, to Gregory Gentry, Indiana University, Robert H. McKinney School of Law Research Assistant to Professor Jennifer Drobac (June 11, 2013, 16:39:36 -0400) (on file with author).

37. PBS, *Is Your Daughter Safe At Work?*, *on* NOW ON PBS (PBS, 2009), *available at* www.pbs.org/now/shows/508/index.html (last accessed Nov. 4, 2014).

38. The Schuster Institute for Investigative Journalism, Brandeis University, *Sexual Harassment of Teens at Work*, www.brandeis.edu/investigate/teenSH1/index.html (last accessed Nov. 4, 2014).

39. Email from Rebecca Short, *supra* note 36.

40. Susan Fineran and James E. Gruber, *Youth at work: Adolescent employment and sexual harassment*, 33 CHILD ABUSE & NEGLECT 550, 554 (2009).

41. *Id.* at 555.

42. Eve Tahmincioglu, *Many teens face sexual harassment on the job*, CAREERS ON NBCNEWS.COM, June 7, 2010 (quoting Mary O'Neill), *available at* www.nbcnews.com/id/37320747/ns/business-careers/t/many-teens-face-sexual-harassment-job/#.UbzL4RZCok8 (last accessed Nov. 4, 2014).

43. Email from Rebecca Short, *supra* note 36.

44. Tahmincioglu, *supra* note 42.

45. Bureau of Labor Statistics, *Labor Force Statistics from the Current Population Survey, Household Data Seasonally Adjusted Quarterly Averages* Table E-1. Employment status of the civilian noninstitutional population by sex and age, seasonally adjusted, *available at* www.bls.gov/web/empsit/cpsee_e01.htm (last accessed Nov. 4, 2014).

46. Tahmincioglu, *supra* note 42.

47. Mary Sanchez, *Fast-Food Industry Serves Up Sexual Harassment*, TALLAHASSEE DEMOCRAT, May 10, 2003, at 8.

48. *Id.*

49. Dina Berta, *Sexual Harassment Remains Nagging Issue for Foodservice Industry*, NATION'S RESTAURANT NEWS, Dec. 16, 2002, at 1.

50. This case alleged the rape of a fourteen-year-old girl by her store manager. Sanchez, *supra* note 47, at 8.

51. Press Release, EEOC, Sexual Harassment Charged at Cannery Row Restaurant (Apr. 10, 2003) (on file with author); Press Release, EEOC, Two Victims To Share $85,000 For Sex Harassment by Company Founder (Apr. 2, 2003) (on file with author).

52. Peter Shinkle, *Restaurant Manager Is Accused of Harassing Workers; EEOC Official Voices Concern About Teen Workers*, ST. LOUIS POST DISPATCH, Jan. 31, 2003, at B2.

53. EEOC Regional Attorney William R. Tamayo explained that many young workers may not know their rights. Press Release, EEOC, EEOC Settles Sex Harassment Suit with Fresno Chain Uncle Harry's Bagels (Mar. 13, 2003) (on file with author). On March 13, 2003, the EEOC settled a sexual harassment case against a Fresno, California–based chain, Uncle Harry's Bagels. *Id.* A store manager allegedly sexually harassed several teenage workers, among other employees. *Id.* Uncle Harry's agreed to pay $150,000 to the six female victims. *Id.* According to EEOC trial attorney, Sanya Hill Maxion, teens may not recognize

sexual harassment and may not know what to do when they experience it. Alexei Oreskovic, *Targeted Teens*, THE RECORDER, July 15, 2003, at 1.

54. Press Release, EEOC, Owner of 25 McDonald's Restaurants to Pay $1 Million in EEOC Sexual Harassment Suit (July 18, 2012) (on file with author).

55. Shinkle, *supra* note 52, at B2.

56. Sanchez, *supra* note 47, at 8.

57. Shinkle, *supra* note 52, at B2.

58. Oreskovic, *supra* note 53, at 1.

59. Press Release, EEOC, EEOC Sues Footaction USA for Sexual Harassment of Teen Employee (Sept. 29, 1999) (on file with author).

60. AACAP, Policy Statement: Sexual Harassment (Oct. 1992), *at* www.aacap.org/cs/root/policy_statements/sexual_harassment (last accessed Nov. 4, 2014).

61. Women's Sports Foundation, *Sexual Harassment and Sexual Relationships Between Coaches, Other Athletic Personnel and Athletes* 1 (undated), *available at* www.womenssportsfoundation.org/home/advocate/title-ix-and-issues/title-ix-positions/sexual_harassment (last accessed Nov. 4, 2014).

62. Safe4Athletes, *Confronting Sexual Abuse and Harassment by Sport Coaches: A Need for a National Effort* 1, www.safe4athletes.org/blog/item/15-confronting-sexual-abuse-and-harassment-by-sport-coaches-a-need-for-a-national-effort (last accessed Nov. 4, 2014). Safe4Athletes relied on several news sources in its list, including: Assoc. Press and T.J. Quinn, *46 coaches on banned list*, ESPN.COM, May 26, 2010, http://sports.espn.go.com/oly/swimming/news/story?id=5220940 (last accessed Nov. 4, 2014); Christine Willmsen and Maureen O'Hagan, *Coaches continue working for schools and private teams after being caught for sexual misconduct*, THE SEATTLE TIMES, Dec. 4, 2003 ("Nearly all were male coaches victimizing girls. At least 98 of these coaches continued to coach or teach."), *available at* http://seattletimes.nwsource.com/news/local/coaches/news/dayone.html (last accessed Nov. 4, 2014);

63. Robert W. Wood, *Penn State's $60M Abuse Settlement Won't Erase Sandusky Name*, FORBES, July 19, 2013, *available at* www.forbes.com/sites/robertwood/2013/07/19/penn-states-60m-abuse-settlement-wont-erase-sandusky-name (last visited Nov. 4, 2014).

64. FREEH SPORKIN & SULLIVAN, LLP, REPORT OF THE SPECIAL INVESTIGATIVE COUNSEL REGARDING THE ACTIONS OF THE PENNSYLVANIA STATE UNIVERSITY RELATED TO THE CHILD SEXUAL ABUSE COMMITTED BY GERALD A. SANDUSKY 16, July 12 2012, *available at* www.scribd.com/doc/99901850/Freeh-Report-of-the-Actions-of-Penn-State-University (last accessed Nov. 4, 2014).

65. *See, e.g.*, USA Gymnastics, *Clubs Care Campaign*, http://usagym.org/pages/education/ClubsCare (last accessed Nov. 4, 2014). While USA Gymnastics puts valuable resources, including child abuse telephone helplines, on its Clubs Care web page, it does not indicate that it is tracking complaints of abuse or harassment.

66. *See, e.g.*, DONALD H. MATTHEWS, SEXUAL ABUSE OF POWER IN THE BLACK CHURCH: SEXUAL MISCONDUCT IN THE AFRICAN AMERICAN CHURCHES (2012); SEXUAL ABUSE IN THE CATHOLIC CHURCH: A DECADE OF CRISIS, 2002–2012 (Thomas G. Plante and Kathleen L. McChesney, eds., 2011); HAMILTON, *supra* note 2, at 67–96, 144–51 (2008).

67. KAREN T. TERRY ET AL., THE CAUSES AND CONTEXT OF SEXUAL ABUSE OF MINORS BY CATHOLIC PRIESTS IN THE UNITED STATES, 1950–2010 8 (2011*), available at* www.usccb.org/issues-and-action/child-and-youth-protection/upload/The-Causes-and-Context-of-Sexual-Abuse-of-Minors-by-Catholic-Priests-in-the-United-States-1950–2010.pdf (last accessed Nov. 4, 2014).

68. *Id.* at 9–10.

69. Staff, *The military's sexual assault epidemic*, THE WEEK, Mar. 31, 2013 *available at* http://theweek.com/article/index/242066/the-militarys-sexual-assault-epidemic (last accessed Nov. 4, 2014).

70. James Dao, *In Debate Over Military Sexual Assault, Men Are Overlooked Victims*, N.Y. TIMES, June 23, 2013, *available at* www.nytimes.com/2013/06/24/us/in-debate-over-military-sexual-assault-men-are-overlooked-victims.html (last visited Nov. 4, 2014).

71. *See, e.g.*, 10 U.S.C.A. § 1561 (originally enacted Pub.L. 105–85, Div. A, Title V, § 591(a)(1), Nov. 18, 1997, 111 Stat. 1760) (requiring investigation of sexual harassment by commanding officers) and § 6980 (2013) (originally enacted Pub.L. 109–364, Div. A, Title V, § 532(a)(2), Oct. 17, 2006, 120 Stat. 2201)) (establishing a Navy policy on sexual harassment and sexual violence). A Pentagon survey estimated that 26,000 people had been sexually assaulted in the military in 2012. Jennifer Steinhauer, *Joint Chiefs' Answers on Sex Crimes Dismay Senators*, N.Y. TIMES, June 5, 2013, at A12, *available at* www.nytimes.com/2013/06/05/us/politics/joint-chiefs-testimony-on-sexual-assault-dismays-senators.html?_r=0&pagewanted=print (last accessed Nov. 4, 2014).

72. Michael Martinez, *Daughters and moms now consider rape before applying to military*, CNN.COM, www.cnn.com/2013/06/16/us/military-recruitment (last accessed Nov. 4, 2014).

73. DEP'T OF DEFENSE, DOD FISCAL YEAR 2012 ANN. REP. ON SEXUAL ASSAULT IN THE MIL., Volume 1, at 81, exhibit 18. DoD received a total of 3,374 reports of sexual assault in FY2012. *Id.* at 57.

74. *Id.* at 83, exhibit 21.

75. MIKE A. MALES, TEENAGE SEX AND PREGNANCY 17 (2010).

76. Amanda Marcotte, *Teenage Hormones Cause Rape and Other Myths Spouted at Senate Hearing on Military Sex Assault*, SLATE.COM, June 5, 2013, www.slate.com/blogs/xx_factor/2013/06/05/senate_hearing_on_sexual_assault_in_the_military_republicans_think_teen.html (last accessed Nov. 4, 2014).

77. Liz Halloran, *Stunned By Military Sex Scandals, Advocates Demand*

Changes, NPR, May 25, 2013, www.npr.org/2013/05/23/186335999/stunned-by-military-sex-scandals-advocates-demand-changes (last accessed Nov. 4, 2014).

78. *Jeffrey Krusinski, Air Force Officer In Charge Of Sexual Assault Prevention Program, Arrested For Alleged Sexual Assault*, THE HUFFINGTON POST, May 7, 2013, *available at* www.huffingtonpost.com/2013/05/06/jeffrey-krusinski-arrested_n_3225155.html (last accessed Nov. 4, 2014).

79. Thom Shanker, *South Carolina: General Faces Adultery Investigation*, N.Y. TIMES, May 21, 2013, *available at* www.nytimes.com/2013/05/22/us/south-carolina-general-faces-adultery-investigation.html?pagewanted=print (last accessed Nov. 4, 2014).

80. Angela K. Brown & Lolita C. Baldor, *Brad Grimes, Fort Hood Soldier, Accused Of Paying Woman For Sex*, THE HUFFINGTON POST, June 12, 2013, *available at* www.huffingtonpost.com/2013/06/12/brad-grimes-soldier-prostitute_n_3429967.html?view=print&comm_ref=false (last accessed Nov. 4, 2014).

81. Thom Shanker, *Women Were Secretly Filmed at West Point, the Army Says*, N.Y. TIMES, May 22, 2013, *available at* www.nytimes.com/2013/05/23/us/sergeant-accused-of-secretly-filming-female-cadets.html?_r=0 (last accessed Nov. 4, 2014).

82. Sig Christiansen, *Court told recruiter became a predator*, SAN ANTONIO EXPRESS-NEWS, Jan. 8, 2013, *available at* www.mysanantonio.com/news/military/article/Court-told-recruiter-became-a-predator-4174226.php (last accessed Nov. 4, 2014).

83. *See* THE INVISIBLE WAR (a film by Kirby Dick 2012) (depicting the military's failure to prevent, investigate, and properly remedy military rape by US soldiers).

84. *See* Rebecca Huval, Feres *Doctrine and the Obstacles to Justice for Military Rape Victims*, INDEPENDENT LENS BLOG, May 9, 2012 (discussing the *Feres* doctrine in the context of military rape).

85. Andrea J. Sedlack et al., US Dept. of Justice, Office of Juvenile Justice and Delinquency Prevention, *Nature and Risk of Victimization*, JUVENILE JUSTICE BULLETIN 4 (June 2013), *available at* www.ojjdp.gov/pubs/240703.pdf (last accessed Nov. 4, 2014).

86. Press Release, DOJ, Bureau of Justice Assistance, In 2005 And 2006 More Than 4,000 Allegations Of Sexual Violence Were Reported In Juvenile Facilities 1 (July 31, 2008), www.ojp.usdoj.gov/newsroom/pressreleases/2008/bjs08095.htm (last accessed Nov. 4, 2014).

87. *Id.* at 2.

88. DEPT. OF JUST., BUREAU OF JUSTICE ASSISTANCE, JUVENILES IN ADULT PRISONS AND JAILS 8 (2000), *available at* www.ncjrs.gov/pdffiles1/bja/182503.pdf (last accessed Nov. 4, 2014).

89. HOLLY KEARL, STOP STREET HARASSMENT: MAKING PUBLIC PLACES SAFE AND WELCOMING FOR WOMEN 21 (2010).

90. Kirsten Gillibrand, Off the Sidelines 129 (2014); Jake Miller, *Sen. Kirsten Gillibrand: Male colleague called me "porky,"* CBSNews.com, Aug. 27, 2014, *available at* www.cbsnews.com/news/sen-kirsten-gilllibrand-male-colleague-called-me-porky (last accessed Nov. 4, 2014).

91. *See* AMC Network Entertainment, *Mad Men*, *available at* www.amctv.com/shows/mad-men (last accessed Nov. 4, 2014).

92. For a listing of laws that prohibit street harassment of various forms, see Talia Hagerty et al., Know Your Rights: Street Harassment and the Law 15–291 (2013) (state-by state listing of laws that prohibit some form of street harassment).

93. Stop Street Harassment, *Companies That Trivialize Street Harassment*, www.stopstreetharassment.org/our-work/listofcompanies (last accessed Nov. 4, 2014).

94. Carla Baranauckas, *Montana judge's comments show ignorance about rape*, The Wash. Post, Aug. 30, 2013, *available at* www.washingtonpost.com/blogs/she-the-people/wp/2013/08/30/montana-judges-comments-show-ignorance-about-rape (last accessed Nov. 4, 2014).

95. *See* Marcia Amidon Lüsted, Advertising to Children 67 (2009) (suggesting that the teen aspirational age is twenty-years-old and that the tween aspirational age is seventeen-years-old); *but see* Dave Siegel et al., The Great Tween Buying Machine: Capturing Your Share of the Multi-Billion-Dollar Tween Market 61 (2004) (noting that tweens are not aspiring to be teens).

96. Davia Temin, *When Is An Apology NOT An Apology? New Lessons From Abercrombie & Fitch*, Forbes, May 17, 2913, *available at* www.forbes.com/sites/daviatemin/2013/05/17/when-is-an-apology-not-an-apology-new-lessons-from-abercrombie-fitch (last accessed Nov. 4, 2014) (quoting CEO Mike Jeffries, internal quotation marks omitted).

97. Kay S. Hymowitz, *Girls' Sexy Aspirations Are Marketers' Target*, Philadelphia Inquirer, Oct. 7, 2000, *available at* http://articles.philly.com/2000–10–07/news/25586982_1_marketers-industry-empowerment (last accessed Nov. 4, 2014).

98. *Id.*

99. Lynn Neary, *Tweens and Media: What's Too Adult?* (NPR radio broadcast Aug. 1, 2006) (transcript available at www.npr.org/templates/story/story.php?storyId=5595146) (last accessed Nov. 4, 2014).

100. Janis Wolak et al., *Online "Predators" and their Victims: Myths, Realities and Implications for Prevention and Treatment*, 63 American Psychologist 111, 122 (Feb.–Mar. 2008) (citation omitted), *available at* www.apa.org/pubs/journals/releases/amp-632111.pdf (last accessed Nov. 4, 2014).

101. *Id.* (emphasis added); *see also* Diane Levin and Jean Kilbourne, So Sexy So Soon: The New Sexualized Childhood and What Parents Can Do to Protect Their Kids (2009).

102. *See generally* AMANDA LENHART ET AL., PEW INTERNET AND AMERICAN LIFE PROJECT, SOCIAL MEDIA & MOBILE INTERNET USE AMONG TEENS AND YOUNG ADULTS 4, 9 (2010) [hereinafter LENHART, SOCIAL MEDIA], *available at* www.pewinternet.org/~/media//Files/Reports/2010/PIP_Social_Media_and_Young_Adults_Report_Final_with_toplines.pdf (last accessed Nov. 4, 2014).

103. *Id.* at 12.

104. Donald F. Roberts & Ulla G. Foehr, *Trends in Media Use*, 18 THE FUTURE OF CHILDREN, 11, 18 (2008), *available at* http://futureofchildren.org/futureofchildren/publications/docs/18_01_02.pdf (last accessed Nov. 4, 2014) (analyzing data from Donald F. Roberts et al., Kaiser Family Foundation, *Generation M: Media in the Lives of 8–18-year-olds* (2005)). I note here that I served on the Board of Trustees of the Kaiser Family Foundation and am a Kaiser family member. My affiliations as a trustee and family member had, and still have, no impact on the results of any survey evidence reported by the foundation. Additionally, I did not conceive of projects nor set the research goals of the foundation. Finally, I received no compensation tied to particular research projects or outcomes.

105. LENHART, SOCIAL MEDIA, *supra* note 102, at 4.

106. WHITNEY ROBAN ET AL., GIRL SCOUT RESEARCH INSTITUTE, THE NET EFFECT: GIRLS AND NEW MEDIA 15 (2002), *available at* www.girlscouts.org/research/pdf/net_effect.pdf (last accessed Nov. 4, 2014).

107. Michele L. Ybarra & Kimberly J. Mitchell, *How Risky are Social Networking Sites? A Comparison of Places Online Where Youth Sexual Solicitation and Harassment Occurs*, 121 PEDIATRICS e350 (Jan. 2008).

108. *Id.*

109. Wolak, *supra* note 100, at 112–13.

110. *Id.* at 117.

111. *Id.* at 115 (citation omitted).

112. *Id.* (citation omitted).

113. *Id.* (citation omitted).

114. MARY MADDEN, ET AL., PEW INTERNET AND AMERICAN LIFE PROJECT, TEENS AND TECHNOLOGY *2013* 2 (Mar. 2013), *available at* www.pewinternet.org/~/media//Files/Reports/2013/PIP_TeensandTechnology2013.pdf (last accessed Nov. 4, 2014).

115. LENHART, SOCIAL MEDIA, *supra* note 102, at 4; AMANDA LENHART ET AL., PEW INTERNET AND AMERICAN LIFE PROJECT, TEENS & SEXTING 2 (2009) [hereinafter LENHART, TEENS & SEXTING], *available at* www.pewinternet.org/~/media//Files/Reports/2009/PIP_Teens_and_Sexting.pdf.

116. Marc Prensky, *What Can You Learn from a Cell Phone? Almost Anything!* 1 (2004), http://thinkingmachine.pbworks.com/f/Prensky-What_Can_You_Learn_From_a_Cell_Phone-FINAL.pdf (last accessed Nov. 4, 2014).

117. MADDEN, *supra* note 114, at 2.

118. *See, e.g.*, Jan Hoffman, *A Girl's Nude Photo, and Altered Lives*, N.Y. TIMES, Mar. 27, 2011, at A1; Sean D. Hamill, *Students Sue Prosecutor in Cellphone Photos Case*, N.Y. TIMES, Mar. 26, 2009, at A21; *see also* Julia Halloran McLaughlin, *Crime and Punishment: Teen Sexting in Context*, 115 PENN ST. L. REV. 135, 136 (2010) (discussing several sexting cases).

119. LENHART, TEENS & SEXTING, *supra* note 115, at 2, 4 & n.10.

120. Kimberly J. Mitchell et al., *Prevalence and Characteristics of Youth Sexting: A National Study*, 129 PEDIATRICS 13, 16 (Jan. 2012), *available at* http://pediatrics.aappublications.org/content/early/2011/11/30/peds.2011–1730.full.pdf+html (last accessed Nov. 4, 2014).

121. *Id.* at 18.

122. 42 U.S.C. § 16913 (2009).

123. McLaughlin, *supra* note 118, at 149 (footnotes omitted).

124. Janis Wolak et al., *How Often are Teens Arrested for Sexting? Data from a National Sample of Police Cases*, 129 PEDIATRICS 4, 9 (Jan. 2012).

125. Donald F. Roberts et al., Kaiser Family Foundation, *Generation M: Media in the Lives of 8–18-Year-Olds* 10, 13 (Mar. 2005) [hereinafter Roberts, *Generation M*], *available at* http://kaiserfamilyfoundation.files.wordpress.com/2013/01/generation-m-media-in-the-lives-of-8–18-year-olds-report.pdf (last accessed Nov. 4, 2014); *see also* Donald F. Roberts & Ulla G. Foehr, *Trends in Media Use*, 18 THE FUTURE OF CHILDREN 11, 18 (2008).

126. Roberts, *Generation M*, *supra* note 125, at 24.

127. Elizabeth Grauerholz & Amy King, *Prime Time Sexual Harassment*, 3 VIOLENCE AGAINST WOMEN 129, 141 (Apr. 1997), *available at* http://vaw.sagepub.com/content/3/2/129.full.pdf+html (last accessed Nov. 4, 2014).

128. *Id.* at 142.

129. *Id.* at 144.

130. DALE KUNKEL ET AL., THE HENRY J. KAISER FAMILY FOUNDATION, SEX ON TV4 EXECUTIVE SUMMARY 2 (2005).

131. L. Monique Ward & Kimberly Friedman, *Using TV as a Guide: Associations Between Television Viewing and Adolescents' Sexual Attitudes and Behavior*, 16 J. RES. ON ADOLESCENCE 133, 150 (Mar. 2006); *see also* Jochen Peter & Patti M. Valkenburg, *Adolescents' Exposure to a Sexualized Media Environment, and Their Notions of Women as Sex Objects*, 56 SEX ROLES 381, 392–93 (Feb. 2007) (finding that "[e]xposure to sexually explicit movies on the internet was the only exposure measure significantly related to beliefs that women are sex objects in the final regression model").

132. Ward & Friedman, *supra* note 131, at 151.

133. Margaret Hunter, *Shake It, Baby, Shake It: Consumption and the New Gender Relation in Hip-Hop*, 54 SOC. PERSP. 16–17 (2011).

134. bell hooks, *Sexism and misogyny: Who takes the rap? Misogyny, gang-*

sta rap, and piano, Z MAGAZINE, Feb. 1994, *available at* http://race.eserver.org/misogyny.html (last accessed Nov. 4, 2014).

135. Brian A. Primack et al., *Degrading and Non-Degrading Sex in Popular Music: A Content Analysis*, 123(5) PUB. HEALTH REP. 593, 593–600 (2008), *available at* www.ncbi.nlm.nih.gov/pmc/articles/PMC2496932/pdf/phr123000593.pdf (last accessed March 6, 2015). The article conflated the third and fourth attributes, but the point is the same. *Id.* at 594.

136. *Id.* at 597.

137. *Misogynistic Lyrics that aren't Rap*, http://misogynisticlyricsthatarentrap.tumblr.com (last accessed Nov. 4, 2014).

138. Johannes W. J. Beentjes & Rubin P. Konig, *Does Exposure to Music Videos Predict Adolescents' Sexual Attitudes*, 9 EUR. SCI. J. 1–18 (2013).

139. Linda Smolak, *Gender as Culture: The Meanings of Self-Silencing in Women and Men*, *in* SILENCING THE SELF ACROSS CULTURES: DEPRESSION AND GENDER IN THE SOCIAL WORLD 129, 139 (Dana C. Jack & Alisha Ali eds., 2010).

140. WAM! *What we do*, *available at* www.womenactionmedia.org/why-wam/what-we-do (last accessed Nov. 7, 2014).

141. Jaclyn, WAM!, *Harassment of women on Twitter? We're ON IT* (Nov. 6, 2014), *available at* www.womenactionmedia.org/2014/11/06/harassment-of-women-on-twitter-were-on-it (last accessed Nov. 7, 2014).

142. Dar Williams, *When I Was a Boy*, THE HONESTY ROOM (1993).

Chapter Three

This chapter draws from Jennifer Ann Drobac, *Consent, Teenagers, and (un)Civil(ized) Consequences*, *in* CHILDREN, SEXUALITY AND THE LAW (Sacha M. Coupet & Ellen Marrus eds., NYU Press, 2015); Jennifer Ann Drobac & Leslie A. Hulvershorn, *The Neurobiology of Decision-Making in High Risk Youth & The Law of Consent to Sex*, 17 NEW CRIM. L. REV. 502 (Summer 2014); Jennifer Ann Drobac, *Wake Up and Smell the Starbucks Coffee: How* Doe v. Starbucks *Confirms the End of the "Age of Consent" in California and Perhaps Beyond*, 33 B.C. J.L. & SOC. JUST. 1 (2013); Jennifer Ann Drobac, *A* Bee Line *in the Wrong Direction: Science, Teenagers, and the Sting to "The Age of Consent,"* 20 J.L. & POL'Y 63 (2011); Jennifer Ann Drobac, *I Can't to I Kant: The Sexual Harassment of Working Adolescents, Competing Theories, and Ethical Dilemmas*, 70 ALBANY L. REV. 675 (2007); Jennifer Ann Drobac, *"Developing Capacity": Adolescent "Consent" at Work, at Law and in the Sciences of the Mind*, 10 UC DAVIS J. JUVENILE L. & POL'Y 1 (2006); and Jennifer Ann Drobac, *Sex and the Workplace: "Consenting" Adolescents and a Conflict of Laws*, 79 WASH. L. REV. 471 (2004), and supporting citations in these texts. I thank Dr. Leslie Hulvershorn for her substantive and editorial comments and corrections throughout this chapter. I also thank Dr. Tracy Gunter for her comments.

1. Roper v. Simmons, 543 U.S. 551 (2005).

2. Jennifer Soper, *Straddling the Line: Adolescent Pregnancy and Questions of Capacity*, 23 LAW & PSYCHOL. REV. 195, 199 (1999).

3. Kendall Powell, *How Does the Teenage Brain Work?*, 442 NATURE 865, 865 (Aug. 24, 2006) (quoting Dr. Bea Luna).

4. Charles A. Phipps, *Children, Adults, Sex and the Criminal Law: In Search of Reason*, 22 SETON HALL LEGIS. J. 1, 52 n.219 (1997) (citing People v. Hernandez, 393 P.2d 673 (Cal.1964)).

5. *See, e.g.*, LINDA SPEAR, THE BEHAVIORAL NEUROSCIENCE OF ADOLESCENCE 5, 36–190 (2010); *see also*, Jiska S. Peper & Ronald E. Dahl, *The Teenage Brain: Surging Hormones—Brain-Behavior Interactions During Puberty*, 22 CURRENT DIRECTIONS IN PSYCHOLOGICAL SCIENCE 134 (2013); JEFFREY JENSON ARNETT, EMERGING ADULTHOOD: THE WINDING ROAD FROM THE LATE TEENS THROUGH THE EARLY TWENTIES (2004).

6. Botanical-online, *Daisy Plant*, www.botanical-online.com/english/daisy_plant.htm (last accessed Nov. 5, 2014).

7. NATIONAL INSTITUTE OF MENTAL HEALTH [hereinafter NIMH], *Teenage Brain: A Work in Progress* [hereinafter *Teenage Brain*], NIMH Publication No. 01–4929, https://public.health.oregon.gov/HealthyPeopleFamilies/Youth/AdolescentGrowthDevelopment/Documents/teenbrain.pdf (last accessed March 6, 2015); Jay N. Giedd et al., *Brain Development During Childhood and Adolescence: A Longitudinal MRI Study*, 2 NATURE NEUROSCIENCE 861 (Oct. 1999); Paul M. Thompson et al., *Growth Patterns in the Developing Brain Detected by Using Continuum Mechanical Tensor Maps*, 404 NATURE 190 (Mar. 9, 2000); SPEAR, *supra* note 5, at 81–83; FRONTLINE, *Interview with Jay Giedd*, INSIDE THE TEENAGE BRAIN, www.pbs.org/wgbh/pages/frontline/shows/teenbrain/interviews/giedd.html (last accessed Nov. 5, 2014); *see also* Judith L. Rapoport et al., *Progressive Cortical Change during Adolescence in Childhood-Onset Schizophrenia: A Longitudinal Magnetic Resonance Imaging Study*, 56 JAMA PSYCHIATRY 649 (1999) (journal formerly ARCHIVES OF GENERAL PSYCHIATRY).

8. Elizabeth R. Sowell et al., *In Vivo Evidence for Post-Adolescent Brain Maturation in Frontal and Striatal Regions*, 2 NATURE NEUROSCIENCE 859, 860 (Oct. 1999).

9. Sarah Spinks, *Adolescent Brains Are Works in Progress*, INSIDE THE TEENAGE BRAIN, www.pbs.org/wgbh/pages/frontline/shows/teenbrain/work/adolescent.html (last accessed Nov. 5, 2014) (focusing on Dr. Giedd's research).

10. B.J. Casey & Kristina Caudle, *The Teenage Brain: Self Control*, 22 CURRENT DIRECTIONS IN PSYCHOLOGICAL SCIENCE 82, 83–84 (2013) (italics in the original). Other researchers confirm the reward seeking behavior of adolescents.

See, e.g., Adriana Galván, *The Teenage Brain: Sensitivity to Rewards*, 22 CURRENT DIRECTIONS IN PSYCHOLOGICAL SCIENCE 88 (2013).

11. Casey & Caudle, *supra* note 10, at 86.

12. Spinks, *supra* note 9 (Giedd noted that the cerebellum, "involved in coordination of our cognitive process, our thinking processes," does not finish changing until the twenties. He added, "And this ability to smooth out all the different intellectual processes to navigate the complicated social life of the teen . . . seems to be a function of the cerebellum.").

13. Comment to 9-13-2013 draft from Dr. Leslie Hulvershorn to the author (on file with author).

14. Sarah Spinks, *One Reason Teens Respond Differently to the World: Immature Brain Circuitry*, INSIDE THE TEENAGE BRAIN, www.pbs.org/wgbh/pages/frontline/shows/teenbrain/work/onereason.html (last accessed Nov. 5, 2014) (discussing Deborah Yurgelun-Todd's study); Sowell, *supra* note 8; *see also* FRONTLINE, *Interview with Deborah Yurgelun-Todd*, INSIDE THE TEENAGE BRAIN, www.pbs.org/wgbh/pages/frontline/shows/teenbrain/interviews/todd.html (last accessed Nov. 5, 2104) (Yurgelun-Todd noted that hers was a very small pilot study. She urged caution in the interpretation of the results.); Abigail A. Baird et al., *Functional Magnetic Resonance Imaging of Facial Affect Recognition in Children and Adolescents*, 38 J. AM. ACAD. CHILD ADOLESC. PSYCHIATRY 195 (Feb. 1999) (discussing Deborah Yurgelun-Todd's study).

15. Sharon Begley, *Getting Inside a Teen Brain*, NEWSWEEK, Feb. 27, 2000, *available at* www.newsweek.com/2000/02/27/getting-inside-a-teen-brain.html (quoting Dr. Jay Giedd) (last accessed Nov. 5, 2014).

16. FRONTLINE, *Interview with Jay Giedd*, *supra* note 7.

17. Spinks, *supra* note 9. Some researchers caution against premature conclusions based on early scientific findings. *See, e.g.*, Monica A. Payne, *"Use-It-or-Lose-It"? Interrogating an Educational Message from Teen Brain Research*, 35 AUSTL. J. TCHR. EDUC. 79 (Aug. 2010). In particular, Dr. Elizabeth Sowell commented, "'Jay likes to say "use it or lose it" and that we should put kids in enriched environments. That makes perfect intuitive sense, but we just don't have the data to say that.'" Powell, *supra* note 3, at 866 (quoting Dr. Elizabeth Sowell).

18. FRONTLINE, *Interview with Jay Giedd*, *supra* note 7.

19. JUVENILE JUSTICE CENTER, ADOLESCENCE, BRAIN DEVELOPMENT AND LEGAL CULPABILITY 2 (Jan. 2004), www.abanet.org/crimjust/juvjus/Adolescence.pdf (last accessed Nov. 5, 2014).

20. NIMH, *Teenage Brain*, *supra* note 7, at 2.

21. Jay Giedd et al., *Anatomical Brain Magnetic Resonance Imaging of Typically Developing Children and Adolescents*, 48 J. AM. ACAD. CHILD ADOLESC. PSYCHIATRY 465 (May 2009), *available at* www.ncbi.nlm.nih.gov/pmc/articles/PMC2892679 (author manuscript at 2) (last accessed Nov. 5, 2014).

22. SPEAR, *supra* note 5, at 85 (citing R. Douglas Fields, *White Matter in Learning, Cognition, and Psychiatric Disorders*, 31 TRENDS IN NEUROSCIENCE 361 (2008)).

23. NIMH, *Teenage Brain*, *supra* note 7, at 2; Elizabeth Gudrais, *Modern Myelination: The Brain at Midlife*, 103 HARV. MAG. 9 (2001) (discussing Dr. Francine Benes's research), *available at* www.harvardmagazine.com/on-line/050153 .html (last accessed Nov. 5, 2014).

24. Gudrais, *supra* note 23.

25. Carol L. Armstrong, *Age-Related, Regional, Hemispheric, and Medial-Lateral Differences in Myelin Integrity in Vivo in the Normal Adult Brain*, 25 AM. J. NEURORADIOLOGY 977, 981 (May 2004), *available at* www.ajnr.org/content/25/6/977.full.pdf (last accessed Nov. 5, 2014).

26. Hulvershorn Comment, *supra* note 13; *see* Drobac & Hulvershorn, *supra* text preceding note 1.

27. SPEAR, *supra* note 5, at 101, 107–08 (citing Laurence Steinberg, *Cognitive and Affective Development in Adolescence*, 9 TRENDS IN COGNITIVE SCI. 69–74 (2005)).

28. *See, e.g.*, Melinda Schmidt & N. Dickon Reppucci, *Children's Rights and Capacities, in* CHILDREN, SOCIAL SCIENCE, AND THE LAW 76, 96 (Bette L. Bottoms et al. eds., 2002) (discussing L.A. Weithorn & S.B. Campbell, *The Competency of Children and Adolescents to Make Informed Treatment Decisions*, 53 CHILD DEV. 1589–98 (1982)); Tony Freemantle, *Lawmakers Get Tougher on Juvenile Offenders*, HOUS. CHRON., Apr. 26, 1998, at A26; *see also* Evelyn Nieves, *California's Governor Plays Tough on Crime*, N.Y. TIMES, May 23, 2000, at A16.

29. MACARTHUR FOUND. RESEARCH NETWORK ON ADOLESCENT DEV. & JUVENILE JUSTICE, THE MACARTHUR JUVENILE ADJUDICATIVE COMPETENCE STUDY SUMMARY 1–2 (2002) [hereinafter MACARTHUR COMPETENCE STUDY SUMMARY], *available at* www.adjj.org/downloads/58competence_study_summary.pdf (last accessed Nov. 5, 2014); Press Release, Temple University, *Many Kids 15 and Younger May Lack Maturity Necessary to be Competent to Stand Trial, Juvenile Justice Study Finds* (Mar. 2, 2003).

30. MACARTHUR COMPETENCE STUDY SUMMARY, *supra* note 29, at 2.

31. Kurt W. Fischer et al., *Narrow Assessments Misrepresent Development and Misguide Policy*, 64 AM. PSYCHOLOGIST 595, 597–98 (2009).

32. SPEAR, *supra* note 5, at 125.

33. Steinberg, *Adolescent Development and Juvenile Justice*, 5 ANNUAL REV. CLINICAL PSYCH. 459, 468 (2009) [hereinafter Steinberg, *Adolescent Development*].

34. SPEAR, *supra* note 5, at 130–54; Laurence Steinberg, *Adolescent Development*, *supra* note 33, at 469; *see also* Elizabeth Cauffman and Laurence Steinberg, *The Cognitive and Affective Influences on Adolescent Decision-Making*,

68 TEMP. L. REV. 1763, 1767, 1771–72 (1995) (providing examples of adolescents' frequent participation in dangerous activities); Galván, *supra* note 10, at 88.

35. Rachel Tompa, *This is your brain on adolescence: MRI studies of teenage brain show why kids act before they think*, UCBERKELEYNEWS, Oct. 16, 2008, http://berkeley.edu/news/media/releases/2008/10/16_neurolaw.shtml (last accessed Nov. 5, 2014); *see also* Steinberg, *Adolescent Development*, *supra* note 33, at 469; SPEAR, *supra* note 5, at 140 (defining sensation-seeking as "a complex trait associated with the desire for diverse, novel, complex, and intense experiences and the willingness to engage in risks to attain those experiences"); Galván, *supra* note 10, at 88–93 (discussing "the role of dopamine-rich striatal circuitry in adolescent reward sensitivity").

36. Steinberg also distinguishes the maturation of the cognitive control system from the maturation of the frontal lobes through synaptic pruning. He notes that both result in improved thinking abilities but that they happen at different times with different implications for cognitive development. Steinberg, *Adolescent Development*, *supra* note 33, at 466. While risk taking can be problematic or even life threatening, adaptive benefits also exist, including "opportunities to explore adult behaviors and privileges, to face and conquer challenges, to master the developmental difficulties of adolescence, and to increase status and peer affiliation within certain peer groups." SPEAR, *supra* note 5, at 135 (citations omitted).

37. Abigail Baird, *The Developmental Neuroscience of Criminal Behavior*, *in* THE IMPACT OF BEHAVIORAL SCIENCES ON CRIMINAL LAW 26–28 (Nita Farhany, ed., 2009).

38. *Id.* at 29.

39. SPEAR, *supra* note 5, at 143.

40. Cauffman, *supra* note 34, at 1787.

41. Cauffman, *supra* note 34, at 1773, 1787; SPEAR, *supra* note 5, at 143; Steinberg, *Adolescent Development*, *supra* note 33, at 46.

42. SPEAR, *supra* note 5, at 142.

43. SPEAR, *supra* note 5, at 142; Cauffman, *supra* note 34 at 1781–82.

44. Beatriz Luna et al., *The Teenage Brain: Cognitive Control and Motivation*, 22 CURRENT DIRECTIONS IN PSYCHOLOGICAL SCIENCE 98–99 (2013).

45. Cauffman, *supra* note 34, at 1781–82.

46. Steinberg, *Adolescent Development*, *supra* note 33, at 468.

47. Lauren Olsho et al., for the United States Department of Health and Human Services (HHS), *National Survey of Adolescents and Their Parents: Attitudes and Opinions about Sex and Abstinence—Final Report* 3–4 (2009), *available at* www.acf.hhs.gov/sitcs/default/files/fysb/20090226_abstinence1.pdf (last accessed Nov. 5, 2014). The report discusses a 2004 Zogby International study that revealed 96 percent of surveyed parents believed that teens should remain abstinent. *Id.* at 3.

48. Steinberg, *Adolescent Development*, *supra* note 33, at 469.

49. Cauffman, *supra* note 34, at 1775–76, 1778–79.

50. *Id.* at 1773–75. In 1995, when theorizing about traits other than cognition that operate in mature decision making, Steinberg and Cauffman defined *maturity of judgment*:

> These psychosocial traits comprise what we call "maturity of judgment." . . . [M]aturity of judgment can be further broken down into three core components: (1) responsibility, which includes healthy autonomy, self-reliance, and clarity of identity; (2) perspective, or the ability to acknowledge the complexity of a situation and see it as part of a broader context; and (3) temperance, which refers to the ability to limit impulsive and emotional decision-making, to evaluate situations thoroughly before acting (which may involve seeking the advice of others when appropriate), and to avoid decision-making extremes.

Id. at 1764–65. These three core components correspond to the four traits about which Steinberg later writes: peer influence, future orientation, reward sensitivity, and the capacity for self-regulation. Steinberg, *Adolescent Development*, *supra* note 33, at 468–71.

51. Dustin Albert et al., *The Teenage Brain: Peer Influences on Adolescent Decision Making*, 22 Current Directions in Psychological Science 114, 115, 118 (2013).

52. Cauffman, *supra* note 34, at 1780.

53. Richard J. Bonnie and Elizabeth S. Scott, *The Teenage Brain: Adolescent Brain Research and the Law*, 22 Current Directions in Psychological Science 158, 161 (2013).

54. Mary A. Ott et al., *Greater Expectations: Adolescents' Positive Motivations for Sex*, Perspectives on Sexual and Reproductive Health 86, 88 (2006) (citation omitted), *available at* www.guttmacher.org/pubs/journals/3808406.html#4 (last accessed Nov. 5, 2014).

55. Danice K. Eaton et al., CDC, *Youth Risk Behavior Surveillance–United States, 2011*, 61 Morbidity and Mortality Weekly Report No. 4, June 8, 2012, at 1, *available at* www.cdc.gov/mmwr/pdf/ss/ss6104.pdf (last accessed Nov. 5, 2014).

56. Mike A. Males, Teenage Sex and Pregnancy 38 (2010) (italics in the original).

57. Males, *supra* note 56, at 21.

58. *See Id.*

59. *See generally*, Males, *supra* note 56, at 21–38.

60. Eaton, *supra* note 55, Table 63 at 110.

61. Males, *supra* note 56, at 24.

62. Eaton, *supra* note 55, at 10.

63. Gladys Martinez et al., CDC, *Teenagers in the United States: Sexual Activity, Contraceptive Use, and Childbearing, 2006–2010 Nation Survey of Family Growth*, 7, 20 & Table 9 (Oct. 2011), *available at* www.cdc.gov/nchs/data/series/sr_23/sr23_031.pdf (last accessed Nov. 5, 2014).

64. Tina Hoff et al., Henry J. Kaiser Family Foundation, *National Survey of Adolescents and Young Adults: Sexual Health Knowledge, Attitudes, and Experiences* 8, 11, 20 (2003) [hereinafter Hoff], *available at* http://kaiserfamilyfoundation.files.wordpress.com/2013/01/national-survey-of-adolescents-and-young-adults.pdf (last accessed Nov. 5, 2014).

65. *Id.* at 18 (citing K. A. Moore & A. Driscoll, National Campaign to Prevent Teen Pregnancy [hereinafter NCPTP]), Partners, Predators, Peers, Protectors: Males and Teen Pregnancy: New Data Analyses of the 1995 National Survey on Family Growth (1997).

66. Jacqueline E. Darroch et al., *Age Differences Between Sexual Partners in the United States*, 31 Fam. Plan. Persp. 160, 164 (1999) (also finding that 29 percent of minors versus 18–21 percent of women older than nineteen had partners three to five years older than they were). The pregnancy rate for teens dating someone three to five years older was 1.4 times as high as for those dating someone closer in age. *Id.* Darroch and her colleagues raise "the concern that the age difference may make it more difficult for young women to resist pressure to have sex and to become pregnant." *Id.* at 167.

67. NCPTP, 14 and Younger: The Sexual Behavior of Young Adolescents 11 (B. Albert et al. eds., 2003) [hereinafter 14 and Younger].

68. Hannah Brückner & Peter Bearman, *Dating Behavior and Sexual Activity of Young Adolescents: Analyses of the National Longitudinal Study of Adolescent Health*, *in* 14 and Younger 31, *supra* note 67, at 54 & Table 31 (relying on the 1994–96 Nat'l Longitudinal Study of Adolescent Health).

69. Olsho, *supra* note 47, at 73.

70. Press Release, Planned Parenthood, Half of All Teens Feel Uncomfortable Talking to Their Parents About Sex While Only 19 Percent of Parents Feel the Same, New Survey Shows (Oct. 2, 2012), *available at* www.plannedparenthood.org/about-us/newsroom/press-releases/half-all-teens-feel-uncomfortable-talking-their-parents-about-sex-while-only-19-percent-parents-40375.htm (last accessed Nov. 5, 2014).

71. Susan Philliber, *Community Concerns and Communication Among Young Teens and Their Parents: Data from California Communities*, *in* 14 and Younger 91, *supra* note 67, at 98. Olsho, *supra* note 47, at 73.

72. *Id.*

73. Press Release, *supra* note 70.

74. Olsho, *supra* note 47, at 73–74.

75. Jeannette Moninger, *Everything You Always Wanted to Know About the Sex Talk (But Were Afraid to Ask)*, Family Circle, Nov. 2012, at 143, *available at*

www.familycircle.com/teen/dating-sex/talking-to-your-teens-about-sex (last accessed Nov. 5, 2014) (discussing the Planned Parenthood/*Family Circle* study).

76. FRONTLINE, *Interview with Deborah Yurgelun-Todd*, *supra* note 14.

77. Olsho, *supra* note 47, at 4.

78. Gladys Martinez et al., CDC, *Educating Teenagers About Sex in the United States*. 6 (2010), *available at* www.cdc.gov/nchs/data/databriefs/db44.pdf (last accessed Nov. 5, 2014) (citations omitted).

79. Kaiser Family Foundation, *Sexsmarts Survey—Teens and Sexual Health Communication, Questionnaire and Detailed Results* 1 (2002), *available at* http://kaiserfamilyfoundation.files.wordpress.com/2013/01/teens-and-sexual-health-communication-toplines-survey.pdf (last accessed Nov. 5, 2014).

80. Hoff, *supra* note 64, at 4, 34.

81. CYNTHIA A. GÓMEZ ET AL., *The Development of Sex-Related Knowledge, Attitudes, Perceived Norms, and Behaviors in a Longitudinal Cohort of Middle School Children*, *in* 14 AND YOUNGER 67, *supra* note 67, at 72 Table 5.

82. Esme Cullen and Alina Salganicoff, The Kaiser Family Foundation, kaiserEDU.org, *Issue Modules, Adolescent Health, Background Brief* (2011), www.kaiseredu.org/Issue-Modules/Adolescent-Health/Background-Brief.aspx#footnote5 (last accessed Nov. 5, 2014).

83. Novella Ruffin (original publication by Angela Huebner), VIRGINIA COOPERATIVE EXTENSION, *Adolescent Growth and Development*, Publication, 350–850 4 (2009), *available at* https://pubs.ext.vt.edu/350/350-850/350-850.html (last accessed March 6, 2015).

84. Ruffin, *supra* note 83, at 4, 2.

85. Ott, *supra* note 54, at 87 (citation to table omitted). A 2000 Kaiser Family Foundation and *Seventeen* magazine survey of teens lends support for the notion that intimacy is a goal for adolescents. Kaiser Family Foundation, SEXSMARTS, *Decision Making About Sex* (2000). Kaiser polled 510 teens between the ages of 12 to 17. In response to a question regarding the "major reason" sexually active teens chose to have sex the first time, 28 percent of 15–17-year-olds "hoped it would make the relationships closer." SEXSMARTS, *Decision Making About Sex*, at 2. Thus, more than a quarter of sexually active teens were searching for a more intimate relationship through sexual intercourse.

86. Ott, *supra* note 54, at 86.

87. *Id.* at 87.

88. SEXSMARTS, *Decision Making About Sex*, *supra* note 85, at 2; Hoff, *supra* note 64, at 3. In 2003, the Kaiser Family Foundation reported that one-third of survey respondents said that sexual activity had progressed faster than they desired in at least one relationship. Nearly a third of responding adolescents (15–17) also said "that they have experienced pressure to have sex." Hoff, *supra* note 64, at 3, 7–8.

89. SEXSMARTS, *Decision Making About Sex*, *supra* note 85, at 2.

90. SEXSMARTS, *Decision Making About Sex*, *supra* note 85, at 1.

91. *See* SHERYL SANDBERG, LEAN IN: WOMEN, WORK, AND THE WILL TO LEAD (2013) and *Lean In*, http://leanin.org/about (last accessed Nov. 6, 2014).

92. Michelle Oberman, *Turning Girls Into Women: Re-Evaluating Modern Statutory Rape Law*, 85 J. CRIM. L. & CRIMINOLOGY 15, 55–56 (1994).

93. *See, e.g.*, Derek A. Kreager and Jeremy Staff, *The Sexual Double Standard and Adolescent Peer Acceptance*, 72(2) SOCIAL PSYCHOLOGY QUARTERLY (June 2009) at 143–164 (confirming "the existence of an adolescent sexual double standard and suggest[ing] that sexual norms vary by both gender and socioeconomic origins."); *but see* Planned Parenthood, *Parents and Teens Talk About Sexuality: A National Poll Overview* 3 (2012), *available at* www.plannedparenthood.org/files/8313/9610/5916/LT_2012_Poll_Fact_Sheet_final_2.pdf (last accessed Nov. 6, 2014) ("There's no double standard—teen girls were only slightly more likely than teen boys to say their parent would disapprove of them dating or having sex.").

94. Bill Albert, NCPTP, *With One Voice 2007: America's Adults and Teens Sound Off About Teen Pregnancy*, 4 (Feb. 2007), *available at* https://thenationalcampaign.org/sites/default/files/resource-primary-download/wov2007_fulltext.pdf (last accessed Nov. 6, 2014).

95. Oberman, *supra* note 92, at 57.

96. Price Waterhouse v. Hopkins, 490 U.S. 228, 235 (1989) (quoting Hopkins v. Price Waterhouse, 618 F. Supp. 1109, 1117 (D.C. Cir. 1985)).

97. Price Waterhouse, 490 U.S. at 257.

98. *Id.* at 58.

99. Catherine Hill & Holly Kearl, AMERICAN ASSOCIATION OF UNIVERSITY WOMEN [hereinafter AAUW], CROSSING THE LINE: SEXUAL HARASSMENT AT SCHOOL, 2–3 (2011), *available at* www.aauw.org/files/2013/02/Crossing-the-Line-Sexual-Harassment-at-School.pdf (last accessed Nov. 6, 2014).

100. Hill, *supra* note 99, at 2–3.

101. *Id.* at 3.

102. Jennifer J. Frost et al., The Alan Guttmacher Institute, *Teenage Sexual and Reproductive Behavior in Developed Countries, Occasional Report No. 8*, Country Report for the United States 10 (Nov. 2001), *available at* www.guttmacher.org/pubs/us_teens.pdf (last accessed Nov. 6, 2014), at 18.

103. Heather Boonstra, *Teen Pregnancy: Trends and Lessons Learned*, 5 The Guttmacher Report, Feb. 2002, at 6, *available at* www.guttmacher.org/pubs/tgr/05/1/gr050107.html (last accessed Nov. 6, 2014).

104. Suzanne M. Sgroi, M.D., *Discovery, Reporting, Investigation, and Prosecution of Child Sexual Abuse*, 29 SIECUS REP., Oct./Nov. 2000, at 6. One of the tort opinions that I reviewed in *Sex and the Workplace* treated the mentally challenged female victim as a conniving seductress. Drobac, *Sex and the Workplace*, *supra* text preceding note 1, at 530–31.

105. Olsho, *supra* note 47, at ix. The report discusses a 2004 Zogby International study that revealed 96 percent of surveyed parents believed that teens should remain abstinent. *Id.* at 3.

106. *Id.* at 30.

107. *See, e.g.*, Drobac, *Sex and the Workplace*, *supra* text preceding note 1, at 527–33.

108. Doe by Roe v. Orangeburg County School District No. 2, 518 S.E.2d 259, 261 (S.C. 1999) (quoting Barnes v. Barnes, 603 N.E.2d 1337, 1342 (Ind. 1992); *see also*, Drobac, *Sex and the Workplace*, *supra* text preceding note 1, at 529–31.

109. Spear, *supra* note 5, at 36–59, 156–57.

110. American Psychological Association [hereinafter APA], *Child sexual abuse: What parents should know*, *available at* http://web.archive.org/web/20140419045524/https://www.apa.org/pi/families/resources/child-sexual-abuse.aspx (last accessed Nov. 7, 2014) (bold in original), at 1. For a fuller definition of child sexual abuse by HHS, see HHS, *Definitions, Scope, and Effects of Child Sexual Abuse, available at* www.childwelfare.gov/pubs/usermanuals/sexabuse/sexabuseb.cfm (last accessed Nov. 6, 2014).

111. *See generally* Child Sexual Abuse: Disclosure, Delay, Denial (Margaret-Ellen Pipe et al., eds., 2007); Rebecca M. Bolen, Child Sexual Abuse: It's Scope and Our Failure (2002).

112. AACAP, *Child Sexual Abuse*, Facts for Families No. 9, Mar. 2011, *available at* www.aacap.org/AACAP/Families_and_Youth/Facts_for_Families/Facts_for_Families_Pages/Child_Sexual_Abuse_09.aspx (last accessed Nov. 6, 2014) at 1; Marci A. Hamilton, Justice Denied: What America Must Do to Protect Its Children 4 and 129–30 n.2 (2008) (finding that 25 percent of girls and 20 percent of boys are sexually abused during their childhood).

113. Hill, *supra* note 99, at 2–3; *see also* Hamilton, *supra* note 112, at 7 (asserting that only about ten percent of abuse survivors report their abuse to authorities).

114. Melissa Brodowski, HHS, Children's Bureau, *Child Maltreatment 2011* 22, 45 (2011), *available at* www.acf.hhs.gov/sites/default/files/cb/cm11.pdf#page=57 (last accessed Nov. 6, 2014).

115. ABA [American Bar Association] Center on Children and the Law, A Judicial Primer on Child Sexual Abuse 3–4 (Josephine Bulkley & Claire Sandt, eds., 1994) [hereinafter A Judicial Primer]; Inger J. Sagatun & Leonard P. Edwards, Child Abuse and The Legal System 220 (1995).

116. Verena Schönbucher et al., *Disclosure of Child Sexual Abuse by Adolescents: A Qualitative In-Depth Study*, 27 J. Interpersonal Violence 3486–87 (Oct. 2012).

117. Hamilton, *supra* note 112, at 9.

118. A Judicial Primer, *supra* note 115, at 3.

119. Complaint at 9, [Sara Doe] v. Culver Theaters, Inc., No. CV139513 (Cal. Santa Cruz Cnty. Super. Ct. Oct. 1999) [hereinafter Sara Doe Complaint 1999]);

Report of Deputy R. Mitchell, #73–2801, Aug. 9, 1999, at 3 (on file with author and Santa Cruz County Sheriff's Department) [hereinafter Mitchell, Aug. 9, 1999]; *see* Report of Deputy R. Mitchell, #73–2801, Oct. 29, 1999, at 4–7 (on file with author and Santa Cruz County Sheriff's Department) [hereinafter Mitchell, Oct. 29, 1999]; Report of Deputy R. Mitchell #73–2801, Nov. 1, 1999, at 4 (on file with author and Santa Cruz County Sheriff's Department) [hereinafter Mitchell, Nov. 1, 1999].

120. Sara Doe Complaint 1999, *supra* note 119, at 2–7; Mitchell, Aug. 9, 1999, *supra* note 119, at 3; *see* Mitchell, Oct. 29, 1999, *supra* note 119, at 4.

121. Sara Doe Complaint 1999, *supra* note 119, at 9; Mitchell, Nov. 1, 1999, *supra* note 119, at 4.

122. Letter from Sara Doe to Michael Cosio (Aug. 12, 1999) (on file with author and Santa Cruz County Sheriff's Department).

123. *See* Mitchell, Aug. 9, 1999, *supra* note 119, at 3.

124. Press Release, McLean Hospital, McLean Researchers Document Brain Damage Linked to Child Abuse and Neglect (Dec. 14, 2000) [hereinafter McLean Researchers] (on file with author).

125. *See* David P. H. Jones & Paul Ramchandani, Child Sexual Abuse: Informing Practice From Research 15–16 (1999) (finding that about half of children studied suffered such symptoms).

126. McLean Researchers, *supra* note 124, at 1–2.

127. *Id.* at 2.

128. *Id.*

129. Carryl P. Navalta et al., *Effects of Childhood Sexual Abuse on Neuropsychological and Cognitive Function in College Women*, 18 J. Neuropsychiatry & Clinical Neurosciences 45, 46 (Winter 2006).

130. *Id.* at 2–3.

131. B. Bower, *Child Sex Abuse Leaves Mark on the Brain*, 147 Sci. News, 340, 340–41 (1995).

132. *See, e.g.*, Ida Frugård Strøm, et al., *Violence, Bullying and Academic Achievement: A Study of 15-Year-Old Adolescents and Their School Environment*, 37 Child Abuse & Neglect 243–51 (Apr. 2013).

133. Jones, *supra* note 125, at 16; A Judicial Primer, *supra* note 115, at 5–6. For further discussion of the effects of child sexual abuse, *see* Sagatun, *supra* note 117, at 24–25 and 220 (describing "Child Sexual Abuse Accommodation Syndrome"); William E. Prendergast, Sexual Abuse of Children and Adolescents 69–102 (1996); Elizabeth Adams, Understanding the Trauma of Childhood Psycho-Sexual Abuse 34–39 (1994); Sexualized Violence Against Women and Children 153–54 (B. J. Cling, ed., 2004).

134. Jones, *supra* note 125, at 16; A Judicial Primer, *supra* note 115, at 5.

135. A Judicial Primer, *supra* note 115, at 5.

136. Michael D. De Bellis, et al., *Neurodevelopmental Biology Associated with Child Abuse*, 20 J. Child Abuse 548, 565 (2011).

137. Navalta, *supra* note 129, at 45, 46.

138. Bower, *supra* note 131, at 341.

139. De Bellis, *supra* note 136, at 555, 572.

140. Hulvershorn Comment, *supra* note 13.

141. Catherine L. Satterwhite, et al., *Sexually Transmitted Infections Among U.S. Women and Men: Prevalence and Incidence Estimates, 2008*, 40 SEXUALLY TRANSMITTED DISEASES 187, 191 (Mar. 2013).

142. Kaiser Family Foundation, *Sexual Health of Adolescents and Young Adults in the United States* 2 (citing Shayna D. Cunningham et al., *Relationships Between Perceived STD-Related Stigma STD-Related Shame and STD Screening Among a Household Sample of Adolescents*, 41 PERSP. SEXUAL REPROD. HEALTH 225–30 (Dec. 2009)) [hereinafter *Sexual Health of Adolescents*], *available at* http://kaiserfamilyfoundation.files.wordpress.com/2013/04/3040–06.pdf (last accessed Nov. 7, 2014).

143. Advocates For Youth, *Adolescents and Sexually Transmitted Infections: A Costly and Dangerous Global Phenomenon* (2010) (citing A. Bralock & D. Koniak-Griffin, *What Do Sexually Active Adolescent Females Say About Relationship Issues?* 24 J. OF PEDIATRIC NURSING 131–40 (Apr. 2009) and J. L. Raiford et al., *Effects of Fear of Abuse and Possible STI Acquisition on The Sexual Behavior of Young African American Women*. 99 AM. J. PUB. HEALTH, 1067–71 (June 2009)), *available at* www.advocatesforyouth.org/storage/advfy/documents/thefacts_adolescents_sti.pdf (last accessed Nov. 7, 2014).

144. *Sexual Health of Adolescents*, *supra* note 142, at 2.

145. ABA CENTER ON CHILDREN AND THE LAW, SEXUAL RELATIONSHIPS BETWEEN ADULT MALES AND YOUNG TEEN GIRLS 2 (Sharon G. Elstein & Noy Davis, eds., 1997) [hereinafter SEXUAL RELATIONSHIPS] (citing THE ALAN GUTTMACHER INSTITUTE, SEX AND AMERICA'S TEENAGERS (1994)). Kaiser reports that "those ages 13–24 accounted for 26%" of new HIV infections in 2010. Kaiser Family Foundation, *The HIV/AIDS Epidemic in the United States* 3 (Apr. 2014), *available at* http://kaiserfamilyfoundation.files.wordpress.com/2014/04/3029–15-the-hivaids-epidemic-in-the-united-states1.pdf (last accessed Nov. 7, 2014).

146. SEXUAL RELATIONSHIPS, *supra* note 145, at 2 (citing M. A. Males, *Adult Involvement in Teenage Childbearing and STD*, THE LANCET 346 (1995)).

147. Advocates For Youth, *supra* note 143, at 2 (citing CDC, *Sexually Transmitted Disease Surveillance, 2008*. (Nov. 2009)).

148. SEXUAL RELATIONSHIPS, *supra* note 145, at 3 (quoting M. A. Males, *Adult Liaison in the 'Epidemic' of 'Teenage' Birth, Pregnancy, and Venereal Disease*, J. SEX RESEARCH 29 (1992) (internal quotation marks omitted)).

149. Mitchell, Aug. 9, 1999, *supra* note 119, at 3.

150. Sara Doe Complaint 1999, *supra* note 119, at 9, 11, 17–18; *see* Sara Doe, *Forgiveness* (a surrealistic poem) (Sept. 2, 1999) (on file with author and Santa Cruz County Sheriff's Department).

Chapter Four

This chapter draws from Jennifer Ann Drobac, *Consent, Teenagers, and (un)Civil(ized) Consequences, in* CHILDREN, SEXUALITY AND THE LAW (Sacha M. Coupet & Ellen Marrus eds., NYU Press, 2015); Jennifer Ann Drobac & Leslie A. Hulvershorn, *The Neurobiology of Decision-Making in High Risk Youth & The Law of Consent to Sex*, 17 NEW CRIM. L. REV. 502 (Summer 2014); Jennifer Ann Drobac, *Wake Up and Smell the Starbucks Coffee: How* Doe v. Starbucks *Confirms the End of the "Age of Consent" in California and Perhaps Beyond*, 33 B.C. J.L. & SOC. JUST. 1 (2013); Jennifer Ann Drobac, *A* Bee Line *in the Wrong Direction: Science, Teenagers, and the Sting to "The Age of Consent,"* 20 J.L. & POL'Y 63 (2011); Jennifer Ann Drobac, *I Can't to I Kant: The Sexual Harassment of Working Adolescents, Competing Theories, and Ethical Dilemmas*, 70 ALBANY L. REV. 675 (2007); Jennifer Ann Drobac, *"Developing Capacity": Adolescent "Consent" at Work, at Law and in the Sciences of the Mind*, 10 UC DAVIS J. JUVENILE L. & POL'Y 1 (2006); and Jennifer Ann Drobac, *Sex and the Workplace: "Consenting" Adolescents and a Conflict of Laws*, 79 WASH. L. REV. 471 (2004), and supporting citations in these texts.

1. In Miller v. Alabama, 132 S. Ct. 2455 (2012), the Court found a prison sentence that subjects a juvenile to life without the possibility of parole unconstitutional.

2. 428 U.S. 52, 74 (1976).

3. Thompson v. Oklahoma, 487 U.S. 815, 823 (1988) (quoting Goss v. Lopez, 419 U.S. 565, 590–91 (1975) (Powell, J., dissenting)).

4. The US Constitution grants eighteen-year-olds the right to vote. US Const. amend. XXVI. The *Thompson* Court noted that no state had lowered its voting age below eighteen. 487 U.S. at 839.

Concerning the right to serve on a jury, in *Thompson*, the Court noted that no state had granted that right to persons under eighteen. 487 U.S. at 840.

Regarding the right to marry, only Mississippi permits persons younger than eighteen to marry without parental consent or judicial authorization. Nebraska permits marriage without parental consent only at nineteen. *See* Legal Info. Inst., *Marriage Laws of the Fifty States, District of Columbia and Puerto Rico*, at www.law.cornell.edu/topics/Table_Marriage.htm (last accessed Nov. 7, 2014); *see also* 487 U.S. at 824. Fifteen states (Arkansas, Delaware, Florida, Georgia, Indiana, Maryland, New Jersey, New Mexico, North Carolina, Ohio, Oklahoma, South Carolina, South Dakota, Virginia, West Virginia) allow young minors to marry if they are pregnant or have a child.

The *Thompson* Court noted that in all states but one, the minimum requirement for a driver's license without parental consent was at least sixteen. 487 U.S. at 842.

By 1988, all states had established a legal minimum drinking age of twenty-one. Robert H. Mnookin & D. Kelly Weisberg, Child, Family, and State 1087 (4th ed. 2000); *see generally* 487 U.S. at 823. In 1984, Congress amended federal law to withhold highway construction funds from states that failed to impose a minimum drinking age of twenty-one by 1986. *Id.*; *see* 23 U.S.C. § 158(a)(2) (1994). Research confirms that a disproportionately high percentage of fatal car accidents still involve teenagers. *See* Mnookin & Weisberg, *supra*, at 1099–1100; Nat'l Highway Traffic Safety Admin. (NHTSA), US Dep't of Transp., Traffic Safety Facts (1997), at www-nrd.nhtsa.dot.gov/Pubs/TSF1997.PDF (last accessed Nov. 7, 2014). Mnookin and Weisberg explain, "As a group, teenagers have had the least amount of experience with either activity [drinking or driving] and thus are more likely to misjudge their abilities and reactions. They are affected by small amounts of alcohol to a greater degree than more experienced drinkers." Mnookin & Weisberg, *supra*, at 1100.

The *Thompson* Court stated that no state allowed a minor to purchase obscene materials. 487 U.S. at 845; *see also* Ginsberg v. New York, 390 U.S. 629 (1968).

The CDC reported that in 1998, all states prohibited the sale of tobacco products to minors. CDC, *State Laws on Tobacco Control—United States 1998*, 48 MMWR Highlights No. SS-3, at 1 (1999), at www.cdc.gov/mmwr/preview/mmwrhtml/ss4803a2.htm (last accessed Nov. 7, 2014); *see Thompson*, 487 U.S. at 823.

The *Thompson* Court explained that thirty-nine of the forty-eight states that permitted gambling prohibited participation by minors. Another three prohibit it without the consent of the parents. 487 U.S. at 847.

5. *Thompson*, 487 U.S. at 834–35 & n.43 (citing Eddings v. Oklahoma, 455 U.S. 104, 115–16 (1982); Bellotti v. Baird, 443 U.S. 622, 635 (1979)). The *Bellotti* Court noted three reasons for limiting the rights of children: "the peculiar vulnerability of children; their inability to make critical decisions in an informed, mature manner; and the importance of the parental role in child rearing." 443 U.S. at 634..

6. Arthur L. Corbin, Corbin on Contracts § 227, at 318 (1952).

7. Mnookin & Weisberg, *supra* note 4, at 1081; Donald T. Kramer, Legal Rights of Children § 10:5, at 842–45 (rev. 2d ed. 2005).

8. 492 U.S. 361, 394 (1989) (Brennan, J., dissenting); *see* In re Stanford, 537 U.S. 968, 969–70 (2002) (Stevens, J., dissenting). Currently, parents retain the legal authority to consent to medical treatment for their children "based on the principle that young people generally lack the maturity and judgment to make fully informed decisions before they reach the age of majority." Cynthia Dailard, *New Medical Records Privacy Rule: The Interface with Teen Access to Confidential Care*, 6 The Guttmacher Rep. On Pub. Pol'y No. 1, at 6 (The Alan Guttmacher Inst. 2003), at www.guttmacher.org/pubs/tgr/06/1/gr060106.html (last accessed Nov. 7, 2014).

9. *See, e.g.*, Porter v. Triad of Arizona, 52 P.3d 799, 803 (Ariz. Ct. App. 2002) (holding that a minor may not bring an action in his own name but may sue through a representative); Am. Alternative Energy Partners II v. Windridge, Inc., 49 Cal. Rptr. 2d 686, 690–91 (Cal. Ct. App. 1996) (finding that the incapacity of minors bars them from representing their own interests in court); Newman v. Newman, 663 A.2d 980, 987 (Conn. 1995) (holding that a child may bring an action only through a next friend or guardian); Cleaver v. George Staton Co., 908 S.W.2d 468, 669 (Tex. Ct. App. 1995) (finding a lack of capacity because of the disability of minority pertaining to the right to sue in one's own name); Jensen *ex rel.* Stierman v. McPherson, 655 N.W.2d 487, 491 (Wis. Ct. App. 2002) (relying on Wis. Stat. § 803.01(3)(c) that requires that an adult represent the minor); *see also* Klak v. Skellion, 741 N.E.2d 288, 298–90 (Ill. App. Ct. 2000) (stating that a minor has no capacity to maintain an action in his name).

10. 29 U.S.C. §§ 203, 212, 213 (2000). Some minimum age exceptions exist for certain jobs such as newspaper delivery and farm work on the family farm. *See, e.g.*, US Dep't of Labor, *State Child Labor Laws Applicable to Agricultural Employment* (Jan. 1, 2014), *available at* www.dol.gov/whd/state/agriemp2.htm (last accessed Nov. 7, 2014). Every state also has child labor laws. When both federal and state laws apply to the employment of a minor, employers must obey the more stringent of the two laws. Federal law allows employers to pay workers under twenty less than minimum wage for the first ninety days of their employment. US Dep't of Labor, *Fact Sheet #32: Youth Minimum Wage—Fair Labor Standards Act* (Revised July 2008), *available at* www.dol.gov/whd/regs/compliance/whdfs32.pdf (last accessed Nov. 7, 2014).

11. Guttmacher Institute, *State Policies in Brief: An Overview of Minors' Consent Laws* 1 (July 2013), *available at* www.guttmacher.org/statecenter/spibs/spib_OMCL.pdf (last accessed Nov. 7, 2014).

12. Dr. Michael J. Bradley discusses the trend to perceive adolescents as adults in his 2002 book. MICHAEL J. BRADLEY, YES, YOUR TEEN IS CRAZY! (2002). He writes:

> [W]e've somehow come to view adolescents as if they were adults and not children. From the kid's perspective, this is nothing new. Teenagers of all generations have lobbied for adult privileges with the swaggering assurances that they can handle "it." The fact is that they cannot handle "it" and they know this. . . . What's new is that we've somehow signed onto this disastrous notion that they are adults, capable of handling "it" completely solo. It's not working. Teens left on their own as small adults not only screw up big-time, they become depressed and rageful in the bargain.

Id. at 16–17.

13. CAL. WELF. & INST. CODE § 707(d)(2), (e) (West 1998). For a discussion of how states treat juvenile criminal offenders as adults, see Elizabeth S. Scott, *The Legal Construction of Adolescence*, 29 HOFSTRA L. REV. 547, 583–86 & nn.140–52 (2000).

14. Graham v. Florida, 130 S. Ct. 2011 (2010).

15. *Id.*

16. Roper v. Simmons, 543 U.S. 551 (2005).

17. *Graham*, 130 S. Ct. at 2026 (citing Brief for American Medical Association et al. as Amici Curiae (AMA Brief) 16–24; Brief for American Psychological Association et al. as Amici Curiae (APA Brief) 22–27).

18. *Id.* (quoting *Thompson*, 487 U.S. 815, 835 (1988) (plurality opinion)).

19. *Id.* (quoting Roper v. Simmons, 543 U.S. at 569–70 (quoting Johnson v. Texas 509 U.S. 350, 367 (1993))).

20. *Id.* at 2028 (quoting *Johnson,* 509 U.S. at 367).

21. *Id.* at 2029 (quoting *Roper*, 543 U.S. at 572).

22. *See* Michelle Oberman, *Turning Girls into Women: Re-Evaluating Modern Statutory Rape Law*, 85 J. CRIM. L. & CRIMINOLOGY 15, 24–25 (1994).

23. Michael M. v. Sonoma County, 450 U.S. 464, 492 (1981) (Brennan, J., dissenting). Alabama, Arkansas, Delaware, Georgia, Idaho, Kentucky, Louisiana, Missouri, New Hampshire, Nevada, New Jersey, North Carolina, North Dakota, Pennsylvania, and Texas protected only female minors from predation by males. Oberman, *supra* note 22, at 32 n.88.

24. *See supra* App. 2 pp. 243–62.

25. Charles A. Phipps, *Children, Adults, Sex and the Criminal Law: In Search of Reason*, 22 SETON HALL LEGIS. J. 1, 55–62 (1997). For a more current summary, see ASAPH GLOSSER ET AL., US DEPT. HEALTH & HUMAN SERV., STATUTORY RAPE: A GUIDE TO STATE LAWS AND REPORTING REQUIREMENTS, *available at* http://aspe.hhs.gov/hsp/08/sr/statelaws/index.shtml (last accessed Nov. 7, 2014).

26. *Id.* at 18–19 (citing MODEL PENAL CODE § 213.1 cmt. 6 at 324 (1985)).

27. *See* App. 2 (summarizing the laws for Arkansas, Hawaii, Illinois (13), Iowa, Maine, Maryland, Michigan (13), Minnesota (13), Mississippi, New Hampshire (13), New Jersey (13), New Mexico (13), South Carolina, Tennessee (13), Utah, Virginia (13), and Wyoming (13)). One can see from App. 2 that many more states set age demarcations at 14 or younger but those differences relate more to penalties imposed than the credence given teenage “consent.”

28. *See* App. 2 (summarizing the laws for Alaska (16), Colorado (15), Connecticut (16), Delaware (16), Florida (16), Idaho (16), Illinois (17), Indiana (16), Kentucky (16), Louisiana (17), Maine (16), Michigan (16), Minnesota (16), New Jersey (16), New Mexico (17/19), Ohio (16), Oklahoma (16), Oregon (16), Pennsylvania (16), Rhode Island (15), Utah (14), Vermont (16), Virginia (13), Washington (16), and Wyoming (13)). Again, one can tell from App. 2 that the varia-

tion in state laws make it difficult to pigeonhole states as having set demarcations regarding "the age of consent."

29. *Id.*; Phipps, *supra* note 25, at 66–69; *see also* Michelle Oberman, *Regulating Consensual Sex with Minors: Defining a Role for Statutory Rape*, 48 BUFF. L. REV. 703, 767–68 (2000).

30. *See, e.g.*, Phipps, *supra* note 25, at 68 n.264.

31. Doe v. Estes, 926 F. Supp. 979, 988 (D. Nev. 1996).

32. Phipps, *supra* note 25, at 23–24.

33. MODEL PENAL CODE § 213.3 cmt. 4, at 389 (1980).

34. *See* App. 2 (summarizing the laws for Alaska, Arizona, Arkansas, California, Colorado, Connecticut, Delaware, Florida, Idaho, Illinois, Indiana, Iowa, Kentucky, Louisiana, Maine, Michigan, Minnesota, New Hampshire, New Jersey, New Mexico (19), North Dakota, Ohio, Oregon, Pennsylvania, Rhode Island, Tennessee, Utah, Vermont, Virginia, Washington (21), Wisconsin, and Wyoming setting the age of consent at eighteen or older in special circumstances).

35. *See* App. 2 (summarizing the laws for Missouri, Nebraska, New York, and Texas setting the age of consent at seventeen).

36. *See* App. 2 (summarizing the laws for Alabama, Georgia, Hawaii, Kansas, Maryland, Massachusetts, Mississippi, Montana, Nevada, North Carolina, Oklahoma, South Carolina, South Dakota, West Virginia, setting the age of consent at sixteen or younger).

37. *See* App. 2 (summarizing the laws for Arizona, California, North Dakota, and Wisconsin setting the age of consent at eighteen).

38. Phipps, *supra* note 25, at 51–52 & n.219; *but see* People v. Teague, No. A104705, 2005 WL 1324792 *7–8 (1st Dist. Cal.) (unpublished opinion citing People v. Scott, 83 Cal. App. 4th 784, 797, fn. 8 (2000) and finding that the defendant's belief that a juvenile was under eighteen, but older than she her actual age, constitutes no defense).

39. *Id.* at 70–71 & n.275 (citing MASS. GEN. LAWS ANN. ch. 272, § 4 (West 1990); MISS. CODE ANN. §§ 97-3-67, -5-21 (1994)).

40. *See* MISS. CODE ANN. § 97-3-65 (1999).

41. Hernandez v. State, 861 S.W.2d 908, 909–10 (Tex. 1993) (finding that § 22.011(d)(1) of the Texas Penal Code permits the accused to raise a statutory promiscuity defense in a case in which the minor's mother "sold" her to the accused and other men). The Texas legislature deleted this defense when it revised the penal code in 1993. *Id.* at 910 (Miller, J., concurring).

42. 861 S.W.2d 908 (Tex. 1993).

43. *Id.* at 909 n.1 (emphasis added).

44. *Hernandez*, 861 S.W.2d at 910 (McCormick, J., dissenting).

45. KENNETH V. LANNING, NATIONAL CENTER FOR MISSING & EXPLOITED CHILDREN, CHILD MOLESTERS: A BEHAVIORAL ANALYSIS 6 (5th ed. 2010) (emphasis in original).

46. *Starbucks*, 2009 WL 5183773, at *1, *4. Doe v. Starbucks, Inc., No. SACV 08–0582 AG (CWx), 2009 WL 5183773, at *1 (C.D. Cal. Dec. 18, 2009) (granting in part and denying in part motions for summary judgment). This case was set to go to trial the week of June 15, 2010. However, according to the court clerk, the case settled. E-mail from Lisa Bredahl, Court Clerk to the Honorable Andrew J. Guilford, to author (Aug. 24, 2010) (on file with author).

47. *Id.* at *2 (quoting Starbucks's Objections to Plaintiff's Evidence at 9:9–10:8, Doe v. Starbucks, Inc., No. SACV 08–0582 AG (CWx), 2009 WL 5183773 (C.D. Cal. Dec. 18, 2009)).

48. *Starbucks*, 2009 WL 5183773, at *1, *4 (citing Doe Declaration ¶ 4, Doe v. Starbucks, Inc., No. SACV 08–0582 AG (CWx), 2009 WL 5183773 (C.D. Cal. Dec. 18, 2009)).

49. *Starbucks*, 2009 WL 5183773, at *2.

50. *Id.* at *3, *4 (quoting Doe Declaration, *supra* note 48, ¶ 20).

51. *Starbucks*, 2009 WL 5183773, at *5.

52. *Id.* (quoting Plaintiff's Statement of Material Facts ¶¶ 20, 25, Doe v. Starbucks, Inc., No. SACV 08–0582 AG (CWx), 2009 WL 5183773 (C.D. Cal. Dec. 18, 2009)).

53. *Starbucks*, 2009 WL 5183773, at *5.

54. *Id.* at *6 (citing Plaintiff's Statement of Material Facts, *supra* note 52, ¶ 59).

55. *Starbucks*, 2009 WL 5183773, at *6.

56. Phipps, *supra* note 25, at 70 n.275; *see* FED. R. EVID. 412 & advisory committee's note. *But see* Barnes v. Barnes, 603 N.E.2d 1337, 1342–43 (Ind. 1992) (holding that in a tort action, the Indiana Rape Shield Statute did not preclude the defendant from introducing evidence of plaintiff's other sexual activities); Doe by Roe v. Orangeburg County Sch. Dist., 495 S.E.2d 230, 233 (S.C. Ct. App. 1997) (finding that the South Carolina rape shield statute did not apply in civil cases).

57. FED. R. EVID. 412 (emphasis added).

58. *See, e.g.*, CAL. EVID. CODE § 1106 (West 1995); CAL. GOV'T CODE § 11513 (West 1992).

59. *See, e.g.*, Susan Estrich, *Sex at Work*, 43 STAN. L. REV. 813, 849 (1991) (arguing that exposure of a woman's sexual history will "lead not only to shame in the courtroom but acquiescence in the workplace").

60. Jon Cassidy, *Woman sues Starbucks over underage sex* 1, THE ORANGE COUNTY REGISTER, Jan. 25, 2010 (updated Jan. 26, 2010*), available at* www.ocregister.com/articles/moore-230812-starbucks-records.html (last accessed Nov. 7, 2014) (internal quotation marks omitted).

61. CAL. PENAL CODE § 288a (West 1999).

62. *See* People v. Cosio, No. S9–09852 (Cal. Santa Cruz Cnty. Super. Ct. 1999).

63. Absent the special facts of her case (*e.g.*, the age disparity and Cosio's managerial position), the number of states that would not protect her increases to perhaps forty. *See* App. 2.

64. *See* Charles A. Phipps, *Children, Adults, Sex and the Criminal Law: In Search of Reason*, 22 SETON HALL LEGIS. J. 1, 27 (1997); *see, e.g.*, CAL. GOV'T CODE § 26500 (West 1988) ("The public prosecutor shall attend the courts, and within his or her discretion shall initiate and conduct on behalf of the people all prosecutions for public offenses.").

65. *See* Phipps, *supra* note 25, at 28–29.

66. Phipps, *supra* note 25, at 34–40. Phipps noted that in 1996 the increasing birth of children to teenagers on public assistance renewed legislative interest in statutory rape laws. *Id.* at 4–5.

67. *Michael M.*, 450 U.S. at 470–71.

68. Oberman, *Regulating Consensual Sex with Minors*, *supra* note 29, at 714, 748, 751.

69. *Compare* Gary B. Melton, *Toward "Personhood" for Adolescents' Autonomy and Privacy as Values in Public Policy*, 38 AM. PSYCHOL. 99–102 (1983) *with* Elizabeth S. Scott et al., *Evaluating Adolescent Decisionmaking in Legal Contexts*, 19 LAW & HUM. BEHAV. 221, 224–31, 240 (1995).

70. Phipps, *supra* note 25, at 33–34 (quoting 4 WILLIAM BLACKSTONE, COMMENTARIES ON THE LAWS OF ENGLAND 212 (William S. Hein ed., 1992) (1769)).

71. Virginia v. Black, 538 U.S. 343, 397 (2003) (Thomas, J., dissenting) (quoting Warrick v. State, 538 N.E.2d 952, 954 (Ind. 1989) (citing IND. CODE 35-42-4-3)) (internal quotation marks and other code citations omitted).

72. *Id.*

73. *See generally* Robert Batey, *The Rights of Adolescents*, 23 WM. & MARY L. REV. 363 (1982); Henry H. Foster & Doris Jonas Freed, *A Bill of Rights for Children*, 6 FAM. L.Q. 343 (1972). Virginia Coigney, who advocated for A Child's Bill of Rights, listed "The Right to Self Determination" as the first right. VIRGINIA COIGNEY, CHILDREN ARE PEOPLE TOO: HOW WE FAIL OUR CHILDREN AND HOW WE CAN LOVE THEM 197 (1975)). She wrote:

> Children should have the right to decide the matters which affect them most directly. This is the basic right upon which all others depend. Children are now treated as the private property of their parents on the assumption that it is the parents' right and responsibility to control the life of the child. The achievement of children's rights, however, would reduce the need for this control and bring about an end to the double standard of morals and behavior for adults and children.

Id. See generally RICHARD E. FARSON, BIRTHRIGHTS (1974).

74. JUDITH LEVINE, HARMFUL TO MINORS: THE PERILS OF PROTECTING CHILDREN FROM SEX xxxv (2002).

75. *Id.*

76. *Id.* at 88.

77. *See generally* MedlinePlus, Abortion, www.nlm.nih.gov/medlineplus/abortion.html (last accessed Nov. 7, 2014) (providing links to various sources discussing the result and potential risks of abortions).

78. *See, e.g.*, Sylvia A. Law, *Abortion Compromise—Inevitable and Impossible*, 1992 U. Ill. L. Rev. 921, 933–35 (1992) (examining underlying issues in the debate about abortion).

79. *See, e.g.*, MedlinePlus, Safe Sex, www.nlm.nih.gov/medlineplus/ency/article/001949.htm (last accessed Nov. 7, 2014) (discussing sexually transmitted diseases and safe sex).

80. One might argue that the right to liberty guaranteed by the United States Constitution protects her right to make a choice in both cases. US Const. amend. XIV, § 1; *see also* Lawrence v. Texas, 539 U.S. 558, 578 (2003) (finding a substantive due process right to make decisions about adult private sexual conduct, but not extending that right to minors); Carey v. Population Servs. Int'l, 431 U.S. 678, 693 (1977) (finding a right to privacy and abortion services for minors); Skinner v. Oklahoma, 316 U.S. 535, 536 (1942) (finding a right to procreate).

81. *See generally* Nat'l Campaign to Prevent Teen Pregnancy, Teen Pregnancy, *available at* http://thenationalcampaign.org/why-it-matters/teen-pregnancy (last accessed Nov. 7, 2014) (providing links to reports that discuss the social, economic, and health risks associated with teen pregnancy).

82. Innocenti Research Ctr., United Nations Children's Fund, Early Marriage: Child Spouses 11 (2001), *available at* www.unicef.org/publications/files/Early_Marriage_12.lo.pdf (last accessed Nov. 7, 2014).

83. Adolescent Health and Dev. Programme, World Health Org., The Second Decade: Improving Adolescent Health and Development 6 (1998), *available at* http://whqlibdoc.who.int/hq/1998/WHO_FRH_ADH_98.18_Rev.1.pdf (last accessed Nov. 7, 2014).

84. *See, e.g.*, Planned Parenthood, *Parent Consent and Notification Laws*, www.plannedparenthood.org/health-topics/abortion/parental-consent-notification-laws-25268.htm (last accessed Nov. 7, 2014) (confirming that thirty-seven states have laws in effect that require parental consent or notification for a minor to access abortion).

85. The Washington State Department of Health determined:

> Infants born to teen mothers are one and a third times more likely to be born prematurely, and 50 percent more likely to be low birthweight babies (under 5.5 pounds). Low birthweight and prematurity raise the probability of a number of adverse conditions, including infant death, blindness, deafness, mental retardation and cerebral palsy.
>
> . . . .
>
> Children born to single teenage mothers "are more likely

> to drop out of school, to give birth out of wedlock, to divorce or separate, and to become dependent on welfare, compared to children with older parents." Sons of adolescent mothers are almost 3 times more likely to be incarcerated than sons of mothers who delay childbearing until older.

Washington State Department of Health, TEEN HEALTH AND THE MEDIA, *Teen Sexuality: Family Planning*, http://depts.washington.edu/thmedia/view.cgi?section=familyplanning&page=fastfacts (last accessed Nov. 7, 2014).

86. *See* Oberman, *Regulating Consensual Sex with Minors*, *supra* note 29, at 778.

87. *Id.* at 777.

88. *Id.* at 778–79. Oberman also allowed for exceptions to the rule for conduct that appeared obviously coercive or "offensive to societal mores." *Id.* at 779. Oberman stated, "It strikes me that mandating victim cooperation would be problematic for several reasons" and then discussed those reasons. *Id.* at 779–82.

89. *Id.* at 778–79.

90. For a more in-depth analysis of a mixed approach to adolescent rights, see generally FRANKLIN ZIMRING, THE CHANGING LEGAL WORLD OF ADOLESCENCE (1982).

91. *See* 42 U.S.C. § 2000e-2(a)(1) (2006); *see, e.g.*, Faragher v. City of Boca Raton, 524 U.S. 775, 787 (1998).

92. 524 U.S. 775, 787 (1998) (citing Harris v. Forklift Sys., 510 U.S. 17, 21–22 (1993)).

93. *See, e.g.*, CAL. GOV'T CODE § 12940 (West 2011); Fisher v. San Pedro Peninsula Hosp., 262 Cal. Rptr. 842, 851 (Ct. App. 1989) (holding a claim of sexual harassment under section 12940 requires "unwelcome" sexual harassment).

94. *See Starbucks*, 2009 WL 5183773, at *158–59, *166.

Chapter Five

This chapter draws from Jennifer Ann Drobac, *Consent, Teenagers, and (un)Civil(ized) Consequences*, *in* CHILDREN, SEXUALITY AND THE LAW (Sacha M. Coupet & Ellen Marrus eds., NYU Press, 2015); Jennifer Ann Drobac & Leslie A. Hulvershorn, *The Neurobiology of Decision-Making in High Risk Youth & The Law of Consent to Sex*, 17 NEW CRIM. L. REV. 502 (Summer 2014); Jennifer Ann Drobac, *Wake Up and Smell the Starbucks Coffee: How* Doe v. Starbucks *Confirms the End of the "Age of Consent" in California and Perhaps Beyond*, 33 B.C. J.L. & SOC. JUST. 1 (2013); Jennifer Ann Drobac, *A* Bee Line *in the Wrong Direction: Science, Teenagers, and the Sting to "The Age of Consent,"* 20 J.L. & POL'Y 63 (2011); Jennifer Ann Drobac, *I Can't to I Kant: The Sexual Harassment of Work-*

ing Adolescents, Competing Theories, and Ethical Dilemmas, 70 ALBANY L. REV. 675 (2007); Jennifer Ann Drobac, *"Developing Capacity": Adolescent "Consent" at Work, at Law and in the Sciences of the Mind*, 10 UC DAVIS J. JUVENILE L. & POL'Y 1 (2006); and Jennifer Ann Drobac, *Sex and the Workplace: "Consenting" Adolescents and a Conflict of Laws*, 79 WASH. L. REV. 471 (2004), and supporting citations in these texts.

1. These personal injury claims relate to lost contract opportunities, the lost companionship of loved ones, outrageous or negligent conduct that results in emotional distress, injuries caused by fear or offensive touching, wrongful detention, and reputational injuries associated with false rumors, misrepresentations, or the disclosure of private facts.

2. JENNIFER ANN DROBAC, SEXUAL HARASSMENT LAW: HISTORY, CASES, AND THEORY 691 (2005).

3. KENNETH ABRAHAM, THE FORMS AND FUNCTION OF TORT LAW 32–35 (1997).

4. BLACK'S LAW DICTIONARY 1569 (7th ed. 1999) (referring also to assumption of risk); *see also* Lea VanderVelde, *The Legal Ways of Seduction*, 48 STAN. L. REV. 817, 860 (1996).

5. 265 N.Y.S. 284 (2d Dept. 1933). This case is a classic "he said, she said" case. I acknowledge the continuing problematic nature of credibility determinations in alleged rape cases and the bias against complaining women who sue for civil damages. I addressed such bias in Chapter 9.

6. This adjusted sum, based on the consumer price index, is available by calculation from *Measuring Worth* www.measuringworth.com/uscompare/result.php?use%5B%5D=DOLLAR&use%5B%5D=GDPDEFLATION&use%5B%5D=VCB&use%5B%5D=UNSKILLED&use%5B%5D=MANCOMP&use%5B%5D=NOMGDPCP&use%5B%5D=NOMINALGDP&year_source=1933&amount=3000&year_result=2011 (last accessed Nov. 7, 2014).

7. Bee Line, 265 N.Y.S. at 284.

8. Bee Line, 265 N.Y.S. at 285.

9. Bee Line, 265 N.Y.S. at 285 (quoting Smith v. Richards, 29 Conn. 232 (1860)).

10. The "age of consent" commonly refers to the age at which a minor, someone under 18 years old, may legally consent to engage in sexual activity with an adult and, thereby, insulate that adult from criminal prosecution. *But see* Donaldson v. Dep't of Real Estate, 36 Cal. Rptr. 3d 577, 588–89 (Cal. Ct. App. 2005) (discussing that "the age of consent" may refer to the age a minor can legally consent to marry).

11. *See, e.g.*, Doe v. Starbucks, Inc., No. SACV 08–0582 AG (CWx), 2009 WL 5183773, at *2, *7–8 (C.D. Cal. Dec. 18, 2009) (granting in part and denying in part motions for summary judgment).

12. *Cf.* Detmer v. Bixler, 642 N.W.2d 170, 176–77 (Neb. Ct. App. 2002) (affirming rejection of negligence claims because minor consented to sexual inter-

course and, therefore, no tort claim existed against her partner). *See generally* ABRAHAM, *supra* note 3, at 137–58.

13. In the criminal system, this rule is also known as the infancy defense. *See generally* MARTIN R. GARDNER, UNDERSTANDING JUVENILE LAW 1880–81 (1997) (discussing the infancy defense and capacity to commit a crime); WAYNE R. LAFAVE & AUSTIN W. SCOTT, HANDBOOK ON CRIMINAL LAW 351 (1972).

14. *See* Doe v. Mama Taori's Premium Pizza, No. M1998–00992-COA-R9-CV, 2001 WL 327906, at *5 (Tenn. Ct. App. Apr. 5, 2001).

15. Another bright-line rule similar to the rule of sevens is the "mature minors" doctrine. The *Mama Taori's* court recognized that some mature minors may consent to conduct reserved for adults. *Id.* at *5. *See generally* GARDNER, *supra* note 13, at 6 (discussing the mature minor and consent to medical treatment).

16. Joseph Rhee et al., *Sandusky Victim 1 Steps Out of Shadows, Says Justice Took Too Long*, ABC NEWS, Oct. 19, 2012, http://abcnews.go.com/US/sandusky-victim-reveals-identity-justice-long/story?id=17511612#.UcHCchZCok8 (last accessed Nov. 7, 2014).

17. Jason Wheeler, *Sandusky's 'Victim No. 1' talks about preventing child sex abuse*, WFAA.COM, Aug. 13, 2013, *available at* www.wfaa.com/news/local/dallas/Sanduskys-Victim-No-1-in-Dallas-talking-about-preventing-child-sex-abuse-219345961.html (last accessed Nov. 7, 2014) (internal quotation marks omitted).

18. Rhee, *supra* note 16, at 2.

19. Adam Lidgett, *Person Identified as 'Victim 1' Reaches Settlement with Penn State in Sandusky Abuse Case*, STATECOLLEGE.COM, Sept. 6, 2013, *available at* www.statecollege.com/news/local-news/person-identified-as-victim-1-reaches-settlement-with-penn-state-in-sandusky-abuse-case,1379706 (last accessed March 3, 2015).

20. *See generally* GARDNER, *supra* note 13, at 6 (discussing the mature minor and consent to medical treatment).

21. *See* VanderVelde, *supra* note 4, at 847.

22. *See id.* at 846–48.

23. Charles A. Phipps, *Children, Adults, Sex and the Criminal Law: In Search of Reason*, 22 SETON HALL LEGIS. J. 1, 14 & n.63 (1997); VanderVelde, *supra* note 4, at 818–19; *cf.* Bostic v. Smyrna Sch. Dist., No. 01–0261, 2003 WL 723262, at *7 (D. Del. Feb. 24, 2003) (rejecting loss of filial consortium claim based upon an 1828 Kentucky seduction action that allowed a family to recover for the "dishonor and disgrace" of a seduced child).

24. VanderVelde, *supra* note 4, at 819. Originally, the writ of seduction, a feudal writ, allowed masters (employers) to recover for the lost work of their servants (employees). Thus, when a female servant became pregnant, the master could seek reimbursement for his financial losses. This system ignored the servant's losses and the needs of her newborn. The law extended these rights to fathers with daughters working outside of the fathers' households. *Id.* at 821.

25. *Id.* at 825.

26. *Id.* at 828–29.

27. *See, e.g.*, CAL. FAM. CODE § 7500 (West 1994); Singer v. Brookman, 578 N.E.2d 1, 6 (Ill. App. Ct. 1991) (finding that "in the absence of specific fiduciary relationship, a parent has the right to the use of a minor child's earnings and services"); Biermann v. Biermann, 584 S.W.2d 106, 108 (Mo. Ct. App. 1979) (holding that a parent having custody may give the minor child license to work and retain the earnings of that child); Peot v. Ferraro, 266 N.W.2d 586, 731 (Wis. 1978) (ruling that a "parent is entitled to a minor child's wages and services as a matter of right").

28. BLACK'S LAW DICTIONARY, *supra* note 4, at 1011 (defining minor as "a person who has not reached full legal age" and an emancipated minor as a "minor who is self-supporting and independent of parental control, [usually] as a result of a court order"). *See generally* GARDNER, *supra* note 13, at 31–32 (examining the concept of emancipation).

29. Joanna Grossman, *Is the Tort of Wrongful Seduction Still Viable?*, FINDLAW, Feb. 11, 2003, http://writ.news.findlaw.com/grossman/20030211.html. Professor Melissa Murray confirms this perspective. She wrote, "Indeed, for many critics [of seduction laws], it appeared that those most in need of law's protection were men, who, because of civil and criminal seduction laws, could be tricked and duped by scheming women." Melissa Murray, *Marriage As Punishment*, 112 COLUM. L. REV. 1, 38 (2012).

30. Grossman, *supra* note 29.

31. Murray, *supra* note 29, at 38.

32. *Id.* at 33.

33. Suzanne M. Sgroi, M.D., *Discovery, Reporting, Investigation, and Prosecution of Child Sexual Abuse*, 29 SIECUS REP, Oct./Nov. 2000, at 6. One of the tort opinions that I reviewed in *Sex and the Workplace* treated the mentally challenged female victim as a conniving seductress. Drobac, *Sex and the Workplace*, *supra* text preceding note 1, at 530–31.

34. RESTATEMENT (SECOND) OF TORTS § 892C(2) (1979).

35. *See* Wilson v. Tobiassen, 777 P.2d 1379, 1384 (Or. Ct. App. 1989) (holding that a minor's incapacity to consent to sexual acts under Oregon Revised Statute § 163.315(1) extends to civil cases).

36. RESTATEMENT (SECOND) OF TORTS § 892B(2).

37. *See* W. PAGE KEETON ET AL., PROSSER AND KEETON ON THE LAW OF TORTS § 18, at 119 (5th ed. 1984); *see also* Hackett v. Fulton County Sch. Dist., 238 F. Supp. 2d 1330, 1369–70 (2002); In re Neal, 179 B.R. 234, 237 (Bankr. D. Idaho 1995).

38. *See* Leleux v. United States, 178 F.3d 750, 755 (5th Cir. 1999) (finding that a naval officer's fraudulent concealment of venereal disease invalidated consent of partner to sexual intercourse). *But cf.* Food Lion, Inc. v. Capital Cities/ABC,

Inc., 194 F.3d 505, 518–19 (4th Cir. 1999) (giving legal effect to consent to an entry and allowing consent as a defense to a claim of trespass, even though it was obtained by misrepresentation or concealed intentions).

39. ABRAHAM, *supra* note 3, at 14–19.

40. *Id.* at 15. Abraham ultimately decided that tort law "does not serve any single goal . . . [but] performs a 'mixed' set of functions." *Id.* at 19.

41. Abraham modified this goal by calling it "optimal deterrence." *Id.* at 19. He explained that, under this justification, liability should deter only excessively risky conduct. Some conduct is not risky enough to justify the deterrence costs that people might incur. *See id.* at 15.

42. *Id.* at 16–17.

43. *Id.* at 14–17.

44. *Id.* at 19.

45. Eight cases found consent relevant. Beul v. ASSE Int'l, Inc., 233 F.3d 441 (7th Cir. 2000); Teti v. Huron Ins. Co., 914 F. Supp. 1132 (E.D. Pa. 1996); Cynthia M. v. Rodney E., 279 Cal. Rptr. 94 (Cal. Ct. App. 1991); McNamee v. A.J.W., 519 S.E.2d 298 (Ga. Ct. App. 1999); Robinson v. Roberts, 423 S.E.2d 17 (Ga. Ct. App. 1992); LK v. Reed, 631 So. 2d 604 (La. Ct. App. 1994); Doe by Roe v. Orangeburg County Sch., 518 S.E.2d 259, 261 (S.C. 1999); and Michelle T. by Sumpter v. Crozier, 495 N.W.2d 327 (Wis. 1993). Nine cases found consent irrelevant. *Bostic*, 2003 WL 723262; Doe v. City of Murietta, 126 Cal. Rptr. 2d 213 (Cal. Ct. App. 2002); Angie M. v. Hiemstra, 44 Cal. Rptr. 2d 197 (Cal. Ct. App. 1995); Bohrer v. DeHart, 943 P.2d 1220 (Colo. Ct. App. 1996); Landreneau v. Fruge, 676 So. 2d 701 (La. Ct. App. 1996); Pettit v. Erie Ins. Exch., 699 A.2d 550 (Md. Ct. Spec. App. 1997); *Wilson*, 777 P.2d at 1379; Doe by Doe v. Greenville Hosp. Sys., 448 S.E.2d 564 (S.C. Ct. App. 1994), *cert. dismissed as improvidently granted*, 464 S.E.2d 124 (S.C. 1995); and Robinson v. Moore, 408 S.W.2d 582 (Tex. Ct. App. 1966).

46. *See* Hackett v. Fulton County Sch. Dist., 238 F. Supp. 2d 1330, 1369 (N.D. Ga. 2002) (finding that the lies the science teacher told his male student induced the student's consent to inappropriate sexual touching). The court held, "[C]onsent to the act by the person affected negates the contact as an actionable tort. 'As a general rule, there can be no tort committed against a person consenting thereto, if that consent is free and not obtained by fraud, and is the action of a sound mind.'" *Id.* (quoting Mims v. Boland, 138 S.E.2d 902, 906 (1964)).

47. *Greenville Hosp.*, 448 S.E.2d at 564. The lower court returned a verdict for Mary in the sum of $545,000. The trial judge reduced the award to $250,000 under the South Carolina Tort Claims Act. *Id.* at 565. The jury rejected a claim by Mary's father "for loss of custody, companionship, and service." *Id.* The father's claim appears to be akin to a seduction claim already discussed.

48. The Workers' Compensation Act did not preclude Mary Doe's tort claims because she received only classroom credit and job skills training in exchange for her services. *Greenville Hosp.*, 448 S.E.2d at 567–68. Thus, the court did not

consider her an employee. *Id.* Non-employee status also would preclude someone like Mary Doe, engaged in volunteer work, from suing under an applicable state fair employment practices statute. *See, e.g.*, O'Connor v. Davis, 126 F.3d 112, 114–16 (2d Cir. 1997) (finding that volunteer student intern did not qualify as an employee under Title VII), *cert. denied*, 522 U.S. 1114 (1998); Lippold v. Duggal Color Projects, Inc., No. 96 CIV 5869(JSM), 1998 WL 13854, at *2 (S.D.N.Y. Jan. 15, 1998) (confirming that unpaid volunteer cannot sue under Title VII because she is not an employee).

49. S.C. Code Ann. § 16–3-655(3) (Law. Co-op. 1985).

50. *Greenville Hosp.*, 448 S.E.2d at 566.

51. *See, e.g., Teti*, 914 F. Supp. at 1139–40 (finding that because the criminal law permits a consent defense when the victim is sixteen, the civil law must recognize the capacity of minors sixteen and older).

52. *Wilson*, 777 P.2d at 1384; *see also Angie M.*, 44 Cal. Rptr. 2d at 202 (acknowledging "the strong public policy that underlies the Legislature's enactment of the multiple statutes directed at protecting minors from sexual exploitation"). The *Angie M.* court distinguished another sexual battery statute, California Civil Code § 1708.5, which required a lack of consent. *Angie M.*, 44 Cal. Rptr. at 202–03. Despite the *Angie M.* court's focus on public policy regarding minors, that reference suggests that the court would have denied a claim by Angie M. under § 1708.5.

53. *Bostic*, 2003 WL 723262, at *6 (citing Mary M. v. N. Lawrence Cmty. Sch. Corp., 131 F.3d 1220, 1227 (11th Cir. 1997), *cert. denied*, 524 U.S. 952 (1998)). The *Bostic* court discussed consent in the context of the Title IX claim as well as the other civil claims and, therefore, referred to whether the plaintiff welcomed the sexual relationship. *Id.*

54. *Robinson*, 408 S.W.2d at 583. The court was incorrect that other courts in this country have uniformly adopted this position.

55. *Pettit*, 699 A.2d at 557 (evaluating Restatement (Second) of Torts § 892A, cmt. b); *Wilson*, 777 P.2d at 1384 (discussing Restatement (Second) of Torts § 892C).

56. *Bohrer*, 943 P.2d at 1227; *Landreneau*, 676 So. 2d at 707; *Pettit*, 699 A.2d at 557.

57. *City of Murietta*, 126 Cal. Rptr. 2d at 226 (footnote omitted).

58. *McNamee*, 519 S.E.2d at 302. *See generally Beul*, 233 F.3d at 450–51.

59. *Cynthia M.*, 279 Cal. Rptr. at 97; *McNamee*, 519 S.E.2d at 302.

60. *Cynthia M.*, 279 Cal. Rptr. at 97.

61. *Id.* (quoting Prosser & Keeton, *supra* note 37, § 18, at 115) (citation and internal quotation marks omitted); *see also McNamee*, 519 S.E.2d at 302 (using the same words as the *Cynthia M.* decision).

62. *Orangeburg*, 518 518 S.E.2d at 261.

63. *Barnes*, 603 N.E.2d at 1342.

64. *Orangeburg*, 518 S.E.2d at 261 (quoting *Barnes*, 603 N.E.2d at 1342).

65. *See* FED. R. EVID. 403 (directing that "[a]lthough relevant, evidence may be excluded if its probative value is substantially outweighed by the danger of unfair prejudice").

66. *Orangeburg*, 518 S.E.2d at 261; *see also Cynthia M.*, 279 Cal. Rptr. at 98; *LK*, 631 So. 2d at 607.

67. *See, e.g., Beul*, 233 F.3d at 451 (opting for a comparative fault rule); *Robinson*, 423 S.E.2d at 18 (evaluating contributory negligence and assumption of risk to find that a thirteen-year-old can "appreciate dangers of his environment and . . . avoid consequences associated with exposure to such dangers"); *LK*, 631 So. 2d at 608 (determining that their "analysis must include the principles of comparative fault").

68. *See, e.g., Cynthia M.*, 279 Cal. Rptr. at 98; *LK*, 631 So. 2d at 607; *Orangeburg*, 518 S.E.2d at 259–60 (noting that the "District proffered testimony tending to dispute the claim Doe was a sweet, innocent young girl with testimony that she had been overheard making sexually explicit statements").

69. *Cynthia M.*, 279 Cal. Rptr. at 98.

70. *Id.* (quoting Overhultz v. Row, 92 So. 716, 717 (La. 1922)) (internal quotation marks omitted). Having stated that *Overhultz* was "directly on point," the *Cynthia M.* court then applied reasoning formulated for an adult. *Id.* In its final footnote, the *Cynthia M.* court admitted that the *Overhultz* plaintiff was not a minor. *Id.* at 98 n.14. The court then stated, "However, we are not inclined to dwell on outdated legal fictions concerning the ability of underage females to consent to sex." *Id.* Commenting upon the current prevalence of underage sexual activity and the problem of pregnancy among unwed teenagers, the court added, "To cling to vestiges of a bygone era, is to ignore the contemporary realities of nature." *Id.* In this footnote, the *Cynthia M.* court arguably blamed teenagers for their promiscuity and particularly teenage girls for their nonmarital pregnancies. The court's treatment of their consent and effective denial of their damages may not prove to be the best way to handle these social ills.

71. *LK*, 631 So. 2d at 605, 607; *see also Orangeburg*, 518 S.E.2d at 261 (reasoning that "[t]o prohibit such evidence [of consent] would effectually allow a victim to come in and tell a one-sided version of events, without being subject to any real cross-examination or impeachment as to the damages actually suffered").

72. Ironically, in the novel, Lolita was not the narrating protagonist but was the object of a pedophile's desire. *See generally* VLADIMIR NABOKOV, LOLITA (Vintage Books 1989) (1955) (telling the story of a man sexually obsessed with his landlady's twelve-year-old daughter).

73. *See* Marybeth Hamilton Arnold, *"The Life of a Citizen in the Hands of a Woman": Sexual Assault in New York City, 1790–1820, in* PASSION AND POWER: SEXUALITY IN HISTORY 35, 40–45 (Kathy Peiss & Christina Simmons eds., 1989) (discussing sexual assault of women at the turn of the nineteenth century and highlighting the popular myth of sexually voracious working class women). Ar-

nold noted the rape of a thirteen-year-old girl who was likened to a harlot. *Id.* at 42. Counsel for the defense argued:

> [If] anything of an improper nature passed between them, I am inclined to believe that it has been with her consent. The passions may be as warm in a girl of her age as in one of more advanced years, and with very little enticement she may have consented to become his mistress. . . . [It] is said her youth renders it impossible she should have been a lewd girl. Who is acquainted with the dissolute morals of our city, and does not know that females are to be found living in a state of open prostitution at the early ages of 12 and 13 years?

Id. (citing Report of the Trial of Richard D. Croucher, on an Indictment for a Rape of Margaret Miller, on Tuesday, the 8th day of July, 1800, at 15, 18 (New York: 1800)); *see also* Estelle B. Freedman, *"Uncontrolled Desires": The Response to the Sexual Psychopath, 1920–1960, in* PASSION AND POWER, *supra*, at 199, 212 (explaining that victims of sexual predators were described "as 'seductive,' 'flirtatious,' and sexually precocious"). *But see* Kathy Peiss, *"Charity Girls" and City Pleasures: Historical Notes on Working Class Sexuality, 1880–1920, in* PASSION AND POWER, *supra*, at 57, 64 (discussing "charity girls," working women who traded sex for gifts and attention).

74. *LK*, 631 So. 2d at 605.

75. *Id.* at 608.

76. *McNamee*, 519 S.E.2d at 302–03.

77. *Angie M.*, 44 Cal. Rptr. 2d at 200 (noting the partner's age, position of authority, and position of confidence).

78. *Bohrer*, 943 P.2d at, 1227 (citing E. Cruz, *When the Shepherd Preys on the Flock: Clergy Sexual Exploitation and the Search for Solutions*, 19 FLA. ST. U. L. REV. 499 (1991)).

79. Davis v. Monroe County Bd. of Educ., 526 U.S. 629, 646 (1999) (quoting Vernonia Sch. Dist. 47J v. Acton, 515 U.S. 646, 655 (1995), in holding that "the nature of [the State's] power [over public schoolchildren] is custodial and tutelary, permitting a degree of supervision and control that could not be exercised over free adults").

80. *Bostic*, 2003 WL 723262, at *6.

81. *Orangeburg*, 518 S.E.2d at 260 (reviewing S.C. CODE § 16–3-655(3)).

Chapter Six

This chapter draws from Jennifer Ann Drobac, *Consent, Teenagers, and (un)Civil(ized) Consequences, in* CHILDREN, SEXUALITY AND THE LAW (Sacha M. Coupet

& Ellen Marrus eds., NYU Press, 2015); Jennifer Ann Drobac & Leslie A. Hulvershorn, *The Neurobiology of Decision-Making in High Risk Youth & The Law of Consent to Sex*, 17 NEW CRIM. L. REV. 502 (Summer 2014); Jennifer Ann Drobac, *Wake Up and Smell the Starbucks Coffee: How* Doe v. Starbucks *Confirms the End of the "Age of Consent" in California and Perhaps Beyond*, 33 B.C. J.L. & SOC. JUST. 1 (2013); Jennifer Ann Drobac, *A* Bee Line *in the Wrong Direction: Science, Teenagers, and the Sting to "The Age of Consent,"* 20 J.L. & POL'Y 63 (2011); Jennifer Ann Drobac, *I Can't to I Kant: The Sexual Harassment of Working Adolescents, Competing Theories, and Ethical Dilemmas*, 70 ALBANY L. REV. 675 (2007); Jennifer Ann Drobac, *"Developing Capacity": Adolescent "Consent" at Work, at Law and in the Sciences of the Mind*, 10 UC DAVIS J. JUVENILE L. & POL'Y 1 (2006); and Jennifer Ann Drobac, *Sex and the Workplace: "Consenting" Adolescents and a Conflict of Laws*, 79 WASH. L. REV. 471 (2004), and supporting citations in these texts.

1. Martha Chamallas, *Consent, Equality, and the Legal Control of Sexual Conduct*, 61 S. CAL. L. REV. 777, 780 (1988).

2. *Id.* at 781, 784.

3. *See* Lea VanderVelde, *The Legal Ways of Seduction*, 48 STAN. L. REV. 817, 846 & n.140 (1996). Professor Chamallas has explained that the marital rape exemption insulated husbands from rape prosecution or limited penalties, thereby negating the sexual freedom of women. Chamallas, *supra* note 1, at 797–98, 797 n.95 ("Only ten states authorize prosecutions of husbands for the rape of their wives on the same terms as other rape defendants.").

4. *See* Michelle Oberman, *Regulating Consensual Sex with Minors: Defining a Role for Statutory Rape*, 48 BUFF. L. REV. 703, 777 (2000) (advocating for statutory rape laws to set normative parameters, enabling boys and girls to discover their own sexual autonomy).

5. VanderVelde, *supra* note 3, at 846 & n.140.

6. William N. Eskridge, Jr., *The Many Faces of Sexual Consent*, 37 WM. & MARY L. REV. 47, 56 & n.29 (1995) (citing VA. CODE ANN. § 18.2–66 (1995)).

7. Chamallas, *supra* note 1, at 789 & n.56 (citing MODEL PENAL CODE § 213.6(3) cmt. at 419–20 (1980)).

8. Ceci Connolly, *Some Abstinence Programs Mislead Teens, Report Says*, WASH. POST, Dec. 2, 2004, at A01 (noting that the Bush administration planned to give $170 million in 2005 to groups that teach abstinence-only).

9. Chamallas, *supra* note 1, at 790, 793.

10. *Id.* at 793. *See, e.g.*, Carey v. Population Servs. Int'l, 431 U.S. 678, 685 (1977) ("That the constitutionally protected right of privacy extends to an individual's liberty to make choices regarding contraception. . . ."); Roe v. Wade, 410 U.S. 113, 153 (1973) (holding that a woman's right to privacy, either grounded in the Fourteenth or Ninth Amendments, "is broad enough to encompass a woman's decision whether or not to terminate her pregnancy"); Griswold v. Con-

necticut, 381 U.S. 479, 485 (1965) (holding that the right to use contraception "concerns a relationship lying within the zone of privacy created by several fundamental constitutional guarantees").

11. Chamallas, *supra* note 1, at 782.

12. *Id.* at 795 (footnotes omitted).

13. The notion of abnormality includes the view that teen-adult sex may be damaging to the minor. It also includes the view that even if the sex is not physically or psychologically damaging, teen-adult sex is morally wrong, consistent with the traditional view. While adults may not hold the teen responsible for her participatory conduct in the first case, they might in the second. *See* Doe v. Oberweis Dairy, 456 F.3d 704, 714 (7th Cir. 2006).

14. Many states prohibit minors from filing lawsuits unless represented by a parent, next friend, or guardian. *See, e.g.*, Porter v. Triad of Arizona, 52 P.3d 799, 802 (Ariz. Ct. App. 2002) (holding that a minor may not bring an action in his own name but may sue through a representative); Am. Alternative Energy Partners II v. Windridge, Inc., 49 Cal. Rptr. 2d 686, 690–91 (Ct. App. 1996) (finding that the incapacity of minors bars them from representing their own interests in court); Newman v. Newman, 663 A.2d 980, 987 (Conn. 1995) (holding that a child may bring an action only through a next friend or guardian); Klak v. Skellion, 741 N.E.2d 288, 289–90 (Ill. App. Ct. 2000) (stating that a minor has no capacity to maintain an action in his name); Cleaver v. George Staton Co., 908 S.W.2d 468, 469 (Tex. Ct. App. 1995) (finding a lack of capacity because of the disability of minors pertaining to the right to sue in one's own name); Jensen ex rel. Stierman v. McPherson, 655 N.W.2d 487, 491 (Wis. Ct. App. 2002) (relying on section 803.01(3)(c)(2) of the Wisconsin Statues that requires an adult to represent the minor).

15. *See* LK v. Reed, 631 So. 2d 604 (La. Ct. App. 1994)). LK v. Reed involved a thirteen-year-old special education student. *Id.* at 605. The Reed trial court suggested that girls might deliberately initiate sexual liaisons, "provoke" criminal prosecution, and recover damages. *Id.* at 607.

16. Paul Igasaki, *Civil Rights for Young Workers*, IMDiversity.com, Dec. 2004, http://imdiversity.com/channels/internships/civil-rights-for-young-workers (last accessed Nov. 7, 2014).

17. *See, e.g.*, Suzanne M. Sgroi, *Discovery, Reporting, Investigation, and Prosecution of Child Sexual Abuse*, 29 Siecus Rep., Oct./Nov. 2000, at 6.

18. Doe v. Oberweis Dairy, No. 03 C 4774, 2005 WL 782709, *6–7 (N.D. Ill. Apr. 6, 2005), *rev'd*, 456 F.3d 704 (7th Cir. 2006).

19. *Id.* at *7.

20. *Oberweis Dairy*, 456 F.3d at 712–13.

21. *Oberweis Dairy*, 456 F.3d at 715, 717.

22. 518 S.E.2d 259, 261 (S.C. 1999).

23. *Id.* at 259.

24. *Oberweis Dairy*, 456 F.3d at 715.

25. The question arose in *Oberweis* whether Nayman was, in fact, a supervisor. The court concluded in dictum that he was. *Id.* at 717.

26. *Id.* at 713, 715.

27. William Shakespeare, *Romeo and Juliet* act 2, sc. 3.

28. In *Oberweis*, Doe's alleged harasser, Matt Nayman, was tried, convicted, and imprisoned under Illinois criminal law for his sexual conduct with Doe. *Oberweis Dairy*, 456 F.3d at 707.

29. *See, e.g.*, JENNIFER J. FROST ET AL., THE ALAN GUTTMACHER INST., TEENAGE SEXUAL AND REPRODUCTIVE BEHAVIOR IN DEVELOPED COUNTRIES, OCCASIONAL REPORT NO. 8, at 16 (2001), *available at* www.guttmacher.org/pubs/us_teens.pdf (explaining that disapproval motivates concern over teenage pregnancy) (last accessed Nov. 7, 2014).

30. *See* Miller v. Maxwell's Int'l Inc., 991 F.2d 583, 587 (9th Cir. 1993) (finding no individual liability under Title VII).

31. Chamallas, *supra* note 1, at 796–801, 810–11.

32. Kim Bell, *Teens Told to Speak Out Against Harassment*, ST. LOUIS POST-DISPATCH, June 26, 2006, at B1.

33. Cathleen Flahardy, *EEOC Responds to Harassment Complaints from Teens: Finish Line Tailors Policy to Target Younger Workers*, INSIDECOUNSEL, Nov. 2005, *available at* www.insidecounsel.com/2013/06/25/eeoc-responds-to-sexual-harassment-complaints-from (last accessed Nov. 7, 2014).

34. Youth @ Work, US Equal Employment Opportunity Comm'n, *Sixteen-year-old Claims She Was Sexually Harassed at Pennsylvania Mexican Restaurant*, http://youth.eeoc.gov/case2.html (last accessed Nov. 7, 2014).

35. Youth @ Work, US Equal Employment Opportunity Comm'n, *Fourteen-year-old Reports Sexual Harassment and Assault at Kansas Fast Food Restaurant*, http://youth.eeoc.gov/case3.html (last accessed Nov. 7, 2014).

36. Bell, *supra* note 32.

37. Igasaki, *supra* note 16.

38. Dana Knight, *Sexual Harassment and Bias Complaints Surging Among the Young*, INDIANAPOLIS STAR, Aug. 14, 2005, *available at* http://archive.indystar.com/article/20050814/BUSINESS/508140346/Sexual-harassment-bias-complaints-surging-among-young (quoting Michael Blickman, internal quotations omitted) (last accessed Nov. 7, 2014).

39. Bell, *supra* note 32.

40. *See generally* JENNIFER ANN DROBAC, SEXUAL HARASSMENT LAW: HISTORY, CASES, AND THEORY 511–28 (2005) (reviewing the harassment of student interns).

41. Amy Joyce, *Lawsuits Shed New Light on Sexual Harassment of Teens; More Young Workers File Complaints*, WASH. POST, Dec. 2, 2004, at A01 (quoting the experts, internal quotation marks omitted).

42. Complaint at 3–9, [Sara Doe] v. Culver Theaters, Inc., No. CV139513 (Cal. Santa Cruz Cnty. Super. Ct. Oct. 1999).

43. Ctr. on Children and the Law, ABA, A Judicial Primer on Child Sexual Abuse 3 (Josephine Bulkley & Claire Sandt, eds., 1994) [hereinafter A Judicial Primer].

44. Igaski, *supra* note 16.

45. Bolon v. Rolla Pub. Schs., 917 F. Supp. 1423, 1429 n.3 (E.D. Mo. 1996). *Quid pro quo* literally translates to "this for that" and references the demanded trade of benefits (or protection from punishment) in exchange for sexual favors.

46. State v. Holm,137 P.3d 726, 752 (Utah 2006) (citing and quoting State v. Elton, 680 P.2d 727, 732 (Utah 1984)).

47. Chamallas, *supra* note 1, at 814–15.

48. Eskridge, *supra* note 6, at 48.

49. *Id.* at 50 & n.16 (citing Va. Code Ann. § 18.2–361(A) (1995)).

50. Lawrence v. Texas, 539 U.S. 558, 578–79 (2003).

51. *Id.* at 564, 578.

52. Eskridge, *supra* note 6, at 53.

53. *Id.* at 49–55.

54. *Id.* at 52. Eskridge gave no citation for his reference to national surveys concerning the sexual behavior of fourteen- and fifteen-year-olds.

55. *Id.* at 62–64.

56. *Id.* at 65.

57. *See generally* Wandi Bruine de Bruin *et al.*, *Adolescents' Thinking About the Risks of Sexual Behaviors* 421–34, *in* Thinking With Data (Marsha C. Lovett and Priti Shah, eds., 2007).

58. Jennifer Ann Drobac, *Pansexuality and the Law*, Wm. & Mary J. Women & L., 297, 298 (1999).

59. *Id.* at 300–01.

60. The Merriam-Webster Dictionary defines *pan-* as "**1:** all **:** completely." Merriam Webster Dictionary, www.merriam-webster.com/dictionary/pan (last accessed March 3, 2015). It defines *sexual* as "**1:** of, relating to, or associated with sex or the sexes." *Id.*, www.merriam-webster.com/dictionary/sexual (last accessed March 3, 2015). Logically, it defines *pansexual* as "**:** exhibiting or implying many forms of sexual expression." *Id.*, www.merriam-webster.com/dictionary/pansexual (last accessed March 3, 2015).

61. *See, e.g.*, Jennifer A. Drobac, *The Oncale Opinion: A Pansexual Response*, 30 McGeorge L. Rev. 1269, 1272 (1999).

62. Janis Wolak et al., *Online "Predators" and their Victims: Myths, Realities and Implications for Prevention and Treatment*, 63 American Psychologist 111, 122 (Feb.–Mar. 2008), *available at* www.apa.org/pubs/journals/releases/amp-632111.pdf (last accessed Nov. 7, 2014).

63. CATHARINE A. MACKINNON, SEXUAL HARASSMENT OF WORKING WOMEN 1, 174, 177 (1979).

64. *See id.* at 220–21.

65. *Id.* at 204.

66. LARRY S. MILNER, HARDNESS OF HEART/HARDNESS OF LIFE: THE STAIN OF HUMAN INFANTICIDE 29 (2000).

67. James E. Robertson, *Cruel and Unusual Punishment in United States Prisons: Sexual Harassment Among Male Inmates*, 36 AM. CRIM. L. REV. 1, 8–9, 18 (1999).

68. *See id.* at 7, 11, 36, 47.

69. Katherine M. Franke, *What's Wrong with Sexual Harassment?*, 49 STAN. L. REV. 691, 758 (1997) [hereinafter Franke, *Sexual Harassment*].

70. *See* MACKINNON, *supra* note 63, at 151–58.

71. Franke, *Sexual Harassment*, *supra* note 69, at 767–68 & n.400 (quoting Quick v. Donaldson Co., 90 F.3d 1372, 1374–75 (8th Cir. 1996)).

72. *Id.* at 767–68 (quoting Quick v. Donaldson Co., Inc., 895 F. Supp. 1288, 1296 (S.D. Iowa 1995), *rev'd*, 90 F.3d 1372, 1380 (8th Cir. 1996)).

73. Oncale v. Sundowner Offshore Servs., Inc., 523 U.S. 75, 81 (1998).

74. Parker v. General Extrusions, Inc., 491 F.3d 596, 603 (6th Cir. 2007) (emphasis added).

75. Gray v. Genlyte Group, Inc., 289 F.3d 128, 140 (1st Cir. 2002).

76. *See generally* Dorothy Roberts, *The Collective Injury of Sexual Harassment*, *in* DIRECTIONS IN SEXUAL HARASSMENT LAW 365, 370–72 (Catharine MacKinnon & Reva B. Siegel eds., 2004); Kimberle Crenshaw, *Demarginalizing the Intersection of Race and Sex: A Black Feminist Critique of Antidiscrimination Doctrine, Feminist Theory and Antiracist Politics*, 1989 U. CHI. LEGAL F. 139 (1989); Peggie R. Smith, *Separate Identities: Black Women, Work, and Title VII*, 14 HARV. WOMEN'S L.J. 21 (1991); Judith A. Winston, *Mirror, Mirror on the Wall: Title VII, Section 1981, and the Intersection of Race and Gender in the Civil Rights Act of 1990*, 79 CAL. L. REV. 775, 796–801 (1991).

77. Kathryn Abrams, *The New Jurisprudence of Sexual Harassment*, 83 CORNELL L. REV. 1169 (1998); Vicki Schultz, *Reconceptualizing Sexual Harassment*, 107 YALE L.J. 1683 (1998).

78. Abrams, *supra* note 77, at 1195–98, 1220, 1205–17, 1219; *see also* Nadine Taub, *Keeping Women in Their Place: Stereotyping Per Se as a Form of Employment Discrimination*, 21 B.C. L. REV. 345 (1980).

79. Schultz, *supra* note 77, at 1687, 1689.

80. Robert Bozick, *Precocious Behaviors in Early Adolescence: Employment and the Transition to First Sexual Intercourse*, 26 J. EARLY ADOLESCENCE 60 (2006). Bozick explained:

> The opportunity-cost hypothesis . . . predicts that young adults who have strong ties to the labor force will perceive there to be

> viable and achievable economic opportunities and consequently refrain from risky behaviors that could potentially jeopardize their chances of attainment. Sexual behavior in this sense is considered risky as it could lead to unwanted pregnancy or sexually transmitted diseases. (*Id.* at 63).

81. *Id.* at 65.

82. *Id.* at 80. According to Bozick, several studies "suggest that opportunities in the labor force suppress risky sexual behavior among older adolescents and young adults." *Id.* at 64. These studies examined the use of birth control and the incidents of pregnancy, however, and did not appear to focus on sexual development generally.

83. *See generally* Katherine Hunt Federle, *On the Road to Reconceiving Rights for Children: A Postfeminist Analysis of the Capacity Principle*, 42 DEPAUL L. REV. 983, 983 (1993) (questioning whether children have the capacity to consent).

84. *See* Bozick, *supra* note 80, at 69–73 (not considering adolescent partners or mutuality as variables).

85. Susan Fineran & James E. Gruber, *Youth at work: Adolescent employment and sexual harassment*, 33 CHILD ABUSE & NEGLECT 550, 554 (2009).

86. MACKINNON, *supra* note 63, at 44.

87. Linda Kelly Hill, *The Feminist Misspeak of Sexual Harassment*, 57 FLA. L. REV. 133, 135, 186 (2005) (footnotes omitted).

88. Elizabeth Anderson, *Recent Thinking About Sexual Harassment: A Review Essay*, 34 PHIL. & PUB. AFF. 284, 289–92 (2006).

89. *Id.* at 290–91. *See generally* Susanne Baer, *Dignity or Equality? Responses to Workplace Harassment in European, German, and U.S. Law*, *in* DIRECTIONS IN SEXUAL HARASSMENT LAW, *supra* note 76, at 582 (differentiating the European Union and German legal reaction to sexual harassment based on dignity from the United States's legal reaction to sexual harassment based on equality); Orit Kamir, *Dignity, Respect, and Equality in Israel's Sexual Harassment Law*, in DIRECTIONS IN SEXUAL HARASSMENT LAW, *supra* note 76, at 561–62 (presenting the Israeli approach to sexual harassment laws); Rosa Ehrenreich, *Dignity and Discrimination: Toward a Pluralistic Understanding of Workplace Harassment*, 88 GEO. L.J. 1, 4 (1999) ("This article argues for a comprehensive re-examination of how workplace harassment is conceptualized.").

90. *See* Onora O'Neill, *Between Consenting Adults*, 14 PHIL. & PUB. AFF. 252 (1985) [hereinafter O'Neill, *Between Consenting Adults*]; R. George Wright, *Consenting Adults: The Problem of Enhancing Human Dignity Non-Coercively*, 75 B.U. L. REV. 1397, 1398, 1426–30 (1995) [hereinafter Wright, *Consenting Adults*].

91. R. George Wright, *Treating Persons as Ends in Themselves: The Legal*

Implications of a Kantian Principle, 36 U. RICH. L. REV. 271, 271 (2002) [hereinafter Wright, *Treating Persons*] (quoting IMMANUEL KANT, GROUNDWORK OF THE METAPHYSICS OF MORALS 38 (Mary Gregor ed. & trans., Cambridge Univ. Press 1998) (1785)); *see also* ALLEN W. WOOD, KANT'S ETHICAL THOUGHT 119–20 (1999) (discussing Kant's means to an end).

92. *See* Onora O'Neill, *The Moral Perplexities of Famine and World Hunger*, *in* MATTERS OF LIFE AND DEATH: NEW INTRODUCTORY ESSAYS IN MORAL PHILOSOPHY 294, 319–24 (Tom Regan ed., 2d ed. 1986) (considering Kant's moral theory in the context of dealing with famine).

93. O'Neill, *Between Consenting Adults*, *supra* note 90, at 252.

94. Wright, *Consenting Adults*, *supra* note 90, at 1398.

95. O'Neill, *Between Consenting Adults*, *supra* note 90, at 253, 258–60; Wright, *Consenting Adults*, *supra* note 90, at 1414.

96. O'Neill, *Between Consenting Adults*, *supra* note 90, at 254–59.

97. *Id.* at 253–54.

98. Wright, *Consenting Adults*, *supra* note 90, at 1435.

99. *See, e.g.*, Tamar Lewin, *After Harvard Controversy, Conditions Change but Reputation Lingers*, N.Y. TIMES, Mar. 5, 2010, *available at* www.nytimes.com/2010/03/06/education/06iht-ffharvard.html?scp=3&sq=harvard&st=cse (last accessed March 7, 2015).

100. Carla Baranauckas, *Montana judge's comments show ignorance about rape*, THE WASH. POST, Aug. 30, 2013, *available at* www.washingtonpost.com/blogs/she-the-people/wp/2013/08/30/montana-judges-comments-show-ignorance-about-rape (last accessed Nov. 7, 2014).

101. Wright, *Consenting Adults*, *supra* note 90, at 1413.

102. O'Neill, *Between Consenting Adults*, *supra* note 90, at 253.

103. *Id.* at 269.

104. *Id.* at 270 (footnotes omitted).

105. Robin L. West, *The Difference in Women's Hedonic Lives: A Phenomenological Critique of Feminist Legal Theory*, 3 WIS. WOMEN'S L.J. 81, 92 (1987).

106. Katherine Hunt Federle, *On the Road to Reconceiving Rights for Children: A Postfeminist Analysis of the Capacity Principle*, 42 DePaul L. Rev. 983, 987–95 (1993) (questioning whether children have the capacity to consent).

107. *Id.* at 985–86.

108. *Id.* at 1025.

109. MACKINNON, *supra* note 63, at 1.

Chapter Seven

This chapter draws from Jennifer Ann Drobac, *Consent, Teenagers, and (un)Civil(ized) Consequences*, *in* CHILDREN, SEXUALITY AND THE LAW (Sacha M. Coupet

& Ellen Marrus eds., NYU Press, 2015); Jennifer Ann Drobac & Leslie A. Hulvershorn, *The Neurobiology of Decision-Making in High Risk Youth & The Law of Consent to Sex*, 17 NEW CRIM. L. REV. 502 (Summer 2014); Jennifer Ann Drobac, *Wake Up and Smell the Starbucks Coffee: How* Doe v. Starbucks *Confirms the End of the "Age of Consent" in California and Perhaps Beyond*, 33 B.C. J.L. & SOC. JUST. 1 (2013); Jennifer Ann Drobac, *A* Bee Line *in the Wrong Direction: Science, Teenagers, and the Sting to "The Age of Consent,"* 20 J.L. & POL'Y 63 (2011); Jennifer Ann Drobac, *I Can't to I Kant: The Sexual Harassment of Working Adolescents, Competing Theories, and Ethical Dilemmas*, 70 ALBANY L. REV. 675 (2007); Jennifer Ann Drobac, *"Developing Capacity": Adolescent "Consent" at Work, at Law and in the Sciences of the Mind*, 10 UC DAVIS J. JUVENILE L. & POL'Y 1 (2006); and Jennifer Ann Drobac, *Sex and the Workplace: "Consenting" Adolescents and a Conflict of Laws*, 79 WASH. L. REV. 471 (2004), and supporting citations in these texts.

1. Civil Rights Act of 1964, Pub. L. No. 88–352, Title VII, 78 Stat. 241 (codified as amended at 42 U.S.C. §§ 2000e to e-17). One finds examples of the influence of tort law on Title VII in several US Supreme Court cases. In 1998, the Supreme Court noted, "Title VII borrows from tort law the avoidable consequences doctrine and the considerations which animate that doctrine would also support the limitation of employer liability in certain circumstances." Burlington Indus., Inc. v. Ellerth, 524 U.S. 742, 764 (1998) (citation omitted). More recently the Court explained, "In defining the proper causation standard for Title VII retaliation claims, it is presumed that Congress incorporated tort law's causation in fact standard. . . ." Univ. of Texas Sw. Med. Ctr. v. Nassar, 133 S. Ct. 2517, 2520 (2013).

2. CATHARINE A. MACKINNON, SEXUAL HARASSMENT OF WORKING WOMEN 1, 165 or 169 or 171–73 (1979).

3. Title IX of the Education Amendments of 1972 (discrimination based on sex or blindness), 20 U.S.C.A. §§ 1681–1688 (West Supp. 2006).

4. 42 U.S.C. § 2000e-2(a)(1) (2000); *See* Faragher v. City of Boca Raton, 524 U.S. 775, 786 (1998).

5. Meritor Sav. Bank v. Vinson, 477 U.S. 57, 67 (1986).

6. MACKINNON, *supra* note 2.

7. *Faragher*, 524 U.S. at 787–88 (quoting Harris v. Forklift Sys., Inc., 510 U.S. 17, 23 (1993)).

8. Under Title VII, both male and female workers enjoy protection from sexual harassment by members of either sex, as long as the harassment is "because of . . . sex." 42 U.S.C. § 2000e-2(a)(1); Oncale v. Sundowner Offshore Servs., Inc., 523 U.S. 75, 78 (1998).

9. *See* Henson v. City of Dundee, 682 F.2d 897, 903–05 (11th Cir. 1982).

10. Miller v. Maxwell's Int'l, Inc., 991 F.2d 583, 588 (9th Cir. 1993).

11. *See, e.g.*, CAL. GOV'T CODE § 12940 (1992); Matthews v. Superior Court,

40 Cal. Rptr. 2d 350, 351 (1995); Page v. Superior Court, 37 Cal. Rptr. 2d 529, 532 (1995).

12. JENNIFER ANN DROBAC, SEXUAL HARASSMENT LAW: HISTORY, CASES, AND THEORY 68–71 (2005) (quoting 29 C.F.R. § 1604.11).

13. *Faragher*,524 U.S. at 787 (citing Harris v. Forklift Sys., Inc., 510 U.S. 17, 21–22 (1993)).

14. *See* EEOC, *Policy Guidance on Current Issues of Sexual Harassment* 8, ENFORCEMENT GUIDANCE N-915–050, Mar. 19, 1990, *available at* www.eeoc.gov/eeoc/publications/upload/currentissues.pdf (last accessed Nov. 8, 2014).

15. *See, e.g.*, CAL. GOV'T CODE § 12940.

16. Meritor Sav. Bank v. Vinson, 477 U.S. 57, 68 (1986).

17. *Cf.* T.L. v. Toys R Us, Inc., 605 A.2d 1125, 1135 (N.J. Super. Ct. App. Div. 1992) (finding that unwelcomeness is an implicit requirement for sexual harassment and that consent will not negate this element as a matter of law and holding that "[t]he issue is one of fact, dependent on the surrounding circumstances").

18. *See* DEBORAH RHODE, SPEAKING OF SEX 102–04 (1997).

19. *Ellerth*, 524 U.S. at 765 (citations omitted); *see also Faragher*, 524 U.S. at 807–08.

20. *Faragher*, 524 U.S. at 805–06; *Ellerth*, 524 U.S. at 764.

21. Ashton *ex rel.* Ashton v. Okosun, 266 F. Supp. 2d 399 (D. Md. 2003).

22. *See* Lea VanderVelde, *The Legal Ways of Seduction*, 48 STAN. L. REV. 817, 847 (1996).

23. *See id.* at 846–48.

24. *Cf.* In re Neal, 179 B.R. 234, 237 (Bankr. D. Idaho 1995) (holding that consent to sexual relations will not negate, as a matter of law, a prior ineffective consent to sexual relations).

25. Letters from Sara Doe to Michael Cosio (July 18, 1999–Aug. 25, 1999), Report No. 99–7955 (No. S9–09852) (on file with author and Santa Cruz County Sheriff's Department).

26. *See, e.g.*, Complaint at 9, [Sara Doe] v. Culver Theaters, Inc., No. CV139513 (Cal. Santa Cruz Cnty. Super. Ct. Oct. 1999).

27. *See* 110 CONG. REC. 2577–84, 2718–21, 2728, 2804–05, 13825, 13837–38, 14511, 15896–97 (1964).

28. MACKINNON, *supra* note 2, at 7.

29. *Id.* at 174.

30. *See* Kathryn Abrams, *The New Jurisprudence of Sexual Harassment*, 83 CORNELL L. REV. 1169, 1171–72 (1998); Anita Bernstein, *Treating Sexual Harassment with Respect*, 111 HARV. L. REV. 445, 450–51 (1997); Martha Chamallas, Essay, *Writing About Sexual Harassment: A Guide to the Literature*, 4 UCLA WOMEN'S L.J. 37, 37–39 (1993) (reviewing the early scholarship); Katherine M. Franke, *Gender, Sex, Agency and Discrimination: A Reply to Professor Abrams*, 83 CORNELL L. REV. 1245, 1245, 1248–49 (1998); Katherine M. Franke, *What's*

Wrong with Sexual Harassment?, 49 STAN. L. REV. 691, 691 (1997) [hereinafter Franke, *Sexual Harassment*]; Vicki Schultz, *Reconceptualizing Sexual Harassment*, 107 YALE L.J. 1683 (1998).

31. RHODE, *supra* note 18, at 101.

32. This adjusted sum, based on the consumer price index, is available by calculation from *Measuring Worth*, www.measuringworth.com/uscompare/result.php?year_source=1997&amount=8000000&year_result=2015 (last accessed Nov. 8, 2014).

33. *Ellerth*, 524 U.S. at 764.

34. *Faragher*, 524 U.S. at 805–06 (quoting Albemarle Paper Co. v. Moody, 422 U.S. 405, 418 (1975)) (citations omitted); *but see* Gebser v. Lago Vista Ind. Sch. Dist., 524 U.S. 274, 287 (1998) (finding, "Title VII, moreover, seeks to 'make persons whole for injuries suffered through past discrimination'" and quoting Landgraf v. USI Film Products, 511 U.S. 244, 254 (1994)).

35. Similarly, the admission of consent evidence in an evaluation of fault and damages interferes with Title VII's deterrent effect by redistributing responsibility for the conduct.

36. Patricia J. Sulak *et al.*, *Analysis of knowledge and attitudes of adult groups before and after attending an educational presentation regarding adolescent sexual activity*, 193 AMER. J. OBSTETRICS & GYNECOLOGY 1945, 1951–52 (2005), *available at* http://download.journals.elsevierhealth.com/pdfs/journals/0002–9378/PIIS0002937805007404.pdf (last accessed Nov. 8, 2014).

37. *See* App. 2 (summarizing the laws for Alaska, Arizona, Arkansas, California, Colorado, Connecticut, Delaware, Florida, Idaho, Illinois, Indiana, Iowa, Kentucky, Louisiana, Maine, Michigan, Minnesota, New Hampshire, New Jersey, New Mexico (19), North Dakota, Ohio, Oregon, Pennsylvania, Rhode Island, Tennessee, Utah, Vermont, Virginia, Washington (21), Wisconsin, and Wyoming setting the age of consent at eighteen or older in special circumstances).

38. Oncale v. Sundowner Offshore Servs., Inc., 523 U.S. 75, 78 (1998).

39. Doe v. Mama Taori's Premium Pizza, No. M1998–00992-COA-R9-CV, 2001 WL 327906 (Tenn. Ct. App. Apr. 5, 2001).

40. *Id.* at *2.

41. *Id.* at *1-*2.

42. *Id.*

43. *Id.* at *4.

44. *Id.* (citing Cardwell v. Bechtol, 724 S.W.2d 739, 746 (Tenn. 1987)).

45. *Id.* at *8.

46. *Id.* at *5 (quoting Cardwell, 724 S.W.2d at 744–45).

47. *Id.* at *5 (citing Cardwell, 724 S.W.2d at 748) (internal quotations omitted).

48. *Id.*, at *5, *8.

49. *Id.* at *5.

50. *See* Tenn. Code Ann. § 37–10–303 (2001).

51. Elizabeth S. Scott, *The Legal Construction of Adolescence*, 29 Hofstra L. Rev. 547, 568 (2000).

52. *Id.* at 568 & n.80.

53. *Mama Taori's*, 2001 WL 327906, at *6.

54. Allstate Ins. Co. v. Patterson, 904 F. Supp. 1270, 1282 (D. Utah 1995) (quoting Allstate Ins. Co. v. Jack S., 709 F. Supp. 963, 966 (D. Nev. 1989), internal quotation marks omitted).

55. *Mama Taori's*, 2001 WL 327906, at *6.

56. *Id.* (citing Tenn. Code Ann. § 36–1-110(a) (1996)).

57. *Id.*

58. The court postponed this more detailed analysis for subsequent proceedings. *Id.* at *11.

59. *Id.* at *7.

60. *Id.* (citing Beul v. ASSE Int'l, Inc., 233 F.3d 441, 450–51 (7th Cir. 2000); McNamee v. A.J.W., 519 S.E.2d 298, 302 (Ga. Ct. App. 1999); Cynthia M. v. Rodney E., 279 Cal. Rptr. 94, 97 (Cal. Ct. App. 1991)); LK v. Reed, 631 So. 2d 604, 607 (La. Ct. App. 1994); Doe by Roe v. Orangeburg County Sch., 518 S.E.2d 259, 261 (S.C. 1999)).

61. *Faragher*, 524 U.S. at 805–06 (1998).

62. *Mama Taori's*, 2001 WL 327906, at *1.

63. Hernandez v. State, 861 S.W.2d 908, 910 n.1 (Tex. 1993).

64. *See generally* Andrew Walkover, *The Infancy Defense in the New Juvenile Court*, 31 UCLA L. Rev. 503, 510–11 (1984); Franklin E. Zimring, *Penal Proportionality for the Young Offender: Notes on Immaturity, Capacity, and Diminished Responsibility*, *in* Youth On Trial 267, 272 (Thomas Grisso & Robert G. Schwartz eds., 2000).

65. Elizabeth Cauffman et al., *Justice For Juveniles: New Perspectives on Adolescents' Competence and Culpability*, 18 Quinnipiac L. Rev. 403, 405 (1999); Elizabeth S. Scott & Laurence Steinberg, *Blaming Youth*, 81 Tex. L. Rev. 799, 801, 829–34 (2003); *see also* Scott, *supra* note 51, at 589–96; Laurence Steinberg & Elizabeth Cauffman, *The Elephant in the Courtroom: A Developmental Perspective on the Adjudication of Youthful Offenders*, 6 Va. J. Soc. Pol'y & L. 389, 399, 405–06 (1999).

66. *Mama Taori's*, 2001 WL 327906, at *7.

67. *Id.* Mama Taori's had responded with a comparative fault defense, directed at the parents as non-parties. The court affirmed the lower court's decision not to strike that defense as to the parents. *Id.* at *8–9.

68. Michael D. De Bellis et al., *Neurodevelopmental Biology Associated with Child Abuse*, 20 J. Child Sexual Abuse 548, 565 (2011), *available at* www.ncbi.nlm.nih.gov/pmc/articles/PMC3769180 (last accessed Nov. 8, 2014).

69. Elizabeth Scott and Laurence Steinberg argued for formal recognition of

developmental characteristics to avoid racist and other discriminatory results in criminal adjudications. Scott & Steinberg, *supra* note 65, at 837. They reasoned,

> A developmentally-informed boundary constraining decisionmakers represents a collective pre-commitment to recognizing the mitigating character of youth in assigning blame. Otherwise, immaturity often may be ignored when the exigencies of a particular case engender a punitive response. . . . This concern is critical, given the evidence that illegitimate racial and ethnic biases influence attitudes about the punishment of young offenders and that decisionmakers appear to discount the mitigating impact of immaturity in minority youths.

Id. One can see the parallel concern for how sexist attitudes might cause the discounting of immaturity in a sexual harassment case. Decision makers might blame the victim without understanding the nature of the target's developing capacity.

70. Susan Estrich, *Sex at Work*, 43 STAN. L. REV. 813, 831 (1991).

71. *Id.* at 833.

72. Scott and Steinberg noted how prejudices threaten any maturity evaluation. They emphasized,

> [W]e currently lack the diagnostic tools to evaluate psychosocial maturity reliably on an individualized basis or to distinguish young career criminals from ordinary adolescents who, as adults, will repudiate their reckless experimentation. Litigating maturity on a case-by-case basis is likely to be an error-prone undertaking, with the outcomes determined by factors other than immaturity.

Scott & Steinberg, *supra* note 65, at 836–37.

73. *Mama Taori's*, 2001 WL 327906, at *11.

Chapter Eight

This chapter draws from Jennifer Ann Drobac, *Consent, Teenagers, and (un)Civil(ized) Consequences*, *in* CHILDREN, SEXUALITY AND THE LAW (Sacha M. Coupet & Ellen Marrus eds., NYU Press, 2015); Jennifer Ann Drobac & Leslie A. Hulvershorn, *The Neurobiology of Decision-Making in High Risk Youth & The Law of Consent to Sex*, 17 NEW CRIM. L. REV. 502 (Summer 2014); Jennifer Ann Drobac, *Wake Up and Smell the Starbucks Coffee: How* Doe v. Starbucks *Confirms the End of the "Age of Consent" in California and Perhaps Beyond*, 33 B.C. J.L. & SOC. JUST. 1 (2013); Jennifer Ann Drobac, *A* Bee Line *in the Wrong Direction: Science, Teenagers, and the Sting to "The Age of Consent,"* 20 J.L. & POL'Y 63

(2011); Jennifer Ann Drobac, *I Can't to I Kant: The Sexual Harassment of Working Adolescents, Competing Theories, and Ethical Dilemmas*, 70 ALBANY L. REV. 675 (2007); Jennifer Ann Drobac, *"Developing Capacity": Adolescent "Consent" at Work, at Law and in the Sciences of the Mind*, 10 UC DAVIS J. JUVENILE L. & POL'Y 1 (2006); and Jennifer Ann Drobac, *Sex and the Workplace: "Consenting" Adolescents and a Conflict of Laws*, 79 WASH. L. REV. 471 (2004), and supporting citations in these texts.

1. No. SACV 08–0582 AG (CWx), 2009 WL 5183773, at *6–8 (C.D. Cal. Dec. 18, 2009).

2. *See id.* at *7–8; People v. Tobias, 21 P.3d 758, 761 (Cal. 2001).

3. *See, e.g.*, CAL. PENAL CODE § 261.5 (West Supp. 2012).

4. *See* App. 2 (noting clear inconsistencies in California, Georgia, Illinois, Louisiana, Maryland, Mississippi, New Hampshire, New York, North Dakota, South Carolina, Tennessee, Virginia, and Wisconsin).

5. 21 P.3d 758, 759 (Cal. 2001).

6. *Id.* at 761–62; *see* People v. Stratton, 75 P. 166, 168 (Cal. 1904) (holding that a woman too young to consent to sexual intercourse is not an accomplice to incest), *superseded by statute*, CAL. PENAL CODE § 261.5, *as stated in Tobias*, 21 P.3d at 758; People v. Stoll, 257 P. 583, 584 (Cal. Ct. App. 1927) (same), *superseded by statute*, CAL. PENAL CODE § 261.5, *as stated in* Donaldson v. Dep't of Real Estate, 36 Cal. Rptr. 3d 577 (Cal. Ct. App. 2005).

7. *Tobias*, 21 P.3d at 761 (citing *Stratton*, 75 P. at 166).

8. CAL. PENAL CODE § 261.5(a) (West Supp. 2012).

9. *Id.* § 261.5(b)-(e).

10. Act of May 19, 1913, ch. 122, sec. 1, § 261, 1913 Cal. Stat. 212, 212 (amending section 261 of the Penal Code relating to the crime of rape).

11. *Tobias*, 21 P.3d 761–62 (comparing CAL. PENAL CODE § 261.5(b)-(d) [offense classification and punishment for unlawful sexual intercourse with a minor], with CAL. PENAL CODE § 264(a) (West 2008) [punishment for rape]). Note, the *Tobias* case dealt with violations of Cal. Penal Code § 285 (incest), not with § 261.5, thus much of this discussion was dictum. *See id.* at 759, 761–62.

12. *Id.* at 762 (emphasis added).

13. *See Tobias*, 21 P.3d at 762 ("[A] minor may be capable of giving *legal* consent to sexual relations.") (emphasis added).

14. *See Starbucks*, 2009 WL 5183773, at *7 (quoting *Tobias*, 21 P.3d at 761–62); *see also, e.g.*, People v. Verdegreen 39 P. 607, 608 (Cal. 1895), *superseded by statute*, CAL. PENAL CODE § 261.5 (West Supp. 2012), *as stated in Tobias*, 21 P.3d at 758 ("It is the declared policy of our law . . . that any female under the age there fixed shall be incapable of consenting to the act of sexual intercourse. . . ."). Note, it was not until 1993 that the California Legislature modified section 261.5 to make it gender neutral. *See* Act of Sept. 29, 1993, ch. 596, sec. 1, § 261.5, 1993 Cal. Stat. 3139 (amending section 261.5 of the Penal Code, relating to crime).

15. *See* People v. Hillhouse, 1 Cal. Rptr. 3d 261, 263, 268 (Ct. App. 2003) (quoting People v. Griffin, 49 P. 711, 712 (Cal. 1897)) (internal quotations omitted).

16. Restatement (Second) of Torts § 892A(2)(a) & cmt. b (1979) (emphasis added).

17. 477 U.S. 57, 68 (1986).

18. *Hillhouse*, 1 Cal. Rptr. 3d at 268–69 (quoting Am. Acad. of Pediatrics v. Lungren, 940 P.2d 797, 855 (Cal. 1997) (Mosk, J., dissenting)).

19. *Id.* at 269 (quoting *Lungren*, 940 P.2d at 855 (Mosk, J., dissenting)) (citations omitted and first set of internal quotation marks omitted).

20. Jones v. United States, 990 A.2d 970, 975–76, 978 n.17 (D.C. 2010).

21. *Id.* at 972–73, 975–76, 976 n.8, 979.

22. *Id.* at 975–76.

23. *Id.*

24. *Id.*

25. Complaint at 2–9, Sara Doe [alias] v. Culver Theaters, Inc., No. 139513 (Cal. Super. Ct. Oct. 27, 2000) [hereinafter Sara Doe Complaint 2000].

26. *Id.* at 6–7.

27. *Jones*, 990 A.2d at 975–76.

28. *Id.* at 976 (internal quotation marks omitted).

29. *Id.* at 975–76.

30. AACAP, *Policy Statement: Sexual Harassment* (Oct. 1992), *at* www.aacap.org/cs/root/policy_statements/sexual_harassment (last accessed Nov. 4, 2014).

31. 15 F.3d 443, 449 (5th Cir. 1994).

32. No. EV98-0196 C-Y/H, 2000 WL 33309376, at *2–3 (S.D. Ind. May 30, 2000).

33. 926 F. Supp. 979, 988 (D. Nev. 1996).

34. Joseph Rhee et al., *Sandusky Victim 1 Steps Out of Shadows, Says Justice Took Too Long*, ABC News, Oct. 19, 2012, http://abcnews.go.com/US/sandusky-victim-reveals-identity-justice-long/story?id=17511612#.UcHCchZCok8 (last accessed Nov. 8, 2014).

35. Kenneth V. Lanning, National Center for Missing & Exploited Children, Child Molesters: A Behavioral Analysis 4 (5th ed. 2010) (emphasis in original).

36. Sara Doe Complaint 2000, *supra* note 25, at 6.

37. *Id.* at 6–8.

38. *Id.* at 10; *see* Minute Order Entering Guilty Plea, People v. Cosio, No. S9-09852 (Cal. Super. Ct. Nov. 29, 1999) (order entering defendant-manager's guilty plea to count one for unlawful sexual intercourse with Sara).

39. Sara Doe Complaint 2000, *supra* note 25, at 8–9.

40. *Id.* at 8.

41. *See id.* at 8–10; B. Cole, Jail Incident Report #99-R-174, at 1–2 (Aug. 16, 1999) (on file with Santa Cruz County Sheriff's Department) (documenting defendant-manager's use of contraband cell phone to telephone Sara); R. Mitch-

ell, Santa Cruz Sheriff's Office, Incident Report #99–7955, at 4 (Aug. 9, 1999) (on file with Santa Cruz County Sheriff's Department) (documenting conversation between Sara's mother and deputy at sheriff's office regarding phone calls between defendant-manager and Sara).

42. *Tobias*, 21 P.3d at 762–63.

43. *Id.*; *see* CAL. PENAL CODE § 261.5 (West Supp. 2012).

44. *See* Tamar Lewin, *Rethinking Sex Offender Laws for Youths Showing Off Online*, N.Y. TIMES, Mar. 21, 2010, at A1.

45. Renguette v. Board of School Trustees ex rel. Brownsburg, 2007 WL 1536841, at *1–2, *5 (S.D. Ind. May 23, 2007).

46. *Id.* at *6.

47. 73 Cal. Rptr. 2d 331, 339 (Ct. App. 1998); *see* CAL. PENAL CODE § 261.5(b).

48. *T.A.J.*, 73 Cal. Rptr. 2d at 341.

49. *See generally* Meredith Cohen, Note, *No Child Left Behind Bars: The Need to Combat Cruel and Unusual Punishment of State Statutory Rape Laws*, 16 J.L. & POL'Y 717, 724–25 (2007) (arguing for the decriminalization of consensual teenage sex).

50. *See* Brenda Goodman, *Man Convicted as Teenager in Sex Case Is Ordered Freed by Georgia Court*, N.Y. TIMES Oct. 27, 2007, at A9. The Supreme Court of Georgia held,

> [The Superior Court of Monroe County] properly ruled that Wilson's sentence of ten years in prison for having consensual oral sex with a fifteen-year-old girl when he was only seventeen years old constitutes cruel and unusual punishment, but erred in convicting and sentencing Wilson for a misdemeanor crime that did not exist when the conduct in question occurred. (Humphrey v. Wilson, 652 S.E.2d 501, 502 [Ga. 2007]).

The case was remanded to the habeas court to reverse Wilson's conviction and discharge him from custody. *Id.*

51. *Tobias*, 21 P.3d at 766–67 (George, C.J., concurring). Chief Justice George quoted the 1970 version of section 261, stating that "sexual intercourse with a female constituted rape if, among other things, she was 'incapable, through lunacy or other unsoundness of mind, . . . of giving legal consent,' or her resistance was overcome by force or violence." *Id.* at 766. The current version of the statute confirms George's reading. Section 261(a)(1) refers to those "incapable, because of a mental disorder or developmental or physical disability, of giving legal consent." CAL. PENAL CODE § 261(a)(1) (West 2008). Section 261(a)(2) refers to force and violence. *Id.* § 261(a)(2). Section 261(a)(3) mentions intoxication and anesthetic substances. *Id.* § 261 (a) (3). Other subsections raise loss of consciousness, fraud, and duress. *Id.* § 261(a)(4)–(7). None of these subsections apply to developmental immaturity. *See id.* § 261 (a)(1)–(7).

52. *Tobias*, 21 P.3d at 767 (George, C.J., concurring) (emphasis added).

53. *Tobias*, 21 P.3d at 767 (George, C.J., concurring) (emphasis added). In discussing *People v. Young*, 235 Cal. Rptr. 361 (Ct. App. 1987), George argued,

> The [Young] Court of Appeal thus properly recognized that a defendant might violate section 261.5 without also violating section 261, and that, although a minor cannot give legal consent to sexual intercourse, he or she voluntarily and willingly can participate in the act, and thus actually consent within the meaning of section 261.6.

Id. at 768 (footnotes omitted).

54. 450 U.S. 464, 466, 469–70 (1981).

55. *Michael M.*, 450 U.S. at 469–76, 479.

56. *See* Act of May 19, 1913, ch. 122, § 261, 1913 Cal. Stat. 212, 212 (amending section 261 of the Cal. Penal Code relating to the crime of rape).

57. IMAGINE NATION: THE AMERICAN COUNTERCULTURE OF THE 1960S AND '70S 7, 189 (Peter Braunstein & Michael William Doyle eds., 2002).

58. *Michael M.*, 450 U.S. at 494–96 (Brennan, J., dissenting).

59. *Id.* at 495 n.9.

60. *Id.* at 495 n.10 (quoting People v. Hernandez, 393 P.2d 673, 674 (Cal. 1964) (internal quotations omitted).

61. *Hernandez*, 393 P.2d at 674.

62. Michael M. v. Superior Court, 601 P.2d 572, 575–76 (Cal. 1979), *aff'd*, 450 U.S. 464 (1981) (emphasis added).

63. *Tobias*, 21 P.3d at 761–62.

64. *Tobias*, 21 P.3d at 767–68 (George, C.J., concurring).

65. *Michael M.*, 601 P.2d at 576 (emphasis added). For example, the court noted other statutes regulating conduct regardless of consent, including section 308 (furnishing or selling tobacco to a minor), section 310 (minors under sixteen years of age cannot attend a prizefight), and section 326.5 (minors are prohibited from participating in bingo games). *Id.*

66. 36 Cal. Rptr. 3d 577, 585–88 (Ct. App. 2005).

67. *Donaldson*, 36 Cal. Rptr. 3d at 579.

68. *Id.* at 579 n.1 (first alteration in original).

69. *Id.* at 579–80.

70. *Compare* Jones v. United States, 990 A.2d 970, 976 n.8 (D.C. 2010) (describing situational offenders as opportunistically taking advantage of children), *with Donaldson*, 36 Cal. Rptr. 3d at 579–80 (describing the sexual misconduct as "an isolated situational incident").

71. *Donaldson*, 36 Cal. Rptr. 3d at 579, 583 n.6.

72. *Jones*, 990 A.2d at 976.

73. *Donaldson*, 36 Cal. Rptr. 3d at 580 & n.2.

74. *Id.* at 582 (quoting CAL. CODE REGS. tit. 10, § 2910(a)(5) (2002)).

75. *Id.* at 580–81 & n.3.

76. *Id.* at 578–79, 586–88.

77. *Id.* at 583–92 & n.12.

78. *Id.* at 588–89 (citations omitted) (citing CAL. CIV. CODE § 49, subd. (b) (West 2007)) (internal quotations omitted). The *Donaldson* court also considered Cal. Fam. Code section 302 which "declares that upon the filing of parental consents and an order of court, a minor 'is capable of *consenting* to *and consummating* marriage.'" *Id.* at 588 n.17. The court suggested that this section was perhaps incompatible with the notion of incapacity to consent to sexual relations. *Id.* Other readers might think that this section is completely compatible with the notion of juvenile incapacity because the code requires two parental consents *and* a court order before the juvenile can marry and consummate the relationship. *See* CAL. FAM. CODE § 302 (West Supp. 2012).

79. *Id.* at 589.

80. *See* CAL. PENAL CODE § 261 (West 2008); Act of Sept. 29, 1993, ch. 596, § 261.5, 1993 Cal. Stat. 3139 (amending section 261.5 of the Penal Code, relating to crime).

81. *Donaldson*, 36 Cal. Rptr. 3d at 587–88.

82. *See id.*

83. *See* 16 C.F.R. § 429.1 (2012) (requiring door-to-door salespeople to notify buyer of the right to cancel the order).

84. *Donaldson*, 36 Cal. Rptr. 3d at 586, 588.

85. *See id.* at 587–88 (supporting notion that minors may be able to give legal consent by quoting *Tobias*, not by providing evidence of this capacity).

86. *Id.* at 588.

87. *See id.*, 36 Cal. Rptr. 3d at 584 n.10. In footnote 10, the court stated,

> We readily agree that licensee's conduct is "troubling." So did the Legislature when it criminalized such conduct. The question, of course, is not how troubling a licensee's conduct may be, but whether it has any bearing on his or her qualifications as a real estate professional under prescribed criteria. Similarly, we have no quarrel with the Department's repeated observation that the victim belonged to a "protected class." She was, in fact, protected by the criminal law, which intervened here to sanction licensee with a felony conviction. The Commissioner's function is to protect the public from unqualified practitioners of the real estate profession, not to amplify the sanctions of criminal law by further punishing its transgressors. (*Id.* [emphasis added]).

88. *See id.*; *c.f.* Lahny R. Silva, *Clean Slate: Expanding Expungements and Pardons for Non-Violent Federal Offenders*, 79 U. CIN. L. REV. 155, 167–68

(2010) (describing state and federal law revocation of licenses for convicted felons).

89. *Starbucks*, 2009 WL 5183773, at *1, *4.

90. *Id.* at *2 (quoting Starbucks's Objections to Plaintiff's Evidence at 9:9–10:8, Doe v. Starbucks, Inc., No. SACV 08–0582 AG (CWx), 2009 WL 5183773 (C.D. Cal. Dec. 18, 2009)).

91. *Starbucks*, 2009 WL 5183773, at *1, *4 (citing Doe Declaration ¶ 4, Doe v. Starbucks, Inc., No. SACV 08–0582 AG (CWx), 2009 WL 5183773 (C.D. Cal. Dec. 18, 2009)).

92. *Starbucks*, 2009 WL 5183773, at *2.

93. *Id.* at *3, *4 (quoting Doe Declaration, *supra* note 91, ¶ 20).

94. *Starbucks*, 2009 WL 5183773, at *5.

95. *Id.* (quoting Plaintiff's Statement of Material Facts ¶¶ 20, 25, Doe v. Starbucks, Inc., No. SACV 08–0582 AG (CWx), 2009 WL 5183773 (C.D. Cal. Dec. 18, 2009)) (internal quotations omitted).

96. *Starbucks*, 2009 WL 5183773, at *5.

97. *Id.*

98. *Starbucks*, 2009 WL 5183773, at *5 (citing J.M. Deposition at 158:10–15, Doe v. Starbucks, Inc., No. SACV 08–0582 AG (CWx), 2009 WL 5183773 (C.D. Cal. Dec. 18, 2009)).

99. *Id.* (citing Kelly Deposition at 65:13–66:3, Doe v. Starbucks, Inc., No. SACV 08–0582 AG (CWx), 2009 WL 5183773 (C.D. Cal. Dec. 18, 2009)). Kelly testified that she did not think the Starbucks's sexual harassment policy applied to Doe's situation because no one had complained about harassment. *Id.*

100. *Id.* at *6 (citing J.M. Deposition, *supra* note 98, at 187:18–24).

101. *Id.*

102. *Id.* (quoting Plaintiff's Statement of Material Facts, *supra* note 95, ¶ 40).

103. *Id.* (citing Plaintiff's Statement of Material Facts, *supra* note 95, ¶ 59).

104. Jon Cassidy, *Woman sues Starbucks over underage sex* 2, The Orange County Register, Jan. 25, 2010 (updated Jan. 26, 2010), *available at* www.ocregister.com/articles/moore-230812-starbucks-records.html (last accessed Nov. 8, 2014).

105. *Id.*

106. *Id.* at *7–8.

107. *Id.* at *7 (emphasis omitted) (quoting *Tobias*, 21 P.3d at 762).

108. *Id.*

109. *Starbucks*, 2009 WL 5183773, at *7; *see* Doe v. Oberweis Dairy, 456 F.3d 704 (7th Cir. 2006).

110. *Starbucks*, 2009 WL 5183773, at *7.

111. Doe v. Oberweis Dairy, No. 03 C 4774, 2005 WL 782709, *6–7 (N.D. Ill. Apr. 6, 2005), *rev'd*, 456 F.3d 704 (7th Cir. 2006).

112. *Id.* at *7.

113. *Oberweis Dairy*, 456 F.3d at 712–13.

114. *Compare Jones*, 990 A.2d at 976 n.8 (describing situational offenders as opportunistically taking advantage of children), *with Oberweis Dairy*, 456 F.3d at 712–13 (explaining Nayman "regularly hit" on the teenage girls he supervised, and engaged in sexual intercourse with other employees, one a minor, before Doe).

115. *Oberweis Dairy*, 456 F.3d at 713. The court cited to the Illinois statutory rape law. *Id.*; *see* 720 ILL. COMP. STAT ANN. 5/12–15(c), 16(d) (West 2011).

116. *Id.* at 713; *compare Oberweis Dairy*, 456 F.3d at 713 (explaining that the policy behind the Illinois statutory rape law is that "below a certain age a person cannot . . . make a responsible decision about whether to have sex"), *with Hillhouse*, 1 Cal. Rptr. 3d at 268–69 (explaining the "communal experience" that minors' "judgment and impulse control . . . tend to be problematic").

117. *Oberweis Dairy*, 456 F.3d at 713 (internal quotations omitted).

118. *Id.*

119. *Id.* at 714.

120. *See* App. 2 (summarizing conflicts regarding liability in California, Illinois, Louisiana, Maryland, Mississippi, New Hampshire, New York, North Dakota, Tennessee, and Wisconsin and with consent relevant only at the damage phase of trial in South Carolina and Virginia).

121. Drobac, *Sex and the Workplace*, *supra* text preceding note 1, at 538–39.

122. *See* App. 2.

123. Cnty. of San Luis Obispo v. Nathaniel J., 57 Cal. Rptr. 2d 843, 844 (Ct. App. 1996) (internal quotations omitted).

124. *Id.* at 845.

125. *See Tobias*, 21 P.3d at 759, 761–62.

126. Order Entering Judgment Against Defendant Culver Theaters, Inc. Pursuant to Settlement Agreement, Sara Doe [alias] v. Culver Theaters, Inc., NO. CV139513 (Cal. Super. Ct. Dec. 2, 2002); *see Donaldson*, 36 Cal. Rptr. 3d at 587–88.

127. *Starbucks*, 2009 WL 5183773, at *7–8; E-mail from Lisa Bredahl, Court Clerk, to author (Aug. 24, 2010, 1:03 PM) (on file with author).

Chapter Nine

This chapter draws from Jennifer Ann Drobac, *Consent, Teenagers, and (un)Civil(ized) Consequences*, *in* CHILDREN, SEXUALITY AND THE LAW (Sacha M. Coupet & Ellen Marrus eds., NYU Press, 2015); Jennifer Ann Drobac & Leslie A. Hulvershorn, *The Neurobiology of Decision-Making in High Risk Youth & The Law of Consent to Sex*, 17 NEW CRIM. L. REV. 502 (Summer 2014); Jennifer Ann Drobac, *Wake Up and Smell the Starbucks Coffee: How* Doe v. Starbucks *Confirms the End of the "Age of Consent" in California and Perhaps Beyond*, 33 B.C. J.L. & Soc. Just. 1 (2013); Jennifer Ann Drobac, *A* Bee Line *in the Wrong Direction: Science, Teenagers, and the Sting to "The Age of Consent,"* 20 J.L. & Pol'y 63 (2011); Jennifer Ann Drobac, *I Can't to I Kant: The Sexual Harassment of Working Adolescents, Competing Theories, and Ethical Dilemmas*, 70 Albany L. Rev. 675 (2007); Jennifer Ann Drobac, *"Developing Capacity": Adolescent "Consent" at Work, at Law and in the Sciences of the Mind*, 10 UC Davis J. Juvenile L. & Pol'y 1 (2006); and Jennifer Ann Drobac, *Sex and the Workplace: "Consenting" Adolescents and a Conflict of Laws*, 79 Wash. L. Rev. 471 (2004), and supporting citations in these texts.

1. William Shakespeare, Othello, act 1, sc. 3, 331–37.

2. Gebser v. Lago Vista Indep. Sch. Dist., 524 U.S. 274, 280, 292 (1998); *see* 20 U.S.C. § 1681 (2000).

3. *See, e.g.*, Alaska Stat. § 14.18.010 (2009); Ark. Code Ann. § 6–18–514 (West 2009); Cal. Educ. Code § 201 (2009); Conn. Gen. Stat. Ann. § 10–15c (West 2009); Iowa Code Ann. § 216.9 (West 2009); La. Rev. Stat. Ann. § 416.13 (2009); Mass. Gen. Laws Ann. ch. 151C, § 2 (West 2008); N.H. Rev. Stat. Ann. § 193-F:3 (2009); R.I. Gen. Laws § 16–21–26 (2009); W. Va. Code § 18–2C (2009) (exemplifying various state statutes that address discrimination or harassment in schools); *see also* L.W. ex rel. L.G. v. Toms River Regional Schools Bd. of Educ., 189 N.J. 381, 915 A.2d 535 (2007) (applying New Jersey Law Against Discrimination (LAD), N.J. Stat. Ann. §§ 10:5–1 to 10:5–49) and Emily Montgomery, *Me and Julio Down by the Schoolyard: An Analysis of School Liability for Discriminatory Peer Sexual Harassment Under Vermont Law*, 35 Vt. L. Rev. 515, 521–22 and accompanying notes (2010).

4. Mary M. v. N. Lawrence Cmty. Sch. Corp., 131 F.3d 1220, 1227–28 (7th Cir. 1997) (deciding both Title IX and § 1983 claims), *cert. denied*, 524 U.S. 952 (1998); Bostic v. Smyrna Sch. Dist., No. 01–0261 KAJ, 2003 WL 723262, at *4–8 (D. Del. Feb. 24, 2003) (disposing of Title IX and state common law claims); Hackett v. Fulton County Sch. Dist., 238 F. Supp. 2d 1330, 1346, 1356–60 (N.D. Ga. 2002) (resolving Title IX, § 1983 and Georgia common law claims); Benefield v. Bd. of Trs. of the Univ. of Ala., 214 F. Supp. 2d 1212, 1218 (N.D. Ala. 2002) (deciding only a Title IX claim); Doe v. Taylor Indep. Sch. Dist., 15 F.3d 443, 449–50 (5th Cir. 1994) (resolving only a § 1983 claim).

5. 42 U.S.C. § 1983 (2000). Some courts have rejected § 1983 claims brought with Title IX claims, reasoning that the "Sea Clammers Doctrine," *see* Middlesex County Sewerage Auth. v. Nat'l Sea Clammers Ass'n, 453 U.S. 1 (1981), prevents overlapping claims and that Title IX preempts any § 1983 claim. *See, e.g.*, Leach v. Evansville-Vanderburgh Sch. Corp., No. EV98–0196 C-Y/H, 2000 WL 33309376, at *11–12 (S.D. Ind. May 30, 2000). *But see* DiSalvio v. Lower Merion Sch. Dist., No. CIV.A. 00–5463, 2002 WL 734343, at *1 (E.D. Pa. Apr. 25, 2002) (holding that the Sea Clammers Doctrine does not preempt a Title IX claim).

6. 526 U.S. 629, 631 (1999) (emphasis added).

7. Doe v. Lago Vista Indep. Sch. District, 106 F.3d 1223, 1224 (1997), *aff'd sub nom.*, Gebser v. Lago Vista Indep. Sch. District, 524 U.S. 274 (1998).

8. Mary Deibel, *Court Sides With Schools On Abuse Harassment Victims Can't Sue Institution Unless Incident Report Ignored*, DENVER ROCKY MOUNTAIN NEWS, June 23, 1998, at 2A.

9. Richard E. Berg-Andersson, *United States Supreme Court Justices*, THE GREENPAPERS.COM (updated Aug. 8, 2010) (listing information, including birth dates, of the justices) (last accessed Nov. 9, 2014).

10. *Doe v. Lago Vista Indep. Sch. District*, 106 F.3d at 1224.

11. *Id.* at 1224–25.

12. *Id.*

13. Deibel, *supra* note 8.

14. *Id.*

15. *Doe v. Lago Vista Indep. Sch. District*, 106 F.3d at 1225.

16. *Gebser*, 524 U.S. at 299 n.10.

17. *Id.* at 278–79.

18. *Id.* at 279–80.

19. *Id.* at 287.

20. *Faragher*, 524 U.S. 775, 805–06 (1998) (quoting Albemarle Paper Co. v. Moody, 422 U.S. 405, 418 (1975)) (citation omitted).

21. *Gebser*, 524 U.S. at 300 (Stevens, J., dissenting).

22. *Id.* at 290, 292.

23. *Id.* at 304 (quoting Franklin v. Gwinnett County Public Schools, 503 U.S. 60, 74 (1992)).

24. *Id.* at 302 n.12.

25. *Id.* at 306.

26. 214 F. Supp. 2d 1212, 1215, 1220 (N.D. Ala. 2002).

27. *Benefield*, 214 F. Supp. 2d at 1218.

28. *Id.* at 1220.

29. BLACK'S LAW DICTIONARY (9th ed, 2009).

30. 131 F.3d 1220, 1220–23 (7th Cir. 1997).

31. *Id.* at 1224.

32. *Id.* at 1226 (citation omitted).

33. *Id.* at 1225 n.6.

34. *Id.* at 1226–27 (citing Davis v. Monroe County Bd. of Educ., 74 F.3d 1186, 1193 (11th Cir. 1996)).

35. *Id.* at 1227.

36. *Compare id. with* Doe by Roe v. Orangeburg County Sch., 518 S.E.2d 259, 261 (S.C. 1999). Ironically, the *Orangeburg* court took its guidance from *Barnes v. Barnes*, 603 N.E.2d 1337 (Ind. 1992), an Indiana case. The *Mary M.* case also originated in Indiana. *Mary M.*, 131 F.3d at 1220.

37. *Mary M.*, 131 F.3d at 1227.

38. 501 F. Supp. 2d 695 (E.D. Pa. 2007).

39. *Id.* at 699.

40. *Id.*

41. *Id.* at 695.

42. *Id.* at 705 (footnote omitted).

43. *Id.* at 706.

44. *Id.* at 705 (footnote omitted).

45. *Id.* at 706 (citations omitted).

46. *Id.* at 706 (footnote omitted).

47. *Id.* at 708.

48. 2010 WL 2524587 (N.D. Cal.).

49. *Id.* at *5.

50. Glenda Anderson, *Willits teacher admits sex with student*, The Press Democrat, Apr. 7, 2009, *available at* www.pressdemocrat.com/article/20090407/ARTICLES/904079881?Title=Willits-teachers-admits-sex-with-student (last accessed Nov. 9, 2014); Glenda Anderson, *Jail term for former Willits teacher who had sex with student*, The Press Democrat, Aug. 4, 2009, *available at* www.pressdemocrat.com/article/20090804/ARTICLES/908049914?Title=Jail-term-for-former-Willits-teacher-who-had-sex-with-student (last accessed Nov. 9, 2014).

51. The *Willits* court explained:

> While some cases within the Ninth Circuit recite "welcomeness" among the elements in a Title IX sexual harassment claim, none have actually analyzed that element in the Title IX context. See, e.g., Doe by and Through Doe v. Petaluma City Sch. Dist., 949 F. Supp. 1415, 1427 (N.D. Cal. 1996) (importing the Title VII hostile environment standard—including "unwelcome" harassment—to the Title IX context, but not analyzing the unwelcome element); Stanley v. Trs. of the Cal. State Univ., 433 F.3d 1129, 1137 (9th Cir. 2006) (quoting Title VII's sexually hostile workplace standard—including the "unwelcome" element—in the context of determining the statute of limitations for Title IX claim); Ray v. Antioch Unified Sch. Dist., 107 F. Supp. 2d 1165, 1170 (N.D. Cal. 2000) (referring to "unwelcome sexual comments and advances" as an example of sexual harassment, but not analyzing welcomeness as an element of a Title IX claim); Gallant v. Board of Trustees of Cal. State Univ., 997 F. Supp. 1231, 1234 (N.D. Cal. 1998) (applying Title VII principles—including the "unwelcome conduct" element—to guide resolution of a Title IX claim, but focusing on the "sufficiently severe or pervasive" element).

Id. at *3 (footnote omitted)).

52. *Willits*, 2010 WL 2524587, at *4.

53. *Id.* at *4–5.

54. *Id.* at *4 n.4.

55. *Id.* at *5.

56. Glenda Anderson, *Willits Man Gets Jail for Sex with Pupil*, PRESS DEMOCRAT (Santa Rosa, Cal.), Aug. 5, 2009, at B1; Glenda Anderson, *Willits Teacher Accused of Sex with Student*, PRESS DEMOCRAT (Santa Rosa, Cal.), Feb. 6, 2009, at B1.

57. A jury acquitted O. J. Simpson of charges for the murder of his ex-wife, Nicole Brown Simpson, and her friend Ronald Goldman. Following a civil trial for wrongful death and survival statute damages, the jury found Simpson liable by a preponderance of the evidence. *See* Rufo v. Simpson, 103 Cal. Rptr. 2d 494 (Cal. Ct. App. 2001) (affirming judgments in wrongful death and survival case brought by family members of Nicole Brown Simpson and Ronald Goldman against O. J. Simpson). This case highlights how differing criminal and civil law burdens can lead to seemingly contradictory results.

58. *See* In the Matter of B.W.,—- S.W.3d—-, 2010 WL 2431630 at *6 (Tex.) The Texas Supreme Court rejected the notion that a thirteen-year-old prostitute's activities proved her maturity:

> The dissent emphasizes B.W.'s "long and sad history of delinquent behavior," presumably suggesting that her bad behavior is indicative of her mental capacity to commit this crime [of prostitution]. The United States Supreme Court has recognized that juveniles "are more vulnerable or susceptible to negative influences and outside pressures," and that "[i]t is difficult even for expert psychologists to differentiate between the juvenile offender whose crime reflects unfortunate yet transient immaturity, and the rare juvenile offender whose crime reflects irreparable corruption."

Id. (quoting Roper, 543 U.S. at 569, 573 (internal citations omitted)).

59. Tom Lininger, *Is It Wrong To Sue For Rape*, 57 DUKE L.J. 1557, 1560–62 (2008) (footnotes omitted).

60. *Michael M. v. Sup. Ct.*, 450 U.S. 464, 495 n.10 (Brennan, J. dissenting) (quoting People v. Hernandez, 61 Cal. 2d 529, 531 (1964)).

61. Lininger, *supra* note 59, at 1564.

62. Agnvall, *In Western Europe*, THE WASH. POST, May 16, 2006, *available at* www.washingtonpost.com/wp-dyn/content/article/2006/05/15/AR200605150 0809_pf.html (last accessed Nov. 9, 2014).

63. Suzanne M. Sgroi, *Discovery, Reporting, Investigation, and Prosecution of Child Sexual Abuse*, 29 SIECUS REP., Oct./Nov. 2000, at 6.

64. According to the National Survey of Family Growth (2002) by the CDC, 46.9% of males and 49% of females have had sexual intercourse by 17. These numbers increase to 55.7% and 55.5% respectively for oral sex by 17. For 18 year olds the rates are 62.4% and 70.3% for sexual intercourse and 65.4% and 70.2% respectively for oral sex. Sharon Jayson, *Teens Define Sex in New Ways*, USA Today, Oct. 19, 2005, at http://usatoday30.usatoday.com/news/health/2005-10-18-teens-sex_x.htm (last accessed March 8, 2015).

65. Bruce Anderson, *Loving the kids, Willits Style*, Anderson Valley Advertiser Online, Aug. 12, 2009, *available at* http://theava.com/archives/1157 (last accessed Nov. 9, 2014).

66. *Revelation* 2:20–22 (New International Version).

67. *Donaldson v. Dep't of Real Estate*, 36 Cal. Rptr. 3d 577, 585–88 (Cal. Ct. App. 2005) 584 n.10.

68. Anderson, *supra* note 65.

69. Susan Estrich, *Sex at Work*, 43 Stan. L. Rev. 813, 831 (1991).

70. Drobac, *Sex and the Workplace*, *supra* text preceding note 1, at 523.

71. "loose, adj., n.2, and adv." OED online (Sept. 2014) (defining loose as "7. Of persons, their habits, writings, etc.: Free from moral restraint; lax in principle, conduct, or speech; chiefly in narrower sense, unchaste, wanton, dissolute, immoral."), www.oed.com.proxy2.ulib.iupui.edu/view/Entry/110192?rskey=XbzE8H&result=2 (last accessed Nov. 09, 2014).

72. Edward Rubin and Malcolm Feeley, *Creating Legal Doctrine*, 69 S. Cal. L. Rev. 1989, 1991–92 (1996).

73. *Id.* at 1991–92.

74. Edward Rubin and Malcolm Feeley, *Judicial Policy Making and Litigation Against the Government*, 5 U. Pa. J. Const. L. 617, 630–36 (2003). Rubin and Feeley suggested, "Comparative institutional analysis is arguably the single most important theme in the legal process school, and the role of courts in relation to the politically accountable branches is certainly the most important application of this theme." *Id.* at 635.

75. *See* Rubin and Feeley, 5 U. Pa. J. Const. L. at 643–47.

76. *Id.* at 644.

77. *See id.* at 646.

78. *Id.* at 663.

79. *Id.* at 627.

80. 518 S.E.2d 259 (S.C. 1999).

81. *Id.* at 261 (quoting *Barnes*, 603 N.E.2d at 1342 (internal quotation marks omitted)).

82. 631 So. 2d 604, 607 (La. Ct. App. 1994) (emphasis in the original).

83. Nancy Reagan embraced the "Just Say No" campaign against drugs, named after her response to an Oakland, California school girl's question about what to do when offered drugs. The Ronald Reagan Presidential Foun-

dation & Library, at http://reaganlibrary.com/details_f.aspx?session_args=pHbOt+41xYlvI/OaIeRTME2rH3g0vKaRwfxv+GaNajWmRlG3uzFng4Tr9luD2EIZIbZWaQit+1J4D1GbGmr8675UrYmS5FOsX48MEmCscBUqlbRdDR9DBDEAup5MgQ31&p=RR1008NRHC&tx=6&h1=3&h2=7&sw=rr_nr_causes&lm=reagan&args_a=cms&args_b=12&argsb=Y (last accessed Nov. 9, 2014).

84. Certainly employer liability for the misconduct of an adult supervisor complicates this matter. However, employers have control over whom they hire and can presumably pass on the "costs of doing business" with teenaged employees to their clients or customers.

85. 456 F.3d at 715; "siren, n." OED ONLINE (Sept. 2014) (defining siren as "[o]ne of several fabulous monsters, part woman, part bird, who were supposed to lure sailors to destruction by their enchanting singing"), www.oed.com.proxy2.ulib.iupui.edu/view/Entry/180372?rskey=dNhhPG&result=1 (last accessed Nov. 9, 2014).

86. Mike P., Senior Creative Manager, *Bringing the Siren to Life*, STARBUCKS.COM, Jan. 5, 2011, www.starbucks.com/blog/bringing-the-siren-to-life (last accessed Nov. 9, 2014).

87. Doe v. Oberweis Dairy, 456 F.3d 704, 716 (7th Cir. 2006).

88. *See* "badinage, v." OED ONLINE (Sept. 2014) (defining the verb as meaning "to banter playfully"), www.oed.com.proxy2.ulib.iupui.edu/view/Entry/14572?rskey=9U1yHW&result=2&isAdvanced=false (last accessed Nov. 09, 2014).

89. *Oberweis*, 456 F.3d at 713.

90. *Id.* at 715 (italics added).

91. *Id.* at 713. The appellate court noted that a witness described Naymen's sexual conduct and added, "These things he did in the store, but he would also invite the girls to his apartment. He had sexual intercourse in the apartment with two of them, one of them a minor, before it was the plaintiff's turn." *Id.*

92. *Id.* at 713. (citation omitted).

93. *Id.* at 714 (quoting Beul v. ASSE Int'l, Inc., 233 F.3d 441, 450–51 (7th Cir. 2000)) (internal quotation marks omitted).

94. *Id.* One can readily imagine what sexual predators think of this ruling.

95. *See* Lawrence v. Texas, 539 U.S. 558, 577 (2003). The Supreme Court held in *Lawrence* that "[t]he fact that the governing majority in a State has traditionally viewed a particular practice as immoral is not a sufficient reason for upholding a law prohibiting the practice. . . ." *Id.* The practice of basing judicial decisions on morality alone is a risky one because social mores change over time. The question in the case of teenagers is what other purpose judges serve by crediting adolescent "consent." I doubt such decisions deter teenagers in the future or make them any more mature as a population.

96. Andrea Longbottom, *The Myth of the Teen Brain: A Q&A With Dr. Epstein*, THE HOME SCHOOL COURT REPORT, July/Aug. 2007, *available at* www

.crosswalk.com/family/homeschool/the-myth-of-the-teen-brain-a-qanda-with-dr-epstein-11551480.html (last accessed Nov. 9, 2014).

97. Richard Epstein, *The Myth of the Teen Brain*, SCIENTIFIC AMERICAN MIND 57, Apr./May 2007, *available at* http://drrobertepstein.com/pdf/Epstein-THE_MYTH_OF_THE_TEEN_BRAIN-Scientific_American_Mind-4–07.pdf (last accessed Nov. 9, 2014).

98. *Id.* at 58–59.

99. *Id.* at 60.

100. *Id.* at 63.

101. *Id.*

102. *See* Wandi Bruine de Bruin et al., *Adolescents' Thinking About the Risks of Sexual Behavior, in* THINKING WITH DATA 421, 432 (Marsha C. Lovett and Priti Shah, eds., 2007) (suggesting that "comprehensive sex education has not led to earlier or increased sexual activity, although it has increased condom and contraceptive use among those teens who do have sex." (citations omitted)).

103. Epstein, *supra* note 97, at 63.

104. KAHLIL GIBRAN, THE PROPHET 56 (1923).

Chapter Ten

This chapter draws from Jennifer Ann Drobac, *Consent, Teenagers, and (un)Civil(ized) Consequences, in* CHILDREN, SEXUALITY AND THE LAW (Sacha M. Coupet & Ellen Marrus eds., NYU Press, 2015); Jennifer Ann Drobac & Leslie A. Hulvershorn, *The Neurobiology of Decision-Making in High Risk Youth & The Law of Consent to Sex*, 17 NEW CRIM. L. REV. 502 (Summer 2014); Jennifer Ann Drobac, *Wake Up and Smell the Starbucks Coffee: How* Doe v. Starbucks *Confirms the End of the "Age of Consent" in California and Perhaps Beyond*, 33 B.C. J.L. & SOC. JUST. 1 (2013); Jennifer Ann Drobac, *A* Bee Line *in the Wrong Direction: Science, Teenagers, and the Sting to "The Age of Consent,"* 20 J.L. & POL'Y 63 (2011); Jennifer Ann Drobac, *I Can't to I Kant: The Sexual Harassment of Working Adolescents, Competing Theories, and Ethical Dilemmas*, 70 ALBANY L. REV. 675 (2007); Jennifer Ann Drobac, *"Developing Capacity": Adolescent "Consent" at Work, at Law and in the Sciences of the Mind*, 10 UC DAVIS J. JUVENILE L. & POL'Y 1 (2006); and Jennifer Ann Drobac, *Sex and the Workplace: "Consenting" Adolescents and a Conflict of Laws*, 79 WASH. L. REV. 471 (2004), and supporting citations in these texts.

1. Planned Parenthood of Southeastern Pennsylvania v. Casey, 505 U.S. 833, 851 (1992).

2. Lawrence v. Texas, 539 U.S. 558, 571 (2003) (quoting Planned Parenthood of Southeastern Pennsylvania v. Casey, 505 U.S. 833, 851 (1992)).

3. Lawrence, 539 U.S. at 578.

4. Casey, 505 U.S. at 895 (citations omitted).

5. Declaration of Ruben C. Gur, Ph.D. at 15, Patterson v. Texas, 528 U.S. 826 (1999) (No. 98–8907), *available at* www.americanbar.org/content/dam/aba/publishing/criminal_justice_section_newsletter/crimjust_juvjus_Gur_affidavit.authcheckdam.pdf (last accessed Nov. 9, 2014).

6. *See* Email from Professor R. George Wright, Indiana University, Robert H. McKinney School of Law, Indianapolis, to author (Apr. 30, 2010) (on file with author).

7. R. George Wright, *Consenting Adults: The Problem of Enhancing Human Dignity Non-Coercively*, 75 B.U. L. REV. 1397, 1425 (1995) [hereinafter Wright, *Consenting Adults*].

8. *Id.* at 1414.

9. *Id.* at 1413–14 (quoting N.C. Freed Co. v. Bd. of Governors of the Fed. Reserve Sys., 473 F.2d 1210, 1216 (2d. Cir. 1973)) (footnotes and internal quotation marks omitted).

10. R. George Wright, *Treating Persons as Ends in Themselves: The Legal Implications of a Kantian Principle*, 36 U. RICH. L. REV. 271, 299 (2002) [hereinafter Wright, *Treating Persons*].

11. *Id.* at 318.

12. *See* EEOC, Youth@Work, http://youth.eeoc.gov/index.html (last accessed Nov. 9, 2014); Press Release, EEOC, EEOC Reaches Out to High Schoolers to Combat Workplace Harassment of Teens (Dec. 15, 2004), *available at* www.eeoc.gov/eeoc/newsroom/release/12–15–04.cfm (last accessed Nov. 9, 2014).

13. *See, e.g.*, Tom Precious, *New York minimum-wage law sparks controversy over state subsidy*, THE BUFFALO NEWS.COM, Mar. 28, 2013, *available at* 2013 WLNR 7569467 (announcing a $.75/hr. subsidy for teen employees, age sixteen to nineteen, at N.Y. taxpayer expense); *see also* LaDonna Pavetti et al., Center on Budget and Policy Priorities, *Creating Subsidized Employment Opportunities for Low-Income Parents: The Legacy of the TANF Emergency Fund* 2, 6, Feb. 16, 2011, *available at* www.cbpp.org/files/2–16–11tanf.pdf (last accessed Nov. 9, 2014) (describing subsidized jobs for youth created by the TANF Emergency Fund).

14. *See* EEOC v. Taco Bell Corp., No. 1:05-cv-0998-SEB-TAB, Consent Decree (S.D. Ind. Feb. 16, 2006) (on file with author).

15. Jennifer A. Drobac, *'Please Don't; I Have My Standards!'*, 27 BNA EMP. DISCRIMINATION REP., July 12, 2006, at 55, 57.

16. Elizabeth Cauffman & Laurence Steinberg, *The Cognitive and Affective Influences on Adolescent Decision-Making*, 68 TEMP. L. REV. 1763, 1772 (1995).

17. United States Department of Labor, *elaws—Fair Labor Standards Act Advisor*, *available at* www.dol.gov/elaws/faq/esa/flsa/003.htm (explaining that "a special minimum wage of $4.25 per hour applies to employees under the age of 20 during their first 90 consecutive calendar days of employment with an employer") (last accessed Nov. 9, 2014).

18. JOHN DEWITT GREGORY, ET AL., UNDERSTANDING FAMILY LAW 220 (2013).

19. Ellen Crean, *Letourneau marries former student*, CBS NEWS, May 21, 2005, *available at* www.cbsnews.com/news/letourneau-marries-former-student (last accessed Nov. 9, 2014).

20. Tracy Johnson, *Fualaau's suit says he wasn't protected from Letourneau*, SEATTLE POST-INTELLIGENCER, May 20, 2002, *available at* www.seattlepi.com/news/article/Fualaau-s-suit-says-he-wasn-t-protected-from-1083448.php#photo-623804 (last accessed Nov. 9, 2014).

21. Sam Skolnik, *Schools, police absolved in Fualaau case*, SEATTLE POST-INTELLIGENCER, Mar. 21, 2002, *available at* www.seattlepi.com/news/article/Schools-police-absolved-in-Fualaau-case-1087664.php (last accessed Nov. 9, 2014).

22. Crean, *supra* note 19.

23. Skolnik, *supra* note 21.

24. *Id.*

25. Karen Foshay, *LAUSD argued middle schooler can consent to sex with teacher*, 89.3 KPCC, Nov. 13, 2014, *available at* www.scpr.org/news/2014/11/13/48034/lausd-argued-middle-schooler-can-consent-to-sex-wi/ (interview begins at 2:28) (last accessed Aug. 5, 2015); *see also* Larry Mantle, *KPCC investigation reveals questionable tactics LAUSD used to defend rape lawsuit*, 89.3 KPCC, Nov. 13, 2014, *available at* www.scpr.org/programs/airtalk/2014/11/13/40321/kpcc-investigation-reveals-questionable-tactics-la/ (interview begins at 4:19) (last accessed Aug. 5, 2015).

26. Arun Rath, *Criminal Law Says Minors Can't Consent—But Some Civil Courts Disagree*, NPR ALL THINGS CONSIDERED, Nov. 16, 2014, *available at* www.npr.org/player/v2/mediaPlayer.html?action=1&t=1&islist=false&id=364538087&m=364561418 (interview begins at 3:44) (last accessed Aug. 5, 2015).

27. Patrick McGreevy, *Gov. Brown signs bill closing loophole in sexual assault law*, L.A. TIMES, July 16, 2015, *available at* www.latimes.com/local/political/la-me-pc-gov-brown-closes-loophole-in-sexual-assault-law-20150716-story.html (last accessed Aug. 5, 2015).

Appendix 1

1. CATHERINE HILL AND HOLLY KEARL, AAUW, CROSSING THE LINE: SEXUAL HARASSMENT AT SCHOOL 11 (2011).

2. UCSC Title IX / Sexual Harassment Office, *What is Sexual Harassment?*, www2.ucsc.edu/title9-sh/whatissh.htm (some punctuation omitted) (last visited Nov. 4, 2014).

Index